FOCUS ON GRAMMAR

A **BASIC** Course for Reference and Practice

SECOND EDITION

Irene E. Schoenberg

Longman

For Harris, Dan, and Dahlia

FOCUS ON GRAMMAR: A BASIC COURSE FOR REFERENCE AND PRACTICE

Pearson Education, 10 Bank Street, White Plains, NY 10606

Editorial director: Allen Ascher
Executive editor: Louisa Hellegers
Director of design and production: Rhea Banker
Development editor: Carolyn Viola-John
Production manager: Alana Zdinak
Managing editor: Linda Moser
Senior production editor: Virginia Bernard
Production editor: Christine Lauricella
Senior manufacturing manager: Patrice Fraccio
Manufacturing supervisor: David Dickey
Photo research: Matthew McConnochie and Marianne Carello
Cover design: Rhea Banker
Cover image: *Elm, Middleton Woods, Yorkshire,
  6 November 1980*. Copyright © Andy Goldsworthy
  from his book *A Collaboration with Nature*,
  Harry N. Abrams, 1990.
Text design: Charles Yuen
Text composition: Preface, Inc.
Illustrators: Ronald Chironna: pp. 10, 83, 119, 165, 170, 171, 184, 185, 200; Jock MacRae: pp. 63, 158,
  161, 262, 275, 334, 414; Paul McCusker: pp. 52, 53, 62, 67, 73, 121, 129, 174, 188, 199, 207, 222, 226,
  241, 316, 333, 388, 408, 411, 413; Dusan Petricic: pp. 11, 25, 30, 41, 98, 108, 120, 190, 201, 211, 298,
  323, 324, 360, 412; Len Shalansky: pp. 308, 321, 419; Dave Sullivan: pp. 1, 2, 3, 5, 8, 9, 12, 14, 15, 16,
  19, 22, 23, 24, 27, 38, 39, 40, 44, 46, 51, 53, 55, 58, 59, 68, 70, 78, 78, 82, 93, 96, 106, 112, 113, 118,
  119, 122, 126, 131, 133, 134, 136, 139, 140, 148, 162, 166, 182, 188, 193, 197, 208, 224, 233, 238, 242,
  249, 252, 260, 269, 278, 285, 290, 294, 306, 314, 327, 331, 335, 338, 339, 358, 359, 361, 365, 376, 385,
  400, 402, 407, 426, 453, 455.
Photo credits: see p. xiv

Library of Congress Cataloging-in-Publication Data

Schoenberg, Irene
  Focus on grammar; a basic course for reference and grammar / Irene E. Schoenberg.—2nd ed.
    p. cm.
  Includes index.
  ISBN 0-201-34676-1
  1. English language—Textbooks for foreign speakers. 2. English language—Grammar—Problems,
exercises, etc. I. Title.

PE1128.S34568 1999
428.2'4—dc21

99-050164
CIP

2 3 4 5 6 7 8 9 10—CRK—04 03 02 01 00

CONTENTS

PUTTING IT ALL TOGETHER

APPENDICES

ABOUT THE AUTHOR

Irene E. Schoenberg has taught ESL for over twenty-five years at Hunter College's *International English Language Institute* and for eighteen years at Columbia University's *American Language Program*. She has trained ESL and EFL teachers at the New School for Social Research and has lectured at conferences and English language schools and universities in Brazil, Mexico, Thailand, Taiwan, Japan, and the United States. She is the author of *Talk about Trivia* and *Talk about Values* and co-author of the *True Colors* series with Jay Maurer. Ms. Schoenberg holds an MA in TESOL from Columbia University. *Focus on Grammar: A Basic Course for Reference and Practice* has grown out of the author's experience as a practicing teacher of English.

AUTHOR'S GOAL AND PURPOSE

In writing *Focus on Grammar*: *A Basic Course for Reference and Practice*, I have tried to avoid presenting grammar divorced from practical use. It has been my pleasure in the classroom and my goal here to integrate grammar into informative and amusing units which, because they reflect real life, will motivate students to learn and use English. I hope this material will provide your students with as much pleasure and confidence with grammar as it has mine.

INTRODUCTION

THE **FOCUS ON GRAMMAR** SERIES

Focus on Grammar: A Basic Course for Reference and Practice, Second Edition, is the first text in the four-level **Focus on Grammar** series. Written by practicing ESL professionals, the series focuses on English grammar through lively listening, speaking, reading, and writing activities. Each of the four Student Books is accompanied by an Answer Key, a Workbook, an Audio Program (cassettes or CDs), a Teacher's Manual, and a CD–ROM. Each Student Book can stand alone as a complete text in itself, or it can be used as part of the series.

BOTH CONTROLLED AND COMMUNICATIVE PRACTICE

Research in applied linguistics suggests that students expect and need to learn the formal rules of a language. However, students need to practice new structures in a variety of contexts to help them internalize and master them. To this end, **Focus on Grammar** provides an abundance of both controlled and communicative exercises so that students can bridge the gap between knowing grammatical structures and using them. The many communicative activities in each unit enable students to personalize what they have learned in order to talk to each other with ease about hundreds of everyday issues.

A UNIQUE FOUR-STEP APPROACH

The series follows a unique four-step approach. In the first step, **grammar in context,** new structures are shown in the natural context of conversations, and narratives. This is followed by a **grammar presentation** of structures in clear and accessible grammar charts, notes, and examples. The third step is **focused practice** of both form and meaning in numerous and varied controlled exercises with objective answers. In the fourth step, **communication practice,** students use the new structures freely and creatively in motivating, open-ended activities.

A COMPLETE CLASSROOM TEXT AND REFERENCE GUIDE

A major goal in the development of **Focus on Grammar** has been to provide Student Books that serve not only as vehicles for classroom instruction but also as resources for reference and self-study. In each Student Book, the combination of grammar charts, grammar notes, and expansive appendices provides a complete and invaluable reference guide for the student. And exercises in the focus practice sections of each unit are also ideal for individual study.

THOROUGH RECYCLING

Underpinning the scope and sequence of the series as a whole is the belief that students need to use target structures many times in many contexts at increasing levels of difficulty. For this reason new grammar is constantly recycled so that students will feel thoroughly comfortable with it.

COMPREHENSIVE TESTING PROGRAM

SelfTests at the end of each part of the Student Book allow for continual assessment of progress. In addition, diagnostic and final tests in the Teacher's Manual provide a ready-made, ongoing evaluation component for each student.

THE BASIC STUDENT BOOK

Focus on Grammar: A Basic Course for Reference and Practice, Second Edition, is written for the beginning and false beginning student. Activities take both levels into account and allow students to demonstrate their ability at different levels.

ORGANIZATION

This book is divided into eleven parts comprising forty-four units. A final section called *Putting It All Together* reviews the major structures of the book. Each of the eleven parts begins with a preview that incorporates the grammar of the part into a lighthearted conversation. Though the characters in the preview are featured throughout the book, parts or units can be studied in any order, allowing the instructor to tailor this text to his or her particular class. Each unit contains the four sections that comprise the essence of *Focus on Grammar:* Grammar in Context, Grammar Presentation, Focused Practice, and Communication Practice. A Review or SelfTest (with answers) and a From Grammar to Writing section conclude each part.

PREVIEW

The preview presents the grammar of the entire part in a natural context. An important belief of the *Focus on Grammar* series is that grammar is an aid to the meaningful use of language. Since students usually understand the meaning of a structure before they master its use, they begin by reading and listening to a conversation that includes the new grammar structures. This initial introduction makes it easier for students to then understand and use grammar appropriately. It also helps them realize that the grammar focus is a means to an end, the end being the appropriate use of the structure in a natural context.

GRAMMAR IN CONTEXT

Grammar in Context presents the grammar of the unit in a natural setting. The texts, all of which are recorded, present language in various formats.

These include telephone conversations, letters, questionnaires, radio talk shows, quiz shows, folktales, essays, and conversations among friends and relatives. In addition, the introductory sections motivate students and provide an opportunity for incidental learning and lively classroom discussion. Topics include a mystery, a discussion of the role of women, a letter to a psychologist, the problems of perfectionists, a matchmaker's questions, suggestions for public speaking, and the use of white lies. A **Warm Up** precedes each text and gives students a chance to express their thoughts and opinions on the topic.

GRAMMAR PRESENTATION

This section is made up of grammar charts, notes, and examples. The Grammar **charts** focus on the form of the unit's target structure. Clear and easy-to-understand boxes present each grammatical form in all its combinations. These charts provide students with a clear visual reference for each new structure. The Grammar **notes** explain the grammar shown in the preceding chart. These notes give definitions, describe the form, offer distinctions between the spoken and written language, and point out potential problems. Every note includes at least one example, and reference notes provide cross-references to related units and the Appendices.

FOCUSED PRACTICE

This section provides practice of the form and meaning of the structures presented in the Grammar Presentation. In the first exercise, **Discover the Grammar**, students indicate their awareness and recognition of the grammar. After this activity, students do a variety of contextualized exercises that progress from more controlled to more productive. Exercises are cross-referenced to the appropriate grammar notes so that students can review the notes if necessary. In addition, a variety of listening activities provide another dimension in which students can practice and incorporate the target grammar. A complete **Answer Key** is provided in a separate booklet.

COMMUNICATION PRACTICE

The Communication Practice activities give students an opportunity to use the structures in more creative ways, allowing them to express their own thoughts and opinions in pair or group work. Through class surveys, discussions, information gaps, games, value clarifications, and problem solving activities, students gain confidence in the target structure as well as many other structures in the language.

REVIEW OR SELFTEST

After the last unit of each part, there is a review section that can be used as a self-test. The exercises test the form and use of the grammar content of the part. These tests include questions in the format of the Structure and Written Expression sections of the TOEFL®. An **Answer Key** is provided after each test.

FROM GRAMMAR TO WRITING

At the end of each part there is a section that gives students practical information about different aspects of writing such as the rules of punctuation and capitalization, models of business letters or informal letters, and ways to organize a paragraph. Students practice writing short passages that review the structures of the part.

APPENDICES

The appendices provide useful information including current maps, lists of the days, months, numbers, common irregular verbs, common non-count nouns, modals with their meaning and examples, tense form charts, spelling and pronunciation rules of tenses, and a phonetic pronunciation chart.

NEW IN THIS EDITION

In response to users' requests, this edition has:

- a revised table of contents with the introduction of the tenses earlier in the text (allowing students to say more sooner)
- a Grammar in Context and a Warm Up providing a theme and context for every unit
- a new easy-to-read format for grammar notes and examples
- vocabulary enrichment through the grouping of vocabulary items by topics such as occupations, relationships, clothing
- cross-references that link exercises to corresponding grammar notes
- more photos and art
- more listening exercises
- more information gaps
- the inclusion of editing exercises
- a From Grammar to Writing section at the end of each part

SUPPLEMENTARY **COMPONENTS**

All supplementary components of *Focus on Grammar, Second Edition,* —the Audio Program (cassettes or CDs), the Workbook, and the Teacher's Manual—are tightly keyed to the Student Book. Along with the CD-ROM, these components provide a wealth of practice and an opportunity to tailor the series to the needs of each individual classroom.

AUDIO PROGRAM

All of the Preview conversations as well as the Grammar in Context passages and many of the Focus practice exercises are recorded on cassettes and CDs. These include clozes, task-based listening, and pronunciation exercises. The symbol [icon] appears next to these activities. The scripts appear in the Teacher's Manual and may be used as an alternative way of presenting these activities.

WORKBOOK

The Workbook accompanying *Focus on Grammar: A Basic Course for Reference and Practice, Second Edition,* provides a wealth of additional exercises appropriate for self-study of the target grammar of each unit in the Student Book. These exercises follow the sequence of the unit. This enables the instructor to make daily homework assignments or allows the instructor to work with individuals or small groups while students are doing the exercises.

TEACHER'S MANUAL

The Teacher's Manual, divided into five parts, contains a variety of suggestions and information to enrich the material in the Student Book. The first part gives general suggestions for each section of a typical unit. The next part offers practical teaching suggestions and cultural information to accompany specific material in each unit. The Teacher's Manual also provides ready-to-use diagnostic and final tests for each of the eleven parts of the Student Book. In addition, a complete script of the audio program is provided, as is an answer key for the diagnostic and final tests.

CD-ROM

The *Focus on Grammar* CD-ROM provides individualized practice with immediate feedback. Fully contextualized and interactive, the activities broaden and extend practice of the grammatical structures in the reading, listening, and writing skill areas. The CD-ROM includes grammar review, review tests, and all relevant reference material from the Student Book. It can also be used alongside the *Longman Interactive American Dictionary* CD-ROM.

CREDITS

PHOTOGRAPHS

Grateful acknowledgment is given to the following for providing photographs:

p. 4 Courtesy of Oregon State University; **p. 10 (Celine Dion)** AP/Wide World Photos; **p. 10 (Arnold Schwarzenegger)** AP/Wide World Photos; **p. 10 (Leonardo DiCaprio)** © Armando Gallo/Retna; **p. 10 (Prince William)** CORBIS/AFP ©; **p. 10 (Romario)** AP/Wide World Photos; **p. 40** PhotoDisc, Inc.; **p. 50** © TSM/DiMaggio/Kalish; **p. 50** TSM/Alan Schein, 1998; **p. 60** Courtesy of Mrs. Duane Hanson, © 1997; **p. 75** PhotoDisc, Inc.; **p. 85** PhotoEdit; **p. 85** Tony Stone Images; **p. 85** CORBIS/Stephanie Maze ©; **p. 92 ("Seinfeld")** Photofest; **p. 92 (Football)** AP/Wide World Photos; **p. 92 ("E.R.")** Sygma Photo News; **p. 92 (Interview)** Richard A. Bloom; **p. 92 (Murder She Wrote)** Photofest; **p. 92 (Mariah Carey)** SIPA Press; **p. 93** Photos International/Archive Photos; **p. 98** ©Archive Photos; **p. 122** Omni-Photo Communications, Inc.; **p. 128** "Lizard Waiting" by Chad Johnstone. © Tobwabba Art, 1998; **p. 130** CORBIS; **p. 130** Tony Stone Images; **p. 130** PhotoEdit; **p. 173** CORBIS/Burnstein Collection ©; **p. 189** © TSM/Alan Schein, 1998; **p. 201** Tony Stone Images; **p. 235** Tony Stone Images; **p. 235** Photo Researchers, Inc.; **p. 242** Omni-Photo Communications, Inc.; **p. 242** Photo Researchers, Inc.; **p. 242** Photographic Resources; **p. 242** AP/Wide World Photos; **p. 266** © Walt Disney; **p. 270** Rijksmuseum Amsterdam; **p. 270** AP/Wide World Photos; **p. 273** Collection of The New-York Historical Society; **p. 284** Photo Researchers, Inc.; **p. 342** Omni-Photo Communications, Inc.; **p. 369** The Image Bank; **p. 392** PhotoDisc, Inc.; **p. 410** PhotoEdit; **p. 410** Tony Arruza Photography; **p. 421** Will Hart; **p. 422** PhotoDisc, Inc.; **p. 422** CORBIS; **p. 423** Photo Researchers, Inc.; **p. 423** Tony Stone Images; **p. 423** PhotoDisc, Inc.

THE STORY BEHIND THE COVER

The photograph on the cover is the work of **Andy Goldsworthy**, an innovative artist who works exclusively with natural materials to create unique outdoor sculpture, which he then photographs. Each Goldsworthy sculpture communicates the artist's own "sympathetic contact with nature" by intertwining forms and shapes structured by natural events with his own creative perspective. Goldsworthy's intention is not to "make his mark on the landscape, but to create a new perception and an evergrowing understanding of the land."

So, too, *Focus on Grammar* takes grammar found in its most natural context and expertly reveals its hidden structure and meaning. It is our hope that students everywhere will also develop a new perception and an evergrowing understanding of the world of grammar.

ACKNOWLEDGMENTS

As a mother, I know never to compare my children. But as an author preparing a second edition I know that everyone will compare it with the first. For that reason I not only have relied on my own teaching experience with the book, but have also sought the reaction of colleagues and students to what works best and what does not. For indicating what is most enjoyable and effective, I want to thank my students at the International English Language Institute at Hunter College and readers around the world who have spoken or written to me about *Focus on Grammar: A Basic Course for Reference and Practice.*

My gratitude to the consultants who read the manuscript and offered numerous excellent suggestions: **Marcia Edwards Hijaab**, Virginia Commonwealth University, Richmond; **Kevin McClure**, ELS Language Center, San Francisco; **Tim Rees**, Transworld Schools, Boston; **Alison Rice**, International English Language Institute, Hunter College, New York. I also thank **Ellen Shaw**, University of Nevada, Las Vegas, **Ann Larson**, Oregon State University, Corvallis, and **Fran Golden**, Applied Language Institute, Kansas City, Missouri, for their insightful comments on the first edition.

My developmental editor **Carolyn Viola-John**'s devotion to this new edition has been exemplary, and she has offered creative solutions to the problems we have encountered. I thank **Christine Lauricella** for expertly guiding the book through the production process and **Matt McConnochie** for his work as a photo researcher. I thank **Sammy Eckstut** and **Deborah Gordon** for their apt comments and **Penny Laporte** for her keen awareness of the fine points of grammar. **Joan Saslow**, while not directly involved in this project, nonetheless influenced its outcome with her insights into language learning. I appreciate, too, the thoughtful comments of **Marjorie Fuchs** who helped strengthen the Grammar in Context sections and generously remarked on other aspects of the text.

Finally, a book of this type cannot be published without a talented director. I thank **Louisa Hellegers** for overseeing this project with her natural tact and humor. I appreciate too her always being available to answer any of my concerns.

Since this edition results from the popularity of the first, I want to thank the marketing team. My gratitude to **Anne Boynton-Trigg** and all those who presented this book to programs around the world.

And I want to acknowledge those who had a role in the first edition: **Nancy Perry**, **Penny Laporte**, **Louisa Hellegers**, **Joan Saslow**, **Allen Ascher**, **Alison Rice**, **Michelle Rayvid**, **Carlin Good**, **Pamela McPartland-Fairman**, **Laura T. LeDrean**, **Ellen Rosenfield**, **Cynthia Wiseman**, **Helen Ambrosio**, and **Lisa Hutchins**.

To **Joanne Dresner** who first directed this project, I owe more than words. This book would not have been possible without her initial ideas, support, and enthusiastic encouragement.

In the first edition of Focus on Grammar I wrote that being a parent of teenagers and writing a basic level grammar book are both humbling experiences. Now that my children are no longer teenagers, I seem to have become a bit smarter. I only hope that this is reflected in the second edition. To my family, **Harris**, **Dan**, and **Dahlia**, thank you for your love and support.

I.E.S

THE FIRST DAY OF CLASS

James Belmont is a photography teacher. Lulu is a new student. Listen and read their conversation.

LULU WINSTON:	Is this photography 101?
JAMES BELMONT:	Yes, it is. Please come in. I'm James Belmont.
LULU:	Nice to meet you. I'm Lucille Winston.
JAMES:	Is that W-I-N-S-T-O-N?
LULU:	That's right.
JAMES:	Ah yes. Here it is. And your first name is Lucille?
LULU:	Yes, but please call me Lulu.
JAMES:	Okay. Hello, Lulu. Welcome to class.
LULU:	It's good to be here.

THE ALPHABET

Listen and repeat the letters of the alphabet.

Aa Bb Cc Dd Ee Ff Gg Hh Ii Jj Kk Ll Mm Nn Oo Pp Qq Rr Ss Tt Uu Vv Ww Xx Yy Zz

CONVERSATION PRACTICE

Listen to this conversation. Work with a partner. Practice the conversation. Use your own names.

A: What's your name?

B: Milton Costa, but please call me Milt.

A: Okay, Milt. How do you spell that?

B: M-I-L-T.

A: Nice to meet you.

B: Nice to meet you, too.

Write the names of your classmates in a notebook.

THE VERB *BE:* PRESENT AND PAST

PREVIEW

Pete Winston is in New York, and Milt Costa is in Oregon. Listen and read their telephone conversation.

THE MYSTERY OF ROCKY

MILT: Hello.

PETE: Hi, Milt?

MILT: Yes.

PETE: This is Pete Winston.

MILT: Hi, Pete. How are you? How's business?

PETE: I'm fine, and business is great. But I'm worried.

MILT: Why? What's wrong?

PETE: I'm worried about my daughter Carol.

MILT: Why?

2

PETE: She's a student at Oregon State University, and she's in love.

MILT: That's wonderful!

PETE: No, it isn't. I don't know her boyfriend.

MILT: Is he a student?

PETE: No, he isn't.

MILT: Is he a teacher?

PETE: No, he isn't.

MILT: What's his name?

PETE: Rocky.

MILT: Rocky?

PETE: Yes, Rocky! Who is this Rocky? Milt, you're an old friend. You're in Oregon now. You're a great detective. Please help me.

MILT: I'll do my best.

PETE: Thanks, Milt. Bye.

MILT: Bye.

SUN WANG: Who was that?

MILT: That was Pete, an old friend.

COMPREHENSION CHECK

Check (✓) **That's right** *or* **That's wrong**.

	That's right.	That's wrong.
1. Pete and Milt are old friends.	☐	☐
2. Pete is worried about his business.	☐	☐
3. Pete is worried about his daughter.	☐	☐
4. Rocky is a student.	☐	☐
5. Milt was not alone.	☐	☐

WITH A PARTNER

Practice the conversation on pages 2 and 3.

THE PRESENT AFFIRMATIVE OF *BE*

GRAMMAR **IN CONTEXT**

WARM UP Is your school big? Is your school in a big city?

Oregon State University

Corvallis, Oregon

Location: small city

Student population: 15,000

Number of foreign students: 1,200

	Yes	No
1. Oregon State University is a big school.	☐	☐
2. Oregon State University is in a big city.	☐	☐

Milt Costa **is** from Brazil. He **is** in Oregon now. He **is** at Oregon State University. He **is** a detective.

Carol Winston **is** from New York. Yoko Mori **is** from Japan. They **are** new students at Oregon State University. They **are** roommates.

Oregon State University **is** big. It **is** clean and beautiful. The people **are** friendly. It **is** a nice place.

Carol, Yoko, and Yoko's dog **are** with Milt.

GRAMMAR **PRESENTATION**
AFFIRMATIVE STATEMENTS AND CONTRACTIONS WITH *BE*

AFFIRMATIVE STATEMENTS

SINGULAR		
SUBJECT	***BE***	
I	**am**	a student.
You	**are**	happy.
Milt He Carol She	**is**	in the United States.
Oregon It	**is**	a state. beautiful. in the United States.

PLURAL		
SUBJECT	***BE***	
Carol and I We	**are**	students.
You and Carol You Carol and Milt They	**are**	happy. in the United States.
Oregon and New York They	**are**	states. beautiful. in the United States.

CONTRACTIONS

I am	→ **I'm**	we are	→ **we're**
you are	→ **you're**	you are	→ **you're**
he is	→ **he's**	they are	→ **they're**
she is	→ **she's**	Pete is	→ **Pete's**
it is	→ **it's**		

NOTES

1. Every sentence has a subject. The subject is a noun or pronoun. **Subject pronouns** replace **subject nouns**. The subject pronouns are *I, you, he, she, it, we,* and *they.*

EXAMPLES

subject
noun
• **Milt** is a detective.

• **The girls** are students.

subject
pronoun
• **He** is in Oregon.

• **They** are roommates.

2. Every sentence has a verb. The **present tense** of the verb *be* has three forms: *am, are,* and *is*.

- I **am** from Taiwan.
- We **are** doctors.
- It **is** in the United States.

3. Use the verb *be* before **nouns, adjectives,** or **prepositional phrases**.

A noun can be singular (one) or plural (more than one). Plural nouns usually end in **-s**.

- He is **a detective**. *(singular noun)*
- They are **friends**. *(plural noun)*
- It is **big**. *(adjectives)*
- We are **happy**.
- Milt is **from Brazil**. *(prepositional phrases)*
- He is **in Oregon**.

4. Contractions are short forms. Contractions join two words together. Use contractions in speaking and informal writing.

A contraction joins subject pronouns and the verb *be*.

A contraction also joins a singular noun with *is*.

In a contraction, **an apostrophe (')** replaces a letter.

- **I'm** a teacher.
- **You're** from Caracas.
- **She's** in love.
- **It's** a boy!
- **We're** friends.
- **They're** roommates.

- Pete**'s** worried.
- His daughter**'s** in love.

FOCUSED PRACTICE

1 DISCOVER THE GRAMMAR

Read about the Wangs. Underline the subject and circle the verb in each sentence.

The Wangs are my friends. Sun and Nora Wang are teachers at Oregon State University. They are from Taipei in Taiwan. Sun is a biology teacher. Nora is a chemistry teacher. We are good friends and neighbors.

2 STUDENTS AT OREGON STATE   Grammar Notes 1–3

Complete the sentences. Use **am**, **is**, *or* **are**.

1. Oregon _____ a state.

2. It _____ in the United States.

3. Carol _____ in Oregon.

4. Yoko and Carol _____ in Oregon.

5. They _____ roommates.

6. They _____ new students.

7. We _____ students.

8. I _____ a student.

9. You _____ happy.

10. He _____ a detective.

3 MEET THE WANGS

Write contractions.

1. They _____ from Taipei.
   (are)
2. Sun _____ a biology teacher.
   (is)
3. We _____ good friends and neighbors.
   (are)

4 EDITING

Correct the passage. Add the verb **be** *in seven more places.*

This ʌ(is) my family. They in Brazil. This my sister Alessandra. She a teacher. This my brother Joao. He a businessman. My family far away, but thanks to e-mail, we close.

COMMUNICATION PRACTICE

5 WHERE ARE THEY FROM?

Work with a partner. Talk about the people. Match the people, the stamps, and the coins with the countries they're from.

EXAMPLES:
Leonardo DiCaprio is from the United States.
Coin O is from Great Britain.

a. Celine Dion

b. Arnold Schwarzenegger

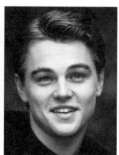
c. Leonardo DiCaprio

d. Prince William

e. Romario

f.   g.   h.   i.   j.   k.   l.   m.   n.   o.

1. Canada   2. the United States   3. Austria   4. Brazil   5. Great Britain

6 OCCUPATIONS

Check (✔) your occupation and the occupations of people in your family. Tell your partner. Any surprises? Tell the class.

EXAMPLE:

A: My sister's a detective. My uncle Sam is an artist. My mother is a businesswoman. I'm a student.

B: My father is a writer . . .

Occupations

- [ ] a businessman
- [ ] a businesswoman
- [ ] a detective
- [ ] a salesperson
- [ ] a student
- [ ] a teacher
- [ ] other _____
- [ ] a nurse
- [ ] a homemaker
- [ ] a doctor
- [ ] an athlete
- [ ] an electrician
- [ ] an artist
- [ ] a plumber
- [ ] a writer
- [ ] a singer
- [ ] a carpenter
- [ ] a lawyer

THE PRESENT NEGATIVE OF *BE*

GRAMMAR **IN CONTEXT**

WARM UP   Do you like mysteries? Is it difficult to be a detective? What do you think?

Listen and read Milt's thoughts.

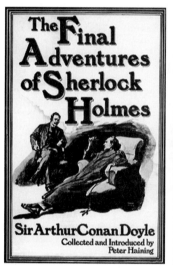

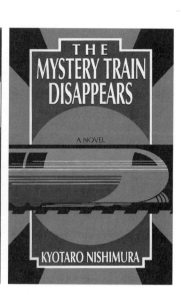

My work **is not** easy. Where is Rocky? He**'s not** on campus. He**'s not** in the telephone book. He**'s not** with Carol. Who is Rocky? He**'s not** a student. He**'s not** a teacher. Carol's happy, but Pete**'s not** happy. Pete's worried. But I**'m not** worried. After all, I'm Milt, the great detective.

GRAMMAR **PRESENTATION**
NEGATIVE STATEMENTS AND CONTRACTIONS WITH *BE*

SINGULAR	
SUBJECT *BE* / *NOT*	
I **am not** I**'m not**	a new teacher. old. from Japan.
You **are not** You**'re not** You **aren't**	
He **is not** He**'s not** He **isn't**	
She **is not** She**'s not** She **isn't**	

PLURAL	
SUBJECT *BE* / *NOT*	
We **are not** We**'re not** We **aren't**	teachers. old. from Japan.
You **are not** You**'re not** You **aren't**	
They **are not** They**'re not** They **aren't**	

It **is not** It**'s not** It **isn't**	a state. beautiful. from Japan.

They **are not** They**'re not** They **aren't**	states. beautiful. from Japan.

NOTES

1. Use *not* after the verb *be* in negative statements.

2. There are two ways to make **negative contractions**:

Join the subject pronoun and the verb *be*.

Join the verb *be* and *not*.

▶ **BE CAREFUL!** There is only one way to make a negative contraction with *I am not*—that is, **I'm not**.

EXAMPLES

• He **is not** a student.

• You**'re not** old.

• You **aren't** old.

• I**'m not** an engineer.

FOCUSED PRACTICE

1 DISCOVER THE GRAMMAR

Read Pete's thoughts. Then read the sentences. Check (✓) what's true.

> Carol's in Oregon. She's far away. I don't know her boyfriend. He isn't a teacher. He isn't a student. Who is he? I don't know. What's his occupation? I don't know. Milt's a good friend and a good detective, but his work is not easy.

1. Carol is far away.	✓	She isn't far away.	☐
2. Rocky is a teacher.	☐	He isn't a teacher.	☐
3. Milt and Pete are friends.	☐	They aren't friends.	☐
4. Pete's a detective.	☐	He's not a detective.	☐

2 A LETTER   Grammar Notes 1–2

Listen and read this letter from Milt to his sister. Listen again and complete the sentences. Use **I'm, He's, She's, He's not,** *or* **is not**.

                                                                    September 8

Hi Alessandra,

_____I'm_____ *in Oregon. I'm working for Pete Winston from New York.* _____
         1.   2.
an old friend. _____ *a nice man and a great businessman.* _____ *worried*
                      3.   4.
about his daughter, Carol. _____ *a new student at Oregon State University.*
                                    5.
_____ *in love. Rocky is her boyfriend.* _____ *a student.* _____ *a*
         6.   7.   8.
teacher. Pete _____ *happy. I want to help him.*
                       9.

   Write soon. Give my love to the family.

                                              Love,
                                              Milt

---

3 PEOPLE, PLACES, AND OCCUPATIONS   Grammar Notes 1–2

Read the story on page 5. Complete the sentences. Use **'m, 's, 're,** *or* **'m not, isn't,**
or **aren't.**

1. Yoko ___isn't___ in Japan now. She ___'s___ in Oregon.

2. Carol _____ from Oregon. She _____ from New York.

3. Milt, Yoko, and Carol _____ in New York now. They _____ in Oregon.

4. Milt _____ a teacher. He _____ a detective.

5. We _____ English teachers. We _____ students.

6. I _____ a student. I _____ an English teacher.

7. New York is a city. It _____ a state, too.

4 WHO ARE THEY?   Grammar Notes 1–2

*Read the conversation on pages 2 and 3. Complete the sentences. Use the words in
the box.*

He's, She's	He's not, She's not	They're	They're not

1. ___He's not___ a teacher. ___He's___ a
businessman.

2. _____ worried. _____ relaxed.

3. _____ friends. _____ cousins.

4. _____ young. _____
middle-aged.

5. _____ a teacher. _____

a student.

6. _____ from New York. _____

from Oregon.

7. _____ students. _____

detectives.

8. _____ in school. _____

at work.

Now say each negative statement another way. Use contractions.

EXAMPLE:

1. He _____isn't_____ a teacher.

COMMUNICATION PRACTICE

5 DESCRIBING YOURSELF

Check (✓) what is true for you. Read those sentences to a partner.

❏ I'm in love.	❏ I'm not in love.
❏ I'm a detective.	❏ I'm not a detective.
❏ I'm a new student.	❏ I'm not a new student.
❏ I'm worried.	❏ I'm not worried.
❏ I'm from an old city.	❏ I'm not from an old city.
❏ I'm busy.	❏ I'm not busy.
❏ I'm a businessman.	❏ I'm not a businessman.
❏ I'm an athlete.	❏ I'm not an athlete.
❏ I'm a plumber.	❏ I'm not a plumber.

In what ways are you and your partner alike?

EXAMPLE:
We're both new students.

6 THAT'S RIGHT / THAT'S WRONG

Introduce a classmate. Then make true and false statements about your classmate. The class listens and says **That's right** *or* **That's wrong** *and corrects the false statements.*

EXAMPLE:

PABLO: This is Juan Herrera. He's from Colombia. He's a student and an athlete. He's in love.

MARTHA: That's wrong. Juan's not from Colombia. He's from Venezuela.

PABLO: That's right. Juan's from Venezuela.

RICARDO: Juan's not in love.

PABLO: That's wrong. Juan's in love, but it's a secret.

RICARDO: Not anymore!

7 A GEOGRAPHY GAME

Work with a partner. Partner A reads sentences 1–4. Partner B reads sentences 5–8.
After each sentence, your partner says **That's right** *or* **That's wrong** *and corrects*
the wrong sentences. (See map on pages A-0 and A-1.)

EXAMPLE:

A: São Paulo is in Brazil.

B: That's right.

A: France is in Paris.

B: That's wrong. France isn't in Paris. Paris is in France.

Partner A

1. Great Britain is in Africa.

2. Mongolia is near China.

3. The United States is in Argentina.

4. Australia is near the United States.

Partner B

5. Mali is in Asia.

6. France is not near Spain.

7. Taiwan is near Hong Kong.

8. The United States is in New York.

Now use the map and make more sentences about the world. Your partner
answers **That's right** *or* **That's wrong** *and corrects the wrong sentences.*

8 THINK ABOUT IT

Work with a partner. Read the sentences and discuss them. Two sentences are
always true. Find them.

EXAMPLE:

A: Detectives are friendly.

B: No, that's not always true.

1. Detectives are friendly.

2. Teachers are women.

3. Taipei and Lima are capital cities.

4. Businessmen are clean.

5. Korea and Colombia are places.

6. New York is clean.

7. Students are happy.

8. Roommates are friends.

9. Washington, D.C. is in Washington.

10. English is easy.

THE PRESENT OF *BE:*
YES / NO QUESTIONS

GRAMMAR **IN CONTEXT**

WARM UP   What do you think? Is the first day of school difficult for new students? Is it difficult for new teachers?

It is the first day of school. Yoko and Al Brown are outside an English class. Listen and read their conversation.

YOKO: Excuse me. **Am I** late for class? **Is the teacher** here?

AL BROWN: **No**, **you're on time**. And **yes, the teacher is here.**

YOKO: Oh, good. I'm Yoko Mori. **Are you new here**?

AL BROWN: **Yes, I am**.

YOKO: I am, too. What's your name?

AL BROWN: Al Brown. Where are you from, Yoko?

YOKO: I'm from Japan. What about you?

AL BROWN: I'm from Michigan.

YOKO: Michigan? Then you're not a new student in this English class.

AL BROWN: You're right. I'm not a new student. I'm a new teacher. I'm *your* new teacher.

GRAMMAR **PRESENTATION**
YES / NO QUESTIONS AND SHORT ANSWERS WITH *BE*

YES / NO QUESTIONS

SINGULAR		
BE	**SUBJECT**	
Am	I	
Are	you	
	he	from Mexico?
Is	she	
	it	

PLURAL		
BE	**SUBJECT**	
	we	
Are	you	from Mexico?
	they	

SHORT ANSWERS

SINGULAR				
	YES		**NO**	
Yes,	you **are.**	**No,**	you**'re not.** you **aren't.**	
	I **am.**		I**'m not.**	
	he **is.**		he**'s not.** he **isn't.**	
	she **is.**		she**'s not.** she **isn't.**	
	it **is.**		it**'s not.** it **isn't.**	

PLURAL				
	YES		**NO**	
Yes,	you **are.**	**No,**	you**'re not.** you **aren't.**	
	we **are.**		we**'re not.** we **aren't.**	
	they **are.**		they**'re not.** they **aren't.**	

OTHER SHORT ANSWERS

I don't know.
Yes, I think so.
No, I don't think so.

NOTES	EXAMPLES
1. In **questions**, a form of *be* comes before the subject.	subject • **Am** I happy?
2. We usually answer *yes / no* questions with short answers.	**A:** Are you from Korea? **B: Yes.** OR **Yes, I am.**
▶ **BE CAREFUL!** Don't use contractions for short answers with *yes*.	**A:** Are they students? **B: Yes, they are.** NOT ~~Yes, they're.~~
3. We sometimes answer questions with long answers.	**A:** Are they students? **B: Yes, they are students.** OR **Yes, they're students.**
4. When we are unsure of an answer, we say, **"I don't know."**	**A:** Is Lima the capital of Peru? **B: I don't know.**
When we think something is true, we say, **"Yes, I think so."**	**A:** Is she a good athlete? **B: Yes, I think so.**
When we think something is untrue, we say **"No, I don't think so."**	**A:** Is it hot today? **B: No, I don't think so.**

FOCUSED PRACTICE

1 DISCOVER THE GRAMMAR

Look at the picture. Then match the questions and answers.

_____ **1.** Is it September 1st?

_____ **2.** Is it 9 o'clock?

_____ **3.** Is Al Brown in class?

_____ **4.** Is Yoko Mori late?

_____ **5.** Are the students worried?

a. No, they aren't.

b. No, she isn't.

c. No, it isn't.

d. Yes, he is.

e. Yes, it is.

2 PEOPLE AND PLACES

Grammar Notes 1–3

*Write **yes / no** questions. Then write short and long answers to the questions.*
Use contractions when possible.

1. Al Brown / from New York

   A: ___Is Al Brown from New York?___

   B: ___No, he's not. (No, he isn't.)___
     OR

   B: ___No, he's not from New York. He's from Michigan.___

2. you / from Australia

   A: _____

   B: _____
     OR

   B: _____

3. Rio de Janeiro / in Colombia

A: _____

B: _____

   OR

B: _____

4. Canada / near India

A: _____

B: _____

   OR

B: _____

5. Caracas and Mexico City / capital cities

A: _____

B: _____

   OR

B: _____

3 **A DETECTIVE AT WORK**   **Grammar Notes 1–2**

Listen and complete the sentences.

4 THE MYSTERY ENDS

Milt and Pete are talking on the telephone. Listen and read their conversation.

MILT: Hello.

PETE: Hi. Is that you, Milt?

MILT: Yes.

PETE: This is Pete.

MILT: Pete, it's 5 A.M. here.

PETE: Oh, I'm sorry. Any news about Rocky?

MILT: No.

PETE: Carol says, "Rocky is big and strong. With Rocky here, I'm safe. I love him."

MILT: Let me think. She says, "He's big and strong." She's safe with Rocky. Wait a second. I've got it.

PETE: You do?

MILT: Yes. Rocky *is* big and strong. And he lives with Carol and Yoko. I know him.

PETE: What?

MILT: Relax, Pete. Rocky is a dog. Rocky is Yoko's dog.

PETE: Rocky's a dog! Oh, Milt. You *are* a great detective. And I worry too much. Please Milt, don't tell Carol. This is our secret.

Now answer the questions. Use short answers.

1. Is it 5 A.M. in New York? ___No, it's not. (No, it isn't.)___

2. Is it 5 A.M. in Oregon? _____

3. Is Rocky big and strong? _____

4. Is Rocky a man? _____

5. Is Pete worried now? _____

6. Are you surprised? _____

COMMUNICATION PRACTICE

5 FIND SOMEONE WHO'S . . .

hungry

right-handed

a good soccer player

thirsty

from an island

left-handed

Go around the class. Use the words and phrases below to ask classmates **yes / no** *questions. Tell the class some interesting facts about your classmates.*

a good singer	hungry	from a new city
a good dancer	thirsty	from a capital city
a good writer	homesick	from an island
a good artist	right-handed	from an old city
a good soccer player	left-handed	usually early / late

EXAMPLE:

A: Mohammed, are you a good writer?

B: Yes, I am.

6 CARS

Work in small groups. Match the cars and countries.

_____ **1.** Fiats and Ferraris are from   **a.** Sweden

_____ **2.** Jeeps are from   **b.** France

_____ **3.** Hyundais are from   **c.** Japan

_____ **4.** Renaults and Peugeots are from   **d.** Korea

_____ **5.** Toyotas and Nissans are from   **e.** the United States

_____ **6.** Volvos and Saabs are from   **f.** Italy

Now play a game. A student in one group asks a student in another group a
yes / no *question about the cars above or other cars. If the answer is correct,
the student who answers wins a point for his or her group. The first group with
10 points wins.*

> **EXAMPLE:**
>
> **GROUP A STUDENT:** Are Hyundais from Korea?
>
> **GROUP B STUDENT:** Yes, they are.
>
> **GROUP A STUDENT:** You're right. (Group B wins a point)

7 EXPRESSING OPINIONS

Work with a partner. Ask each other **yes / no** *questions. Answer* **Yes, I think so**,
No, I don't think so, *or* **I don't know**. *Check (✔) your partner's answers.*

	Yes, I think so.	No, I don't think so.	I don't know.
1. Is Leonardo DiCaprio a good actor?	❑	❑	❑
2. Is Arnold Schwarzenegger a good actor?	❑	❑	❑
3. Is Celine Dion a good singer?	❑	❑	❑
4. Are Volvos good cars?	❑	❑	❑
5. Are Volvos popular cars?	❑	❑	❑
6. Are Jeeps expensive?	❑	❑	❑
7. Are Jeeps popular?	❑	❑	❑
8. (your own idea)	❑	❑	❑

THE **PAST TENSE** OF **BE;**
PAST TIME MARKERS

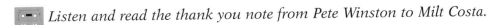

GRAMMAR **IN CONTEXT**

WARM UP   Are thank you notes easy for you to write?

 Listen and read the thank you note from Pete Winston to Milt Costa.

Dear Milt,

   Thanks for your help **last week**.
You **were** wonderful. I **was** very
worried about Carol. I know
she's 20 and she's an adult, but
for me she's still a little girl.

   Regards to your sister.

                              Fondly,
                              Pete

P.S. You're right, Milt. You really
   are Milt, the Great Detective!

Peter Winston
345 West 76 Street
New York, New York 10024

          Mr. Milt Costa
          2 Maple Street
          Corvallis, Oregon 97333

GRAMMAR **PRESENTATION**
THE PAST TENSE OF *BE*; PAST TIME MARKERS

AFFIRMATIVE STATEMENTS

SINGULAR			
SUBJECT	**BE**		**TIME MARKER**
I	**was**		
You	**were**	at a restaurant	**last night.**
He She It	**was**		

PLURAL			
SUBJECT	**BE**		**TIME MARKER**
We You They	**were**	at a restaurant	**last night.**

NEGATIVE STATEMENTS

SINGULAR			
SUBJECT	**BE / NOT**		**TIME MARKER**
I	**was not wasn't**		
You	**were not weren't**	at home	**last night.**
He She It	**was not wasn't**		

PLURAL			
SUBJECT	**BE / NOT**		**TIME MARKER**
We You They	**were not weren't**	at home	**last night.**

YES / NO QUESTIONS

SINGULAR			
BE	**SUBJECT**		**TIME MARKER**
Was	I		
Were	you	at work	**two weeks ago?**
Was	he she it		

PLURAL			
BE	**SUBJECT**		**TIME MARKER**
Were	we you they	at work	**two weeks ago?**

NOTES	EXAMPLES
1. The **past tense** of *be* has two forms: *was* and *were*.	• Bekir **was** late. • They **were** worried.
2. In informal writing and in speaking, use the contractions *wasn't* and *weren't* in negative statements and short answers.	• I **wasn't** in London. • They **weren't** students. • Were they at work? No, they **weren't**.
3. Past time markers can go at the beginning or the end of a sentence.	• **Yesterday** he was absent. • He was in Taipei **last week**.

PAST TIME MARKERS

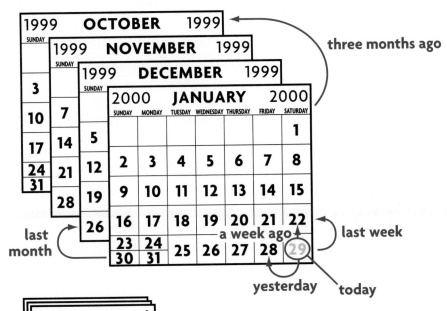

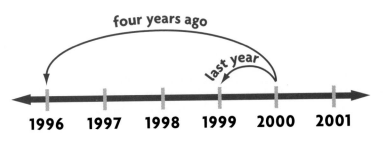

FOCUSED PRACTICE

1 DISCOVER THE GRAMMAR

Read the cartoon. Then circle the correct answer.

> How's your teacher?

> I don't know. Yesterday 2+2 was 4. Today 3+1 is 4!

1. Was the teacher right yesterday?

   a. Yes, she was.   **b.** No, she wasn't.

2. Is the teacher right today?

   a. Yes, she is.   **b.** No, she isn't.

3. Is the story funny?

   a. Yes, I think so.   **b.** No, I don't think so.

2 CLASS ATTENDANCE   Grammar Notes 1–2

Look at yesterday's attendance sheet (✔ = here). Complete the sentences with **was**, **wasn't**, **were** *and* **weren't**.

1. Pierre and Emiko _____*were*_____ absent yesterday.

   Yesterday they _____ here.

2. Juan and Gloria _____ here yesterday.

3. Anna _____ absent yesterday.

4. Gloria _____ absent yesterday.

	Yesterday
Pierre	*absent*
Juan	✔
Gloria	✔
Emiko	*absent*
Anna	*absent*

What about you?

I _____ yesterday.

3 AL BROWN'S CLASS

Al Brown is taking attendance. Listen. Then listen again and write a check (✔), **absent**, *or* **late** *next to the names.*

	Yesterday	**Today**
Yoko Mori	absent	✔
Bekir Ada		
Eun Young Kim		
Hector Gonzales		

4 THE WEATHER

Look at the chart and learn the words for different kinds of weather. Then complete the sentences about the weather in different places.

hot   warm   cool   cold

sunny   windy   rainy   cloudy

🌐 World Weather

	LAST WEEK	ONE MONTH AGO
Alaska	cold / cloudy	cold / sunny
Bangkok	hot / sunny	hot / sunny
Bogotá	warm / sunny	warm / cloudy

1. A: How was the weather in Bangkok last week?

B: It __was__ __hot__ and __sunny__.

A: And one month ago?

B: One month ago it _____ _____ and _____, too.

2. A: _____ it warm in Alaska last week?

B: No, it _____.

3. A: Was it sunny in Bogotá last week?

B: _____, _____ _____.

A: How was the weather in Bogotá one month ago?

B: It _____ _____ and _____.

4. A: Was it warm and sunny in Bogotá _____ _____?

B: Yes, it _____.

COMMUNICATION PRACTICE

5 INFORMATION GAP: THE WEATHER IN CAPITAL CITIES

Work in pairs.

Student A, look at this page. Ask your partner questions to complete the chart.

Student B, look at the Information Gap on page 37 and follow the instructions there.

World Weather					
	Yesterday		**Today**		
Mexico City	cool / cloudy		cool / cloudy		
São Paulo	warm / sunny		warm / sunny		
Washington, D.C.	cool / cloudy		cool / rainy		
Tokyo	_____		_____		
Seoul	_____		_____		
Taiwan	_____		_____		

EXAMPLES:

1. Is it hot in Tokyo today?

2. Was it hot in Tokyo yesterday?

3. How's the weather in Seoul today?

4. How was the weather in Seoul yesterday?

6 GAME

Work with a partner. Write three true and three false sentences. Use the words in the box.

hot	warm	cloudy	rainy	late	absent
cold	cool	sunny	windy	early	here

Now read your sentences to a partner. Your partner says **That's right** *or* **That's wrong** *and corrects the false sentences.*

EXAMPLES:

A: It's hot today.
B: That's right.

A: Juan was late yesterday.
B: That's wrong. Juan was early.

REVIEW OR SELFTEST

I. *Read each conversation. Circle the letter of the underlined word or group of words that is not correct.*

1. **YOKO:** Are you <u>a</u> new student?
      A

   BEKIR: Yes, <u>I'm</u>. I'm from Turkey. Where <u>are you</u>
              B   C

   from?

   YOKO: <u>I'm</u> from Japan.
             D

   A B C D

2. **JUAN:** You're old <u>student</u>.
                          A

   YOKO: No, you're wrong. We <u>aren't</u> old students.
                                    B

   Bekir and I <u>are</u> <u>new</u> students.
                C   D

   A B C D

3. **CAROL:** <u>It's</u> hot here.
               A

   YOKO: No, <u>it's not</u>. It's sixty degrees. <u>It's cold</u>.
                  B   C

   CAROL: Well, <u>I hot</u>.
                     D

   A B C D

4. **JUAN:** <u>Was</u> it hot in your room <u>last night</u>?
              A   B

   YOKO: No, it <u>isn't</u>. <u>It was</u> cold.
                     C   D

   A B C D

5. **JUAN:** <u>Was</u> Yoko and Bekir in class <u>yesterday</u>?
              A   B

   MARIA: <u>I don't know</u>. I <u>was</u> absent.
                C   D

   A B C D

II. *Circle the answer that best completes each sentence.*

1. Last week we _____ in Paris.
   (A) was   (C) is
   (B) are   (D) were

   A B C D

2. Yoko and Carol _____ absent yesterday.
   (A) were   (C) are
   (B) was   (D) is

   A B C D

3. _____ a detective?
   (A) Is you   (C) Are you
   (B) You   (D) You are

   A B C D

(continued on next page)

4. John _____ the United States.　　　　　　　　**A　B　C　D**
    (A) is from　　　　　(C) are from
    (B) am from　　　　(D) were from

5. Are you tired? Yes, _____.　　　　　　　　　　**A　B　C　D**
    (A) we tired　　　　(C) we be
    (B) we're　　　　　(D) we are

6. _____ Carol and Yoko at home last night?　　　**A　B　C　D**
    (A) Was　　　　　(C) Are
    (B) Were　　　　　(D) Be

III. *Write* **yes / no** *questions. Use the words in parentheses.*

A: (cloudy / yesterday) _____

B: No, it wasn't. It was sunny.

A: (cloudy / now) _____

B: Yes.

A: (you / in school / last week) _____

B: Yes, I was.

IV. *Correct this e-mail from Carol to her father. There are three mistakes.*

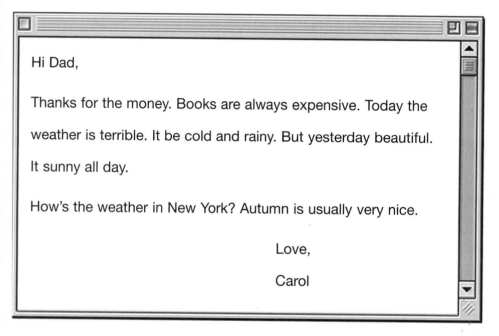

Hi Dad,

Thanks for the money. Books are always expensive. Today the weather is terrible. It be cold and rainy. But yesterday beautiful. It sunny all day.

How's the weather in New York? Autumn is usually very nice.

Love,

Carol

▸ *To check your answers, go to the Answer Key on page 37.*

FROM GRAMMAR TO WRITING
CAPITALIZATION

 Look at A and B. What's wrong with A?

A	B
mr. john smith 342 dryden road ithaca, new york 14850	Mr. John Smith 342 Dryden Road Ithaca, New York 14850

Study the information about capitalization.

Capitalization	
1. Use a **capital letter** for the first word in every sentence.	• **We** are new students.
2. Use capital letters for **titles**.	• This is **Mr.** Winston. • She is **Dr.** Jones.
3. Use capital letters for the names of **people** and **places** (proper nouns).	• **Lulu Winston** is from **Vancouver, Canada**.
4. Use capital letters for the names of **streets**, **cities**, **states**, **countries**, and **continents**.	• 5 **Elm Street** **West Redding, Connecticut** **U.S.A.**
5. Use a capital letter for the word *I*.	• **I** am happy to be here.

2 *Add capital letters.*

1. this is ms. herrera.

2. her address is 4 riverdale avenue.

3. i'm her good friend.

4. she was in bangkok and taiwan last year.

3 *Correct the postcard from Ellen to Ruth. Add capital letters.*

 Paradise Hotel

Hi ruth,

john and i are in acapulco this week. it's beautiful here. the people are friendly and the weather is great. it's sunny and warm.

last week we were in mexico city for two days. i was there on business. my meetings were long and difficult, but our evenings were fun.

hope all is well with you.

Regards,

ellen

To:

ms. ruth holland

10 oldwick court

ringwood, new jersey 07456

u.s.a.

Write a postcard to a friend.

To:

REVIEW OR SELFTEST
ANSWER KEY

I.
1. B
2. A
3. D
4. C
5. A

II.
1. D
2. A
3. C
4. A
5. D
6. B

III.
1. Was it cloudy yesterday?
2. Is it cloudy now?
3. Were you in school last week?

IV. It *is* cold and rainy. But yesterday *was* beautiful. It *was* sunny all day.

INFORMATION GAP FOR STUDENT B   Unit 4, Exercise 5

Student B, answer your partner's questions. Then ask your partner questions to complete the chart.

World Weather

	Yesterday			Today		
Mexico City	_____			_____		
São Paulo	_____			_____		
Washington, D.C.	_____			_____		
Tokyo	cool / sunny			cool / sunny		
Seoul	cool / sunny			cold / windy		
Taiwan	warm / cloudy			hot / cloudy		

EXAMPLES:
1. Is it hot in Mexico City today?
2. Was it hot in Mexico City yesterday?
3. How's the weather in São Paulo today?
4. How was the weather in São Paulo yesterday?

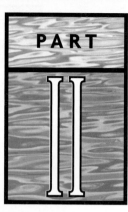

PART II
NOUNS, ADJECTIVES, AND PREPOSITIONS; THE PRESENT PROGRESSIVE

PREVIEW

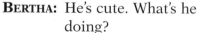 *Lulu Winston and Bertha Bean are friends. Lulu is looking at pictures of her family. Listen and read the conversation.*

WONDERFUL SONS, LUCKY DAUGHTERS-IN-LAW

LULU: Come, look at my pictures.

BERTHA: Not more pictures!

LULU: But these are special. They're my favorite pictures.

BERTHA: Okay, okay. Show me your pictures.

LULU: This is Bob at five.

BERTHA: He's cute. What's he doing?

LULU: He's fixing the toilet.

BERTHA: Oh?

LULU: You know, today he's a plumber. He's a very *successful* plumber.

BERTHA: I know. I know. Is this Pete?

LULU: Yes. He was eight years old in this photo.

BERTHA: Is he selling drinks?

LULU: Uh-huh. He's selling lemonade and orange juice. Today he's buying and selling businesses.

BERTHA: Are these your grandchildren?

LULU: Yes. They're my wonderful grandchildren.

BERTHA: Who are the women behind your grandchildren?

LULU: They're my daughters-in-law. My sons are so handsome!

BERTHA: They're pretty.

LULU: Pretty? My sons aren't pretty. They're handsome.

BERTHA: Your daughters-in-law are pretty.

LULU: My daughters-in-law are *lucky*. They're married to my wonderful sons.

BERTHA: They're not so lucky. You're their mother-in-law.

COMPREHENSION CHECK

Check (✔) **That's right**, **That's wrong**, *or* **I don't know**.

	That's right.	That's wrong.	I don't know.
1. Lulu thinks her sons are wonderful.	❏	❏	❏
2. Lulu thinks her grandchildren are wonderful.	❏	❏	❏
3. Lulu thinks her daughters-in-law are wonderful.	❏	❏	❏
4. Bertha thinks Lulu's daughters-in-law are lucky.	❏	❏	❏
5. Lulu thinks Bertha's lucky.	❏	❏	❏

WITH A PARTNER

Practice the conversation on pages 38 and 39.

COUNT NOUNS; *A / AN*

GRAMMAR **IN CONTEXT**

WARM UP Do you like to take pictures of your family and friends?

 *Lulu is showing her friend Adele photos of her granddaughters. Listen and read the conversation.*

ADELE: Who are they?

LULU: They're my **granddaughters**.

ADELE: Your **granddaughters**? They're lovely. Are they married?

LULU: No, they're single. This is **Norma** on the right. She's **a** Spanish **teacher**. And **Carol's** on the left. She's **a student**.

ADELE: My **grandson** is **a chef** and **an athlete**. He's single too, and he's new here. Do you think they'd like to meet **a chef**?

LULU: Of course. Everyone loves to eat. But they're not here. **Carol's** in **Oregon** and **Norma's** in **Massachusetts**.

ADELE: Invite them here this **winter**. Everyone loves **Florida** in **winter**. I'll introduce them to him.

GRAMMAR **PRESENTATION**
COUNT NOUNS; A / AN

SINGULAR NOUNS (ONE)	PLURAL NOUNS (MORE THAN ONE)

He is **a plumber**.

She is **an artist**.

Florida is **a state**.

They are **plumbers**.

They are **artists**.

Oregon and Florida are **states**.

NOTES

EXAMPLES

1. Nouns are the names of people, places, and things. Use *a* before singular **count nouns** that begin with a consonant sound.

▶ **BE CAREFUL!** Use *a* before a *u* that is pronounced like *u* in *university*.

- She's **a s**tudent.
- He's **a b**usinessman.
- It's **a h**ouse.

- It's **a u**niversity.

(continued on next page)

2. Use *an* before singular count nouns that begin with a vowel sound.

- She's **an a**ctress.
- He's **an e**ngineer.
- It's **an i**ce-cream cone.
- It's **an o**ven.
- It's **an u**mbrella.

▶ **BE CAREFUL!** Use *an* before an *h* that is silent.

- It's **an h**our too early.

3. Do not put *a* or *an* before plural nouns.

- **Lemons** are yellow.

4. The names of people and places are **proper nouns**. These are always capitalized. Do not put *a* or *an* before proper nouns.

- **Bangkok** is the capital of **Thailand**.
- **Lulu** is a grandmother.

5. Do not use *a* or *an* before non-count nouns.

- His **hair** is brown.

REFERENCE NOTE
See Unit 33 for a discussion of non-count nouns.
See Appendix 7, pages A-7 and A-8, for the spelling rules for plural nouns.
See Unit 33 and Appendix 10, page A-10, for the use of the definite article *the*.
See Appendix 18, page A-18, for pronunciation of the phonetic alphabet.

FOCUSED PRACTICE

1 DISCOVER THE GRAMMAR

Read about James Belmont.

James Belmont is a photographer and an artist. He takes photos from all over the world. James is now in Miami. He's a photography teacher at a local college.

Look at the reading again and find the following.

1. Find a noun that begins with a vowel sound. _____

2. Find a proper noun. _____

3. Find a plural noun. _____

2 PEOPLE, PLACES, THINGS
Grammar Notes 1–2

Listen and complete the sentences. Use **a** or **an** before a singular noun. Leave a blank before a plural noun.

1. He's ___*a*___ plumber.

2. We are _____ students.

3. It's _____ house.

4. These are _____ watches.

5. It's _____ hour.

6. They are _____ businessmen.

7. We're _____ teachers.

8. These are _____ earrings.

9. She's _____ actress.

10. This is _____ orange.

3 PLURAL NOUNS

Look at the spelling rules for plural nouns on pages A-7 and A-8 in Appendix 7.
Complete the sentences. Use the plural form of each noun.

1. (son) These are my _____ sons _____ .

2. (woman) They are _____ women _____ .

3. (country) We're from different _____ .

4. (city) Our _____ are far from here.

5. (picture) They are new _____ .

6. (brother) My _____ are tall.

7. (class) My _____ are in room 302 and room 410.

8. (watch) Our _____ are from Japan.

9. (potato) These _____ are big.

10. (dictionary) These _____ are good.

4 EDITING

*Yoko and Marcos are in their English class. Read their conversation. Add **a***
*or **an** in two places. Then listen and check your work.*

MARCOS: What's this?

YOKO: It's ^a^ pen.

MARCOS: Is that eraser?

YOKO: Yes.

MARCOS: Is he teacher?

YOKO: Yes, he is. He's Al Brown.

COMMUNICATION PRACTICE

 LEARNING THE NAMES OF CLASSROOM OBJECTS

Work with a partner. Look at the picture on page 44 and learn the names of objects in the classroom. Point to the objects and ask your partner questions.

EXAMPLES:

A: Is that a pen? **A:** What's that?
B: Yes, it's a pen. **B:** It's a book bag.

Classroom Objects

a desk	an audio cassette recorder	a CD player	a wastepaper basket
a book		a CD (compact disc)	a pen
a notebook	a VCR (video cassette recorder)	a chalkboard	an eraser
a book bag		a map	a computer
a table	a video cassette	a ruler	a television
an audio cassette			

Now make a list of singular and plural objects in your classroom.

Singular	**Plural**
a VCR	pens

 **MY FAVORITE MONTH, DAY, CITY**

Work with a partner. Add words to each list. Tell your partner about your favorites.

EXAMPLES:
My favorite day is Friday.
My favorite month is December.

Days of the Week	**Months of the Year**	**Cities**
Sunday	January	Venice
Monday	February	Kyoto

Now tell the class about your partner's favorites.

EXAMPLES:
Maria's favorite day is Friday.
Her favorite month is December.

6 DESCRIPTIVE ADJECTIVES

GRAMMAR **IN CONTEXT**

WARM UP Circle the words that describe your home.

big - small	new - old	comfortable - uncomfortable
messy - neat	clean - dirty	safe - dangerous

Listen and read the letter from Carol to Lulu.

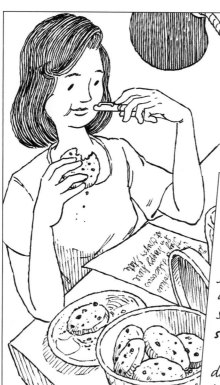

Dear Grandma Lulu,

Thanks so much for the cookies. They're **delicious**. I'm **happy** here at Oregon State. My roommate, Yoko, is from Japan. She's a **new** student, too. She's **nice** and very **neat**. She looks like an actress. She's **tall** and **thin**. Her hair is **short** and **straight**.

We have a **small** apartment and a **big** dog. Our dog's name is Rocky. He's **loud** and **lovable**. We're **safe** with Rocky around.

My classes are **interesting**, and my teachers are **friendly**. I'm **lucky** to be here. I hope you're **fine**. Please write.

Love,
Carol

GRAMMAR **PRESENTATION**
DESCRIPTIVE ADJECTIVES

NOUN	BE	ADJECTIVE
Arnold Schwarzenegger	is	**strong**.
Arnold Schwarzenegger and Sylvester Stallone	are	

	ADJECTIVE	NOUN
He is a	**famous**	actor.
They are		actors.

NOTES

EXAMPLES

1. Adjectives describe nouns.

- Arnold Schwarzenegger is **strong**.

2. Adjectives can come after the verb *be*. Adjectives come before a noun.

- Yoko is **young**.
- He is a **famous** man.
  NOT ~~He is a man famous.~~

3. Adjectives do not change form.

singular
- **new** student, **tall** boy

plural
- **new** students, **tall** boys
  NOT ~~news students, talls boys~~

4. When a noun follows an adjective, use *an* before the adjective if the adjective begins with a vowel sound.

- He's **an** interesting actor.

Use *a* before the adjective if the adjective begins with a consonant sound.

- She's **a** strong athlete.

5. Do not use *a* or *an* when the adjective is not followed by a noun.

- It is important.
- He is tall.

FOCUSED PRACTICE

1 DISCOVER THE GRAMMAR

Underline the adjective or adjectives in each sentence.

1. The movie was <u>interesting</u>, but it was long.

2. The tall man is a carpenter.

3. That pie was delicious.

4. They are wonderful actors.

2 OPPOSITES
Grammar Note 1

Read Carol's letter to her grandmother again. Find an adjective in the letter that means the opposite of each adjective below.

1. big _____ small _____

2. boring _____

3. curly _____

4. heavy _____

5. old _____

6. quiet _____

7. long _____

8. unfriendly _____

9. unhappy _____

10. unlucky _____

Dear Grandma Lulu,
    Thanks so much for the cookies. They're **delicious**. I'm **happy** here at Oregon State. My roommate, Yoko, is from Japan. She's a **new** student, too. She's **nice** and very **neat**. She looks like an actress. She's **tall** and **thin**. Her hair is **short** and **straight**.
    We have a **small** apartment and a **big** dog. Our dog's name is Rocky. He's **loud** and **lovable**. We're **safe** with Rocky around.
    My classes are **interesting**, and my teachers are **friendly**. I'm **lucky** to be here. I hope you're **fine**. Please write.
                    Love,
                    Carol

3 CLASSROOM OBJECTS
Grammar Notes 1–2

Write questions to complete the conversations. Use the words in slashes.

1. Was / new / it / a / notebook

    A: ___ Was it a new notebook _____ ?

    B: Yes, it was.

2. new / Is / tape / the / long

    A: _____?

    B: Yes, it's three hours long.

3. interesting / Are / the / videos

    A: _____?

    B: Yes, they're very interesting.

---

4 EDITING

Grammar Notes 1–4

Correct the mistakes in the conversations.

1. A: Are those ~~olds~~ ^old^ videos?

    B: Yes, they are. They're from 1985.

    A: Are they interestings?

    B: I think so.

2. A: That's a computer expensive. Is it new?

    B: Yes, it is.

    A: Are you happy with it?

    B: Yes, it's a good.

3. A: Those news books were longs.

    B: Were they interestings?

    A: I don't think so.

4. A: Athens is a city old.

    B: It's a place interesting.

    A: You're right.

COMMUNICATION PRACTICE

5 OUR CITY

Work with a partner. Write adjectives to describe your city.

EXAMPLE:
Our city is clean.

Our city is _____.

6 OBJECTS IN OUR CLASSROOM

Work with a partner. Look around the classroom. Describe objects in your classroom. Use the adjectives in the box.

big	brown	dark	interesting	long	new	small	straight

EXAMPLE:
That's a new notebook.

7 FRIENDS

Work in small groups. Study the adjectives. Use your dictionary for new words. Then check (✓) the words that describe good qualities.

_____ **1.** honest   _____ **5.** cold   _____ **9.** good-looking   _____ **13.** helpful

_____ **2.** friendly   _____ **6.** forgetful   _____ **10.** understanding _____ **14.** quiet

_____ **3.** warm   _____ **7.** funny   _____ **11.** serious   _____ **15.** shy

_____ **4.** dishonest   _____ **8.** loyal   _____ **12.** kind   _____ **16.** talkative

EXAMPLE:
It's good to be honest.

Now tell about a friend.

EXAMPLE:
A: My friend Janet is very funny. I love to be with her.
B: My friend Sue is not funny, but she's very helpful and kind. That's important to me.

PREPOSITIONS OF PLACE

GRAMMAR **IN CONTEXT**

WARM UP Look at the picture. Where is Pete?

Listen and read the conversation.

DR. GRUEN: Hi, Pete.

PETE WINSTON: Hello, George. It's nice to see you. How's your family?

DR. GRUEN: Everyone's fine. How are you?

PETE: OK, but I think I need new glasses.

DR. GRUEN: Well, Pete, let's see. Look at the chart and answer these questions. Where's the Q?

PETE: It's **next to** the W.

DR. GRUEN: Good. And the W?

PETE: The W is **between** the Q and the Z. And the O is **under** the W.

DR. GRUEN: Wonderful. And what's **under** my nose?

PETE: Your nose? That's easy. A handsome, new mustache.

DR. GRUEN: Your eyesight is excellent. See you here next year.

PETE: Great. And see you at the concert next week.

GRAMMAR **PRESENTATION**
PREPOSITIONS OF PLACE

These are common prepositions of place.

under **behind** **on** **next to**

between **near** **in**

The briefcase is **under** the desk.

The blackboard is **behind** the desk.

The dictionary is **on** the desk.

The apple is **on** the desk, too.
It is **next to** the dictionary.

The apple is **between** the
dictionary and the computer.

The computer is **near** the
apple and the dictionary.

The newspaper is **in** the
wastepaper basket.

NOTES

1. Prepositions of place tell where
something is. Some common prepositions
of place are *under, behind, on, next to,
between, near, in*.

▶ **BE CAREFUL!** *Near* and *next to* are not the
same. Look at the letters of the alphabet:

ABCDEFGHIJKLMNOPQRSTUVWXYZ

EXAMPLES

- My book bag is **under** my seat.
- Your umbrella is **near** the door.

- The letter A is **next to** the letter B. It is
  near the letter B, too.
- The letter A is **near** the letter C, but it
  is not **next to** the letter C.
- The letter J is not **next to** the letter A.
- It is not **near** the letter A, either.

FOCUSED PRACTICE

1 DISCOVER THE GRAMMAR

Look at the pictures. Complete the sentences.

__e__ **1.** The teacher is

_____ **2.** The briefcase, dictionary, apple, and computer are

_____ **3.** The wastepaper basket is

_____ **4.** The VCR is

_____ **5.** The apple is on the desk. It's

_____ **6.** The dictionary is on the desk. It's

_____ **7.** The blackboard is

_____ **8.** The newspaper is

a. on the desk.

b. under the television.

c. in the wastepaper basket.

d. between the computer and the dictionary.

e. under the desk.

f. behind the desk.

g. near the desk.

h. next to the apple.

2 A COCKROACH IN THE KITCHEN! Grammar Note 1

Look at Yoko and Carol's kitchen.

*Put an **R** on the refrigerator.*
*Put an **N** on the napkin.*
*Put an **S** on the sink.*
*Put an **ST** on the stove.*
*Put a **C** on the counter.*

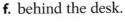 *Listen to the conversation. Yoko and Carol are very unhappy. There's a cockroach in their kitchen. Put checks (✔) where the cockroach was. Then complete the sentence.*

	A			B
1. on the refrigerator	✔	*or*	under the refrigerator	☐
2. on the counter	☐		under the counter	☐
3. on the napkin	☐		under the napkin	☐
4. between the counter and the sink	☐		between the sink and the stove	☐

5. At the end of the conversation, Carol and Yoko are _____.

    a. happy   **b.** unhappy

COMMUNICATION PRACTICE

3 GUESS THE COUNTRY

*Work with a partner. Write sentences about a country's location. Use the prepositions **between**, **near**, **next to**, and **in**. Read your sentences to your partner. Your partner guesses the country. (See the map on pages A-0 and A-1.)*

EXAMPLE:
This country is between Japan and China. It's near Mongolia. It's next to China. It's in Asia. What country is it?

4 TEST YOUR MEMORY

Work with a partner. Your partner closes his or her eyes. Ask your partner where objects in your classroom are. Then ask your partner where classmates are.

EXAMPLES:

A: Where's the chalkboard?   **A:** Where's Maria?
B: It's near the door.   **B:** She's between Luis and Yuriko.

Now ask your partner about places in your school. Use the words in the box.

cafeteria	water fountain	ladies' room	library
elevator	stairs / staircase	mens' room	

EXAMPLE:
A: Where is the cafeteria?
B: It's next to the library.

5 A WORD GAME

One student reads the following clues to the class. The clues spell a word. The class listens and guesses the word.

Clues:

1. There are seven letters in this word.
2. The first letter is *e*.
3. The last letter is *h*.
4. The letter *n* is next to the *e*. What is the word?
5. The letter *s* is next to the *h*. What is the word?

6. The letter *n* is between the *e* and a *g*. What is the word?
7. The letter *s* is between the *h* and an *i*. What is the word?
8. The letter *l* is in the middle. What is the word?

The word is ____ ____ ____ ____ ____ ____ ____.

Write your own word puzzle. Read it to your class.

PRESENT PROGRESSIVE

GRAMMAR **IN CONTEXT**

WARM UP In some countries the jobs of men and women are changing. More women in the United States are becoming police officers, bus drivers, doctors, and lawyers. What's happening in your country?

PERCENTAGE OF WOMEN LAW AND MEDICAL SCHOOL GRADUATES (UNITED STATES)			
Law School		**Medical School**	
1960	2.5%	1960	5.5%
1995	42.6%	1995	38.8%

Elenore is talking to her mother-in-law, Lulu. Listen and read their telephone conversation.

ELENORE: Hello?
　　LULU: Hi, Elenore. This is Lulu.
ELENORE: Hello, Lulu. How are you doing?
　　LULU: I'm fine. How are my wonderful grandchildren?
ELENORE: Everyone's okay. You know, **Norma's working** in Boston. **She's teaching**. Doug's the captain of his soccer team.
　　LULU: That's great. How's Carol?
ELENORE: Well, she's at school. I hope **she's studying**. Carol's not a letter writer, but I'm sure she's fine.
　　LULU: Is Pete there? **Is he watching** the tennis matches on TV?
ELENORE: No, **he isn't watching** TV. He's not here right now. **He's doing** the laundry.
　　LULU: *What's* my son doing?
ELENORE: The laundry.
　　LULU: Oh. My poor baby.
ELENORE: What was that?
　　LULU: Nothing. What's Doug doing now?
ELENORE: He's at the supermarket. **He's shopping**.
　　LULU: And what about you? What are you doing?
ELENORE: **I'm doing** the taxes.
　　LULU: *You're* doing the taxes! That's a man's job.

GRAMMAR **PRESENTATION**
PRESENT PROGRESSIVE

AFFIRMATIVE STATEMENTS

SUBJECT	BE	BASE FORM OF VERB + -ING
I	am	
You	are	
He She It	is	working.
We You They	are	

NEGATIVE STATEMENTS

SUBJECT	BE	NOT	BASE FORM OF VERB + -ING
I	am		
You	are		
He She It	is	not	working.
We You They	are		

YES / NO QUESTIONS

BE	SUBJECT	BASE FORM OF VERB + -ING
Am	I	
Are	you	
Is	he she it	working today?
Are	we you they	

SHORT ANSWERS

	AFFIRMATIVE			NEGATIVE	
	you	are.		you're	
	I	am.		I'm	
Yes,	he she it	is.	No,	he's she's it's	not.
	you we they	are.		you're we're they're	

NOTES

1. Use the **present progressive** (also called the *present continuous*) to talk about an action that is happening now (as you are speaking).

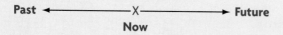

Past ◄————————X————————► Future

Now

EXAMPLES

- The baby **is crying**. She's hungry.
- **It's raining** today.

2. Do not repeat the subject and the verb *be* when the subject is doing two things.

- Doug is **eating** and **drinking**.
  NOT ~~Doug is eating and Doug is drinking.~~

3. The subject and *be* are reversed when asking a *yes / no* question in the present progressive.

statement
- **He is** working.

question
- **Is he** working?

4. Use **contractions** in speaking and in informal writing.

- **I'm** not cooking. **I'm** doing the laundry.
- Elenore **isn't** cleaning. **She's** doing the taxes.
- We **aren't** working. **We're** resting.

5. Use contractions in negative answers in speaking and writing.

- No, **you're not**. OR No, **you aren't**.

6. We usually use short answers in speaking, but we can also use long answers.

- Is she sleeping?
- **No.** OR No, **she's not sleeping**.
- **No, she's not.** OR No, **she's not sleeping**.
- **No, she isn't.** OR No, **she isn't sleeping**.

REFERENCE NOTE
See Appendix 13, page A-13, for spelling rules for the present progressive.
See Unit 26 for verbs that are not usually used in the progressive form.

FOCUSED PRACTICE

1 DISCOVER THE GRAMMAR

Listen and read the weather and traffic report. Underline the present progressive. Then answer the questions.

Good morning. This is Ted Treitel with this morning's weather and traffic. Take your umbrellas. It's raining right now in midtown, and the temperature is 40 degrees Fahrenheit. As for traffic, Route 5 is a good road into the city. Cars are moving quickly. But don't take Highway 11. There's an accident, and cars aren't moving at all.

Check (✔) True or False.

	True	False
1. It's raining in midtown.	☐	☐
2. Cars aren't moving on Route 5.	☐	☐
3. Cars aren't moving on Highway 11.	☐	☐

2 FAMILY PICTURES

Grammar Notes 1, 3–4

Complete the conversation. Use the present progressive and the verb in parentheses.

BERTHA: That's a wonderful picture of Carol.

_____Is_____ she _____wearing_____
1. (wear)

a costume?

LULU: No. That's not a costume. She _____ a
2. (wear)

cape. It was a present from me. Look.

Here's Doug.

BERTHA: He's very serious.

LULU: I know. He _____ because
3. (smile, not)

he's worried about soccer. Soccer is his

life this year.

BERTHA: _____ Elenore and Pete _____
4. (have)

a fight?

LULU: I don't think so. I think they _____.
5. (dance)

It's a strange picture of them.

BERTHA: Okay, Lulu. Enough pictures. Let's go out for lunch.

It's 12:00. They _____ a lunch special at
6. (offer)

China Palace between 11:30 and 12:30.

LULU: Okay. I _____ hungry.
7. (get)

③ WHAT ARE THEY DOING? Grammar Notes 4–6

Write **yes / no** *questions in the present progressive. Then read the conversation on page 55 again and answer the questions. Use short answers.*

1. Lulu / talk to Pete

A: Is Lulu talking to Pete? _____

B: No she's not. (No, she isn't.) _____

2. Doug / shop

A: _____

B: _____

3. Elenore / do laundry

A: _____

B: _____

4. Lulu and Elenore / talk about the weather

A: _____

B: _____

5. Pete / watch TV

A: _____

B: _____

4 A DUANE HANSON SCULPTURE

Duane Hanson is an American artist. His sculptures show Americans doing everyday things. This is a photo of one of his sculptures. Write about it. Use the present progressive in your sentences.

1. sit / at a table

Two people ___are sitting at a table.___

2. wear jeans, a plaid shirt, leather shoes

The _____

3. a house dress

The _____

4. watches

Both of them _____

5. wear glasses

The _____

6. read / eat ice cream

_____

7. look at / the woman

The _____

8. not talk

They _____

COMMUNICATION PRACTICE

5 WHAT AM I DOING NOW?

Check the sentences that are true for you.

1. ☑ I'm holding a pen.   ☐ I'm not holding a pen.
2. ☐ I'm sitting next to a man.   ☐ I'm not sitting next to a man.
3. ☐ I'm sitting next to a woman with glasses.   ☐ I'm not sitting next to a woman with glasses.
4. ☐ I'm looking out the window.   ☐ I'm not looking out the window.
5. ☐ I'm wearing comfortable shoes.   ☐ I'm not wearing comfortable shoes.
6. ☐ I'm wearing a watch.   ☐ I'm not wearing a watch.
7. ☐ I'm wearing jeans.   ☐ I'm not wearing jeans.
8. ☐ I'm thinking about the present progressive.   ☐ I'm not thinking about the present progressive.
9. ☐ I'm daydreaming.   ☐ I'm not daydreaming.
10. ☐ I'm smiling.   ☐ I'm not smiling.
11. ☐ I'm _____ (your own idea)   ☐ I'm not _____.

Read your sentences to a partner. Listen to his or her sentences. What are both you and your partner doing now? Tell the class.

> **EXAMPLES:**
> We are both wearing comfortable shoes.
> We are not holding pens.

6 CAN I CALL YOU BACK LATER?

Work with a partner. Practice the telephone conversation. Use the verbs in the box and your own ideas. Partner A calls Partner B. Partner B is busy and wants to call Partner A back later. Then Partner B calls, but Partner A wants to call back later.

study	write a letter	read my e-mail	watch TV and eat
work	eat	take a bath / shower	clean
your own idea			

> **EXAMPLE:**
> **ALI:** Hello, Juan. This is Ali.
> **JUAN:** Hi, Ali.
> **ALI:** Are you busy, Juan?
> **JUAN:** Well, <u>I'm watching a good movie on TV</u>. Can I call you back in a few minutes?
> **ALI:** Sure.

(continued on next page)

Repeat your telephone conversations for the class. Listen to your classmates'
conversations. Write down what each student is doing.

EXAMPLES:

Juan is watching a movie on TV.

Emiko is reading her e-mail.

7 INFORMATION GAP: WHAT'S THE DIFFERENCE?

Work with a partner.

Partner A, look at this picture. Write
sentences about your picture. Use the verbs
in the box. Then, talk with your partner
about the differences in your pictures. Find
five differences.

Partner B, look at the Information Gap on
page 67 and follow the instructions.

chase	eat	fight	play	rain	read	sleep	watch TV

EXAMPLE:

A: In my picture, the father is watching TV.

B: In my picture, he's . . .

A: Is the mother reading and eating popcorn in your picture?

8 CHARADES

Act out a situation in front of your class. The class guesses what you are doing.

Suggestions

You are watching a sad movie.

You are sleeping and snoring.

You are reading a boring book.

You are telling your friend a secret.

You are eating very spicy food.

You are arguing about your bill at a restaurant.

You are sewing.

9 GAME: WHAT'S EVERYONE WEARING?

A. *Work with a partner. Look at the illustration. Label the clothes and accessories.*

a. watch	**e.** cap	**i.** overalls	**m.** glasses
b. earring	**f.** sweatshirt	**j.** shoes (athletic)	**n.** blouse
c. ring	**g.** skirt	**k.** socks	**o.** vest
d. belt	**h.** shoes (loafers)	**l.** sweater	**p.** pants/slacks

B. *Partner A, look at your classmates for a minute. Close your eyes. Try to answer your partner's questions. Partner B, ask* **yes / no** *questions about students in the class.*

EXAMPLE:

B: Is Maria wearing a short skirt and small earrings?

A: No, she isn't. She's wearing a long skirt and big earrings.

REVIEW OR SELFTEST

I. *Read each conversation. Circle the letter of the underlined word or group of words that is not correct.*

1. **A:** <u>Is</u> <u>it's</u> raining outside?
       A   B

   B: Yes, <u>it is</u>. I'm <u>not</u> leaving.
              C   D

                                                               A   B   C   D

2. **A:** <u>Are they</u> <u>play</u> soccer?
       A   B

   B: <u>No</u>, they're <u>playing</u> baseball.
          C   D

     A   B   C   D

3. **A:** <u>She's wearing</u> <u>a</u> red blouse.
           A   B

   B: No, she's <u>no</u> wearing a red blouse. She's wearing a
                   C

   <u>red</u> sweater.
   D

   A: Oh.

     A   B   C   D

4. **A:** <u>Are</u> <u>they</u> <u>youngs</u> men?
       A   B   C

   B: <u>I think so</u>. They're in college.
          D

     A   B   C   D

5. **A:** They're <u>news</u> <u>students</u>.
                  A   B

   B: No, they <u>aren't</u>. They're <u>old</u> students.
                   C   D

     A   B   C   D

II. *Complete the sentences. Circle the correct answers.*

1. He is _____.

   (A) a man strong   (C) strong man

   (B) a strong man   (D) strong men

   A   B   C   D

2. They are my _____.

   (A) grandchild   (C) a grandchild

   (B) the grandchildren   (D) grandchildren

   A   B   C   D

3. This is _____.

   (A) oranges   (C) an orange

   (B) a orange   (D) an oranges

   A   B   C   D

4. Is this _____?

   (A) clean towel   (C) towels clean

   (B) clean towels   (D) a clean towel

   A   B   C   D

5. Are _____?

   (A) you sleeping   (C) sleeping

   (B) you sleep   (D) you be sleeping

   A   B   C   D

III. *Complete the sentences. Use* **a** *or* **an** *or leave a blank.*

1. He isn't _____ teacher. He's _____ student. He's _____ new in this school.

2. She isn't _____ actress. She's _____ singer.

3. They're _____ famous. They're _____ actors.

4. Our grammar class isn't long. It's _____ hour.

5. This is _____ hospital. It's near the university.

6. He's _____ uncle. She's _____ aunt. This is their nephew.

7. This is _____ grammar book. It's _____ helpful book. It's _____ interesting, too.

IV. *Complete the sentences. Use the words in the box. Look at the world map on pages A-0 and A-1 if you need help.*

between	in	next to

1. France is _____ Europe.

2. The United States is _____ the Atlantic Ocean and the Pacific Ocean.

3. Pakistan is _____ India.

4. Brazil is _____ South America.

V. *Complete the paragraph. Use the affirmative and negative present progressive of each verb in parentheses.*

Carol and her friend Dan are at the library, but they're not studying now.

Carol _____ a letter. Her American history book is on the table, but she
         1. (write)
_____ the history book. Carol _____ next to Dan. Dan's biology
   2. (read)   3. (sit)
book is in front of him, but he _____ his biology book. He _____
                                    4. (read)   5. (look)
at a magazine. Carol and Dan _____ and _____ a break.
                                  6. (relax)   7. (take)
They _____ now.
         8. (work)

▶ *To check your answers, go to the Answer Key on page 67.*

FROM GRAMMAR TO WRITING SUBJECTS AND VERBS

1 *What's wrong with these sentences?*

A

1. He a handsome man.
2. She a red skirt.
3. I from Argentina.

B

1. Am wearing blue pants.
2. Are tired?
3. Is a cool day.

All sentences in A are missing a verb.

All sentences in B are missing a subject.

Study the information about subjects and verbs.

Subjects and Verbs

Every sentence needs a subject and verb.

The **subject** is a noun or pronoun. It tells who or what did something.

- **John** is running.
- **They** are watching TV.

The **verb** tells the action or links the subject with the rest of the sentence.

- It **is raining**.
- He **is** a doctor.

---

2 *Correct this paragraph. Then underline the subject and circle the verb in each sentence.*

I in Central Park. It a sunny day in September. Is crowded. Some children soccer. They're laughing and shouting. Some people are jogging. Three older women on a bench. Are watching the joggers and soccer players. A young man and woman are holding hands. Are smiling. Are in love. Central Park a wonderful place to be on a beautiful September day.

3 *Imagine you are in one of the following places. Write one paragraph about the people you see there.*

1. You are on a bus.

2. You are in a restaurant or cafeteria.

3. You are in a park.

REVIEW OR SELFTEST
ANSWER KEY

I.
1. B
2. B
3. C
4. C
5. A

II.
1. B
2. D
3. C
4. D
5. A

III.
1. a; a; ____
2. an; a
3. ____; ____
4. an
5. a
6. an; an
7. a; a; ____

IV.
1. in
2. between
3. next to
4. in

V.
1. is writing
2. isn't reading
3. 's sitting (is sitting)
4. 's not reading (isn't reading)
5. 's looking (is looking)
6. are relaxing
7. taking
8. aren't working

INFORMATION GAP FOR STUDENT B
Unit 8, Exercise 7

Partner B, look at this picture. Write sentences about your picture. Use the verbs in the box. Then, talk with your partner about the differences in your pictures. Find five differences.

| chase | eat | fight | play | rain | read | sleep | watch TV |

EXAMPLE:

A: In my picture, the father is watching TV.

B: In my picture, he's . . .

A: Is the mother reading and eating popcorn in your picture?

PART III

WH- QUESTIONS; POSSESSIVES; PREPOSITIONS OF TIME

PREVIEW

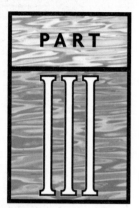

Carol is looking at a photograph of her family. Listen and read the conversation between Yoko and Carol.

THE WINSTON FAMILY

YOKO: What are you looking at?

CAROL: A photo of my family. It was in that package from my Mom.

YOKO: Whose birthday was it?

CAROL: My Dad's. He was fifty.

YOKO: When was that?

CAROL: Last summer.

YOKO: Where were you?

CAROL: In Cape Cod, Massachusetts.

YOKO: Who's standing on the left? Is that your sister?

CAROL: Uh-huh. That's Norma. She lives in Massachusetts. She's a Spanish teacher. We're very different.

YOKO: Oh?

CAROL: She's serious about everything. She wants to save the world. Not like me. She loves animals and she's a vegetarian. I like animals, but I live on chicken and burgers.

YOKO: You *are* different. How old is she?

CAROL: She's twenty-six years old, six years older than me. She's divorced.

YOKO: Who's that?

CAROL: Doug, my younger brother. He's fifteen and in his second year of high school. He lives with my parents. These days Doug and my Dad are having problems.

YOKO: What are they fighting about?

CAROL: About his music, his hair, and his grades.

YOKO: I think he's cute. Who's behind the cake? Is that your Dad?

CAROL: Yes. He's like Norma, very serious. He's a businessman.
My parents and my brother live in New York. My Mom, Elenore, is standing next to Doug.

YOKO: She looks happy.

CAROL: She usually is. She's a writer and a people person. Actually, she gets along well with everyone except my Grandma Lulu.

YOKO: And that's Grandma Lulu.

CAROL: Right. Grandma Lulu lives in Florida. She's seventy-three.

YOKO: Seventy-three? She looks great.

CAROL: I know, but she's lonely. She doesn't work. She lives in Florida and her two sons live far away.

YOKO: How old's your Mom?

CAROL: Forty-nine. And that, of course, is me.

YOKO: It's a great picture of you.

CAROL: Thanks.

COMPREHENSION CHECK

Label the people in the picture. Then complete the chart about the Winstons.

NAME	AGE	OCCUPATION	LIVES IN
Carol			
Norma			
Doug			
Pete			
Elenore			
Lulu			

WITH A PARTNER

Practice the conversation on pages 68 and 69.

9 QUESTIONS WITH *WHO, WHAT,* AND *WHERE*

GRAMMAR **IN CONTEXT**

WARM UP What's a nice birthday gift for an older person?

Listen and read the conversation between Lulu and her friend Bertha.

LULU: **Who**'s there?

BERTHA: It's me, Bertha.

LULU: Oh, come on in.

BERTHA: Hi. You know, I was here an hour ago and you weren't home. **Where** were you?

LULU: At the hairdresser's.

BERTHA: Oh, I *see.* Your hair is beautiful.

LULU: Thanks. **What**'s that?

BERTHA: It's a small gift.

LULU: A gift? **Who**'s it for?

BERTHA: For you. It's October 15th. Happy birthday.

LULU: Oh, Bertha. Thanks so much. It's heavy. **What** is it? Is it a book?

BERTHA: No, it's a photo album.

LULU: How lovely. Thank you, thank you, thank you. I feel like I'm twenty-one, not seventy-one.

BERTHA: You're not seventy-one. You're seventy-three.

LULU: Shh. It's a secret.

WHAT'S YOUR OPINION?

Is it impolite to ask people their age?

GRAMMAR **PRESENTATION**
QUESTIONS WITH *WHO*, *WHAT*, AND *WHERE*

QUESTIONS WITH *WHO*

QUESTIONS			ANSWERS
QUESTION WORD	BE		
Who	is	Lulu's friend?	Bertha. Bertha is. Bertha is Lulu's friend.
Who	are	friends?	Lulu and Bertha. Lulu and Bertha are. Lulu and Bertha are friends.

QUESTIONS WITH *WHAT*

QUESTIONS			ANSWERS
QUESTION WORD	BE		
What	is	lovely?	The photo album. The photo album is. The photo album is lovely.
What	are	these books?	Dictionaries. They're dictionaries. These books are dictionaries.

QUESTIONS WITH *WHERE*

QUESTIONS			ANSWERS
QUESTION WORD	BE		
Where	is	Lulu?	At the hairdresser's. She's at the hairdresser's.
Where	are	the presents?	On the table. They're on the table.

NOTES	EXAMPLES
1. *Wh-* **questions** (or information questions) ask for information. They cannot be answered with a *yes* or *no*.	**A: What** is it? **B:** It's a book.
2. Use *who* for questions about people.	**A: Who**'s seventy-three years old? **B:** Lulu is.
3. Use *what* for questions about things.	**A: What**'s a secret? **B:** Lulu's age.
4. Use *where* for questions about locations.	**A: Where** was Lulu? **B:** At the hairdresser.
5. We sometimes use contractions for *wh-* questions with *is* in speaking and informal writing.	• **Who's** there? • **What's** his last name? • **Where's** the dictionary?

FOCUSED PRACTICE

1 DISCOVER THE GRAMMAR

Read about Pete's business trip. Then match the questions and answers.

Last week Pete was in Bangkok on business. His flight was long and boring, but his trip was a success.

_____ **1.** Who was in Bangkok last week?   **a.** Pete's flight to Bangkok.

_____ **2.** Where was Pete last week?   **b.** In Bangkok.

_____ **3.** What was long and boring?   **c.** Pete was.

2 CAN YOU DO ME A FAVOR?   Grammar Notes 1–5

Read and learn these phrases. Then listen to the telephone conversation between Elenore and Pete.

at the movies	at the theater	at a ball game	at a party
at a concert	at work	at school	at home
in the kitchen	in the living room	in the bedroom	in the bathroom

(continued on next page)

Now circle the correct answers to the questions.

1. Where's Elenore?

  a. at Doug's school   **b.** at home   **c.** at a ball game

2. What's in the living room?

  a. a newspaper   **b.** a notebook   **c.** a book

3. Who's at home?

  a. Bertha   **b.** Elenore   **c.** Pete

4. Where's Lulu?

  a. at a concert   **b.** at the movies   **c.** at the theater

5. What's the name of the book Elenore wants?

  a. *The Color Purple*   **b.** *The Red and the Black*   **c.** *The Color of Water*

3 TELEPHONE CALLS

A. *Listen and complete the phone conversations in Part 1. Use* **who's**, **what**, **what's**, *and* **where**.

Part 1

JEFF'S MOTHER: Hello. _____ this?
                                            1.

DOUG: Hi, Mrs. Kim. It's Doug. Is Jeff there?

JEFF'S MOTHER: Oh, hi Doug. No, I'm sorry. Jeff isn't here.

DOUG: _____ is he?
                    2.

JEFF'S MOTHER: He's at a party.

DOUG: Please tell him I called.

NOAH'S FATHER: Hello?

DOUG: Hi, Mr. Jones. Is Noah there?

NOAH'S FATHER: No, I'm sorry. _____ this?
                                                        3.

DOUG: It's Doug Winston.

NOAH'S FATHER: Oh, hi Doug. I think Noah's at the movies.

DOUG: Well, please tell him I called.

DINO'S SISTER: Hello.

DOUG: Hello. This is Doug. Is Dino there?

DINO'S SISTER: Oh, hi Doug. Dino isn't here now. He's watching a ball game at Sue's house. *[background noise]*

DOUG: Excuse me. _____ was that?
          4.

DINO'S SISTER: He's at Sue's house.

DOUG: Well, please tell him I called.

ELENORE: _____ the matter Doug?
          5.

DOUG: Jeff's at a party, Noah's at the movies, and Dino's at Sue's house. Today is my birthday and all my friends are busy.

B. *Answer the questions. Then listen and complete Part 2.*

1. Where's Jeff? _____

2. Who's at the movies? _____

3. What's special about today for Doug? _____

Part 2

[Ten minutes later the doorbell rings, and Doug opens the door.]

NOAH, JEFF, DINO: _____ _____

DOUG: You guys are really something.

COMMUNICATION PRACTICE

❹ NOBODY IS HOME

Make up a telephone conversation. Practice the conversation with a partner.

A: Hello.

B: _____. This is _____. Is _____ there?

A: _____.

B: Where is he?

A: _____.

B: Well, what about _____?

A: _____.

B: Please tell them I called.

❺ WHERE ARE THEY?

Work with a partner. Read the following sentences. Guess where the people are.
(There are many correct answers.)

1. **LULU:** Hi, Bertha. Please come in.

   Where's Lulu? __I think she's at home._____

2. **DOUG:** This music is great.

   Where's Doug? _____

3. **ELENORE:** Shh! Please be quiet. This book is hard to understand.

   Where's Elenore? _____

4. **CAROL:** Ouch! The water's hot.

   Where's Carol? _____

5. **VALERIE:** Oh Pete, Elenore. I'm so glad you're here. Please come in. The drinks are here
   and the food is over there.

   Where are Pete and Elenore? _____

6 OUR OPINIONS

Complete the questions and answer them for yourself. Then ask a partner the questions and complete the chart with your partner's answers.

	You	**Your Partner**
1.	_____What's_____ your favorite subject?	
2.	_____ two good writers?	
3.	_____ your favorite vegetable?	
4.	_____ two good new movies?	
5.	_____ a good actor?	
6.	_____ two beautiful cities?	
7.	_____ your favorite sport?	
8.	_____ two good TV shows?	

Do you and your partner like the same people and the same things?

7 A MEMORY GAME

One student studies the class and the classroom. Then the student sits in the front of the class with his or her eyes closed. The class asks questions about people and things in the room.

> **EXAMPLE:**
> Who's next to the door?
> What's between the _____ and the _____?
> Where's John?

10 POSSESSIVE NOUNS AND POSSESSIVE ADJECTIVES; QUESTIONS WITH *WHOSE*

GRAMMAR **IN CONTEXT**

WARM UP   Are grades important in a language class? Why?

Al Brown is talking to the students in his class. He has three papers without names. Listen and read the conversation.

AL BROWN: **Whose** composition is this?

BEKIR: Is it a good paper?

AL BROWN: It's excellent.

BEKIR: It's **my** composition.

YOLANDA: No, that's not your handwriting. It's **Yoko's** composition. She's absent today.

AL BROWN: Thanks, Yolanda. **Whose** paper is this?

BEKIR: Is it a good paper?

AL BROWN: It's okay.

BEKIR: I think it's **my** composition.

JUAN: It's not **your** composition. It's **my** composition. See, **my** name is on the back.

AL BROWN: Okay, Juan. Here's **your** composition. **Whose** composition is this?

BEKIR: Is it a good paper?

AL BROWN: Well, it needs work.

BEKIR: It isn't **my** composition.

AL BROWN: Oh yes it is. I have a grade for everyone else.

Whose composition is this?

GRAMMAR **PRESENTATION**
POSSESSIVE NOUNS AND ADJECTIVES; QUESTIONS WITH *WHOSE*

POSSESSIVE NOUNS	
SINGULAR NOUNS	**PLURAL NOUNS**
Lulu's last name is Winston.	The **girls'** gym is on this floor.
That **boy's** book bag is next to mine.	The **boys'** gym is near the elevator.

POSSESSIVE ADJECTIVES		
SUBJECT PRONOUNS	**POSSESSIVE ADJECTIVES**	**EXAMPLE SENTENCES**
I	**my**	**I** am a student. **My** name is Carol.
you	**your**	**You** are next to me. **Your** seat is here.
he	**his**	**He's** a professor. **His** subject is computers.
she	**her**	**She's** my grandmother. **Her** name is Lulu.
it	**its**	**It's** Yoko's dog. **Its** name is Rocky.
we	**our**	**We** are businessmen. **Our** business is in the United States and Asia.
you	**your**	**You** are students. **Your** classroom is near the gym.
they	**their**	**They** are students. **Their** school is in Oregon.

QUESTIONS WITH *WHOSE*	
QUESTIONS	**ANSWERS**
Whose hair is long?	Carol**'s**. Carol**'s** is. Carol**'s** hair is long.
Whose eyes are blue?	Carol**'s**. Carol**'s** are. Carol**'s** eyes are blue.
Whose pen is this?	Yoko**'s**. It's Yoko**'s**. It's Yoko**'s** pen.
Whose pens are these?	Yoko**'s**. They're Yoko**'s**. They're Yoko**'s** pens.

NOTES	EXAMPLES
1. **Possessive nouns** and **possessive adjectives** show belonging.	• **Elenore's car** (the car belongs to Elenore) • **her** car (the car belongs to her)
2. Add an **apostrophe (')** + **s** to a **singular noun** to show possession. Add an **apostrophe (')** to a **plural noun** ending in *s* to show possession.	• That's Yoko**'s** paper. • The boy**s'** gym is on the third floor.
3. **Possessive adjectives** replace **possessive nouns**. Possessive adjectives agree with the possessive noun they replace, not the noun that follows.	**His** • ~~Doug's~~ sisters are in Oregon and Massachusetts. **Her** • ~~Carol's~~ brother is in New York.

4. A **noun** always follows a possessive noun or a possessive adjective.
 	
▶ **BE CAREFUL!** Do not confuse "Carol's" in "Carol's hair is long" with "Carol's" in "Carol's a student."
 	
Do not confuse *its* and *it's*.
its = possessive adjective; *it's* = *it is*
	noun
	• **Yoko's book** is new.
	     noun
	• **Her book** is new.
	
	   subject verb
	• **Carol's hair** is long.
	 subject verb
	• **Carol's** a student.
	
	• This is my turtle. **Its** name is Tubby.
	• **It's** a hot day.

5. Use *whose* for questions about possession. ▶ **BE CAREFUL!** *Who's* is the contraction of *who is*. It sounds like the possessive *whose*.	• **Whose** notebook is this? • **Who's** a student? Carol is. • **Whose** hair is long? Carol's is.

REFERENCE NOTE
See Appendix 8, page A-8, for more rules about possessive nouns.

FOCUSED PRACTICE

1 DISCOVER THE GRAMMAR

Read the conversation between Carol and Yoko. Underline the possessive adjectives. Circle the possessive nouns.

CAROL: Hey, Yoko, the apartment looks great, but where are all <u>my</u> things?

YOKO: What are you looking for?

CAROL: Well, for one, where's (Grandma Lulu's) letter?

YOKO: Her letter? It's in the desk drawer.

CAROL: Oh, I see it. Where's Dan's cap? It was on the sofa before.

YOKO: His cap is in the closet.

CAROL: Got it. And what about my brother's and sister's birthday cards?

YOKO: Their cards are on the table over there. Anything else?

CAROL: No, I think that's all.

2 FAMILY RELATIONSHIPS   Grammar Notes 1–2, 4

Complete the sentences. Use the words in the box.

grandmother	mother	aunt	sister	sister-in-law	niece	me
grandfather	father	uncle	brother	brother-in-law	nephew	

1. My mother's mother is my ___grandmother___. My father's mother is my

   _____, too.

2. My mother's father is my _____. My mother's brother is my

   _____. My mother's sister is my _____.

3. My brother's son is my _____. My brother's daughter is my _____.

4. My husband's brother is my _____. My husband's sister is my

   _____.

5. My grandmother's daughter is my _____ or my _____.

6. My grandfather's son is my _____ or my _____.

7. My father's daughter is my _____ or _____.

8. My mother's son is my _____ or _____.

BONUS POINTS: What's a step-sister? a great-grandmother? a cousin?

3 BELONGINGS

Change the possessive nouns to possessive adjectives.

1. ~~Carol's~~ *Her* school is in Oregon.

2. The cats' food is in a bowl.

3. Pete's mother is in Florida.

4. Yoko's teacher is Al Brown.

5. The dog's fur is brown.

6. Elenore and Pete's apartment is in New York City.

7. My mother-in-law's home is in London.

8. The girls' bicycles are in the garage.

4 QUESTIONS

Complete the questions. Use **where's**, **who's**, **whose**, *and* **what's**.

1. _____ his last name? It's Winston.

2. _____ in the kitchen? Mom is.

3. _____ books are on the floor? Carol's.

4. _____ your homework? It's at home.

5 BERTHA BEAN'S FAMILY

Complete the sentences. Use subject pronouns and possessive adjectives.

____My____ name is Bertha Bean. ____I____ live in Florida.
　　1.　　　　　　　　　　　　　　　　　2.

_____ am a widow. I have two children, a son and a
　3.

daughter. _____ son is a police
　　　　　　　　4.

officer. _____ is forty years
　　　　　5.

old. _____ name is Jack.
　　　6.

_____ wife is a nurse. They
　7.

live in Connecticut. They have three

children. _____ children are seven, six, and three years old.
　　　　　　8.

　　My daughter is a teacher. _____ is thirty-three years
　　　　　　　　　　　　　　　　9.

old.

_____ is single. _____ home is in Boston. _____ lives near
　10.　　　　　　　　11.　　　　　　　　　　　　　12.

Lulu Winston's granddaughter Norma. _____ daughter and Lulu's
　　　　　　　　　　　　　　　　　　13.

granddaughter are neighbors. Lulu and I are neighbors and friends.

COMMUNICATION PRACTICE

6 FAMILY TREES

Draw your family tree. Then work in small groups. Tell your group about different people in your family.

EXAMPLE:
Woo Hyun Lee is my mother's brother. He's my favorite uncle. He's a businessman. He's in the United States now. He's a strong and intelligent man.

Grandfather Grandmother Grandfather Grandmother

Father Mother Uncle

Brother Me

7 GAME: WHOSE BROTHER IS THIS?

Bring in photos of family members. Write how the person is related to you on the back of the photo (my sister, my mother, my aunt, etc.). The teacher collects the photos and gives each student a photo. Students ask questions about the photos.

EXAMPLE:
STUDENT 1: Whose _____sister_____ is this?
STUDENT 2: I think it's Juan's.
JUAN: You're right. She's my sister. (*Now Juan asks a question.*)

8 FIND SOMEONE WHOSE __ / FIND SOMEONE WHO'S __

Complete the questions. Use **whose** *or* **who's**. *Then ask your classmates these questions. Write their answers.*

1. _____Whose_____ birthday is in February? _____Juan's is._____

2. _____ good in art? _____

3. _____ handwriting is beautiful? _____

4. _____ a good athlete? _____

5. _____ eyes are green? _____

6. _____ a good cook? _____

7. _____ first name is long? (eight or more letters) _____

8. _____ book bag is heavy? _____

9. _____ birthday is in the summer? _____

10. _____ a good dancer? _____

QUESTIONS WITH *WHEN* AND *WHAT* + NOUN; PREPOSITIONS; ORDINAL NUMBERS

GRAMMAR **IN CONTEXT**

WARM UP What is your favorite holiday? When is it?

Listen and read the conversation between Doug and his friends Noah and Dino.

NOAH: Hey Doug.

DOUG: Hey Noah, Dino. How're you doing?

NOAH: Okay. And you?

DOUG: Good. By the way, what's the next school holiday?

NOAH: Election Day.

DOUG: **When** is it?

NOAH: It's **on** the **first** Tuesday in November.

DINO: Not always.

NOAH: Yes it is.

DINO: No it's not.

DOUG: Then **what day** is Election Day?

DINO: Election Day is **on** the **first** Tuesday after the **first** Monday **in** November. This year it's *not* **on** the **first** Tuesday **in** November.

NOAH: Okay, okay. You're such a genius.

GRAMMAR **PRESENTATION**
QUESTIONS WITH *WHEN* AND *WHAT* + NOUN;
PREPOSITIONS OF TIME; ORDINAL NUMBERS

WHEN		
WHEN	**VERB**	
When	is	Independence Day?

ANSWERS

It's on July 4th.
On July 4th.
July 4th.

WHAT + NOUN			
WHAT	**NOUN**	**VERB**	**OBJECT**
What	**day**	is	the party?
What	**time**	is	the party?

ANSWERS

It's on Monday.
On Monday.
Monday.

It's at 8:00.
At 8:00.
8:00.

PREPOSITIONS OF TIME	
Her graduation is	**in** December. **in** (the) winter. **in** 1999. **in** the morning. **in** the afternoon. **in** the evening.
Is your birthday	**on** Wednesday? **on** December 25th?
The party is	**at** 7:30. **at** night.

ORDINAL NUMBERS

1st = first	12th = twelfth	32nd = thirty-second
2nd = second	13th = thirteenth	40th = fortieth
3rd = third	14th = fourteenth	43rd = forty-third
4th = fourth	15th = fifteenth	50th = fiftieth
5th = fifth	16th = sixteenth	60th = sixtieth
6th = sixth	17th = seventeenth	70th = seventieth
7th = seventh	18th = eighteenth	80th = eightieth
8th = eighth	19th = nineteenth	90th = ninetieth
9th = ninth	20th = twentieth	100th = hundredth
10th = tenth	21st = twenty-first	101st = one hundred first
11th = eleventh	30th = thirtieth	

NOTES	EXAMPLES
1. Use *when* or *what* + **noun** for questions about time.	• **When** is your party? It's on Tuesday. • **What day** is your party? It's on Tuesday.
2. We usually use **prepositions** when we answer questions about time. *in* + months, seasons, years *in* + *the morning, the afternoon, the evening* *on* + days of the week *on* + the date *at* + the exact time *at* + *night*	• It's **in** January. • Her graduation was **in** 1999. • My son is at camp **in the afternoon**. • It's **on** Monday and Wednesday. • It's **on** January 4. • It's **at** ten o' clock **in the morning** and **at** eight o' clock **at night**.
3. There are two kinds of numbers: **cardinal**—*one, two three*. **ordinal**—*first, second, third*. Use **ordinal numbers** for dates, streets, and floors of a building.	• She has **three** classes on Thursday. • Her **first** class is at 9:00. • His birthday is on January **twentieth**. OR • It's on January **20th**. • Her apartment is on **Seventy-seventh** Street. OR • It's on **77th** Street.
4. Use **ordinal numbers** to number things in a sequence. The spelled form is used.	• Her **first** class is English. Her **second** is math. Her **third** class is history. NOT ~~Her 1st class is English.~~

REFERENCE NOTE
See Appendix 3, pages A-3 and A-4, for a list of cardinal and ordinal numbers.
See Appendix 3, pages A-3 and A-4, for a list of the days, months, and seasons.
See Appendix 4, page A-4, for information about telling time.

FOCUSED PRACTICE

1 DISCOVER THE GRAMMAR

MAY

SUNDAY	MONDAY	TUESDAY	WEDNESDAY	THURSDAY	FRIDAY	SATURDAY
	1	2	3	4	5	6
7	8 Meet Denise at New Age Tea	9	10	11 Book group, 7 P.M.	12	13
14	15	16	17	18	19	20 Pick up theater tickets
21	22	23	24 10 A.M. Dr. Koren	25	26	27
28	29	30 Writer's Conference 6 to 8 P.M.	31			

JUNE

SUNDAY	MONDAY	TUESDAY	WEDNESDAY	THURSDAY	FRIDAY	SATURDAY
				1	2	3
4	5 Return library books	6	7	8	9	10 Doug's soccer game 2 P.M.
11	12	13	14 Meet with editor for lunch	15	16	17 Wedding Natalie and Les 9 P.M.
18	19	20	21	22	23	24
25	26	27	28	29	30	

Look at Elenore's calendar. Match the occasion, the date, and the time.

Occasion	Date	Time
1. The Writer's Conference is	on June 10	in the afternoon
2. Elenore's doctor's appointment is	on June 17	at night
3. Doug's soccer game is	on May 30	in the morning
4. Natalie and Les' wedding is	on May 24	in the evening

2 SCHEDULE OF EVENTS

A. *Look at Pete's old planner. Complete the conversations. Use* **When**, **What time**, **on**, **at**, *and* **in the**.

```
                        WEEKLY PLANNER
   ◯  MONDAY                            January 1st
                                       NEW YEAR'S DAY


      TUESDAY                          January 2nd
         meeting with Doug Nagano-10 A.M.
   ◯     meeting with Carol Loomis-12:30 P.M.
         meeting with Art Kantor, Ray Stone, Marilyn Hooper-4 P.M.

      WEDNESDAY                        January 3rd
         fly to São Paulo- 7 P.M. flight


   ◯  THURSDAY                         January 4th
         free day



      FRIDAY                           January 5th
         talk to marketing directors - 2 P.M.
   ◯     talk to communications directors-3:30 P.M.
```

1. **A:** _____ was Pete's meeting with Doug Nagano?

   B: It was _____ January 2nd _____ _____ morning.

2. **A:** _____ was Pete's flight to São Paulo?

   B: It was _____ night.

   A: _____ _____ was it?

   B: It was _____ 7 P.M.

3. **A:** _____ was Pete's talk?

   B: It was _____ January 5th. It was _____ _____ afternoon.

B. *Complete the sentences with* **first**, **second**, *and* **third**.

1. Pete's ____first____ meeting was on January 2nd at 10 A.M. His _____

   meeting was at 12:30 P.M., and his _____ was at 4 P.M.

2. On January 5th, Pete's _____ talk was at 2 P.M. and his _____ talk

   was at 3:30 P.M.

❸ WHERE'S THE PARTY?   Grammar Notes 3–4

Pete and Elenore are going to a party. They are confused. Listen to their conversation. Then listen again and complete the sentences.

1. John and Sue live _____ Street between _____ and

   _____ Avenue.

2. Their apartment is _____ floor.

3. John and Alice live _____ Street between _____ and

   _____ Avenue.

4. Their apartment is _____ floor.

❹ NATIONAL HOLIDAYS   Grammar Notes 1–2, 4

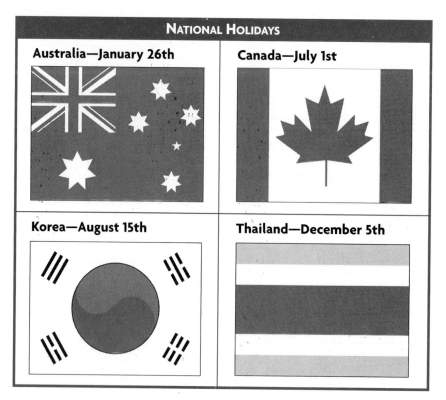

Look at the chart and answer the questions.

1. When is Australia's national holiday? _It's on January 26th._____

2. When is Thailand's national holiday? _____

3. What country's national holiday is on July 1st? _____

4. What country's national holiday is in August? _____

COMMUNICATION PRACTICE

5 INFORMATION GAP: HOLIDAYS AROUND THE WORLD

Work in pairs.

Student A, look at the chart on this page. Ask your partner questions to complete your chart.

Student B, look at the Information Gap on page 105 and follow the instructions there.

EXAMPLES:
What country's national holiday is on _____? (date)
What month is _____'s national holiday?
What's the date of _____'s national holiday?
What country's national holiday is in _____? (month)
When is _____'s national holiday?

NATIONAL HOLIDAYS AROUND THE WORLD						
COUNTRY		**MONTH**	**DAY**	**COUNTRY**		**MONTH**	**DAY**
Argentina			25th	Haiti		January	
Brazil		September		Italy		June	2nd
		April	16th	Japan		December	22nd
Dominican Republic		February	27th	Lebanon		November	22nd
Ecuador		August		Turkey		October	29th
Greece			25th	**United States of America**		July	4th
Your country's national holiday:							

6 SCHOOL HOLIDAYS

Work in small groups. Look at a school calendar. What are your school's holidays? When are they?

 QUESTIONS WITH *WHO, WHOM,* AND *WHY; WH-* QUESTIONS AND THE PRESENT PROGRESSIVE

GRAMMAR **IN CONTEXT**

WARM UP   Check the kinds of TV shows you like.

comedies	☐	news magazines	☐	movies	☐
medical dramas	☐	news	☐	music videos (MTV)	☐
police dramas	☐	sports	☐		
legal dramas	☐	talk shows	☐	mysteries	☐

What's your favorite TV show? _____

 *Bertha calls Lulu. Listen and read their conversation.*

LULU: Hello.

BERTHA: Hi, Lulu? Bertha. How are you doing?

LULU: So-so. My back is still bothering me.

BERTHA: Gee, I'm sorry to hear that. Is that the TV?

LULU: Yes.

BERTHA: It's very loud. **Where are you watching TV?**

LULU: In my bedroom. The phone is near the TV.

BERTHA: **What are you watching?**

LULU: *Sleepless in Seattle.*

BERTHA: Oh. That was a good movie. I just love romantic comedies. Who's in it again?

LULU: Tom Hanks and Meg Ryan.

BERTHA: Oh yeah. **What's happening?**

LULU: Tom Hanks is asking a woman for a date.

BERTHA: **Who's he asking?** Meg Ryan?

LULU: No. That comes later.

BERTHA: **Why are you watching TV now?** Your photography class is in half an hour.

LULU: Not today. Our teacher is away.

BERTHA: Oh. Well then, enjoy the movie. And feel better.

LULU: Thanks. Bye.

BERTHA: Bye.

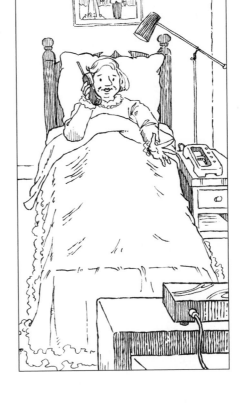

GRAMMAR **PRESENTATION**
QUESTIONS WITH *WHO, WHOM,* AND *WHY;*
WH- QUESTIONS AND THE **PRESENT PROGRESSIVE**

WH- WORD	*BE*	SUBJECT	BASE FORM OF VERB + *-ING*	ANSWERS
Who	is		sleeping?	Lulu is. Lulu is sleeping.
What	is		happening?	I'm cooking for our party.
Who(m)	is	Doug	meeting?	Noah. Doug is meeting Noah.
Why	are	you	hurrying?	I'm late. I'm hurrying because I'm late.
What	are	you	making?	Soup. I'm making soup.
Where	are	they	going?	To the supermarket. They're going to the supermarket.

NOTES

EXAMPLES

1. Every sentence has a subject and a verb.

Some sentences have a subject, a verb, and an object.

Use *who* to ask questions about the subject.

In informal English, use *who* to ask questions about the object.

In formal English, use *whom* to ask questions about the object.

subject verb
• **Lulu is** sleeping.

subject verb   object
• **Lulu is** hugging **Bertha**.

A: **Who** is sleeping?
B: **Lulu** is (sleeping).

A: **Who** is hugging Bertha?
B: **Lulu** is (hugging Bertha).

A: **Who** is Lulu hugging?
B: **Bertha**. (Lulu is hugging **Bertha**.)

A: **Whom** is Professor Walters meeting?
B: **Bekir**. (Professor Walters is meeting **Bekir**.)

2. Use *why* to ask for reasons.

> **A: Why** are they sleeping?
>
> **B:** They're sleeping because they're tired.
>
> OR
>
> **B:** Because they're tired. (spoken English)
>
> OR
>
> **B:** They're tired. (*Because* is understood.)

3. Many *wh-* questions in the **present progressive** use the same word order as *yes / no* questions.

> YES / NO QUESTIONS:
> * **Are you** cooking?
> * Where **are you** cooking?
> * Why **are you** cooking?

▶ **BE CAREFUL!** *Who* and *what* questions about the object use *yes / no* question word order.

> QUESTIONS ABOUT THE OBJECT:
> * Who **are you** meeting?
> * What **are you** cooking?

Who and *what* questions about the subject do not use the same word order as *yes / no* questions.

> QUESTIONS ABOUT THE SUBJECT:
> * Who **is cooking**?
> * What **is happening**?

REFERENCE NOTE
See Unit 9 for a discussion of questions with *who, what,* and *where.*

FOCUSED PRACTICE

1 DISCOVER THE GRAMMAR

Read this passage about Milt.

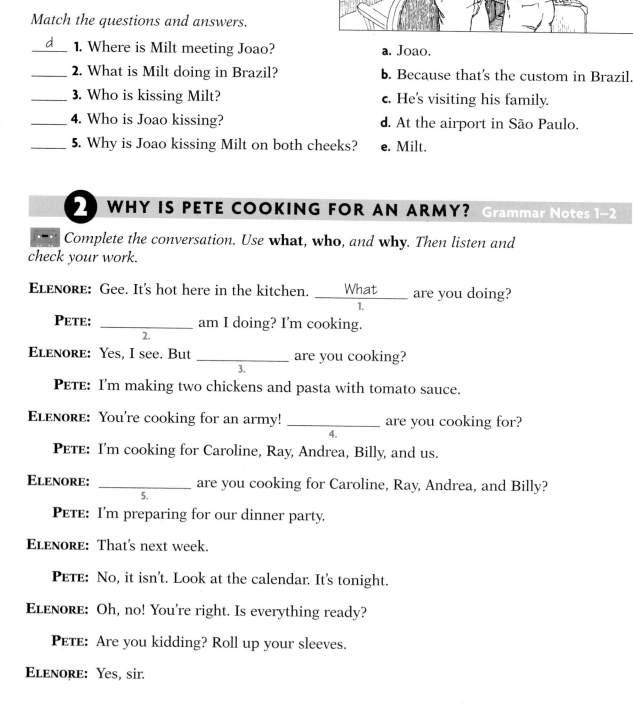

Milt is visiting his family in Brazil. His brother-in-law, Joao, is meeting him at the airport. Joao is kissing Milt on both cheeks. That's the custom in Brazil.

Match the questions and answers.

__d__ **1.** Where is Milt meeting Joao?

_____ **2.** What is Milt doing in Brazil?

_____ **3.** Who is kissing Milt?

_____ **4.** Who is Joao kissing?

_____ **5.** Why is Joao kissing Milt on both cheeks?

a. Joao.

b. Because that's the custom in Brazil.

c. He's visiting his family.

d. At the airport in São Paulo.

e. Milt.

2 WHY IS PETE COOKING FOR AN ARMY? Grammar Notes 1–2

Complete the conversation. Use **what**, **who**, *and* **why**. *Then listen and check your work.*

ELENORE: Gee. It's hot here in the kitchen. _____What_____ are you doing?
1.

PETE: _____ am I doing? I'm cooking.
2.

ELENORE: Yes, I see. But _____ are you cooking?
3.

PETE: I'm making two chickens and pasta with tomato sauce.

ELENORE: You're cooking for an army! _____ are you cooking for?
4.

PETE: I'm cooking for Caroline, Ray, Andrea, Billy, and us.

ELENORE: _____ are you cooking for Caroline, Ray, Andrea, and Billy?
5.

PETE: I'm preparing for our dinner party.

ELENORE: That's next week.

PETE: No, it isn't. Look at the calendar. It's tonight.

ELENORE: Oh, no! You're right. Is everything ready?

PETE: Are you kidding? Roll up your sleeves.

ELENORE: Yes, sir.

3 EDITING

Correct the questions. Then read Exercise 2 and answer them.

_____ **1.** Who's cooking?

    a. Elenore   **b.** Pete

_____ **2.** What Pete is doing?

    a. He's making dinner.   **b.** He's making lunch.

_____ **3.** What he cooking?

    a. Two chickens and pasta with   **b.** Two chickens with mushrooms
        tomato sauce   and rice

_____ **4.** Who is cooking for?

    a. An army   **b.** A few friends

_____ **5.** Where Pete and Elenore are having a conversation?

    a. In the living room   **b.** In the kitchen

_____ **6.** Why Pete is cooking now?

    a. The dinner party is tonight.   **b.** The dinner party is tomorrow night.

4 A BALL GAME   Grammar Notes 1, 3

Doug is returning home. He meets his friend, Noah. Noah is wearing
headphones. Complete their conversation. Then listen and check your work.

Doug: Hey Noah. What _____?
                               1. (listen to)

Noah: The ball game.

Doug: Who _____?
                        2. (play)

Noah: The Mets are playing the Dodgers.

Doug: Where _____?
                        3. (play)

Noah: In New York.

Doug: Who _____?
                        4. (win)

Noah: It's a tie. It's the bottom of the ninth. Wait . . . Something's happening.
        Everyone's shouting.

Doug: What _____?
                        5. (happen)

Announcer: It's a home run.

Noah: A home run. Yes! The Mets are winners.

5 **A FUNNY TV SHOW**

Elenore is sick. Pete is calling her. Listen to their conversation. Then listen again and answer the questions.

1. Who is watching TV?

Elenore is.

2. What program is she watching?

_____

3. Where are Lucy and Ethel working?

_____

4. Is Elenore enjoying the show? _____

5. Who's sneezing? _____

6. Why is this person sneezing? _____

6 **A GOODNIGHT STORY FOR DAD**

Look at the picture. Write questions in the present progressive. Then answer them.

1. Who / sleep

A: Who is sleeping?

B: The father is.

2. Where / the father / sleep

A: _____

B: _____

3. Who / hold / a book

A: _____

B: _____

4. Who / smile

A: _____

B: _____

5. Why / the little girl / smile

A: _____

B: _____ (father / sleep)

COMMUNICATION PRACTICE

7 INFORMATION GAP: SURFING THE CHANNELS

Work in pairs.

Student A, ask your partner questions to complete sentences 1 and 2.

Student B, turn to the Information Gap on page 104 and follow the directions there.

EXAMPLE:
A: Where is a man lying?
B: He's lying on the floor.

1. **CHANNEL 2:** A man is lying on _____. A _____ is sticking out of his chest. _____, _____, _____, and a maid are sitting in the living room and talking.

2. **CHANNEL 4:** Some young men are wearing _____. They're _____ on a playing field. One man is carrying a _____.

3. **CHANNEL 5:** A woman is sitting behind a desk. She is talking about the president's trip to Asia.

4. **CHANNEL 7:** A woman is laughing. She's throwing a pie in a man's face.

Now, work with your partner and decide together what kind of show is on each channel.

1. Channel 2 is a _____.

3. Channel 5 is a _____.

2. Channel 4 is a _____.

4. Channel 7 is a _____.

8 WHAT ARE YOU WATCHING?

Prepare a conversation with a partner.

Student A is watching TV when Student B calls. Student B, ask Student A questions about his or her show. Ask questions in the present progressive.

A: Hello.

B: Hi, _____. This is _____.

Are you busy?

A: Oh hi, _____. I'm _____.
(watch)

B: Oh, what's happening?

A: . . .

REVIEW OR SELFTEST

PART
III

I. *Read each conversation. Circle the letter of the underlined word or group of words that is not correct.*

1. **A:** <u>Who's</u> her mother?
       A

   B: Elenore <u>is</u> <u>Carol</u> <u>mother</u>.
                 B   C   D

   A B C D

2. **A:** <u>What</u> <u>day's</u> is your party?
       A   B

   B: <u>It's</u> <u>on</u> Saturday.
         C   D

   A B C D

3. **A:** <u>When</u> <u>is your class</u>?
       A   B

   B: <u>It's</u> <u>on the afternoon</u>.
         C   D

   A B C D

4. **A:** <u>Where's</u> the library?
       A

   B: It's <u>near</u> the elevator <u>in the</u> <u>third</u> floor.
             B   C   D

   A B C D

5. **A:** <u>What</u> <u>you're</u> <u>doing</u>?
       A   B   C

   B: <u>We're</u> watching the news on TV.
         D

   A B C D

II. *Complete the sentences. Choose the correct word.*

1. My classroom is on the _____ floor.
                        (two, second)

2. My _____ class is at nine-thirty.
      (one, first)

3. Lulu is _____ years old.
          (seventy-three, seventy-third)

4. Her home is on _____ Street.
                 (Twenty-nine, Twenty-ninth)

5. November is the _____ month of the year.
                  (eleven, eleventh)

III. *Read the invitation. Complete the questions. Use* **who, what, where, when, whose.**

BIRTHDAY PARTY

FOR: Jeff

AT: 350 East 77 Street, Apt. 2A

ON: November 2   **AT:** 9 P.M.

RSVP: Noah at 980-2240
         or Doug 876-9898
---

1. _____ is on November 2nd? Jeff's party.

2. _____ birthday party is on November 2nd? Jeff's party.

3. _____ is the party? It's at 350 East 77 Street, Apt. 2A.

4. _____ is the party? It's on November 2nd.

5. _____ time is the party? It's at 9 P.M.

6. _____ is giving the party? Noah and Doug are.

IV. *Write questions about the underlined words.*

1. A: _____?
   B: Lulu's birthday is <u>on October 15th</u>.

2. A: _____?
   B: Doug is <u>at home</u>.

3. A: _____?
   B: Lulu's last name is <u>Winston</u>.

4. A: _____?
   B: <u>Elenore</u> is reading in the living room.

5. A: _____?
   B: Lulu is meeting <u>Bertha</u>.

6. A: _____?
   B: <u>Dan's</u> hat is in the closet.

V. *Cross out the underlined words. Use* **His, Her, Its,** *or* **Their.**

1. <u>Carol's</u> uncle is a plumber.

2. <u>The Winstons'</u> car is old.

3. <u>Doug's</u> sister Norma is a Spanish teacher.

4. This is my turtle. <u>My turtle's</u> name is Mertle.

5. <u>The students'</u> tests are on the teacher's desk.

▶ *To check your answers, go to the Answer Key on page 104.*

FROM GRAMMAR TO WRITING PUNCTUATION I: THE APOSTROPHE, THE COMMA, THE PERIOD, THE QUESTION MARK

 Read this e-mail letter. Then circle all the punctuation marks.

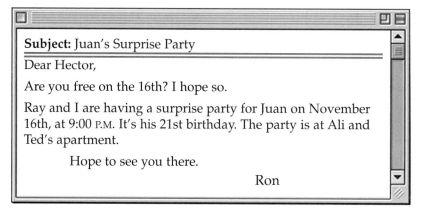

> **Subject:** Juan's Surprise Party
>
> Dear Hector,
>
> Are you free on the 16th? I hope so.
>
> Ray and I are having a surprise party for Juan on November 16th, at 9:00 P.M. It's his 21st birthday. The party is at Ali and Ted's apartment.
>
>   Hope to see you there.
>
>   Ron

Study these rules of punctuation.

The Apostrophe (')

1. Use an apostrophe to show possession and to write contractions.

- **Carol's** book is here.
- We **aren't** late.

The Comma (,)

2. Rules for commas vary. Here are some places where commas are almost always used:

a. in a list of more than two things

- He is wearing **a shirt, a sweater,** and **a jacket**.

b. after the name of a person you are writing to

- Dear **John,**

c. after *yes* or *no* in a sentence

- **Yes,** I am.
  No, I'm not.

d. when you use *and* to connect two sentences.

- His house is **huge,** and his car is expensive.

The Period (.)

3. a. Use a period at the end of every statement.

    b. Use a period after many abbreviations.

- We are English language **students.**

- The party is on **Nov.** 16th.

The Question Mark (?)

4. Use a question mark at the end of a question.

- Are you planning a **party?**
- Where are you **going?**

2 *Add punctuation marks to this note.*

> Dear Uncle John
>
> Bob and I are planning a party for my parents
> 25th wedding anniversary on Sunday Dec 11th
> The party is at our home at 23 Main St Its at
> 3 o'clock I hope you can make it
>
>   Emily

3 *Write an e-mail to a friend or relative. Invite him or her to a party. Include the following information.*

Who's the party for?
Who's giving the party?
What's the occasion?
When is the party?
Where is the party?

PART III
REVIEW OR SELFTEST
ANSWER KEY

I.
1. C
2. B
3. D
4. C
5. B

II.
1. second
2. first
3. seventy-three
4. Twenty-ninth
5. eleventh

III.
1. What
2. Whose
3. Where
4. When
5. What
6. Who

IV.
1. When is Lulu's birthday (When's Lulu's birthday?)
2. Where is Doug? (Where's Doug?)
3. What is Lulu's last name? (What's Lulu's last name?)
4. Who is reading in the living room? (Who's reading in the living room?)
5. Who is Lulu meeting? (Who's Lulu meeting?)
6. Whose hat is in the closet?

V.
1. ~~Carol's~~ Her
2. ~~The Winstons'~~ Their
3. ~~Doug's~~ His
4. ~~My turtle's~~ Its
5. ~~The students'~~ Their

INFORMATION GAP FOR STUDENT B   Unit 12, Exercise 7

Student B, answer your partner's questions. Then ask your partner questions to complete sentences 3 and 4.

EXAMPLE:
A: Where is a man lying?
B: He's lying on the floor.

1. **CHANNEL 2:** A man is lying on the floor. A knife is sticking out of his chest. The man's wife, a family friend, a detective, and a maid are sitting in the living room and talking.

2. **CHANNEL 4:** Some young men are wearing uniforms. They're running on a playing field. One man is carrying a football.

3. **CHANNEL 5:** A woman is sitting behind _____. She is talking about

_____.

4. **CHANNEL 7:** A woman is _____. _____'s throwing a pie in a man's face.

Now, work with your partner and decide together what kind of show is on each channel.

1. Channel 2 is a _____ .

2. Channel 4 is a _____ .

3. Channel 5 is a _____ .

4. Channel 7 is a _____ .

INFORMATION GAP FOR STUDENT B   Unit 11, Exercise 5

Student B, answer your partner's questions. Then ask your partner questions to complete your chart.

EXAMPLES:
What country's national holiday is on _____? (date)
What month is _____'s national holiday?
What's the date of _____'s national holiday?
What country's national holiday is in _____? (month)
When is _____'s national holiday?

NATIONAL HOLIDAYS AROUND THE WORLD						
COUNTRY		**MONTH**	**DAY**	**COUNTRY**		**MONTH**	**DAY**
Argentina		May	25th	**Haiti**		January	1st
Brazil		September	7th			June	2nd
Denmark		April	16th	**Japan**		December	
		February	27th	**Lebanon**			22nd
Ecuador		August	10th			October	29th
Greece		March	25th	**United States of America**		July	4th
Your country's national holiday:							

THE SIMPLE PRESENT TENSE

PREVIEW

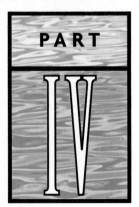 *Doug and his mother, Elenore, are shopping for clothes. Listen and read their conversation.*

CLOTHES FOR A TEENAGER

DOUG: Mom, look at these jeans.

ELENORE: They're nice, but you have a lot of jeans. You're wearing your favorite ones right now.

DOUG: These? They're way too tight.

ELENORE: But those jeans are very expensive. How about this brand here? These cost half as much.

DOUG: No way. Look at the legs. They're not baggy.

ELENORE: Why do you want baggy jeans?

DOUG: They're cool. All the kids wear them.

ELENORE: Doug, how about one of these nice shirts? You really need a long-sleeved shirt and dress shoes.

DOUG: I don't need a long-sleeved shirt. I have one, and I have dress shoes, too. Besides, I hate dress shoes.

ELENORE: But your long-sleeved shirt has a big stain on it, and your dress shoes are tight.

DOUG: My tie covers the stain, and my shoes are okay because I don't wear socks.

ELENORE: No socks?

DOUG: It's the style. The kids at school don't wear socks.

SALESPERSON: Do you need any help?

DOUG: Yes, I'm looking for baggy jeans like these.

SALESPERSON: What size do you want?

DOUG: My waist is 32.

ELENORE: And he needs a shirt and shoes, too.

SALESPERSON: Well, we have the jeans in size 32. These jeans are comfortable and easy to care for, too. And wait, you're in luck. They're on sale today—$20 off.

DOUG: See, Mom?

SALESPERSON: And we have a big sale on long-sleeved shirts and dress shoes.

ELENORE: See, Doug?

COMPREHENSION CHECK

Check (✔) **That's right**, **That's wrong**, *or* **It doesn't say**.

	That's right.	That's wrong.	It doesn't say.
1. Doug's long-sleeved shirt has a stain.	❏	❏	❏
2. Doug wants to be in style.	❏	❏	❏
3. There are no shoes in size 10.	❏	❏	❏
4. Doug and his mother have the same ideas about clothes.	❏	❏	❏

WHAT'S YOUR OPINION?

Do teenagers usually like to shop with their parents?

WITH PARTNERS

Practice the conversation on pages 106 and 107.

SIMPLE PRESENT TENSE: AFFIRMATIVE AND NEGATIVE STATEMENTS

GRAMMAR **IN CONTEXT**

WARM UP   Read the cartoon.

Many people think that clothes are important. What do you think?

 Dr. Kramer is a psychologist. Listen and read a letter to Dr. Kramer.

Dear Dr. Kramer,

My son **is** fourteen years old. He **is** a good student and he **has** many friends. But we **have** one problem with him. He **loves** clothes. He **wants** all the latest styles. We **are** not poor, but I **think** it **is** wrong to spend a lot of money on clothes, especially for a growing boy. We **give** my son money each week, but he **doesn't have** enough to buy all the clothes he **wants**. Now he **wants** to get a part-time job. I **don't want** him to work, but my husband **thinks** it's okay. What **do** you **think**?

Worried Mom

GRAMMAR **PRESENTATION**
SIMPLE PRESENT TENSE: AFFIRMATIVE AND NEGATIVE STATEMENTS

AFFIRMATIVE STATEMENTS	
SUBJECT	**VERB**
I You* We They	**work**.
He She It	**works**.

NEGATIVE STATEMENTS		
SUBJECT	**DO NOT / DOES NOT**	**BASE FORM OF VERB**
I You* We They	**do not don't**	**work**.
He She It	**does not doesn't**	**work**.

*You is both singular and plural.

NOTES

EXAMPLES

---

1. Use the **simple present tense** to tell about things that happen again and again (habits, regular occurrences, customs, and routines).

Past ——X————X——┼——X————X—— Future
 Now
Doug plays soccer every day.

- Doug **plays** soccer every day.
- Many Americans **eat** turkey on Thanksgiving.
- Pete and Elenore **work.**
- Most teenagers **wear** jeans.

---

2. Use the **simple present tense** to tell **facts**.

- This sweatshirt **costs** thirty dollars.

---

3. Use the **simple present tense** with **non-action verbs**.

- Doug and his mother **are** in the store.
- Doug **likes** bright colors.

(continued on next page)

4. Use the contractions *doesn't* and *don't* for negative statements in speaking or in informal writing.

▶ **BE CAREFUL!** When *or* connects two verbs in a negative statement, we do not repeat *don't* or *doesn't* before the second verb.

- Doug **doesn't** wear ties often. He wears T-shirts.
- We **don't** live in Oregon. We live in New York.

- He **doesn't work** or **study** in the summer.
- We **don't eat** or **drink** at work. NOT ~~He doesn't work or doesn't study in the summer.~~

---

5. In affirmative statements, use the **base form** (dictionary form) of the verb for all persons except the third person singular. Put an **-s** (or **-es)** ending on the third person singular (*he / she / it*).

- He need**s** a dress shirt. I need a belt.
- She want**s** an apple. I want bananas.
- He miss**es** me. I miss him.

---

6. PRONUNCIATION NOTE: Pronounce the third person singular ending /s/, /z/, or /ɪz/.

- /s/ He eat**s** cereal for breakfast.
- /z/ She play**s** basketball.
- /ɪz/ He watch**es** TV every day.

---

7. The third person singular affirmative forms of *have*, *do*, and *go* are not regular.

- He **has** a new sweatshirt.
- She **does** the taxes.
- It **goes** in the kitchen.

---

8. The verb *be* has different forms from all other verbs.

- I **am** tired.
- You **are** tall.
- He **is** bored.
- I **look** tired.
- You **look** tall.
- He **looks** bored.

REFERENCE NOTE
See Unit 26 for a fuller discussion of non-action verbs.
See Appendix 14, page A-14, for spelling and pronunciation rules for the third person singular in the simple present tense.
See Unit 1 for a complete presentation of the verb *be*.

FOCUSED PRACTICE

1 DISCOVER THE GRAMMAR

This is Dr. Kramer's answer to the letter from a worried mom (see page 108). Read the letter and circle the verbs in the simple present tense.

> Dear Worried Mom,
>
> Your son's interest in clothes is not unusual. Most teens want to dress the way their friends dress. As for work, a part-time job is good for a teen as long as his or her schoolwork doesn't suffer. It's good that your son likes to wear nice clothes and wants to work. I agree with your husband. When people work, they usually think carefully about the cost of things. There is no reason to worry. Your son sounds fine to me.
>
> Dr. Kramer

2 LISTENING: VERB ENDINGS   Grammar Note 6

Underline the verb in each sentence. Then listen to the sentences and check the sound of the verb endings. (See Appendix 14, page A-14, for an explanation of these pronunciation rules.)

	/s/	/z/	/ɪz/
1. He <u>wears</u> T-shirts.		✔	
2. He misses his girlfriend.			
3. She plays tennis every week.			
4. She drinks coffee in the morning.			
5. It takes an hour to get to school.			
6. He washes his clothes on Sunday.			
7. She lives in Boston.			
8. He worries about his family.			

❸ AL BROWN, AN ENGLISH TEACHER   Grammar Notes 1–7

Complete the sentences. Use the correct form of the verb in parentheses.

Al Brown _____teaches_____ English as a
                   1. (teach)
Second Language. He is unlike the other

teachers in his department. He is only

twenty-seven years old. The other teachers

are over thirty. The other teachers

_____ button-down shirts.
        2. (wear)
Al _____ T-shirts or
        3. (wear)
sweatshirts. After class the other teachers

_____ home. Every afternoon
        4. (go)
Al _____ to the park. Many
        5. (go)
students _____ soccer in the
              6. (play)
park. Sometimes Al _____ his
                       7. (watch)
students, and sometimes he

_____ soccer with them.
        8. (play)

Three evenings a week Al _____ Japanese lessons with a private tutor. His
                             9. (have)
tutor is one of his students. Every evening Al _____ Japanese at the library
                                                  10. (study)
and _____ Japanese homework.
        11. (do)

Al's girlfriend is in Japan. Al _____ her a lot. He _____
                                    12. (miss)   13. (worry)
about her, too. He _____ to see her in the summer.
                      14. (hope)

*Now circle all the verbs in the third person singular. What three verbs are
pronounced with the extra syllable /ɪz/ in the third person singular?*

_____ , _____ , and _____

📼 *Listen and check your work.*

4 **WHAT'S THE STORY?**

Listen to the conversation between Doug and his mother. Check (✔) what their conversation is about.

_____ **1.** Elenore is worried about Doug. He is sick. He has a lot of health problems. It's a holiday, and it's hard to find a doctor.

_____ **2.** Doug says he's sick because he doesn't want to go to school. He doesn't remember that it's a holiday and school is closed.

_____ **3.** Doug is sick. He has a headache, a stomachache, and an earache. He wants to go to school because it's a holiday and school is fun on holidays.

5 **EDITING**

Find and correct the mistakes in this story about Doug.

    My name is Doug Winston. I'm in my second year of high school. I'm captain of my

school's soccer team. I ~~lives~~ ^{live} in New York City with my parents. We lives in a large

apartment in an old building. Both my mother and father works. My mother is a writer.

She write stories for magazines. My father is a businessman. His work take him all over

the world. I has two older sisters, Carol and Norma. Carol live in Oregon and Norma live

in Massachusetts. I no have any brothers. Carol's a student at Oregon State University and

Norma's a Spanish teacher in a high school in Boston. Norma's a good Spanish teacher,

but I'm glad she no is my teacher. She gives her students a lot of homework.

COMMUNICATION PRACTICE

6 MY PARTNER AND I

Check (✔) the sentences that are true for you.

1. _____ I eat breakfast every day.   _____ I don't eat breakfast every day.
2. _____ I speak English after class.   _____ I don't speak English after class.
3. _____ I read in bed.   _____ I don't read in bed.
4. _____ I eat in bed.   _____ I don't eat in bed.
5. _____ I sing in the shower.   _____ I don't sing in the shower.
6. _____ I like big cities.   _____ I don't like big cities.
7. _____ I like leather jackets.   _____ I don't like leather jackets.
8. _____ I like modern art.   _____ I don't like modern art.
9. _____ I like computers.   _____ I don't like computers.

Work with a partner. In what ways are you and your partner alike? In what ways are you different? Write five sentences about you and your partner.

EXAMPLES:
We both eat breakfast every day.
He speaks English after class, but I don't.

7 WEEKEND ACTIVITIES

Listen as each student tells about his or her weekend activities. Take notes. Tell about each student's activities before you tell about your own.

EXAMPLE:
MARIA: On the weekends, I sleep late. I don't go to school.
BEKIR: On the weekends, Maria sleeps late. She doesn't go to school. I work. I don't eat breakfast at home.
CARLOS: Maria sleeps late and she doesn't go to school. Bekir works. He doesn't eat breakfast at home. I play tennis. I don't study.

(8) INFORMATION GAP: CUSTOMS AROUND THE WORLD

Work in pairs.

Student A, complete sentences 1–4.

Then read sentences 1–4 to your partner. Your partner says "That's right" or corrects your sentence. Your partner reads sentences 5–8 to you. Listen and say "That's right" or correct your partner's sentence.

Student B, look at the Information Gap on page 147 and follow the instructions there.

1. People in Japan _____ shoes in their home. When they enter a home,
   a. (wear / don't wear)

   they _____ their shoes and _____ slippers.
   b. (remove / don't remove)   c. (put on / don't put on)

2. People in Korea _____ rice cake soup on New Year's Day. Children
   a. (eat / don't eat)

   often _____ red jackets with sleeves of many colors.
   b. (wear / don't wear)

3. People in Thailand bow to show respect. Younger people usually

   _____ first.
   a. (bow / don't bow)

4. In Brazil during Carnival people wear strange and beautiful costumes. Brazilians

   _____ during Carnival. They _____ in the street.
   a. (work / don't work)   b. (dance / don't dance)

5. In Saudi Arabia at the time of Ramadan, Moslems don't eat or drink during daylight.

   Ramadan lasts for thirty days. At the end of Ramadan there is a three-day celebration.

6. On New Year's Day, Chinese children receive money in red envelopes from their

   parents and grandparents.

7. In the United States, people usually don't work on July 4th. They watch fireworks

   and have barbecues.

8. In Denmark, people bang on their friends' doors and set off fireworks on New Year's Eve.

Now work with your partner. Write about customs you know well. Read your sentences to the class.

_____

_____

_____

SIMPLE PRESENT TENSE: YES / NO QUESTIONS AND SHORT ANSWERS

GRAMMAR **IN CONTEXT**

WARM UP Look at these ads for roommates. What information is important in a roommate ad?

Listen and read this roommate questionnaire and Dan and Jon's answers.

ROOMMATE QUESTIONNAIRE

Names:	Dan YES	Dan NO	Jon YES	Jon NO
1. **Do** you **smoke**?		✔		✔
2. **Does** the smell of smoke bother you?	✔			✔
3. **Do** you **wake up** early?		✔		✔
4. **Do** you **like** to go to bed after midnight?	✔		✔	
5. Are you neat?	✔		✔	
6. **Does** a messy room bother you?	✔		✔	
7. Are you quiet?		✔	✔	
8. Are you talkative?	✔			✔
9. **Do** you **listen** to loud music?	✔		✔	
10. **Do** you **watch** a lot of TV?	✔		✔	
11. **Do** you **study** and **listen** to music at the same time?	✔		✔	
12. **Do** you **study** with the TV on?	✔		✔	

WHAT'S YOUR OPINION?

Are Dan and Jon a good match?

Yes No
☐ ☐

GRAMMAR **PRESENTATION**
SIMPLE PRESENT TENSE: *YES / NO* QUESTIONS AND SHORT ANSWERS

YES / NO QUESTIONS		
Do / Does	**SUBJECT**	**BASE FORM OF VERB**
Do	I you* we they	**work**?
Does	he she it	

SHORT ANSWERS		
AFFIRMATIVE		
Yes,	I you* we they	**do**.
	he she it	**does**.

SHORT ANSWERS		
NEGATIVE		
No,	I you* we they	**don't**.
	he she it	**doesn't**.

*You is both singular and plural.

NOTES

EXAMPLES

1. For *yes / no* questions in the simple present tense, use *do* or *does* before the subject. Use the base form of the verb after the subject.

- subject
Do you **work**?
- **Does** he **speak** Italian?

2. Do not use *do* or *does* for *yes / no* questions with *be*.

- Do you speak French? **Are** you from France?
- Does he speak French? **Is** he from France?
- Do I know you? **Am** I in the right room?

REFERENCE NOTE
See Unit 2 for a discussion of *yes / no* questions with *be*.

FOCUSED PRACTICE

① DISCOVER THE GRAMMAR

Read about Dan and Jon. They're college roommates.

In many ways Dan and Jon are alike. Both Dan and Jon like music and sports, but Dan likes popular music and Jon likes jazz. Both Dan and Jon like basketball, but Jon likes football and Dan doesn't. Dan and Jon are neat. They don't like a messy room. They both like to go to bed late—well after midnight. They watch about two hours of TV at night and they study with the TV on. But in one way Dan and Jon are completely different. Dan is very talkative, but Jon is very quiet. Dan says, "We're lucky about that. It works out very nicely. I talk, he listens." Jon says, "Uh-huh."

Match the questions and answers.

_____ **1.** Do they both like music and sports?

_____ **2.** Do they like to go to bed early?

_____ **3.** Does Dan like popular music?

_____ **4.** Dan is talkative and Jon is quiet. Does it matter?

_____ **5.** Do Dan and Jon like classical music?

a. It doesn't say.

b. Yes, they do.

c. Yes, he does.

d. No, they don't.

e. No, it doesn't.

② AT A DEPARTMENT STORE   Grammar Notes 1–2

Doug is buying a jacket at a department store. Write the correct questions to complete the conversation.

> **a.** Do you want to see anything else?
> **b.** Do you have any winter jackets?
> **c.** Do you need any help?
> **d.** Does this jacket come in brown?

SALESPERSON: Do you need any help _____ ?
                                          1.

DOUG: Yes, please. _____ ?
                                2.

SALESPERSON: Yes, we do. All our jackets are over there.

DOUG: _____ ?
                   3.

SALESPERSON: Let me check. . . . Uh . . . yes. What size are you?

DOUG: Large.

SALESPERSON: Here you go. _____ ?
                                      4.

DOUG: No thanks.

❸ HOW MUCH IS IT?

Complete the **yes / no** *questions. Then look at the picture and answer the questions.*

1. __Do__ the pants cost

   thirty dollars?

   __Yes, they do__ .

2. _____ the pants expensive?

   _____ .

3. _____ the jacket cost three

   hundred and fifty dollars?

   _____ .

4. _____ the jacket expensive?

   _____ .

❹ LEAVING FOR SCHOOL

Doug is leaving for school. Listen to the conversation between Doug and his mother. Then answer the questions with **Yes, he does**, **No, he doesn't**, *or* **I don't know**.

1. Does Doug have his keys?

   __Yes, he does__ .

2. Does Doug have his book bag?

   _____ .

3. Does Doug have his lunch?

   _____ .

4. Does Doug have his wallet?

   _____ .

5. Does Doug have his soccer shoes? _____ .

6. Does Doug have a good day at school? _____ .

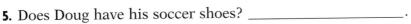

COMMUNICATION PRACTICE

5 FIND SOMEONE WHO . . .

*Find out about your classmates. Ask these questions or add your own. Take notes.
Tell the class something new about a classmate.*

Do you _____?

    speak more than two languages
    watch more than three hours of TV every day
    cook well
    know tai chi
    know sign language
    play a musical instrument
    have more than four sisters or brothers
    ski
    fly a plane

Your questions:

_____

_____

Are you _____?

    an only child
    a good dancer
    good at computers
    good at art
    good at sports

Your questions:

_____

_____

Tell the class some things about a classmate.

EXAMPLE:
Claudia speaks three languages. She speaks Spanish, French, and
English. She knows tai chi, but she doesn't know tae kwon do.
She's good at computers, but she's not a good dancer.

6 A TREASURE HUNT

*Work in small groups. Ask each other questions. Check (✔) the items you have
that are listed in the box. The first group to check ten items wins.*

EXAMPLE:
Do you have a mirror?
OR
Does anyone have a mirror?

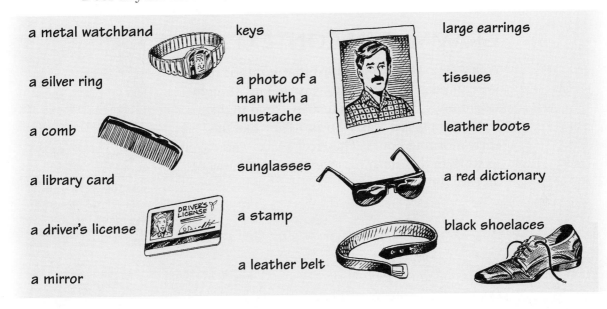

a metal watchband   keys   large earrings

a silver ring   a photo of a man with a mustache   tissues

a comb   leather boots

a library card   sunglasses   a red dictionary

a driver's license   a stamp   black shoelaces

a mirror   a leather belt

7 FACTS ABOUT THE WORLD

Complete the questions with **Do, Does, Is,** *or* **Are.** *Then work with a partner and
answer the questions. Check your answers on page 146.*

1. _____ Canada north of the United States? _____
2. _____ Canada have a king? _____
3. _____ Canada have ten provinces? _____
4. _____ Thailand have a king? _____
5. _____ Thailand famous for its silk? _____
6. _____ Brazilians speak Spanish? _____
7. _____ Brasília the capital of Brazil? _____
8. _____ Switzerland have two official languages? _____
9. _____ many people in Korea eat kimche? _____
10. _____ kimche spicy? _____
11. _____ Mexico north of Texas? _____
12. _____ tacos popular in Mexico? _____

UNIT

15

SIMPLE PRESENT TENSE: *WH-* QUESTIONS

GRAMMAR **IN CONTEXT**

WARM UP   The owl is a bird that hunts at night.
We call people who like to stay up late at night
"night owls." Night owls feel awake at night.
Other people are "early birds." They like the
early morning hours. They feel awake and eager
to work in the morning. Are you a night owl or
an early bird?

*Look at the picture of
Doug and Elenore. Listen and
read the questions and guess
the answers.*

_____ **1. Who likes** to get up
early?

_____ **2. Who does** Elenore
wake up?

_____ **3. What time does**
Doug first **wake up**?

_____ **4. When does** Doug
get up?

_____ **5. Why does** Doug **run**
to the bus stop?

_____ **6. What does** Elenore
say to Doug?

A NIGHT OWL AND AN EARLY BIRD

Doug Winston, a night owl, hates to get up in the morning. On weekends and vacations, Doug goes to bed after 1:00 A.M. and gets up at noon. Unfortunately for Doug, school starts at 8:15, and Doug needs to get up early.

At 7:00 A.M. Doug's alarm rings. He wakes up, but he doesn't get up. He stays in bed and daydreams. He thinks about his friends, his schoolwork, and his soccer games. At 7:20 his mother comes in. She has a big smile on her face. She's cheerful and full of energy. She says, "Dougie, it's time to get up."

Elenore, Doug's mom, is an early bird. Even on vacations, Elenore is up at 6:00 A.M. When Elenore wakes Doug in the morning, he moans and groans. He's a grouch in the morning. He says, "Go away. Leave me alone. I'm tired. I need more sleep."

Finally, at about 7:30 Doug gets up. He jumps out of bed, showers, and gets dressed. At 7:50 he drinks a big glass of orange juice, takes a donut, and runs to the bus stop.

Now match the questions on page 122 with the answers.

a. He doesn't want to be late.

b. Doug.

c. At 7:30.

d. "Dougie, it's time to get up."

e. Elenore.

f. At 7:00.

GRAMMAR **PRESENTATION**
SIMPLE PRESENT TENSE: *WH-* QUESTIONS

WH- QUESTIONS				
WH- WORD	*DO / DOES*	SUBJECT	BASE FORM OF VERB	
1. **What**	do	I	**do**	after breakfast?
2. **Where**		you	**eat**	lunch?
3. **When**		we	**leave**	work?
4. **What time**		they	**come**	home?
5. **Why**	does	he	**live**	in New York?
6. **Who(m)**		she	**call**	on Sunday?

ANSWERS
1. You get dressed after breakfast.
2. I eat lunch in the school cafeteria.
3. We leave work at 5:00.
4. They come home at 6:00.
5. He lives in New York because he works there.
6. She calls her mother on Sunday.

SHORT ANSWERS
1. You get dressed.
2. In the school cafeteria.
3. At 5:00.
4. At 6:00.
5. He works there.
6. Her mother.

WH- QUESTIONS ABOUT THE SUBJECT		
WH- WORD	VERB	
Who	**wears**	sweatshirts?
What	**costs**	a lot?

ANSWERS
Doug's friends (do).
Doug's sweatshirt (does).

NOTES

EXAMPLES

1. *Wh-* **questions** give information and cannot be answered with a *yes* or *no*.	**A: What** does he need? **B:** He needs some milk.

2. Most *wh-* questions in the simple present begin with a question word followed by **do** or **does** followed by the subject and the base form of the verb.

- **When do you eat** breakfast?
- **Where does she live?**
- **What does it mean?**
- **Why do we dream?**
- **How do I get** there?
- **Who does he love?**

3. Do not use **do** or **does** when **who** or **what** begins a question about the subject.

subject
- Noah speaks Spanish.
  Who speaks Spanish?
  NOT ~~Who does speak Spanish?~~
- Twenty comes after nineteen.
  What comes after nineteen?
  NOT ~~What does come after nineteen?~~

4. Always use the third person singular form of the verb when **who** or **what** begins a question about the subject.

- Who **speaks** Spanish?
  Pedro does.
- Who **speaks** Korean?
  Eun Joo and Sun-Keun do.
- What **comes** before *d*?
  A, b, and *c* do.

5. *Who* asks questions about a subject.

Who asks questions about an object in informal English.

Whom asks questions about the object in formal English.

subject
- **Doug** plays soccer.
  Who plays soccer? **Doug** does.

object
- Doug meets **Noah** at the park.
  Who does Doug meet? **Noah**.

object
- The king greets **his guests**.
  Whom does the King greet?

PRONUNCIATION NOTE
In pronunciation we use falling intonation for *wh-* questions: Where do you live?

FOCUSED PRACTICE

1 DISCOVER THE GRAMMAR

It's eight o'clock on a Monday morning. Dan and Carol are in a math class. Read their conversation. Then match the questions with the answers.

DAN: Am I tired! (yawning)

CAROL: I can see that.

DAN: I always have trouble getting to an eight o'clock class, especially on Monday.

CAROL: That's because you sleep until noon on Sunday and stay up late on Sunday night. Do you ever have trouble falling asleep?

DAN: Yes. But then I read our math book. That puts me to sleep.

_____ 1. Who sleeps until noon on Sunday?

_____ 2. What day is it especially hard to get to an eight o'clock class?

_____ 3. Why does Dan have trouble waking up early on Monday?

_____ 4. When does Dan sleep until noon?

_____ 5. What does Dan do when he wants to fall asleep?

a. Monday.

b. Sunday.

c. He reads his math book.

d. Because he stays up late on Sunday.

e. Dan.

What do you do when you have trouble falling asleep?

2 DOUG'S DAY   Grammar Notes 1–5

Read each sentence. Write a question that the underlined words answer.

1. Doug wakes up <u>at 7:00</u>.

   When does Doug wake up?

2. Doug's school begins <u>at 8:15</u>.

   _____

3. Doug eats lunch <u>in the school cafeteria</u>.

   _____

4. Doug eats <u>a hamburger and french fries</u> for lunch on Mondays.

   _____

5. Doug and Noah go <u>to the park</u> after school.

_____

6. Doug and Noah meet <u>Dino and Jeff</u> at the park.

_____

7. <u>Doug</u> plays soccer in the park.

_____

8. Doug practices soccer every day <u>because he is the captain of his team and soccer is important to him.</u>

_____

③ LULU

*Label the **subject (S)** and the **object (O)** in each sentence. Write one question about the subject and one question about the object. Then answer the questions. Use short answers.*

                                       S   O

1. On Sunday afternoon, Pete calls Lulu in Florida.

   Who calls Lulu in Florida on Sunday afternoon? Pete does.

   Who does Pete call on Sunday afternoon? Lulu.

2. Lulu visits Bertha almost every afternoon.

_____

_____

3. Lulu meets her neighbor every Tuesday morning.

_____

_____

4. The neighbor helps Lulu with her grocery shopping.

_____

_____

5. Lulu and Bertha meet Adele and Edith at a restaurant every Monday evening.

_____

_____

4 DREAMS

Use these words to write questions. Then read this magazine article about dreams and answer the questions.

1. Who / dream ___Who dreams_____?

   ___Everyone dreams._____

2. Why / people / dream _____?

   _____

3. When / people / dream _____?

   _____

4. What / psychologists / believe about dreams _____?

   a. _____

   b. _____

   c. _____

5. What / dreams / prove _____?

   _____

Dreams ☆
☆ ☆

Why do we dream? Nobody knows, but everyone dreams. We dream during REM (rapid eye movement) sleep. In eight hours of sleep, people usually have four REM periods. But we remember very little. We usually remember only 20 or 30 seconds of REM sleep.

There are many ideas about dreams. Some psychologists believe we dream because we need a safe way to do things we can't do when we're awake. Some think we dream in order to work out our problems. Others believe dreams don't have any special meaning. They are simply thoughts that come to us when we sleep. Whatever you believe, dreams prove one thing—some people have wonderful imaginations.

COMMUNICATION PRACTICE

5 MORNING AND NIGHT

Work with a partner. Ask questions about your partner's night and weekday mornings. Tell the class two things about your partner.

EXAMPLES:

Do you dream?
If yes, what do you dream about?
When does your alarm clock ring?
Are you a morning person?
What do you usually have for breakfast?

Now write three questions for a class survey. Report the results.

EXAMPLES:

1. What do you drink in the morning?
2. What do you dream about?

Survey Results:

Six students drink coffee. Two students drink tea. One student drinks milk.

6 HOUSEHOLD CHORES

Study the household chores. Then work with a partner. Ask your partner who does what in his or her home.

EXAMPLES:

A: Who does the dishes in your home?
B: My brother does the dishes.

Household Chores

do the dishes

vacuum

take out the garbage

fix things around
the house

cook

make the bed

set the table

7 TRIVIA TIME

Work in groups. Decide together on the correct answer. Check your answers on page 146.

1. Where in Canada do most people speak French?

   a. in Toronto

   b. in Quebec

   c. in Vancouver

2. What famous performing arts center lies on a harbor of the South Pacific Ocean? (some say it looks like a folded dinner napkin)

   a. the Vienna Staatsoper

   b. the Kennedy Center for the Performing Arts

   c. the Sydney Opera House

3. What Southeast Asian city has floating markets early every morning?

   a. Bali

   b. Bangkok

   c. Taiwan

4. Where do bonsai trees, kabuki theater, sumo wrestling, and kendo come from?

   a. Korea

   b. Japan

   c. Mongolia

5. When do most Parisians go on vacation?

   a. in August

   b. in April

   c. in December

6. What European city offers romantic boat rides with singing gondoliers?

   a. Vienna

   b. Verona

   c. Venice

Now work with a partner. Write your own **wh- questions**. *Then ask the class your questions.*

1. _____

2. _____

3. _____

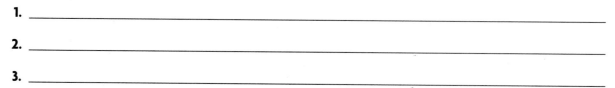

SIMPLE PRESENT TENSE AND *THIS / THAT / THESE / THOSE*

GRAMMAR **IN CONTEXT**

WARM UP   Discuss this question.

Is it difficult for you to throw away letters? books? clothes? CDs?

Elenore is trying to clean a closet. Listen and read the conversation.

ELENORE: Pete, please look at the clothes in **that** box. I want to throw away a few things. Our closet is very full.

PETE: Okay. Elenore! **This** is my favorite sweater. I love **this** sweater.

ELENORE: **That** old thing? You never wear it, and it has a big stain.

PETE: I like it a lot.

ELENORE: Okay. Anything else?

PETE: Yes. I want to keep **these** shoes and **these** pants.

ELENORE: Why? **Those** shoes are tight, and **those** pants have holes.

PETE: Doug wants them.

ELENORE: No, he doesn't.

PETE: Well, I want them.

ELENORE: Okay. Anything else?

PETE: Yes—**this** old hat. I know I don't wear it and it has a hole and some stains, but it has some wonderful memories.

ELENORE: You win. Let's get a new closet.

PETE: That's a great idea. Now please put everything back.

GRAMMAR **PRESENTATION**
SIMPLE PRESENT TENSE AND *THIS / THAT / THESE / THOSE*

SINGULAR		
THIS / THAT	VERB	
This	is	my uncle.
That	's	my jacket.

PLURAL		
THESE / THOSE	VERB	
These	are	my friends.
Those		my gloves.

SINGULAR			
THIS / THAT	NOUN	VERB	
This	man	comes	from Rome.
That	book	has	300 pages.

PLURAL			
THESE / THOSE	NOUN	VERB	
These	women	are	lawyers.
Those	dictionaries		heavy.

NOTES

EXAMPLES

1. Use *this*, *that*, *these*, and *those* to identify persons or things.

- **Soup** is delicious. *(all soup)*
- **This** soup is delicious. *(the soup I'm eating)*

2. *This* refers to a person or thing near you. *That* refers to a person or thing far from you. Use *this* and *that* to talk about a singular noun.

A: **This** is my umbrella. **That's** your umbrella by the door.

B: Oh, sorry. They're both green.

3. *These* refers to people or things near you. *Those* refers to people or things far away. Use *these* and *those* to talk about plural nouns.

A: **These** sweaters are not on sale.

B: **Those** sweaters in the store window are on sale.

4. *This*, *that*, *these*, and *those* can be pronouns or adjectives.

- pronoun
  This is my book.
- adjective
  This book is red.

FOCUSED PRACTICE

1 DISCOVER THE GRAMMAR

Lulu is at a new laundromat. She has a problem. Listen and read the conversation between Lulu and the woman who works at the laundromat. Underline **this**, **that**, **these**, *and* **those***. Circle the nouns they refer to.*

WOMAN: Is something wrong?

LULU: Yes.

WOMAN: What's the problem?

LULU: Well, <u>this</u> isn't my (blouse), and these aren't my socks.

WOMAN: Oh, I'm sorry.

LULU: And this isn't my towel. This towel is yellow. My towels are blue. Those towels over there on that shelf look like my towels. And my brown blouse isn't here.

WOMAN: Oh, no. I don't know what happened.

LULU: And look at these pants. They're size 4. Look at me. Am I size 4? I'm not size 4. I'm size 14.

WOMAN: I'm terribly sorry.

LULU: I am, too.

2 A BABYSITTING JOB   Grammar Notes 1–4

Carol's babysitting for Billy, her history professor's son. Carol is taking Billy home from kindergarten. Carol is holding gloves, a jacket, and a scarf. Complete the conversation. Use **this**, **that**, **these**, *or* **those***.*

CAROL: Hi, Billy, are you ready to go?

BILLY: Hi, Carol. Look, Carol, ____these____ are my paintings.
                                        1.

CAROL: They're beautiful.

BILLY: Thanks. _____ one is for Mommy, _____ one is for Daddy, and
                    2.   3.

_____ four paintings are for you.
      4.

CAROL: Well, thank you. You're very generous. Billy, are _____ your gloves?
                                                              5.

BILLY: No, they're not. _____ are my gloves under the table.
                            6.

(continued on next page)

CAROL: Okay, Billy, get your gloves. Billy, is

_____ your jacket?
        7.

BILLY: Yes, it has my name in it.

CAROL: Is _____ your scarf?
              8.

BILLY: No, _____'s my scarf over there.
               9.

CAROL: Okay. Now let's hurry home.

BILLY: Okay.

③ EDITING

There are five mistakes in these conversations. The first one is corrected. Find and correct the other four.

1. **CAROL:** Helen, ~~this~~ *these* are my friends Dan and Bob, and this is my roommate Yoko.

   HELEN: Nice to meet you.

2. **ELENORE:** Look at these men across the street. I think they're famous.

   VALERIE: I think you're right. Those man looks like Tom Cruise. And that one looks like Steven Spielberg.

3. **NOAH:** Who are that boys near the pizza place? Are they from our school?

   DOUG: I can't tell. They're too far away.

4. **ELENORE:** Is these your earring?

   VALERIE: Yes, it is. Thanks.

COMMUNICATION PRACTICE

4 A NEW LANGUAGE

Are you tired of English? Learn a few words in a new language. Work in small groups. One person in your group probably knows a language that the others don't. Your new language "teacher" points to objects in the room. He or she teaches you vocabulary in the new language. Use **this**, **that**, **these**, *or* **those**.

> **EXAMPLES:**
>
> This is *a door* in English. In French, it's *une porte*.
>
> These are *keys* in English. In Spanish, they're *llaves*.
>
> That's *a window* in English. In Japanese, it's a 窓 or まと (pronounced "mado").
>
> Those are *chairs* in English. In Russian, they're стул (pronounced "stool ya").

5 INFORMAL AND FORMAL INTRODUCTIONS

Read the two conversations. Which conversation is more formal—A or B?

Conversation A

CAROL: These are my friends Bill and Steve.

AMY: Hi. I'm Amy.

BILL: Hi, Amy. Nice to meet you.

STEVE: Hi.

AMY: Nice to meet you, too.

Conversation B

PETE: Bill, this is Sam Jones. He's the new director of finance. Mr. Jones, this is Bill Smith. He's our marketing director.

SAM JONES: It's a pleasure to meet you.

BILL SMITH: Nice to meet you, too.

Now, with a partner, practice making informal and formal introductions. Use your own names.

SIMPLE PRESENT TENSE AND ONE / ONES AND IT

GRAMMAR IN CONTEXT

WARM UP   Read this story. What do you think of it?

A man gets a new umbrella and decides to throw away his old **one**. He puts the old **one** in the wastebasket. A friend recognizes the old umbrella and returns **it**. Then the man leaves the umbrella on the train, but the conductor returns **it** the next day. The man tries very hard to throw away his umbrella, but **it** always comes back. Finally, he lends the umbrella to a friend. He never sees **it** again.

Now listen and read the conversation between Doug and Elenore.

ELENORE: Doug, where's your new sweatshirt?

DOUG: Dino has **it**. I'm wearing his sweatshirt.

ELENORE: Why?

DOUG: Sometimes Dino and I lend each other clothes.

ELENORE: But that **one** is so tight. You like baggy clothes.

DOUG: I like baggy jeans, not baggy sweatshirts. And this **one** has a hood. Hoods are in style now. And look at all these pockets. There are two big **ones** and one small **one**.

ELENORE: I'll never know what you like to wear.

GRAMMAR **PRESENTATION**
SIMPLE PRESENT TENSE AND *ONE* / *ONES* AND *IT*

	SINGULAR			
	A / AN	**SINGULAR COUNT NOUN**		*ONE*
I don't need	**a**	**pen**.	I have	**one**.

	SINGULAR		
	NOUN PHRASE		*ONE*
I don't need	**a long-sleeved shirt**.	I have	**one**.

		SINGULAR					
		ADJECTIVE	**SINGULAR COUNT NOUN**			**ADJECTIVE**	*ONE*
Do you want	a	gray	**sweatshirt**	or	a	blue	**one**?

		PLURAL					
	ADJECTIVE	**PLURAL COUNT NOUN**			**ADJECTIVE**	*ONES*	
The	gray	**sweatshirts**	are twenty dollars.	The	blue	**ones**	are eighteen.

		SINGULAR			
THIS	*ONE*		*THAT*	*ONE*	
This	**one**	is my book and	that	**one**	is **Yoko's**.

	IT		
	THE	**+ NOUN**	*IT*
Where's	**the**	**car**?	**It's** on Main Street.
	POSSESSIVE ADJECTIVE + NOUN		*IT*
Where's	**your**	**watch**?	**It's** on the dresser.
	THIS / THAT	**+ NOUN**	*IT*
Where's	**that**	**book**?	**It's** on my desk.

NOTES	EXAMPLES
1. Use *one* in place of *a* or *an* plus a **singular count noun**.	**A:** Does he need a car? **B:** Yes, he needs **one**. (*one* = a car)
2. Use *one* in place of **a noun phrase**.	**A:** She doesn't want a sweatshirt with pockets. She has **one**. *(one* = a sweatshirt with pockets)
3. Use *one* or *ones* after **an adjective** in place of a singular or plural count noun.	**A:** There are three dictionaries. There are two big **ones** and a small **one**. (*ones* = dictionaries, *one* = dictionary)
4. Use *one* after *this* or *that*. ▶ **BE CAREFUL!** Do not use *ones* after *these* or *those*.	**A:** Do you need this book? **B:** No, I don't need **this one**. I need **that one**. (*one* = book) **A:** Do you want these? **B:** No, I want **those**. NOT <s>No, I want those ones.</s>
5. Use *it* in place of *the* + **a noun**.	**A:** Where is **the letter**? **B:** **It**'s on the floor. (*it* = the letter)
6. Use *it* in place of a **possessive pronoun** (*my, your, his, her, its, our,* or *their*) plus a singular count noun.	**A:** Where is **your lunch**? **B:** **It**'s in my lunch box. (*it* = my lunch)
7. Use *it* in place of *this* or *that* plus a **singular count noun**.	**A:** Where is **that cookie**? **B:** **It**'s on the floor. (*it* = that cookie)

FOCUSED PRACTICE

1 DISCOVER THE GRAMMAR

Yoko is dressing for a party. Read the conversation between Yoko and Carol.

CAROL: Hi Yoko. What's up?

YOKO: Oh, Carol. I'm going to a party. I have a nice blouse, but I need a long black skirt.

CAROL: I have <u>one</u>. Here. You can wear it.
                   1.

YOKO: Are you sure? It's beautiful.

CAROL: Positive. And here are two belts. Choose one.

YOKO: This <u>one</u> is nice. Is it really okay if I borrow <u>it</u> for tonight?
                 2.   **3.**

CAROL: Of course. And here's my silver necklace. <u>It</u> matches the belt.
                                                          4.

YOKO: You're right. Thanks a lot, Carol.

CAROL: No problem. Have a great time.

YOKO: Thanks.

Look at the underlined words. Circle what they refer to.

   1. a. a long black skirt   **b.** a party   **c.** Yoko's skirt

   2. a. skirt   **b.** belt   **c.** belts

   3. a. the nice belt   **b.** a belt   **c.** a skirt

   4. a. my long skirt   **b.** my silver belt   **c.** my silver necklace

② GETTING READY FOR COLD WEATHER   Grammar Notes 1–7

Bertha, who lives in Florida, is planning to visit her daughter in Boston. Read the conversation between Lulu and Bertha. Replace the underlined words in the conversation. Use **one**, **ones**, *or* **it**.

LULU: Well, Bertha, are you ready for your trip? Remember, it gets pretty cold in

Boston.

BERTHA: Yes, I'm ready. I have a new coat. $\overset{\text{It}}{\underset{\text{1.}}{\text{My coat}}}$ is a heavy wool.

LULU: Do you have a scarf?

BERTHA: Two—a white <u>scarf</u> and a red, white, and blue <u>scarf</u>. I think I need a wool hat.
            2.   3.

Do you have <u>a wool hat</u> I could borrow?
            4.

LULU: Sure. I have three wool hats. I have a red <u>wool hat</u> and two white <u>wool hats</u>.
                                                      5.   6.

BERTHA: Oh, let me see the red hat.

LULU: Okay. It's in my hall closet. One minute . . . now where is <u>that hat</u>? . . .
                                                                      7.

Here it is.

BERTHA: Oh, Lulu. This hat isn't for me. I look like a tomato in <u>this hat</u>.
                                                                8.

COMMUNICATION PRACTICE

3 FRUIT AND VEGETABLES

Work with a partner. Look at the pictures and complete the sentences. The first pair to label every fruit or vegetable correctly wins.

1. Rabbits eat many of these. They're long and orange. They're

   c a r r o t s .

2. There's an "egg" in the name of this one. It's purple. It's (a/an)

   ___ ___ ___ ___ ___ ___ ___ ___ .

3. We often put this one in a salad. It's green. It's (a/an)

   ___ ___ ___ ___ ___ ___ ___ ___ .

4. There are red ones, yellow ones, orange ones, and green ones.

   They're ___ ___ ___ ___ ___ ___ ___ .

5. Some of these are poisonous. They grow in damp places.

   They're ___ ___ ___ ___ ___ ___ ___ ___ ___ .

6. There's a saying: "You are the _____ of my eye." There's another saying: "An _____ a day keeps the doctor away." There are red ones, yellow ones, and green ones. They are

   ___ ___ ___ ___ ___ ___ .

7. This one is very sour. It's yellow. It's (a / an)

   ___ ___ ___ ___ ___ .

8. On Halloween people carve faces on this one. It's orange.

   It's (a / an) ___ ___ ___ ___ ___ ___ ___ .

9. We put these in pies. People in the United States eat these pies on Washington's birthday.

   They're ___ ___ ___ ___ ___ ___ ___ ___ .

10. This one is very watery and has a lot of seeds. It's red in the middle and green on the outside. It's (a/an)

    ___ ___ ___ ___ ___ ___ ___ ___ ___ ___ .

Now describe a fruit or vegetable. Ask the class what it is.

PART IV

REVIEW OR SELFTEST

I. *Read each conversation. Circle the letter of the underlined word that is not correct.*

1. **A:** <u>Do</u> you <u>have</u> a good dictionary?
        A   B

   B: Yes, I <u>have</u>. <u>It's</u> on my desk.
          C   B

              A   B   C   D

2. **A:** <u>Where</u> does he <u>works</u>?
       A   B

   B: He <u>works</u> at the bank <u>next to</u> the supermarket.
          C   D

              A   B   C   D

3. **A:** <u>Does</u> he <u>need</u> a doctor?
       A   B

   B: Yes, he <u>needs</u>. He <u>has</u> a terrible earache.
           C   D

              A   B   C   D

4. **A:** <u>Why</u> do you <u>work</u> at night?
       A   B

   B: <u>When</u> I <u>study</u> during the day.
        C   D

              A   B   C   D

5. **A:** <u>Do</u> you <u>have</u> any sweatshirts in medium?
       A   B

   B: Yes, we <u>are</u> <u>have</u> sweatshirts in all sizes.
           C   D

              A   B   C   D

6. **A:** Carol doesn't <u>to</u> <u>live</u> in California.
               A   B

   B: <u>Where</u> does she <u>live</u>?
        C   D

              A   B   C   D

7. **A:** <u>Who</u> <u>does</u> Carol usually <u>eats</u> lunch with?
       A   B   C

   B: She usually <u>eats</u> with Dan and Jon.
             D

              A   B   C   D

II. *Complete the sentences. Use the present tense of the verb in parentheses.*

1. (need) _____ you _____ a suit?

2. He (wash) _____ the windows once a month.

3. Carol (have) _____ a sister and a brother.

4. Pete (be, not) _____ a lawyer.

5. Mrs. Smith (fix) _____ lamps.

6. Pete (go) _____ to the park on Tuesdays.

142

7. She (do) _____ the dishes every morning.

8. (speak) _____ your sister _____ English?

9. (wear) _____ the students _____ uniforms to school?

10. We (eat, not) _____ turkey for breakfast.

11. Pete often (worry) _____ about his family.

12. Who (live) _____ next to the Winstons?

13. What (make) _____ you happy?

14. What time (come) _____ your father _____ home from work?

15. Where (keep) _____ they _____ their money?

III. *Write questions. Use the simple present tense.*

  1. Elenore gets up at 6:00 A.M.

    a. _____? At 6:00 A.M.

    b. _____? Elenore does.

    c. _____? Yes, she does.

    d. _____? She gets up.

  2. Doug calls Noah every night at 9:00 P.M.

    a. _____? Doug does.

    b. _____? Noah.

IV. *Complete the sentences. Use **it**, **one**, or **ones**.*

  1. I have a green sweater and two white _____.

  2. I have a green sweater. _____ is very warm.

  3. Doug has a blue sweater and a gold _____.

  4. Elenore wears that jacket because _____ is very comfortable.

  5. I like green grapes, but I don't like red _____.

  6. On Thursdays, we usually watch an interesting show about animals in Australia.

    _____ is on channel 13 at 8:00.

  7. My old watch is gold, but my new _____ isn't.

V. *Complete the conversations. Use* **this**, **that**, **these**, *or* **those**.

1. **A:** Come and meet my friend. John, _____ is my cousin George.

   B: Nice to meet you.

2. **A:** How much does the tie in your hand cost?

   B: _____ one costs thirty-five dollars. It's silk. But _____ ties on the

   other side of the room only cost ten dollars.

   A: Thanks.

3. **A:** Who's _____ boy across the street?

   B: It's Alex.

4. **A:** You are a very good photographer. _____ photos are excellent.

   B: Thank you. I have some more in my bag.

   A: Please show them to me.

   B: Okay.

   A: They're wonderful. What about _____ photos on the wall? Are they your

   photos, too?

   B: Yes, they are.

   A: Wow! You're really talented!

VI. *Correct these sentences.*

1. Doug ~~like~~ likes soccer.

2. She isn't write a letter every week.

3. Does Carol needs an umbrella?

4. This is my gloves.

5. Do they wants any eggs?

6. Norma is teaches Spanish.

7. Who does cooks in your house?

8. This are my friends.

9. Those magazine has wonderful photos.

10. Does Doug likes basketball?

▶ *To check your answers, go to the Answer Key on page 146.*

FROM GRAMMAR TO WRITING
TIME WORD CONNECTORS:
FIRST, NEXT, AFTER THAT, THEN, FINALLY

❶ *Which paragraph sounds better, Paragraph A or B? Why?*

Paragraph A

I like to watch my roommate prepare tea. She boils water and pours the boiling water in a cup with a teabag in it. She removes the tea bag and adds sugar. She adds lemon. She adds ice. She sips the tea and says, "Mmm. This tea is just the way I like it."

Paragraph B

I like to watch my roommate prepare tea. First, she boils some water and pours the boiling water in a cup with a teabag in it. Next, she removes the teabag and adds some sugar. After that, she adds some lemon. Then she adds some ice. Finally, she sips the tea and says, "Mmm. This tea is just the way I like it."

Study this information about time word connectors.

Time Word Connectors

You can make your writing clearer by using **time word connectors**. They show the order that things happen. Some common ones are: **first**, **next**, **after that**, **then**, and **finally**.

Note the use of the **comma** after these words.

- **First**, you add the water. **Next**, you add the sugar.

---

❷ *Use time word connectors to show the order of things in this paragraph.*

I take a shower. I have breakfast. I drive to the train station. I take a train and a bus. I get to work.

Now write a paragraph about a routine you follow. Use time word connectors. Here are some ideas:

  a. Every Saturday morning . . .

  b. Every New Year's Day . . .

  c. Every year on my birthday . . .

REVIEW OR SELFTEST
ANSWER KEY

I.
1. C 3. C 5. C 7. C
2. B 4. C 6. A

IV.
1. ones 4. it 6. It
2. It 5. ones 7. one
3. one

II.
1. Do, need
2. washes
3. has
4. isn't ('s not) (is not)
5. fixes
6. goes
7. does
8. Does, speak
9. Do, wear
10. don't eat
11. worries
12. lives
13. makes
14. does, come
15. do, keep

V.
1. this 3. that
2. This / those 4. These / those

VI.
2. She <u>doesn't</u> write a letter every week.
3. Does Carol <u>need</u> an umbrella?
4. This is my <u>glove</u>. (<u>These are</u> my gloves.)
5. Do they <u>want</u> any eggs?
6. Norma teaches Spanish.
7. Who cooks in your house?
8. <u>These are</u> my friends. (<u>This is</u> my friend.)
9. Those magazines <u>have</u> wonderful photos. (<u>That magazine</u> has wonderful photos.)
10. Does Doug <u>like</u> basketball?

III.
1. a. When does Elenore get up? (What time does Elenore get up?)
   b. Who gets up at 6:00 A.M.?
   c. Does Elenore get up at 6:00 A.M.?
   d. What does Elenore do at 6:00 A.M.?
2. a. Who calls Noah every night at 9:00 P.M.?
   b. Who does Doug call every night at 9:00 P.M.?

Answers to Exercise 7 on page 121
1. Is; Yes, it is.
2. Does; No, it doesn't.
3. Does; Yes, it does.
4. Does; Yes, it does.
5. Is; Yes, it is.
6. Do; Yes, they do.
7. Is; Yes, it is.
8. Does; No, it doesn't.
9. Do; Yes, they do.
10. Is; Yes, it is.
11. Is; No, it isn't.
12. Are; Yes, they are.

Answers to Exercise 7 on page 130
1. b 4. b
2. c 5. a
3. b 6. c

Student B, complete sentences 5–8. Then listen to your partner read sentences 1–4. Say "That's right" or correct your partner's sentence. Then read sentences 5–8 to your partner. Your partner says "That's right" or corrects your sentence.

1. People in Japan don't wear shoes in their home. When they enter a home, they remove their shoes and put on slippers.

2. People in Korea eat rice cake soup on New Year's Day. Children often wear red jackets with sleeves of many colors.

3. People in Thailand bow to show respect. Younger people usually bow first.

4. In Brazil during Carnival people wear strange and beautiful costumes. Brazilians don't work during Carnival. They dance in the streets.

5. In Saudi Arabia at the time of Ramadan, Moslems _____ or
   _____ during daylight. Ramadan _____ for thirty days. At
     b. (drink / don't drink)   c. (lasts / doesn't last)
   the end of Ramadan there _____ a three-day celebration.
                                 d. (is / isn't)

   a. (eat / don't eat)

6. On New Year's Day, Chinese children _____ money in red envelopes from
                                      a. (receive / don't receive)
   their parents and grandparents.

7. In the United States, people usually _____ on July 4th. They
                                  a. (work / don't work)
   _____ fireworks and _____ barbecues.
    b. (watch / don't watch)   c. (have / don't have)

8. In Denmark, people _____ on their friends' doors and
                     a. (bang / don't bang)
   _____ fireworks on New Year's Eve.
   b. (set off / don't set off)

Now work with your partner. Write about customs you know well. Read your sentences to the class.

_____

_____

_____

_____

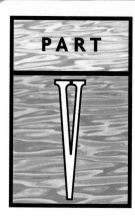

THE SIMPLE PAST TENSE

PREVIEW

Carol is visiting San Francisco. She is talking on the phone to her mother, Elenore, in New York. Listen and read their conversation.

THE WINSTONS' THANKSGIVING DAY

CAROL: Hi, Mom.

ELENORE: Hi, Carol. Gee, we really missed you for Thanksgiving.

CAROL: I missed you, too.

ELENORE: How's San Francisco? When did you and Yoko arrive?

CAROL: We arrived late Wednesday night. San Francisco's great. On Thanksgiving Day we took a sight-seeing bus all around the city. Then we rode on a cable car and walked around Fisherman's Wharf. We ate fish at a restaurant there and had a great time. What about you and Dad? Did you have a nice Thanksgiving?

ELENORE: Well, Uncle Bob and Aunt Valerie invited us for dinner.

CAROL: How was it?

ELENORE: Dinner was delicious. Aunt Valerie made a huge turkey. I brought cranberry sauce, Norma baked a pumpkin pie, and Dad prepared pumpkin curry soup.

CAROL: Pumpkin curry soup? That's different. How did it taste?

ELENORE: I liked it, but Uncle Bob didn't like it at all. He tried one spoonful and shouted, "Fire!" Then he drank four glasses of water.

CAROL: Poor Uncle Bob!

ELENORE: Poor Dad! After dinner Uncle Bob turned on the TV and watched a football game. You know how Dad hates football.

CAROL: Did you stay long?

ELENORE: No, we left early.

CAROL: Well, that was a good idea. Remember last summer when we went to Massachusetts with Aunt Valerie and Uncle Bob? Uncle Bob and Dad had that big fight.

ELENORE: Please, Carol, don't remind me. Well, I hope you and Yoko enjoy the rest of your vacation.

CAROL: Thanks, Mom. I'll call you next week. Bye.

ELENORE: Bye.

COMPREHENSION CHECK

Check (✔) who did what activity.

	Carol	Carol's parents	No one
1. visited San Francisco	☐	☐	☐
2. visited Aunt Valerie and Uncle Bob	☐	☐	☐
3. went to Massachusetts last summer	☐	☐	☐
4. saw a fire	☐	☐	☐
5. rode on a cable car	☐	☐	☐
6. ate turkey, cranberry sauce, and pumpkin pie	☐	☐	☐

WITH A PARTNER

Practice the conversation on pages 148 and 149.

 18 SIMPLE PAST TENSE: REGULAR VERBS—AFFIRMATIVE AND NEGATIVE STATEMENTS

GRAMMAR **IN CONTEXT**

WARM UP   Look at the chart. Were you in any of these cities?
What cities? When?

The World's Ten Largest Cities

Seoul, South Korea
São Paulo, Brazil
Bombay (Mumbai), India
Jakarta, Indonesia
Moscow, Russia
Istanbul, Turkey
Mexico City, Mexico
Shanghai, China
Tokyo, Japan
New York City, United States

Source:
infoplease.com, 1997

 Listen and read the following postcard.

Hi Elenore and Pete,

   Ali and I are having a great time here in
this magical city.

   Last night we **walked** along the Seine River.
Today we **dined** in Montmartre and we **visited**
the Louvre. (I **didn't** really **like** the Mona Lisa,
but maybe I **didn't understand** it.)

   We're now at the Eiffel Tower and it looks
just like it does in the photos.

   Hope all is well with you.

                 Love,
                 Wendy and Ali

France

To:
Mr. and Mrs. Pete Winston
345 West 76th Street
New York, New York 10023
U.S.A.

What city did Wendy and Ali visit?

GRAMMAR **PRESENTATION**
SIMPLE PAST TENSE: REGULAR VERBS— AFFIRMATIVE AND NEGATIVE STATEMENTS

AFFIRMATIVE STATEMENTS

SUBJECT	BASE FORM OF VERB + -ED, -D, IED
I You He She It We You They	cook**ed**. arrive**d**. cr**ied**.

NEGATIVE STATEMENTS

SUBJECT	DID NOT	BASE FORM OF VERB
I You He She It We You They	**did not** **didn't**	**cook**. **arrive**. **cry**.

SOME COMMON PAST TIME MARKERS

YESTERDAY	AGO	LAST
yesterday morning **yesterday** afternoon **yesterday** evening	two days **ago** a week **ago** a month **ago** a year **ago**	**last** night **last** Monday **last** week **last** summer

NOTES	EXAMPLES

1. Use the **simple past tense** to talk about an event that happened in the past.

| | • I **arrived** last night. |

2. There are three endings for the regular simple past tense: **-d, -ed, -ied**.

• I bake**d** a cake.
• We cook**ed** spaghetti.
• They stud**ied** Japanese.

3. In the past tense, the verb form is the same for all persons.

• **I visited** my sister last night.
• **She visited** me this morning.
• **We visited** our aunt this afternoon.

4. For negative statements in the past, use **did not + the base form of the verb**.

Use the contraction **didn't** for negative statements in speaking or informal writing.

• We **did not stay** at a hotel.
• He **did not like** the painting.

• We **didn't stay** at a hotel.

5. **Time markers** usually come at the beginning or at the end of a sentence.

• **Yesterday morning** I studied.
• I studied **yesterday morning**.

6. _Today_, _this morning_, _this afternoon_, and _this evening_ can be past time markers if they mean "before now."

• I studied grammar **today**. (It is now 9:00 P.M. I studied grammar in the afternoon.)
• **This morning** I listened to the news. (It is now afternoon.)

REFERENCE NOTE
See Appendix 15, page A-15, for complete spelling and pronunciation rules for the simple past tense.

FOCUSED PRACTICE

1 DISCOVER THE GRAMMAR

Read these sentences and underline the past-tense verbs. Then write the base form (dictionary form) of the verb next to each sentence. Circle the four other time markers.

1. (Yesterday) we <u>walked</u> around Fisherman's Wharf. _____ walk _____

2. We arrived last Wednesday night. _____

3. Uncle Bob and Aunt Valerie invited us to their house. _____

4. Norma baked a pie this morning. _____

5. Aunt Valerie cooked a huge turkey. _____

6. The bus stopped at the corner a few minutes ago. _____

7. We studied history last night. _____

2 SPELLING AND PRONUNCIATION　　　　Grammar Notes 2–3

Complete the sentences. Use the past tense of the verbs in the box. See Appendix 15 on page A-15 for spelling rules for the regular simple past tense.

watch	visit	cook	arrive	walk	study	bake	joke	want	hug

	/t/	/d/	/ɪd/
1. I'm sorry I'm late. I ____missed____ my train.	✔	❏	❏
2. The plane _____ on time.	❏	❏	❏
3. Last night she _____ her uncle in the hospital.	❏	❏	❏
4. He _____ hot cereal yesterday morning.	❏	❏	❏
5. I'm tired. Yesterday I _____ up a lot of hills in San Francisco.	❏	❏	❏
6. Last year she _____ to live in the city, but now she likes the country.	❏	❏	❏
7. We _____ at the library this afternoon.	❏	❏	❏
8. Last night I _____ a good movie on TV.	❏	❏	❏
9. Uncle Bob _____ about Dad's pumpkin curry soup.	❏	❏	❏
10. Everybody _____ and kissed me at my graduation.	❏	❏	❏

▶ *Now listen to the sentences. Then listen again and check (✔) the final sound of each verb. See Appendix 15 on page A-15 for pronunciation rules for the regular simple past tense.*

3 A POSTCARD FROM SAN FRANCISCO

Carol sent her grandmother a postcard from San Francisco. Complete the sentences. Use the simple past tense of each verb.

The Golden Gate Bridge

Chinatown

San Francisco Sights

Fisherman's Wharf

Cable Car

Sunday

Dear Grandma Lulu,

    Greetings from San Francisco! Yoko and I ___rented___ *a car last*
                                                        1. (rent)

Wednesday morning in Oregon. We _____ *in San Francisco*
                                           2. (arrive)

Wednesday night. We love it here. It's a very modern and open city.

Thursday we _____ *Fisherman's Wharf and Chinatown. Friday*
                   3. (visit)

we _____ *around Berkeley with Yoko's friends. Yoko's uncle*
   4. (walk)

_____ *us to his home in Oakland, but we* _____ *to*
  5. (invite)   **6. (want, not)**

drive anymore, so we _____ *him. We* _____ *our*
                   7. (visit, not)   **8. (pack)**

bags this morning and we're on our way home.

    All my books are at school, so I can't study, but traveling is an

education, isn't it?

    I hope you had a nice Thanksgiving.

                                              Love,

                                              Carol

To: *Mrs. Lulu Winston*
      6103 Collins Ave.
      Miami Beach, FL 33130

4 GETTING AROUND

Complete the conversations. Use **last**, **ago**, *or* **yesterday**.

1.   **PETE:** Hi, Bob. How are you doing?

   BOB: Fine.

   PETE: Were you away?

   BOB: Yes. I attended a conference in Washington _____ week.

   a.

   PETE: Oh, lucky you. Washington's beautiful this time of year. I was there a couple

   of months _____ and the weather was awful. When did you get

   b.

   back to New York?

   BOB: _____.

   c.

2. **ELENORE:** Pete, where are the Strams?

   PETE: In Prague. They arrived there _____ morning.

   a.

   ELENORE: Wow! _____ month they were in Brazil. And a year

   b.

   _____ they were in Bangkok. They really get around.

   c.

5 THE WINSTONS' THANKSGIVING

Read the conversations on pages 148 and 149 again. Write affirmative or negative past-tense sentences.

1. Carol and Yoko / visit / San Francisco / last week

   Carol and Yoko visited San Francisco last week.

2. Carol and Yoko / visit / Boston / last week

   Carol and Yoko didn't visit Boston last week.

3. Uncle Bob / watch / a football game / on Thanksgiving

   _____

4. Carol / watch / a football game / on Thanksgiving

   _____

5. Aunt Valerie / cook / a huge turkey / last Thursday

   _____

6. Carol and Yoko / cook / a turkey / on Thanksgiving

   _____

6 WRONG MESSAGES

Listen to Pete and Elenore's phone messages. Then read this conversation between Elenore and Pete. Correct Pete's three mistakes.

PETE: Hello.

ELENORE: Hi Pete. Listen. I'm at the hairdresser's. I'll be home at about 6:30.

PETE: Okay. Thanks for calling.

ELENORE: Any messages?

PETE: Well, a James Mills called. He and Joe arrived today. They're at the Central Hotel.

ELENORE: Okay. Any other messages?

PETE: Yes. Doug. He invited Noah for dinner.

ELENORE: Oh that's nice. I'm glad I cooked a lot this morning. Well, see you in about an hour.

PETE: Okay. Bye.

7 EDITING

Find and correct the three mistakes in this postcard.

Dear Elenore and Pete,

They say everyone loves Rio. Now we know why.

Yesterday morning we did watch a soccer game on Ipanema Beach. Then we visit Sugarloaf. In the evening we're enjoying a huge and delicious meal at a churrascaria.

The people are friendly and the weather is great. Regards to Norma, Carol, and Doug.

Love,

Dahlia and Josh

Brazil

To:

Mr. and Mrs. Pete Winston
345 West 76th Street
New York, New York 10023
U.S.A.

COMMUNICATION PRACTICE

8 WHAT I DID LAST WEEKEND

*Work in small groups. Check (✔) the activities you did last weekend. Then tell
your group more about them.*

_____ **1.** I watched TV.

_____ **2.** I listened to music.

_____ **3.** I visited friends or relatives.

_____ **4.** I talked on the
telephone.

_____ **5.** I played a sport.

_____ **6.** I worked.

_____ **7.** I studied.

> **EXAMPLE:**
> I watched TV Friday night. I watched Hitchcock's movie *The Birds*. It was scary.

9 TALKING ABOUT FEELINGS

*Work in small groups. Write five sentences that begin, "I feel bad. I didn't . . ."
Then write five sentences that begin, "I'm a little angry. My friend didn't . . ."
Use the verbs in the box or add your own.*

call	visit	talk to	wash	answer	help	thank	clean	return	study

> **EXAMPLES:**
> **1.** I feel bad. I didn't thank Maria for the gift.
> **2.** I'm a little angry. My friend didn't return my sweater. She borrowed it
> a month ago.

Now read a sentence to your group. Your classmates listen and respond.

10 GUESS THE SITUATION

*Work in small groups. Read the sentences. Who is speaking? What happened?
Discuss your answers with your group. Use the verbs in the box.*

delivered	arrived	died	played	dialed	graduated

> **EXAMPLE:**
> "I'm so sorry. Our baby-sitter missed her bus and arrived thirty minutes late."
> A woman is speaking. The woman and her husband arrived late at a party.

1. "Thanks. I enjoyed the game. Let's meet next week."

2. "The pizza smells good. Here's twenty dollars, and keep the change."

3. "Congratulations."

4. "Sorry, wrong number."

5. "I'm so sorry to hear about your grandfather's death."

SIMPLE PAST TENSE: IRREGULAR VERBS—AFFIRMATIVE AND NEGATIVE STATEMENTS

GRAMMAR **IN CONTEXT**

WARM UP   What does, "You never know what will happen" mean to you?

Listen and read this Chinese folktale.

YOU NEVER KNOW WHAT WILL HAPPEN

A long time ago there lived a poor Chinese peasant. One day a beautiful horse appeared. When the peasant's friends **saw** the horse, they **said**, "How lucky you are!"

The peasant answered, "You never know what will happen."

After two days, the horse **ran** away. The peasant's friends **came** and **said**, "What a terrible thing. How unlucky you are! The fine horse ran away." The peasant **didn't get** excited. He simply said, "You never know what will happen."

Exactly one week later the horse returned. And it **brought** three other horses. When the peasant's friends **saw** the horses, they **said** to their friend, "Oh. You are so lucky. Now you have four horses to help you." The peasant looked at them and once again **said**, "You never know what will happen."

The next morning the peasant's oldest son **was** in the field. Suddenly one of the horses **ran** into him, and the boy **fell** to the ground.

He **was** badly hurt. He **lost** the use of his leg. Indeed, this **was** terrible, and many people **came** to the peasant and expressed their sadness for his son's misfortune. But again the peasant simply **said**, "You never know what will happen."

A month after the son's accident, soldiers **rode** into the village. They shouted, "There are problems along the border. We are taking every healthy young man to

fight." The soldiers **took** every other young man, but they **didn't take** the peasant's son. Every other young man **fought** in the border war, and every man died. But the peasant's son lived a long and happy life. As his father **said**, you never know what will happen.

GRAMMAR **PRESENTATION**
SIMPLE PAST TENSE: IRREGULAR VERBS—
AFFIRMATIVE AND NEGATIVE STATEMENTS

AFFIRMATIVE STATEMENTS		
SUBJECT	**VERB**	
I You He She It We You They	**saw**	the horses.

NEGATIVE STATEMENTS			
SUBJECT	**DID NOT / DIDN'T**	**BASE FORM OF VERB**	
I You He She It We You They	**did not didn't**	see	the soldiers.

NOTES	**EXAMPLES**
1. Irregular past tense verbs do not add *-ed* in affirmative sentences. They have different forms.	• We **saw** a beautiful horse. • The horse **ran** home. • She **came** late. • He **brought** a friend to school. • He **ate** a huge lunch.
2. For **negative statements** in the past, use *did not* **+ the base form of the verb.** (except for the verb *be*)	• They **did not visit** Los Angeles. • She **did not eat** lunch.
3. The past tense of *be* is *was* or *were*. The negative of *was* is *was not*, and the negative of *were* is *were not*. The contractions of *was not* and *were not* are *wasn't* and *weren't*.	• I **was** at the library last night. • They **were not** home this morning. • It **wasn't** late. • They **weren't** in Tokyo.

REFERENCE NOTE
See Appendix 12, page A-13, for a list of irregular past tense verb forms.

FOCUSED PRACTICE

1 DISCOVER THE GRAMMAR

Read this story that Al Brown told his students. Underline all the past tense verbs. Circle the irregular verbs.

Many years ago my grandfather, Benjamin Brown, (took) a cruise on the Mediterranean Sea. The first evening at dinner a Frenchman sat down next to my grandfather. Before he sat down, the Frenchman looked at my grandfather and said, "Bon appetit."

My grandfather stood up and said, "Ben Brown." The same thing happened the next evening and the one after that. My grandfather said to an Englishman on the ship, "I

Bon Appétit!

don't understand my dinner partner. Every evening he comes to dinner and introduces himself." The Englishman, who spoke French, asked my grandfather some more questions. Soon he understood my grandfather's mistake. He explained to my grandfather that "bon appetit" was not the man's name, but was French for "Enjoy your meal."

The next night my grandfather came to dinner after the Frenchman. My grandfather smiled and with a perfect French accent said, "Bon appetit." The Frenchman stood up and replied, "Ben Brown."

2 CAROL AND YOKO IN SAN FRANCISCO   Grammar Notes 1–2

Study these irregular verbs.

Base form	Past form
do	did
drive	drove
eat	ate
feel	felt
find	found
go	went
leave	left
meet	met
send	sent

(continued on next page)

Now complete the sentences. Use the verbs in the box on page 161.

1. Carol and Yoko (not) ___didn't eat___ turkey on Thanksgiving. They ___ate___ fish.

2. Carol _____ Yoko's friends from Berkeley for the first time last Wednesday.

3. Lucky Yoko! She _____ twenty dollars on a cable car in San Francisco.

4. Carol didn't get to San Francisco by bus. She rented a car and _____ there with Yoko.

5. Yoko (not) _____ her homework on Thursday or Friday. She _____ it on Saturday and Sunday.

6. After their trip to San Francisco, Yoko and Carol _____ very relaxed.

7. Carol and Yoko (not) _____ to a concert. They _____ to the movies.

8. Carol _____ a postcard to her grandmother.

9. Yoko and Carol _____ San Francisco at noon on Sunday. They arrived home at nine o'clock Sunday night.

3 THANKSGIVING VACATION

Study these irregular verbs. Now complete the conversation. Use the verbs in the box.

Base form	Past form
forget	forgot
have	had
hide	hid
read	read (pronounced /rɛd/)
sleep	slept
speak	spoke
steal	stole
swim	swam

AL BROWN: Welcome back. I hope you all enjoyed your Thanksgiving vacation.

YOLANDA: Oh, I _____had_____ a great time. I visited Los Angeles for four days.
                     1.

I _____ in a pool and played tennis every day.
        2.

AL BROWN: What about you, Maria?

MARIA: On my vacation I _____ late every day, and I _____
                              3.   **4.**

two novels.

AL BROWN: In English?

MARIA: No, in Spanish.

AL BROWN: Oh, well. Yuriko, did you have a nice vacation?

YURIKO: Yes, I did. My boyfriend called me yesterday. We _____ for over
                                                              5.

an hour.

AL BROWN: Bekir, why are you so sad?

BEKIR: I want to forget my vacation. Last Friday I _____ to lock my door
                                                          6.

and someone _____ my TV.
                  7.

AL BROWN: Did the thief take any money?

BEKIR: No. I _____ my money in my grammar book.
                    8.

The thief didn't look there.

COMMUNICATION PRACTICE

4 A MEMORY GAME

Play a memory game with the class. Sit in a circle. The first student tells one thing he or she did yesterday. The next student tells what the first student did and then what he or she did. Continue as long as each student remembers what the others have already said.

> **EXAMPLE:**
>
> **A:** I went to the movies.
>
> **B:** A went to the movies, and I read a novel.

5 HOW WAS YOUR DAY?

Work in small groups. Tell about a wonderful day and a terrible day. Use **First**, **Then**, *and* **After that**.

> **EXAMPLES:**
>
> I had a wonderful day today.   Yesterday I had a terrible day.
>
> *First,* I saw my grandmother.   *First,* I got to school late.
>
> *Then,* I went to the park.   *Then,* I broke my glasses.
>
> *After that,* I rented a video.   *After that,* someone stole my wallet.

6 A SPECIAL PERSON

Complete the story. Use your imagination. Read your story to your classmates. Listen to their stories.

_____ ago I met a _____. He / She had _____

and _____. He / She came from _____. We spoke about

_____ and _____. I said, "_____." He / She said,

"_____." Then he/she left. I felt _____.

7 SURPRISES

Work in small groups. Sometimes you don't know what will happen. Tell your group a story from your life with a surprising ending. Then tell the class one of your group's stories.

> **EXAMPLE:**
>
> As a child, Bob hated school. He never did well in school. His sisters and brothers always brought home prizes for their excellent schoolwork, but not Bob. Bob's parents worried about him. But in his second year of high school Bob had a wonderful chemistry teacher. He became interested in chemistry. From that time on he studied hard. He is now a well-known chemistry professor at a top university.

SIMPLE PAST TENSE: *YES / NO* AND *WH-* QUESTIONS

GRAMMAR **IN CONTEXT**

WARM UP   Do you have anything (a watch, a ring, a necklace) that belonged to an older relative? What is it? Who did it belong to?

EXAMPLE:
I have a beautiful old watch. It belonged to my grandfather's brother. When he died, my grandfather gave it to me.

Look at these questions. Listen and read the conversation on page 166. *Then answer the questions.*

1. **What did** Norma **lose**?

   a. a boyfriend   **b.** a watch   **c.** a ring

2. **Who did** it **belong** to?

   a. her great-   **b.** her best friend   **c.** her father
   grandmother

3. **When did** she **get** it?

   a. many years ago   **b.** a few years ago   **c.** a few days ago

4. **Who called** her?

   a. the new   **b.** her great-   **c.** her friend
   math teacher   grandmother

5. **Did** Norma **get** it back?

   a. No, she didn't.   **b.** Yes, she did.   **c.** It doesn't say.

ALICE: **What happened**, Norma? You look like you lost your best friend.

NORMA: Well, I'm pretty upset. I lost my ring.

ALICE: Oh, that's awful. Was it valuable?

NORMA: Not really. But it was valuable to me. It belonged to my great-grandmother. My mom gave it to me just a few days ago, at Thanksgiving.

ALICE: **Where did** you **lose** it?

NORMA: I'm not sure. Maybe I lost it in the parking lot. The ring was loose.

ALICE: **When did** you last **have** the ring?

NORMA: Well, I know I had it this morning.

[Norma's cell phone rings.]

NORMA: Hello?

MARY: Hello. I'm Mary Connelly. Is this Norma Winston?

NORMA: Yes?

MARY: I'm the new math teacher at Kennedy High School. I found a ring in the teacher's lunchroom. **Did** you, by any chance, **leave** a ring there?

NORMA: Yes, I did. **How did** you **know** it was my ring?

MARY: I found the ring and I asked around. Elaine Brown remembered the ring on your finger.

NORMA: Oh that's wonderful. I'm glad Elaine has a good eye for jewelry.

MARY: Anyway, don't worry. Your ring is safe.

NORMA: Thanks so much. And welcome to Kennedy.

MARY: Thanks. See you tomorrow.

GRAMMAR **PRESENTATION**
SIMPLE PAST TENSE: *YES / NO* QUESTIONS AND SHORT ANSWERS AND *WH-* QUESTIONS

YES / NO QUESTIONS		
DID	**SUBJECT**	**BASE FORM OF VERB**
Did	I you he she it we you they	**work**? **eat**?

SHORT ANSWERS					
AFFIRMATIVE			**NEGATIVE**		
Yes,	you I he she it you we they	**did.**	**No,**	you I he she it you we they	**didn't.**

WH- QUESTIONS ABOUT THE SUBJECT	
WH- WORD	**PAST-TENSE VERB**
Who	**called**?
What	**happened**?

ANSWERS
Norma did. (Norma called.)
She lost her ring.

OTHER WH- QUESTIONS			
WH- WORD	**DID**	**SUBJECT**	**BASE FORM OF VERB**
What		I	**forget**?
Where		you	**go**?
When	**did**	he	**arrive**?
Why		we	**leave**?
Who(m)		you	**call**?
How long		they	**stay**?

ANSWERS
You forgot your book.
I went to San Francisco.
Before lunch.
We didn't want to be late.
The teacher.
A few hours. For a few hours.

NOTES	EXAMPLES
1. *Yes / No* **questions** in the past tense have the same form for regular and irregular verbs except for the verb *be*.	<p>regular verb</p>• **Did** you **enjoy** the movie?<p>irregular verb</p>• **Did** you **write** the letter? • **Were** you at work yesterday?
2. Most *wh-* **questions** in the past begin with the question word followed by *did* + **the subject** + **the base form** of the verb.	• **Where did** Bill **study**? • **Who did** Bill **study** with? • **Why did** Bill **study** there? • **What did** Bill **study**?
Wh- questions in the past do not use *did* when the question is about the subject.	<p>subject</p>• Bill **studied** in the library with Jon. **A: Who studied**? Bill did. NOT <s>Who did study?</s><p>subject</p>• The glass **broke**. **A: What broke**? The glass did. NOT <s>What did break?</s>
Wh- questions in the past with *be* do not use *did*.	**A: Where were** you last night? **B:** I was in the library.
3. Questions that begin with *How* ask about the manner in which something occurred.	**A: How did** you **get** to school? **B:** By bus.
Questions that begin with *How long* ask for the length of time. We often use *for* in the answer.	**A: How long did** you **stay**? **B: For two hours.** (We stayed for two hours.)
Note the form for a question about how long something took.	**A: How long did it take** you to get there? **B:** An hour.

4. We usually give short answers to *yes / no* and *wh-* questions, but we can also give long answers.

A: Did you work yesterday afternoon?

B: Uh-huh.

B: Yes.

B: Yes, I did.

B: Yes, I worked yesterday afternoon.

A: Where did you go?

B: To the park.

B: We went to the park.

PRONUNCIATION NOTE

Yes / no questions use rising intonation. *Wh-* questions use falling intonation.

(Did you hear the story? What did you think about it?)

REFERENCE NOTE

For more notes about *wh-* questions, see Part III and Unit 30.

FOCUSED PRACTICE

1 DISCOVER THE GRAMMAR

First read these questions and write the letter of the two possible answers to each question. Then read the story and circle the correct answer.

a. Yes, he did.	f. A blanket.
b. Paul's mother.	g. Because he wanted to remember his grandfather.
c. Paul lost it.	h. No, he didn't.
d. It tore.	i. A change purse.
e. Paul's son.	j. Because his parents worked.

1. **What happened** to the change purse? __*c*__ or __*d*__

2. **What happened** to the pencil case? _____ or _____

3. **Did** Paul's grandfather **play** with him? _____ or _____

4. **Did** Paul **play** with his grandmother? _____ or _____

5. **What did** Paul's grandfather **give** him? _____ or _____

6. **What did** Paul **make** the pencil case into? _____ or _____

7. **Who made** the book bag into a pencil case? _____ or _____

8. **Who found** Paul's story? _____ or _____

9. **Why did** Paul **spend** a lot of time at his grandparents' house? _____ or _____

10. **Why did** Paul **write** about his grandfather's blanket? _____ or _____

GRANDPA'S BLANKET

As a young child, I was quiet and shy. I was also sick a lot of the time. My parents worked, and I spent a lot of time at my grandparents' house. While my grandmother cleaned and cooked, my grandfather played with me.

I was six when my grandfather died. A few months before he died, he gave me a beautiful blue and white blanket. I loved the blanket very much because it reminded me of my grandfather. But after a couple of years, the blanket didn't look very good. It had holes and stains. I didn't want to throw the

blanket away, so my mother made the blanket into a book bag. I was proud of the book bag, and I used it to carry my books to school every day for a couple of years. Then the book bag tore. I begged my mother to make something out of it. She made it into a pencil case. After a few months, the pencil case tore too. By then I could sew, and I made the pencil case into a small change purse.

I used it for three years, but one day I lost it. I felt bad. My friends and family said, "Forget about it, Paul. You can't make something out of nothing."

I thought about it for a while. I decided my friends and family were wrong. There *was* a way to make something out of nothing. I wrote down the story of my grandfather's blanket. Last week my son found my story in our attic. My son asked me about the blanket. And he asked about my grandfather. Grandpa and his blanket aren't gone.

Grandpa's Blanket

---

② JUAN'S GRANDFATHER   Grammar Notes 1–4

Juan told the class a family story about his grandfather. Write questions about the story. Then listen to the story and answer the questions.

1. Where / this story take place?

  Where does this story take place? _____ ? In ___Senegal.___

2. Juan's grandfather / have / an interpreter?

  _____ ? _____

3. Juan's grandfather / like / his interpreter?

  _____ ? Yes, _____

4. How long / it take / the interpreter to tell a joke?

  _____ ? Ten _____

5. What / the interpreter / say to the crowd?

  _____ ? He said, "_____"

❸ BEKIR'S GRANDPARENTS   Grammar Notes 1–2, 4

Ali asked Bekir questions about his grandparents. Write questions to complete their conversation. Use the words in parentheses.

ALI: As a child, ___did you live with your grandparents___ ?
             1. (did / live / with your grandparents)

BEKIR: No. My mother's parents lived next door. My father's parents lived far away.

ALI: _____ ?
             2. (Where / your father's parents / live)

BEKIR: In the south of Turkey.

ALI: _____ ?
             3. (What / your grandfather / do)

BEKIR: He had a farm.

ALI: _____ ?
             4. (work / long hours)

BEKIR: Oh yes. He worked more than twelve hours a day.

ALI: _____ ?
             5. (have / a large farm)

BEKIR: Yes. It belonged to his father before him.

ALI: _____ ?
             6. (What / your grandmother / do)

BEKIR: She helped my grandfather with the farm. She worked hard, too. She brought up

   my father and his seven sisters and brothers.

ALI: _____ ?
             7. (Where / your grandparents / meet)

BEKIR: Their parents arranged their marriage.

ALI: _____ ?
             8. (When / they / meet)

BEKIR: In the 1940s.

ALI: _____ ?
             9. (have / a happy marriage)

BEKIR: I think so. They never complained.

ALI: Are your grandparents alive today?

BEKIR: My grandfather died six years ago, but my grandmother is still alive. She lives with

   my father's older brother on the farm.

4 **THE HISTORY OF THANKSGIVING** Grammar Notes 2–3

Read about Thanksgiving in the United States. Then write questions that the underlined words answer.

<u>In 1620</u> a group of people came to America from England. They were the Pilgrims.
   1.
They left England <u>because the king of England didn't allow them to practice their religion</u>.
                                              2.

   <u>The Pilgrims</u> wanted to sail to Virginia and join the first English settlers. But their boat
   3.
landed to the north, in Massachusetts.

   Massachusetts has a cold climate, and the Pilgrims had a difficult time. But with the

help of friendly Native Americans, they learned <u>to hunt and grow crops for food</u>.
                                                            4.

   After a difficult year, the Pilgrims gathered their first harvest. They celebrated with a

big feast. They invited <u>the Native Americans</u> to this feast. The feast lasted <u>for three days</u>.
                              5.   **6.**

1. When _did the Pilgrims come to America?_

2. Why _____

3. Who _____

4. What _____

5. Who(m) _____

6. How long _____

5 EDITING

Read the conversation between Eun Young and a classmate. There are six mistakes. The first one has been corrected. Find and correct the other five.

EUN YOUNG: Ch' suk is in some ways like the American Thanksgiving. It's the harvest moon festival. We celebrated it about three months ago.

CLASSMATE: Did you ~~enjoyed~~ *enjoy* it?

EUN YOUNG: Not this year. This year I was here in Oregon, but last year I celebrated it with my family and it was great.

CLASSMATE: What you did last year?

EUN YOUNG: I went to my hometown, Pusan. As usual, traffic was awful.

CLASSMATE: Oh yeah? How long did the trip took?

EUN YOUNG: It usually takes three hours, but it took six hours. Everyone travels on this holiday.

CLASSMATE: Why you did go there?

EUN YOUNG: My grandparents live there. I always visit them on Ch' suk.

CLASSMATE: What did you there?

EUN YOUNG: My cousins and I played games, exchanged gifts, and ate mooncakes. We also visited the graves of our ancestors.

CLASSMATE: Did you missed it this year?

EUN YOUNG: I certainly did.

COMMUNICATION PRACTICE

6 A WONDERFUL VACATION

Write questions about a wonderful vacation. Answer your questions. Then ask your partner about his or her vacation.

VACATION	YOU	YOUR PARTNER
Where / go		
Why / go there		
go there / alone		
Who / go with		
Where / stay		
How long / stay		
How / get there		
What / do		
buy / special souvenirs		
eat / special food		
meet / interesting people		
take / good photos		

EXAMPLE:
A: Where did you go?
B: I went to Hawaii.
A: Did you go there alone?
B: No, I went there with two friends.

Now tell the class about your partner's vacation.

7 MY GRANDPARENTS

Work with a partner. Reread Exercise 3 on page 172. Then ask your partner about his or her grandparents or other older relatives. With the class, talk about life in the past. In what ways was it different from today?

PART
V

REVIEW OR SELFTEST

I. *Read each conversation. Circle the letter of the the underlined word or group of words that is not correct.*

1. **A:** You <u>didn't</u> <u>finished</u> your dinner.
            A   B

   B: That's because <u>it</u> <u>wasn't</u> good.
                 C   D

   A B C D

2. **A:** <u>Who(m)</u> <u>you</u> <u>did</u> call?
            A   B

   B: I <u>called</u> John. I <u>wanted</u> Susan's phone number.
           C   D

   A B C D

3. **A:** When <u>did</u> they <u>visit</u> Hawaii?
            A   B

   B: They <u>visit</u> Hawaii last fall. They <u>were</u> there for
            C   D

   a week.

   A B C D

4. **A:** <u>How long</u> did <u>it took</u> you to get to work?
           A   B

   B: <u>It took</u> me over an hour. <u>Traffic was</u> very heavy.
         C   B

   A B C D

5. **A:** <u>Did</u> she <u>drank</u> a glass of milk?
        A   B

   B: Yes. She <u>drank</u> it with some cookies. Then she <u>did</u>
             C   D

   her homework.

   A B C D

6. **A:** Where <u>did</u> you <u>see</u> them?
            A   B

   B: I <u>did</u> <u>saw</u> them during the Thanksgiving vacation.
         C   D

   A B C D

II. *Read each question. Circle the correct answer.*

1. When did you get up?
   a. At eight-thirty.
   b. Yes, I did.
   c. Because it was early.

2. Who visited us last week?
   a. They do.
   b. They were.
   c. They did.

3. Where did they go yesterday?
   a. To the movies.
   b. At noon.
   c. With their friends.

4. Did they have a good breakfast?
   a. Yes, they do.
   b. Yes, they had.
   c. Yes, they did.

5. How long did she stay?
  a. By bus.
  b. A few hours.
  c. An hour ago.

6. Did she have a good vacation last summer?
  a. No, she hasn't.
  b. No, she didn't.
  c. No, she wasn't.

7. Who did you stay with?
  a. My relatives.
  b. John did.
  c. On Saturday.

8. Did it rain last night?
  a. No, it doesn't.
  b. No, it didn't.
  c. No, it don't.

III. *Complete the story. Use the past tense of each verb in parentheses.*

George Washington was the first president of the United States.

He _____ in a beautiful home in Virginia. His
      1. (live)

mother _____ a special garden with a beautiful little
        2. (have)

cherry tree. Everyone _____ that cherry tree. One day
                    3. (love)

George _____ a hatchet as a present. He _____
        4. (get)   5. (decide)

to try the hatchet. He _____ to the cherry tree and
                    6. (go)

_____ it down. As soon as he _____ the tree on the ground,
  7. (chop)   8. (see)

he _____ terrible. He _____ sadly back to the house
    9. (feel)   10. (walk)

and _____ to his room. He _____ that afternoon. He
      11. (go)   12. (play, not)

_____ that evening. That night George's father said, "Someone
  13. (eat not)

_____ down our cherry tree." George _____ to tell his father
  14. (chop)   15. (decide)

the truth. He _____ toward his father and said, "I _____ it.
              16. (walk)   17. (chop)

I _____ it down with my new hatchet. I cannot tell a lie."
    18. (chop)

  "Thank you for telling the truth," his father _____.
                                              19. (say)

IV. *Complete the conversations. Use the simple present, present progressive, or simple past form of each verb in parentheses.*

1. A: Why (arrive) _____ you _____ so late?

  B: I (forget) _____ to set my alarm clock last night.

2. A: There aren't any grapes. Who (eat) _____ them all?

  B: I don't know. I (eat, not) _____ them. I (like, not) _____ grapes.

(continued on next page)

3. A: I (get) _____ a beautiful gift in the mail last week.

 B: Who (send) _____ it?

 A: Uncle Sam.

4. A: What (say) _____ his answering machine _____?

 B: It says, "I'm sorry I (miss) _____ your call. Please leave your name and a

 short message. Thank you. Have a nice day."

5. A: Let's study together.

 B: Gee, I'm not in the mood to study. I (study) _____ all day yesterday.

 What (do) _____ you _____ yesterday?

 A: I (play) _____ tennis.

6. A: Where are the kids?

 B: Annie (play) _____ outside, and Dave (do) _____ homework.

 A: What about Annie's homework?

 B: She (do) _____ it last night.

7. A: Where are the cookies?

 B: I (hide) _____ them last night.

 A: Why (hide) _____ you _____ them?

 B: I (try) _____ to lose weight.

 A: Well, I'm not. I (want) _____ those cookies.

V. *Complete each sentence. Choose the correct time marker. Write it on the line.*

 1. _____ I wash my clothes.
   a. A week ago   **b.** Every Monday

 2. Did you see your friend _____?
   a. this morning   **b.** now

 3. We visited them two weeks _____.
   a. last   **b.** ago

 4. I spoke to the doctor _____ Thursday.
   a. last   **b.** ago

▶ *To check your answers, go to the Answer Key on page 181.*

FROM GRAMMAR TO WRITING PUNCTUATION II:
The Exclamation Point (!), The Hyphen (-), Quotation Marks (" . . . ")

1 *What's wrong with these sentences?*

1. You're kidding

2. She's twenty one years old

3. He said I love you

4. He worked for many years before he became rich.

Study this information about punctuation. Then add the correct punctuation to the sentences above.

The Exclamation Point (!)	
1. Use the exclamation point after **strong, emotional statements**. (Don't use it too often.)	• What a surprise! • You're kidding! • How wonderful!

The Hyphen (-)	
2. a. Use a hyphen in **compound numbers** from twenty-one to ninety-nine.	• There were **twenty-two** students in the class.
b. Use a hyphen **at the end of a line** when dividing a word. Words must be divided by syllables. (Check your dictionary. If you are unsure, do not hyphenate words.)	• We visited them at the **begin-ning** of the year.

(continued on next page)

Quotation Marks (" . . . ")

3. Use quotation marks **before** and **after the exact words** of a speaker. Use a comma before the quote.

- She said, "I just love your new sweater."

Last week the students in Al Brown's English class told stories they heard as children. Maria told the class a story from the Bible. Read the story. Circle the exclamation marks and hyphens. Add quotation marks where necessary.

WHOSE BABY IS IT?

Solomon was a king. He lived about 3,000 years ago. Everyone came to Solomon because he was very wise.

One day two women approached King Solomon. One carried a baby. The first woman said, We live nearby and had our babies three days apart. Her baby died in the night, and she changed it for mine. This baby is really mine.

King Solomon turned to the other woman. She said, No! That woman is lying. That's my baby.

The two women started shouting and continued until King Solomon shouted, Stop!

He then turned to his guard and said, Take your sword and chop the baby in two. Give one part to this woman and the other to that one. The guard pulled out his sword. As he was about to divide the baby, the first woman screamed, No! Don't do it. Give her the baby. Just don't kill the baby.

King Solomon then said, Now I know the mother. Give the baby to the woman who has just spoken.

Work in small groups.

1. *Brainstorm.*

What was your favorite story as a child?

When did you first hear it? Who told it to you? Why did you like it?

2. *Tell your story to your group.*

3. *Write your story. When you are finished, read your story twice. First read it for the story. Next read it for grammar and punctuation.*

4. *Rewrite your story. Hang it on the wall. Go around and read the stories of your classmates.*

REVIEW OR SELFTEST
ANSWER KEY

I.
1. B
2. B
3. C
4. B
5. B
6. C

II.
1. a
2. c
3. a
4. c
5. b
6. b
7. a
8. b

III.
1. lived
2. had
3. loved
4. got
5. decided
6. went
7. chopped
8. saw
9. felt
10. walked
11. went
12. didn't play
13. didn't eat
14. chopped
15. decided
16. walked
17. chopped
18. chopped
19. said

IV.
1. did arrive, forgot
2. ate, didn't eat, don't like
3. got, sent
4. does, say, missed
5. studied, did, do, played
6. 's playing (is playing), 's doing (is doing), did
7. hid, did, hide, 'm trying (am trying), want

V.
1. b
2. a
3. b
4. a

IMPERATIVES; SUGGESTIONS; THERE IS / THERE ARE

PREVIEW

Elenore and Pete are walking along Third Avenue in New York City. Listen and read their conversation.

LET'S STOP FOR PIZZA

ELENORE: What a beautiful day!

PETE: It sure is. There isn't a cloud in the sky!

ELENORE: I'm getting hungry. Let's stop for pizza.

PETE: Okay. But are there any pizza places around here?

ELENORE: I don't know. There's a young man there. Why don't you ask him?

PETE: Excuse me. Is there a pizza place near here?

YOUNG MAN: Sorry, I don't think so. There's a Chinese restaurant on this street, and there are several small restaurants on the next street. There are a few coffee bars on 43rd Street, but I don't know of any pizza places near here.

PETE: Thanks anyway. Elenore, there's a woman over there. Ask her.

ELENORE: Excuse me. Are there any pizza places near here?

WOMAN: Not here, but Luigi's is on 37th Street and Third. Just walk down Third Avenue. Then turn right on 37th Street. Luigi's has great pizza.

ELENORE: Thanks a lot.

[20 minutes later]

PETE: There it is.

ELENORE: Finally! I'm hungry and tired.

PETE: Uh-oh.

ELENORE: What's wrong?

PETE: Look! "Closed for Renovations."

COMPREHENSION CHECK

Complete the sentences. Circle the right words.

1. Elenore and Pete walk to Luigi's Pizza because _____.
   a. it's the only restaurant in the area
   b. Luigi is their friend
   c. a woman tells them that Luigi's has great pizza

2. Elenore and Pete didn't have pizza because _____.
   a. they were tired and wanted to go home
   b. the pizza place wasn't open
   c. there weren't any pizza places there

WITH PARTNERS

Practice the conversation on pages 182 and 183.

21 IMPERATIVES; SUGGESTIONS WITH *LET'S, WHY DON'T WE . . . ?; WHY DON'T YOU . . . ?*

GRAMMAR **IN CONTEXT**

WARM UP   People eat pizza all over the world. Some say it's the first global food. What do you think about pizza? Do you like it? What's your favorite kind?

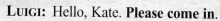 *Listen and read about today's person in the news.*

The Daily Times   Section 2/Page 3

PERSON IN THE NEWS

Today's "Person in the News" is Luigi Paolini. Ten years ago, Luigi came to New York from Naples and opened a tiny pizza shop. Today Luigi has five pizzerias in New York City. Our reporter, Kate Evans, interviewed Luigi in his 37th Street store.

LUIGI: Hello, Kate. **Please come in**.

KATE: Wow. It's busy here.

LUIGI: Yes. We're expanding. Sorry, Kate. It's noisy and messy. **Please be** careful. **Don't touch** anything. . . . **Why don't we step** into my office?

KATE: Good idea. **Let's go**. . . . Luigi, your pizza is a big success. How come?

LUIGI: Well, my food is fresh and my prices are low. But I think the real reason is the dough.

KATE: The dough?

LUIGI: Uh-huh. My grandpa taught me the secret.

KATE: Would you share the recipe?

LUIGI: Sure. But that's not the secret. The secret is how I handle the dough.

LUIGI'S PIZZA DOUGH	
Ingredients:	Directions:
1 package of fast-acting yeast	1. **Stir** the yeast and sugar into the water. **Wait** five minutes.
1 teaspoon sugar	2. **Put** the flour, oil, and salt in a food processor.
1 cup warm water	**Add** the ingredients in #1. **Turn on** the food
1 cup flour	processor for 40 seconds. Now you have the dough.
2 tablespoons olive oil	3. **Put** the dough in a large plastic food bag. **Place** the bag in a bowl. **Leave** it in the bowl for one hour. (It will rise.)
1 teaspoon salt	4. **Make** two large pizza crusts or three small ones.

Match the pictures and the directions.

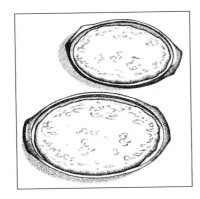

a. _____

c. _____

b. _____

d. _____

GRAMMAR **PRESENTATION**
IMPERATIVES; SUGGESTIONS WITH *LET'S, WHY DON'T WE . . . ?*; ADVICE WITH *WHY DON'T YOU . . . ?*

IMPERATIVES

AFFIRMATIVE	
BASE FORM OF VERB	
Open	the door.

NEGATIVE		
DON'T	**BASE FORM OF VERB**	
Don't	**open**	the door.

SUGGESTIONS

AFFIRMATIVE		
LET'S	**BASE FORM OF VERB**	
Let's	**take**	a walk.

NEGATIVE			
LET'S	**NOT**	**BASE FORM OF VERB**	
Let's	**not**	**take**	a walk.

WHY DON'T WE	**BASE FORM OF VERB**	**. . . ?**
Why don't we	**order**	pizza?

ADVICE

WHY DON'T YOU	**BASE FORM OF VERB**	**. . . ?**
Why don't you	**take**	a break?

NOTES	EXAMPLES
1. The **imperative** uses the **base form of the verb**. The base form is the form in the dictionary. For example: *Walk* is the base form of the verb *walk*. (Other forms are *walking*, *walks*, and *walked*.)	• **Walk** three blocks and **turn** right.

2. Use the imperative to:
  a. give **directions** and **instructions**.
  b. give **orders** or **commands**.
  c. give **advice** or make **suggestions**.
  d. give **warnings**.
  e. make **polite requests**.
	• **Stir** the sugar in the water.
	• **Be** quiet!
	• **Relax**.
	• **Keep** out! Danger!
	• **Please open** the door.

3. ***Don't*** comes before the base form for the negative imperative.	• **Don't turn** left.
4. In an imperative statement, the subject is always ***you***, but we don't say it or write it.	• **Ask** that young man. (You) ask that young man.
5. Use ***Let's*** or ***Let's not*** and the base form for suggestions that include you and another person.	• **Let's go**. • **Let's not stay**.
6. Use ***Why don't we*** and the base form for suggestions that include you and another person. Use ***Why don't you*** and the base form to give advice to another person. REMEMBER: to put a question mark at the end of sentences with *Why don't we* and *Why don't you*.	• **Why don't we go** to my office? • **Why don't you look** on the Internet?

FOCUSED PRACTICE

1 DISCOVER THE GRAMMAR

While Elenore and Pete were walking along Third Avenue, two burglars entered their home. Listen and read their conversation. Then underline the imperatives.

FRANK: Hey, George. I'm nervous. This is my first job.

GEORGE: <u>Relax</u>, Frank. I'm here.

FRANK: Okay, George. What's this? Is this a gold watch?

GEORGE: Yes, it's gold. Take it.

FRANK: How about these pearls next to the watch?

GEORGE: They're good pearls. Put them in our bag.

FRANK: What's that, over there?

GEORGE: Junk. Don't take it.

FRANK: What's under the junk?

GEORGE: It's a ring, but leave it. It's a cheap ring.

FRANK: Are these good earrings?

GEORGE: Yes, give them to me.

FRANK: What's that noise?

GEORGE: A police siren. Drop everything. Let's run!

How many imperatives are there?

a. 5   **b.** 7   **c.** 8

2 TELEPHONE MESSAGES

Grammar Notes 1–4, 6

Elenore and Pete are now home. Listen to their conversation.

Now listen to their conversation again, complete the chart, and answer the question.

	WHO CALLED?	**WHAT'S THE MESSAGE?**	**WHAT'S THE CALLER'S NUMBER?**
Message 1			
Message 2			
Message 3			

Why didn't the third caller leave a telephone number?

❸ GIVING DIRECTIONS   Grammar Notes 1–2, 4

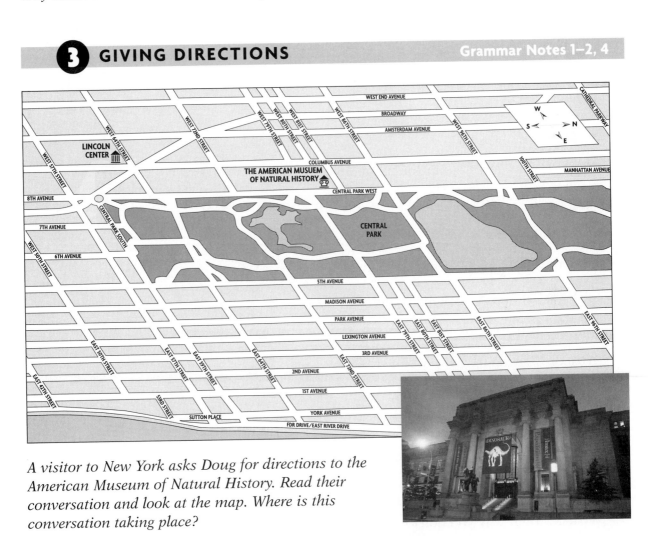

A visitor to New York asks Doug for directions to the American Museum of Natural History. Read their conversation and look at the map. Where is this conversation taking place?

Doug and the visitor are at _____.

VISITOR: Excuse me, how can I get to the American Museum of Natural History?

  DOUG: Do you want to walk or take the subway?

VISITOR: Is it in walking distance?   *(continued on next page)*

Doug: Yes—it's just about a mile.

Visitor: Then I'll walk.

Doug: Okay. Go down to 81st Street.

Visitor: Is that south?

Doug: Yes, walk fifteen blocks. Turn left on 81st Street. Walk three blocks until you get to Central Park West. Turn right and you're at the main entrance to the museum.

Visitor: Thanks.

Now look at the map and write directions to Lincoln Center from the American Museum of Natural History. The entrance to Lincoln Center is on Columbus Avenue and 64th Street. You are leaving the museum at 80th Street and Central Park West.

4 EDITING

A young man delivers a pizza. Find and correct the six mistakes.

Woman: Who's there?

Young Man: Pizza delivery.

Woman: Oh. Please to put the pizza down here. How much do I owe you?

Young Man: $16.95.

Woman: Here's $20. Keeps the change.

Young Man: Thanks. Excuse me, what's the best way to get to 115 East 79th Street?

Woman: Driving up First Avenue to 79th Street and turning left.

Young Man: Thanks.

Woman: Is your car in a parking spot?

Young Man: Yes.

Woman: Then why you don't walk? It's only three blocks from here. Parking is very difficult.

Young Man: Good idea. It's a beautiful night.

Woman: No mention it.

COMMUNICATION PRACTICE

5 FINDING IMPERATIVES

*Work in small groups. Look at the instructions in this textbook and find
imperative statements. Write down ten base-form verbs used in the instructions.
Read your list to the other groups.*

1. _____work_____

2. _____

3. _____

4. _____

5. _____

6. _____

7. _____

8. _____

9. _____

10. _____

6 MAKING SUGGESTIONS / GIVING ADVICE

Work with a partner.

A. *Make three suggestions for each situation. Begin with* **Let's** *or* **Why don't
we**. *Use the ideas in the box or your own ideas.*

> go to the movies, the theater, a concert, the park
> play ball, tennis, soccer
> have a party

A: The weather is great.

B: _____

A: There's no school tomorrow.

B: _____

B. *Advise someone with the following problems. Begin with* **Why don't you**.
Use the ideas in the box or your own ideas.

> take a course in Swedish   ask friends about their computers
> visit Sweden   read about computers
> get some Swedish tapes   go to stores and ask questions about computers

A: I want to learn Swedish.

B: _____

A: I want to buy a computer.

B: _____

Your idea:

A: _____I want_____

B: _____

⑦ GAME: SIMON SAYS

Work with a partner. Label the parts of the body. (See Appendix 5 on page A-5 to check your work.)

head	hip
shoulder	knee
ankle	stomach
back	thigh
waist	toe

Play a game. A leader (a student or the teacher) goes to the front of the class. The leader makes polite requests (using **please***) and commands.*

EXAMPLE:

Please put your hands on your knees. *(polite request)*

Put your hands on your ankles. *(command)*

The class follows only the polite requests (when the leader says **please***). If a student follows a command, the student sits down. The last student standing becomes the next leader.*

⑧ WITH A PARTNER

Work in pairs. Give directions to your partner to . . .

1. your home from school

2. a good restaurant from school

EXAMPLE:

A: How can I get to your home from school?

B: Take the number 4 train and get off at 14th Street. Walk one block south to 13th Street. Then turn right. I live at 124 East 13th Street.

SUBJECT AND OBJECT PRONOUNS; DIRECT AND INDIRECT OBJECTS

GRAMMAR **IN CONTEXT**

WARM UP   Do you know a few sentences in different languages? What languages? Who taught them to you?

🔲 *Listen and read the conversation between Carol and Yoko.*

CAROL: This is a great picture of you. Who are **you** standing with?

YOKO: Bekir and Maria. Do **you** know **them**?

CAROL: I know **him**. **He**'s the guy from Turkey. But **I** don't think **I** know **her**. Who is Maria?

YOKO: **She**'s a friend from Brazil. I met **her** in the library. **She** wants to learn **Japanese**. **I**'m teaching **her some Japanese**. And **she**'s teaching **me a little Portuguese**.

CAROL: That's great. Where was this picture taken?

YOKO: In Bekir's apartment.

CAROL: What's **he** wearing?

Tudo bem

Tudo bem

YOKO: **It**'s my yutaka. My mom sent **it to me** last month.

CAROL: **He** looks cute in **it**.

YOKO: I know. **I** told **him**. **I lent it to him** for the International Students Masquerade Party last Saturday, and he won **first prize**.

CAROL: No kidding! That's cool.

Hajimemashite

Hajimemashite

GRAMMAR **PRESENTATION**
SUBJECT AND OBJECT PRONOUNS; DIRECT AND INDIRECT OBJECTS

SUBJECT AND OBJECT PRONOUNS

SINGULAR			
SUBJECT PRONOUN AND VERB			**OBJECT PRONOUN**
I'm **You**'re **He**'s **She**'s	happy.	He likes	**me**. **you**. **him**. **her**. **it**.
It's	wonderful.		

PLURAL			
SUBJECT PRONOUN AND VERB			**OBJECT PRONOUN**
We're **You**'re **They**'re	happy.	He likes	**us**. **you**. **them**.

DIRECT AND INDIRECT OBJECTS

SUBJECT	VERB	DIRECT OBJECT	*To*	INDIRECT OBJECT	SUBJECT	VERB	INDIRECT OBJECT	DIRECT OBJECT
She	sent	**a gift** it	to	us.	She	sent	us	**a gift**.

NOTES

EXAMPLES

1. A pronoun replaces a noun. A **subject pronoun** replaces a noun in subject position.

subject
- **Carol** loves Rocky.
- **She** loves Rocky.

2. An **object pronoun** replaces a noun in object position (after the verb).

object
- Carol loves **Rocky**.
- She loves **him**.

---

3. When you refer to yourself and another person, the other person comes first.

- **Carol and I** love Rocky.
  NOT ~~I and Carol love Rocky.~~

---

4. Some sentences have only a subject and a verb.

subject   verb
- Pete painted.

Some sentences have a subject, a verb, and an object.

subject   verb   object
- Yoko's mom sent **a yutaka**.

Some sentences have two objects following the verb.

subject   verb   object indirect object
- Yoko's mom sent **a yutaka to Yoko**.

A **direct object** answers the question *whom* or *what*.

- **What** did Yoko's mom send?
  direct object
  Yoko's mom sent **a yutaka**.

An **indirect object** answers the question *to whom* or *to what*.

- **To whom** did she send the yutaka?
  indirect object
- Yoko's mom sent the yutaka **to Yoko**.

---

5. For the verbs *give, hand, lend, pass, read, sell, send, show, write, teach, tell, throw, owe,* and *e-mail,* there are two possible sentence patterns if the direct object is a noun.

direct object   indirect
(noun)   *to* object
- She gave **the yutaka to her**.

OR

indirect direct object
object   (noun)
- She gave **her the yutaka**.

If the direct object is a **pronoun**, it always comes before the indirect object.

direct object   indirect
(pronoun) *to* object
- She gave **it   to her**.

FOCUSED PRACTICE

1 DISCOVER THE GRAMMAR

Read each sentence. Write **d** *above the direct object and* **i** *above the indirect object. Circle the subject pronouns. Underline the object pronouns.*

1. Show the book to me.

2. They told us the truth.

3. Write me a letter.

4. Show your work to your partner.

5. We threw the ball to them.

6. She read us the message.

2 UNDERSTANDING DIRECTIONS   Grammar Note 2

Complete the sentences. Use **me**, **him**, **her**, **it**, **you**, **us**, *or* **them**. *Then draw a line from the object pronoun to the noun or pronoun it replaces.*

1. Find the pronouns. Then circle _____them_____.

2. Underline the sentence. Then circle _____.

3. Read this story. Read _____ to the class.

4. Al Brown is helpful. Ask _____ for help.

5. Please don't help _____. We want to work alone.

6. I'm lost. Please help _____.

7. Carol is good at drawing. Ask _____ to draw it for you.

8. Carol and I are good at drawing. Ask _____ to draw those cartoons for you.

9. Yoko and Ali are good at grammar. Ask _____ for help.

10. There are two bananas on the counter. Please don't eat _____.

3 HELPING OTHERS

Complete the conversations. Use subject and object pronouns.

1. **CAROL:** Yoko, ___I___'m wet. Please give

    ___me___ a towel.

    YOKO: Here ___you___ are.

2. **LULU:** This little boy is on the wrong bus.

    _____'s lost. Please help _____.

    BUS DRIVER: Okay, son. Where are _____ going?

3. **MILT:** Excuse me. We're looking for an

    express train. Can you help _____?

    WOMAN: The express train stops there. Look!

    There _____ is.

4. **ELENORE:** Paul and Mary bought the same

    computer that we did. They're

    having trouble with _____. Please

    show _____ how it works.

    PETE: No problem.

4 IN OTHER WORDS

Underline the direct object in each sentence. Then complete the conversations.
*Use **it** or **them** in place of the direct object. (Remember: When the direct object is*
a pronoun, it always comes before the indirect object.)

1. **A:** I gave my brother <u>my bicycle</u>.

   B: Who did you give it to?

   A: ___I gave it to my brother.___

2. **A:** I handed my boss my report.

   B: Who did you hand it to?

   A: _____

(continued on next page)

3. A: She owes her roommate a lot of money.

   B: Who does she owe a lot of money to?

   A: _____

4. A: Please pass Yoko the salt.

   B: What do you want me to do with the salt?

   A: _____

⑤ EDITING

Read this conversation between Carol and Dan. Find and correct the four errors.

CAROL: Ron's parents are very generous.

  DAN: Oh? Why do you say that?

CAROL: Well, last month they gave him a car. The year before they sent to Europe him. And they often give he expensive gifts.

  DAN: They *are* generous. Ron's lucky. Is he grateful?

CAROL: No. He thinks they owe it to him.

  DAN: I'd like to introduce him to Jack's parents.

CAROL: Why?

  DAN: Well, last summer Jack gave their parents a new car. And he sent them to Hawaii on their anniversary.

CAROL: What a nice guy.

  DAN: I know, but his parents think he owes them it.

COMMUNICATION PRACTICE

 DOING SOMETHING NICE FOR A CLASSMATE

Work in small groups. Discuss things you can do for classmates. Use the verbs **give**, **lend**, **send**, **write**, *and* **e-mail** *in your conversations.*

A classmate is sick.

A classmate's birthday is soon.

A classmate needs a suit for a job interview.

> **EXAMPLE:**
> Let's send him some cards.
> Why don't we give him a gift?

7 **GAME**

Throw a ball (or pass a message or tell a secret) to a student. That student throws the ball to another student. Continue four more times. The last person tells the class who threw the ball (or passed the message or told the secret) to whom.

> **EXAMPLE:**
> José threw it to Erica. Erica threw it to Ali. Ali . . .

8 GIFTS, CARDS, E-MAIL, AND LETTERS

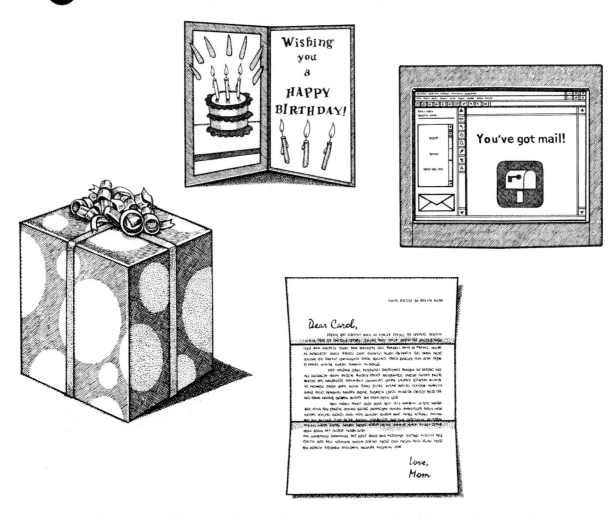

Work in small groups. Talk about the people to whom you give gifts, cards, e-mail messages, and letters.

1. I usually give presents to _____.

2. I send greeting cards to _____.

3. I write letters to _____.

4. I e-mail messages to _____.

Then tell your group about a special card or present that you gave someone or someone gave you.

EXAMPLE:

When my son was four years old, he had a friend from Pakistan. Every day when I took my son to the park, his friend asked to go along. His mother rarely left her home. I never knew why. At the end of the summer, the family moved. When we said good-bye, the mother gave me a very beautiful hand-carved lamp. Whenever I see the lamp, I remember the boy and his mother.

THERE IS / THERE ARE, IS THERE . . . ? / ARE THERE . . . ?

GRAMMAR **IN CONTEXT**

WARM UP **There are shopping malls all over the world.** They attract people of all ages and incomes. Do you shop at malls? Why or why not? Are there any near your home?

 *Listen and read the conversation.*

MAN: Excuse me. **Is there** a mall around here?

WOMAN: Yes. **There's** a huge mall just up ahead. Follow me. I'm going **there**.

MAN: **Is there** a restaurant at the mall?

WOMAN: **There are** at least five different fast food places at the food court.

MAN: **Are there** any nice restaurants?

WOMAN: I'm not sure. I think **there's** one nice restaurant. Anyway, when you get to the mall, go to the third floor. All the food is **there**.

MAN: Thanks.

GRAMMAR **PRESENTATION**
THERE IS / THERE ARE, IS THERE . . . ? / ARE THERE . . . ?

THERE IS / THERE ARE

AFFIRMATIVE			
THERE	**BE**	**SUBJECT**	**PLACE**
There	**is**	a restaurant	on this street.
There	**are**	two restaurants	

CONTRACTIONS
there is → **there's**
there is not → **there isn't**
there are not → **there aren't**

NEGATIVE			
THERE	**BE**	**SUBJECT**	**PLACE**
There	**isn't**	a good restaurant	on this street.
There	**aren't**	any good restaurants	

IS THERE . . . ? / ARE THERE . . . ?

QUESTIONS			
BE	**THERE**	**SUBJECT**	**PLACE**
Is	**there**	a pizza place	near here?
Are	**there**	any banks	

SHORT ANSWERS	
AFFIRMATIVE	**NEGATIVE**
Yes, there is.	No, there isn't.
Yes, there are.	No, there aren't.

NOTES	EXAMPLES
1. Use *there is* or *there's* to say that a person or thing is somewhere.	• **There's** a man at the door.
2. Use *there are* to say that people or things are somewhere. ▶ **BE CAREFUL!** Don't confuse *there are* and *they are*.	• **There are** five fast food places in the mall. subject • **There are** ten women in our class. subject • **They are** all good students.
3. In the negative, use the contractions *isn't* and *aren't*. The full forms, *is not* and *are not*, are rarely used with *there*.	• **There isn't** a cloud in the sky. • **There aren't** any malls near our school.
4. We usually use *any* with *yes / no* questions about plural nouns.	• Are there **any** malls nearby?
5. BE CAREFUL! Don't confuse *there is* and *there are* with *there*. (The last *there* in the example sentence points out something that is not nearby. We use *here* for something nearby.)	• Oregon is a beautiful place. **There are** mountains and beaches *there*. • Last summer we exchanged homes with friends in Lisbon. We went **there** and they came *here*.

FOCUSED PRACTICE

1 DISCOVER THE GRAMMAR

Look at the mall directory. Check the sentences that are true.

Third Floor	3a	3b	3c	3d	3e	
Food Court	Thai food	Chinese food	Burgers	Sushi bar	Coffee bar	
Second Floor	2a	2b	2c	2d	2e	2f
	Women's clothes	Shoe store	Art supply store	Furniture store	Children's clothes	Cosmetics store
First Floor	1a	1b	1c	1d	1e	1f
	Florist	Gift shop	Bookstore	Unisex hair salon	Electronics store	Women's clothes

Mall Directory

_____ **1.** There's a florist on the first floor.

_____ **2.** There's a coffee bar on the second floor.

_____ **3.** There aren't any toy stores.

_____ **4.** There are five places to eat.

_____ **5.** There isn't any Thai food at this mall.

_____ **6.** There's a bookstore on the first floor.

2 WORD ORDER PRACTICE

Grammar Notes 1–4

Put a check (✔) next to each correct sentence. Change sentences that don't make sense.

_____ **1.** There's a mall in the Chinese restaurant. _There's a Chinese Restaurant in the mall._

_____ **2.** There's a second floor on the gift shop. _____

_____ **3.** There are two women's clothes stores at the mall. _____

_____ **4.** There's an electronics store on the first floor. _____

_____ **5.** There isn't any mall at the men's clothing store. _____

③ A TERRIBLE PIZZA PLACE   Grammar Notes 3, 5

Complete the sentences. Use **there isn't, there aren't,** *or* **they aren't.**

ALLEN: This pizza place is terrible. _____ any tablecloths and the placemats
1.

are dirty.

NORMA: You're right. _____ any napkins, either.
2.

ALLEN: There are real knives and forks, but _____ clean.
3.

NORMA: There are waiters, but _____ very polite.
4.

ALLEN: It's very hot, but _____ even a fan.
5.

NORMA: Let's leave.

④ HOW ABOUT SOME MEXICAN FOOD?   Grammar Notes 1–2

Complete the conversation. Use **there's, there are, they're,** *and* **there.**

DAHLIA: Are you in the mood for pizza?

NORMA: Let's not have pizza. I was at a terrible pizza place yesterday. _____
1.

lots of other restaurants around.

DAHLIA: Today is Sunday. Are any of them open?

NORMA: _____ all open seven days a week.
2.

DAHLIA: How about a Mexican restaurant? _____ a good one on the next street.
3.

NORMA: Great. I love Mexican food and I know that restaurant. I was _____
4.

a few months ago.

⑤ EDITING

Find and correct the three mistakes in this reading.

Pizzas come in all shapes and sizes. Are pizzas with mushrooms, with pepperoni, with

broccoli, and with tofu. In the United States they are over 61,000 pizzerias. Their sales

reach 30 billion dollars. People in the United States eat 3 billion pizzas a year. They are

pizza shops in almost every city, town, and village.

COMMUNICATION PRACTICE

6 GAME: ARE THERE ANY TWINS IN YOUR FAMILY?

Use the phrases in the boxes and ask your classmates questions. Begin with **Is there** *or* **Are there any**. *If a student says* yes, *write his or her name in the box. When you have three across or down, call out "I've got it!"*

twins in your family	famous people in your family	detectives in your family
a plant in your home	a black comb in your pocket	pictures in your wallet
a Thai restaurant near your home	pizza places on your street	park near your home

EXAMPLE:

A: Are there any twins in your family?

B: Yes. My mother is a twin. *(A writes B's name in the first box.)*

7 INFORMATION GAP: IS THERE A CLOCK IN THE KITCHEN?

Work in pairs.

Student A, your partner has a picture of a kitchen and a dining room. Ask your partner if the following items are in the kitchen or the dining room. Write the name of the room (or rooms) they are in. Cross out items that are not in your partner's picture.

Student B, turn to the Information Gap on pages 222 and 223 and follow the instructions there.

EXAMPLE:

A: Is there a dining room table in the dining room?

B: Yes, there is.

1. dining room table ___dining room___

2. chairs _____

3. calendar _____

4. refrigerator _____

5. pictures _____

6. stove _____

7. dishwasher _____

8. microwave oven _____

9. toaster _____

10. clock _____

11. cabinets _____

12. counter _____

13. chandelier _____

14. rug _____

Student A, you have a picture of a living room and a bedroom. Answer your partner's questions about your picture.

8 A ROOM IN MY HOME

Work with a partner. Take turns. Describe a room in your home. Your partner draws it. Check each other's drawings.

24 NUMBERS, QUANTIFIERS, AND QUESTIONS WITH *HOW MANY . . . ?*

GRAMMAR **IN CONTEXT**

WARM UP   Is there a cafeteria in your school? Do you have any complaints about it? If yes, what are they?

Carol and Connie are in line at their school cafeteria. Listen and read their conversation.

CONNIE: Hi Carol.

CAROL: Oh, hi Connie. How's it going?

CONNIE: Okay. What are you having for lunch?

CAROL: A hamburger and fries.

CONNIE: Hmm. **There aren't many** choices.

CAROL: What do you mean? **There are five** choices. There are hamburgers, chicken, pasta, fish, and pizza. **How many** do you want?

CONNIE: Well, I want fish, but **there's** only **one** kind of fish.

CAROL: Oh.

CONNIE: And **there aren't any** limes.

CAROL: Limes?

CONNIE: For the fish.

CAROL: But **there are lots of** lemons.

CONNIE: I like limes. What's for dessert?

CAROL: **There are a lot of** desserts. **There are four** different pies, **some** apples, **a few** cupcakes, and **several** kinds of cookies. What are you looking for?

CONNIE: Cherry pie. **There isn't any** cherry pie.

CAROL: Then I guess there's no dessert for you.

CONNIE: I'll settle for a cookie. And maybe a small slice of apple pie.

WHAT'S YOUR OPINION?

Are Connie's complaints reasonable?

GRAMMAR **PRESENTATION**
NUMBERS, QUANTIFIERS, AND QUESTIONS WITH *HOW MANY . . . ?*

NUMBERS AND QUANTIFIERS

AFFIRMATIVE		
SINGULAR		
There's	**a** **one**	mistake.

NEGATIVE		
SINGULAR		
There	**isn't a** **isn't one**	mistake.
There's	**no**	

AFFIRMATIVE		
PLURAL		
There are	**four** **a few** **some** **several** **many** **a lot of** **lots of**	mistakes.

NEGATIVE		
PLURAL		
There	are **no** are**n't any** are**n't many** are**n't a lot of**	mistakes.

HOW MANY . . . ?

QUESTIONS			
HOW MANY	**PLURAL NOUN**	*BE THERE*	
How many	restaurants	**are there**	in this area?

ANSWERS
There are eight restaurants in this area. There are eight. Eight. There are a lot. There's one. There aren't any.

NOTES	EXAMPLES
1. Use **articles, numbers**, or **quantifiers** with *there's, there are, there isn't,* and *there aren't*.	• There's **a** fly in your soup. *article* • There are **three** worms in these apples. *number* • There aren't **many** people in this restaurant. *quantifier*
2. For the **negative**, we usually say ***There aren't any***. ***There isn't a, There are no, There's no***, or ***There isn't one*** are usually used for emphasis.	• There **aren't any** limes. • There **isn't a** thing to eat. • There **are no** carrots. • There's **no** milk! • There **isn't one** piece of bread.
3. Use ***a lot of*** and ***many*** for large numbers. Use ***lots of*** in speaking and very informal writing.	• There are **a lot of** carrots in this soup. • There are **lots of** carrots in this soup.
4. Use ***a few*** and ***not many*** for small numbers.	• There are **a few** oranges. • There **aren't many** apples.
5. Use numbers or quantifiers in answers to questions with ***how many***.	A: **How many people are there?** B: **Four.** OR **A few.**

> **REFERENCE NOTE**
> See Unit 33 and 34 for more notes about quantifiers.
> See Unit 34 for questions with *how much*.

FOCUSED PRACTICE

1 DISCOVER THE GRAMMAR

Look at the picture.

Choose the answer that completes the sentences.

1. There's one _____.

2. There are several _____.

3. There aren't any _____.

4. There are a lot of _____.

a. parking meters

b. people

c. toy stores

d. bakery

2 A BUSY STREET   Grammar Note 5

Write questions about the underlined words. Begin with **How many** *and other* **wh-** *questions.*

1. There's <u>one pizza place</u>. _____

2. <u>A hardware store</u> is next to the supermarket. _____

_____

3. There are <u>six parking meters</u> on the street. _____

4. The pizza place is <u>between the shoe repair store and the hardware store</u>. _____

_____

❸ A FRUIT BOWL

Look at the picture and complete the sentences. Use **There aren't any**, **There are a few**, **There are a lot of**, *or* **There is one**, **There are two**.

1. _____There are a few_____ apples.

2. _____ pears.

3. _____ grapes.

4. _____ banana.

5. _____ pineapples.

6. _____ watermelons.

7. _____ oranges.

❹ TEST RESULTS

Al Brown is returning tests. Listen and match the names with the grades.

_____ **1.** Yoko

_____ **2.** Bekir

_____ **3.** Yolanda

_____ **4.** Michiko

a. 100 percent

b. 99 percent

c. 66 percent

d. 85 percent

COMMUNICATION PRACTICE

5 GUESS THE NUMBER

Guess how many of each item there are in your classroom. Work quickly. Don't count. Then count the items with the class and compare the correct number to your guesses.

EXAMPLE:
How many desks are there?
Your guess: 20
Class count: 23

	Your guess	Class count			Your guess	Class count
1. chairs	_____	_____	6. umbrellas		_____	_____
2. watches	_____	_____	7. newspapers		_____	_____
3. dictionaries	_____	_____	8. book bags		_____	_____
4. students	_____	_____	9. hats		_____	_____
5. erasers	_____	_____	10. doors		_____	_____

How many correct guesses did you make? _____

Who made the most correct guesses? _____

6 GENERAL KNOWLEDGE QUIZ

Work in pairs. Take turns. Ask each other these questions. Begin with **How many**. *(The answers are on page 221.)*

EXAMPLE:
A: How many people are there in China?

1. people/in China
   a. about 1,246,900,000   **b.** about 2,246,900,000   **c.** about 246,900,000

2. people/in Mexico
   a. about 80,294,000   **b.** about 102,026,000   **c.** about 90,294,000

3. members/of the United Nations
   a. about 200   **b.** about 100   **c.** about 300

4. planets/in the Solar System
   a. nine   **b.** ten   **c.** eight

5. players/on a soccer team
   a. eleven   **b.** ten   **c.** twelve

(continued on next page)

6. people/in Brazil

    a. about 173,790,000   **b.** about 120,790,000   **c.** about 100,790,000

7. people/in the United States

    a. about 175,000,000   **b.** about 375,000,000   **c.** about 275,000,000

8. continents/in the world

    a. seven   **b.** five   **c.** four

9. time zones/in the world

    a. twelve   **b.** four   **c.** twenty-four

10. players/on a baseball team

    a. ten   **b.** nine   **c.** twelve

Now ask your own question that begins with **How many**.

---

 7 **PEOPLE IN MY FAMILY**   **Grammar Notes 1–4**

Work with a partner. Talk about people in your family. Use the quantifiers and nouns in the boxes.

Quantifiers

aren't any	a lot of	several
aren't many	many	some
		a few

Nouns

artists	princes/princesses	writers
athletes	detectives	teachers
comedians	soldiers	farmers
doctors	engineers	

    EXAMPLE:

    A: Are there any comedians in your family?

    B: Well, my uncle Bob thinks he's a comedian. He always tells jokes. What about in your family?

    A: There aren't any comedians, but there are several artists. Two of my cousins and my aunt are artists.

---

8 **CAN YOU COUNT THE BLOCKS?**

How many blocks are there in this drawing? Explain your answer to the class.

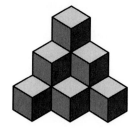

REVIEW OR SELFTEST

I. *Read each conversation. Circle the letter of the underlined word or group of words that is not correct.*

1. A: It's windy. Please <u>to open</u> the window.

                   _A

   B: Are you sure? <u>There's</u> <u>an air conditioner</u>. <u>Let's turn</u> it on.

                      _B   _C   _D

                                      A B C D

2. A: <u>There are</u> <u>a lot of difficult words</u> in this article.

       _A   _B

   B: <u>Are there</u> a dictionary <u>in the bookcase</u>?

        _C   _D

                                        A B C D

3. A: <u>There's</u> a note on the refrigerator. It says Aunt Valerie is

       _A

      in the hospital.

   B: <u>Let's</u> <u>to send</u> <u>her</u> some flowers.

        _B   _C   _D

                                          A B C D

4. A: <u>How many</u> <u>women</u> <u>is there</u> in your class?

        _A   _B   _C

   B: <u>There are</u> twelve including the teacher.

        _D

                                          A B C D

5. A: <u>Are you busy</u>?

        _A

   B: <u>Me and John</u> are going to the computer lab. He's

        _B

      <u>showing me</u> how to use a new program. <u>Why don't you</u>

          _C   _D

      join us?

II. *Complete the questions.*

   1. A: _____ teachers _____ there

       in your school?

   B: There are twenty.

   2. A: _____ any soda machines in the building?

   B: Yes, there are.

   3. A: _____ any malls near your apartment?

   B: No, there aren't.

   4. A: _____ the teacher?

   B: Yes, she is.

(continued on next page)

5. A: _____ late?

B: No, we aren't.

6. A: _____ chairs _____ there?

B: There are six.

A: _____ new chairs?

B: No, they're not.

7. A: _____ a ladies' room on this floor?

B: Yes, there is.

A: _____ near the stairs?

B: Yes, it is.

III. *Complete the paragraph. Choose the correct words.*

Doug's father is a businessman. _____ name is Pete. Doug's mother is
                                         1. (He, Him, His)

a writer. _____ name is Elenore. Pete, Elenore, and Doug live in New York
           2. (His, Her, Our)

City. _____ apartment is on the West Side. _____ a big
      3. (They, Them, Their)   4. (It's, Its, They)

apartment. Many of _____ friends live near _____.
                 5. (they, them, their)   6. (they, them, their)

IV. *Look at this chart about the students in Al Brown's Level 2 English class. Write
statements about the number of students from different countries. Use* **There is,**
There are, *or* **There aren't** *and choose from the words in parentheses.*

English — Level 2		
Teacher: Al Brown		
Number of Students		**Country**
6		Korea
3		Thailand
1		Colombia

1. (a lot of, a few, one, any)   Korea

    There are a lot of students from Korea.

2. (a lot of, a few, one, any)   Thailand

3. (a lot of, a few, one, any)   Colombia

_____

4. (a lot of, a few, one, any)   Turkey

_____

Now look at the chart and write questions. Use **How many**.

5. A: _____?

    B: Only one.

6. A: _____?

    B: A lot.

7. A: _____?

    B: A few.

8. A: _____ Germany?

    B: There aren't any.

V. *One sentence is correct. The other is wrong. Circle the correct sentence.*

    1. a. They are thirteen students in my class.
       b. There are thirteen students in my class.

    2. a. Give it to her.
       b. Give it to she.

    3. a. He's a good scientist, but he's a bad science teacher.
       b. He's a good scientist, and he's a bad science teacher.

    4. a. It is near we.
       b. It is near us.

    5. a. There is three pens on the table.
       b. There are three pens on the table.

    6. a. There aren't any restaurants near here.
       b. There aren't no restaurants near here.

VI. *Correct these sentences.*

1. The pot is hot. ~~You don't~~ Don't touch it!

2. Please you are quiet.

3. Why don't we to take a walk?

4. They's a young man at the door.

5. There aren't some books on the shelf.

6. There is several mistakes in your letter.

▶ *To check your answers, go to the Answer Key on page 221.*

FROM GRAMMAR TO WRITING
SENTENCE COMBINING
WITH *AND* AND *BUT*

1 *Read these sentences. Then complete items 1 and 2.*

1. a. He's tall. He's a good basketball player.
   b. He's tall, **and** he's a good basketball player.

2. a. He's tall. He's a terrible basketball player.
   b. He's tall, **but** he's a terrible basketball player.

1. In number 1b
the word **and** _____.
a. adds information
b. adds a contrast

2. In number 2b
the word **but** _____.
a. adds information
b. adds a contrast

Study this information about **and** *and* **but**.

The Connectors *And* and *But*	
1. We use connectors to help the reader understand our ideas more easily. Use **and** and **but** to connect two sentences.	• The book is good. It is easy to understand.
And adds information to the idea in the first sentence. **But** adds a contrast. This information is often surprising or unexpected.	• The book is good, **and** it is easy to understand. • The book is good, **but** it is difficult to understand.

2. When you use **and** or **but** to connect two sentences, use a comma before **and** or **but**.	• The house is big, **and** it has a lot of rooms. • The house is big, **but** it has only one bathroom.

3. Don't use a comma to separate two descriptive adjectives.	• I am hungry **and** tired. • He is tired **but** happy.

2 *Elenore and Pete Winston are talking about different apartments. Complete their conversation. Use **and** or **but**.*

ELENORE: It's difficult to find a good apartment in this city. Joe's apartment is cheap,

_____ it's far from stores. Our apartment is near stores, _____

it's expensive.

PETE: You're right. My uncle's apartment is cheap, _____ it's small. Dino's

apartment is big _____ cheap, _____ it's very dark.

ELENORE: Carol and Yoko are lucky. Their apartment is cheap _____

comfortable. It's near stores, _____ it's sunny, too.

PETE: They live in a small college town, _____ we live in a big city.

3 *Complete the sentences. Use **and** or **but**.*

1. She's friendly _____ popular.

2. She's friendly _____ unpopular.

3. The meeting is important, _____ few people are here.

4. The meeting is important, _____ many people are here.

5. Her last name is long, _____ it's hard to pronounce.

6. Her last name is long, _____ it's easy to pronounce.

4 *Draw a picture of your favorite city street. Then write a paragraph about the street. Use the connectors **and** and **but** in some of your sentences.*
OR
*Compare stores in your neighborhood. Use the connectors **and** and **but** in some of your sentences.*

EXAMPLE:
My favorite street is Edgehill Avenue in the Bronx. It is an unusual street.
It is long and crooked. There are a lot of stores nearby, but there aren't any
stores on Edgehill Avenue. There are only ten private houses. The houses are
small and old. They are made of wood. The rooms are small, but the ceilings
are high. There are many tall trees and beautiful gardens around the houses.
The trees are very old. The people in the houses are old, too. I often go to
Edgehill Avenue, and I know the street well because my grandparents live at
10 Edgehill Avenue.

REVIEW OR SELFTEST
ANSWER KEY

I.
1. A
2. C
3. C
4. C
5. B

V.
1. b
2. a
3. a
4. b
5. b
6. a

II.
1. How many / are
2. Are there
3. Are there
4. Is she
5. Are we
6. How many / are
   Are they
7. Is there
   Is it

VI.
2. Please be quiet.
3. Why don't we take a walk?
4. There's a young man at the door.
5. There are no books on the shelf.
6. There are several mistakes in your letter.

III.
1. His
2. Her
3. Their
4. It's
5. their
6. them

IV.
2. There are a few students from Thailand.
3. There is one student from Colombia.
4. There aren't any students from Turkey.
5. How many students are there from Colombia?
6. How many students are there from Korea?
7. How many students are there from Thailand?
8. How many students are there from Germany?

Answers to Exercise 6 on pages 213–214
1. a
2. b
3. a
4. a
5. a
6. a
7. c
8. a
9. c
10. b

Student B, you have a picture of a kitchen and a dining room. Answer your partner's questions about your picture.

Your partner has a picture of a living room and a bedroom. Ask your partner if the following items are in the living room or the bedroom. Write the name of the room (or rooms) they are in. Cross out items that are not in your partner's picture.

EXAMPLE:

B: Are there any lamps in the bedroom?

A: Yes, there are. There are two lamps in the bedroom.

B: Are there any lamps in the living room?

A: Yes, there's one lamp in the living room.

1. lamps _____ bedroom, living room _____

2. table _____

3. desk _____

4. sofa _____

5. TV _____

6. rug _____

7. plants _____

8. computer _____

9. VCR _____

10. books _____

11. bed _____

12. dresser _____

13. bookcase _____

14. mirror _____

REVIEW OF THE SIMPLE PRESENT TENSE AND THE PRESENT PROGRESSIVE

PREVIEW

Yoko Mori and Carol Winston are students at Oregon State University. They are roommates. They are not getting along at this time. Listen and read their conversation.

ROOMMATE TROUBLE

CAROL: Yoko, what are you doing?

YOKO: I'm cleaning.

CAROL: But you're moving *my* clothes and *my* papers.

YOKO: Well, that's because you always leave *your* clothes and *your* papers on my desk.

CAROL: What are you talking about? Sometimes I leave my clothes on your chair. Once in a while I put my papers or clothes on your desk, but . . .

YOKO: Carol, look at my desk. All your papers, your dirty blue socks, and your gray sweatshirt are on it.

CAROL: First of all, those socks aren't mine. They're Dan's. And how often do you leave your books on my desk?

YOKO: Almost never. But you like to leave your clothes and books on my chair and desk almost every day.

CAROL: Well, in my opinion, an empty desk goes with an empty mind.

YOKO: That's nonsense. The apartment looks wonderful when it's neat and clean.

CAROL: It looks unnatural.

YOKO: No, it doesn't.

CAROL: Yes, it does. *[Yoko goes to the door.]* Yoko, where are you going?

YOKO: Out.

COMPREHENSION CHECK

Complete the sentences. Circle the right words.

1. Yoko is upset because Carol _____.
   a. doesn't put her clothes and books away
   b. wants to use Yoko's desk and chair
   c. has an empty mind

2. When Carol says "An empty desk goes with an empty mind" she means _____.
   a. a messy desk shows a person is stupid
   b. a messy desk shows a person is working hard
   c. a messy desk shows a person is thinking

WITH A PARTNER

Practice the conversation on pages 224 and 225.

25 PRESENT AND PRESENT PROGRESSIVE; *HOW OFTEN . . . ?*; ADVERBS AND EXPRESSIONS OF FREQUENCY

GRAMMAR IN CONTEXT

WARM UP   Do you ever listen to talk shows on the radio or TV? What shows? What do you think about them?

Listen to psychologist Josh Tal on his weekly radio talk show, Tell Tal Your Troubles. *Read as you listen.*

JOSH TAL: Good morning. This **is** Josh Tal on *Tell Tal Your Troubles*. Right now we **are speaking** to Neat Nita and Bob the Slob. Last week Nita wrote, "My boyfriend, Bob, **is** a slob. He **never puts** his things away. He **never cleans** his apartment. He **has** time for fun and time for work, but he **never has** time to clean. We **plan** to marry in June."

And Bob wrote, "Nita**'s** a nut about neatness. She **always cleans**. She **doesn't leave** her apartment until everything **is** in place. **Every day** she **spends** about two hours cleaning. I think she**'s wasting** her time. Life **is** too short to spend so much time cleaning. What **do** you **think**?"

I **think** Nita and Bob **need** our help. They**'re** on the phone now. Hi, Bob?

BOB: Good morning, Josh.

JOSH: Hi, Bob. Hello, Nita.

NITA: Hi, Josh.

JOSH: Bob, I **have** a few questions for you.

BOB: Go ahead.

JOSH: Bob, Nita **says** you **almost never clean**. Is that true?

BOB: Uh-huh.

JOSH: Well, Bob, **how often do** you **clean** your apartment?

BOB: **Rarely**.

JOSH: So . . . how **does** your apartment **look**?

BOB: Messy, but I**'m almost never** there. I**'m usually** at work or I**'m** out with friends. And I **spend** almost **every weekend** at Nita's place.

JOSH: How**'s** Nita's place?

BOB: It**'s** clean, but she **spends** hours cleaning it.

JOSH: Nita, **is** that true? **Do** you **spend** a lot of time cleaning your home?

NITA: **Yes, I do**. A clean home **is** important for me. And I **want** Bob to clean with me when we're married. Right now I**'m dusting** and **polishing** all my furniture. It **looks** great.

JOSH: Hmm. What **do** you **think** about that, Bob?

BOB: I **don't want** to clean.

JOSH: Well, **do** you **want** to marry Nita?

BOB: Yes, I **love** Nita, but I **don't like** to clean.

JOSH: Let's ask our audience for their advice . . .

GRAMMAR **PRESENTATION**
SIMPLE PRESENT TENSE AND PRESENT PROGRESSIVE; *HOW OFTEN . . .?*; ADVERBS AND EXPRESSIONS OF FREQUENCY

SIMPLE PRESENT TENSE
I **eat** at eight o'clock.
He **eats** at eight, too.
She **doesn't eat** with me.
They **don't eat** with us.
Does he **eat** meat?
Do you **eat** in the cafeteria?

PRESENT PROGRESSIVE
I**'m eating** now.
He**'s eating** now.
She **isn't eating** with him.
They **aren't eating** with us.
Is he **eating** chicken?
Are you **eating** chicken?

HOW OFTEN

How often	do	I / you / we / they	take medicine?
	does	he / she	clean?
		it	snow?

ANSWERS

Three times (a day).
Once (a week).
Every (Sunday).
Rarely.
Once in a while.
Never.

ADVERBS OF FREQUENCY

WITH *BE*			WITH OTHER VERBS		
Yoko **is**	always almost always frequently usually often sometimes rarely / seldom almost never never	neat.	Yoko	always almost always frequently usually often sometimes rarely / seldom almost never never	**cleans** her desk.

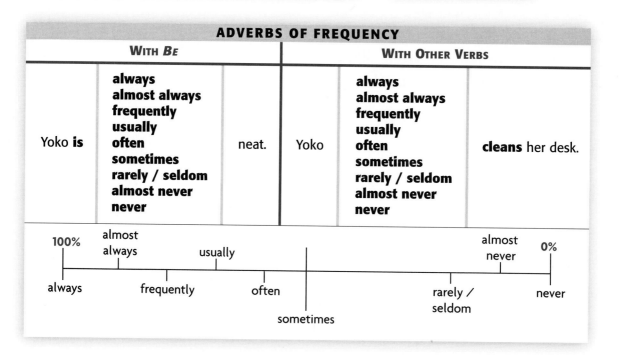

EXPRESSIONS OF FREQUENCY	
	TIME MARKERS
Yoko plays tennis	**every (day).** **twice (a week).** **three times (a month).** **several times (a year).** **once in a while.**

NOTES

EXAMPLES

1. Use the **simple present tense** to tell or ask about habits, customs, regular occurrences, routines, or facts.

Past ————————————————— Future
Now
I listen to the radio every morning.

- I **listen** to the radio every morning.
- **Do** you **listen** to the radio?

---

2. Use the **present progressive** to tell or ask about an action that is happening right now or these days.

Past —————————X————————— Future
Now
I'm listening to the radio right now.

- **I'm listening** to the radio right now.
- **Is** Carol **watching** TV?
- Lulu **is taking** a photography course this year.

---

3. *How often* asks questions about frequency. *How often* is usually used with the simple present or simple past tense. It is rarely used with the present progressive.

- **How often** do you clean your room?
  NOT ~~How often are you cleaning your room?~~

---

4. **Adverbs** and **expressions of frequency** tell how often we do something.

- Yoko **always** makes her bed.
- Carol **never** makes her bed.
- Carol goes to class **every day**.

(continued on next page)

5. Adverbs and expressions of frequency are often used with the simple present tense. They rarely occur with the present progressive.

- They **usually** *eat* breakfast at eight o'clock.
  NOT ~~They are usually eating breakfast at eight o'clock.~~

6. Adverbs of frequency come after the verb *be*.

- Yoko *is* **usually** on time. She isn't **usually** late.

They usually come before other verbs in the simple present tense.

- Carol **rarely** *cleans* her desk.
- She doesn't **often** dust.

Sometimes, *usually*, and *often* can also come at the beginning of a sentence.

- Carol **sometimes** complains about Yoko.
- **Sometimes** Carol complains about Yoko.

7. Expressions of frequency are time markers. They usually come at the beginning or at the end of a sentence.

- He plays tennis **every day**.
- **Every week** she goes to the movies.

REFERENCE NOTE
See Part IV for a more complete discussion of the simple present tense.
See Units 4, 8, and 12 for more complete discussions of the present progressive.

FOCUSED PRACTICE

1 DISCOVER THE GRAMMAR

Circle the verbs in the simple present tense. Underline the verbs in the present progressive tense.

1. Carol usually (listens) to *Tell Tal Your Troubles*, but today, she's <u>listening</u> to another radio program.

2. Yoko is wearing a sweatshirt now. She usually wears sweaters.

3. Every Thursday morning Josh Tal has a radio talk show. It's now Wednesday afternoon and Josh is preparing for his show.

4. Carol often cooks on Wednesday, but today Yoko is cooking.

5. Carol is studying and listening to the radio. She almost always studies and listens to the radio at the same time.

2 LETTER TO PSYCHOLOGIST JOSH TAL   Grammar Notes 1–2

Complete the letter. Use the simple present tense or the present progressive.

Dear Josh,

My girlfriend and I _____have_____ a great relation-
                              1. (have)
ship in every way but one. I'm romantic, but she is not.

Every week I _____ her flowers. She usually
                    2. (buy)

_____, "Don't buy flowers. You _____
    3. (say)   4. (waste)
money." Every time I _____ her a love poem, she
                          5. (write)

_____, "Don't write poems. You _____
    6. (say)   7. (waste)
time." Sometimes I _____ a candlelit dinner. After
                        8. (prepare)
five minutes she _____, "I _____ on
                      9. (say)   10. (turn)
the lights now. I want to see my food."

    What's wrong with her? Or is there something wrong

with me?

                                        Ronnie the Romantic

3 CAROL'S LETTER TO HER GRANDMOTHER Grammar Notes 1–7

Complete Carol's letter to her grandmother. Use the correct form of the verbs and adverbs of frequency in parentheses. Then listen and check your work.

Dear Grandma Lulu,

Thanks for the delicious Florida oranges and grapefruits. It __'s__ so nice of you
                                                          1. (be)
to send me a surprise every month. My roommate and I _____ an orange with our
                                                       2. (have, usually)
breakfast and a grapefruit with our dinner. The fruit _____ wonderful, but my roommate,
                                                         3. (be, always)
Yoko, isn't. She _____ a pest. Right now we _____ to each other.
                  4. (be, sometimes)   **5. (talk, not)**
Yoko _____ because I don't clean the apartment every day. But I do other things
      6. (complain, often)
for us. I _____ our dog, Rocky, every morning and evening. I _____ out the
           7. (walk)   **8. (take, always)**
garbage in the evening, and I _____ to the supermarket every Monday.
                                9. (go)
It _____ easy to share an apartment.
   10. (be, not, always)
I hope you are fine and enjoying the Florida sunshine. _____ you still _____
                                                                                    11. (be, take)
that photography class? I _____ at my desk right now and _____ at the
                           12. (sit)   **13. (look)**
beautiful photo you sent me.

I can't wait to see you.

Love,
Carol

4 QUESTIONS OF FREQUENCY   Grammar Notes 3–5

Write questions. Begin with **How often**. *Use the ideas in the box. Then answer the questions. Use the frequency expressions in the box or your own.*

Ideas	Expressions of Frequency	
you go to the movies	every day	once a week
you write letters to friends	twice a week	once a month
your best friend e-mail you	three times a week	
your family have dinner together		

1. How often do you go to the movies?   I go to the movies once a week.

5 EDITING

Find and correct the seven other mistakes in the telephone conversation.

ELENORE: Hello.

CAROL: Hi, Mom.

ELENORE: Hi, Carol. It's so good to hear your voice. How's school?

CAROL: Fine. I'm really ~~work~~ *working* hard these days. I have a tutor in math.

ELENORE: That's great.

CAROL: I call now about something else. It's my roommate. Always Yoko says, "Carol, let's clean the apartment." She clean the apartment every day. Right now she washing the windows!

ELENORE: What about you?

CAROL: Well, I rarely hangs up my clothes, and sometimes I am leaving some papers on her desk. I never makes my bed. It's a waste of time. And I like to live this way.

ELENORE: Gee, Carol. You have a problem.

---

6 DO PEOPLE CHANGE? Grammar Notes 1–2, 4–5

Complete the conversation. Use the verbs and adverbs in parentheses. Then listen and check your work.

CAROL: Yoko, I'm home. . . . Yoko? What's going on?

YOKO: Hi. It's the new me.

CAROL: Wow! You ____'re wearing____ dirty jeans and a
　　　　　　　　　1. (wear)

wrinkled blouse. Your books and papers are on the

floor, and you _____ them up. That's not
　　　　　　2. (pick, not)

like you. You _____ clean jeans and unwrinkled blouses. You
　　　　　3. (wear, always)

_____ your books or papers on the floor.
4. (leave, almost never)

YOKO: Well, you _____ about moving out, and
　　　　　　　5. (think)

now Dan's calling me "Nita the Neat One."

CAROL: Hey, Yoko, I _____ anywhere. As for Dan,
　　　　　　　　　6. (go, not)

he's joking. Let's forget about this. Let's go for pizza.

YOKO: Oh Carol, that's a super idea.

[Yoko leaves the room]

CAROL: Yoko? What _____ you _____?
　　　　　　　　7. (do)

YOKO: I _____ my clothes. I'm not going out looking like this!
　　　　8. (change)

COMMUNICATION PRACTICE

7 SURVEY: HOW OFTEN DO YOU . . . ?

*Work with three classmates. Ask each classmate five questions that begin with **How often**. Choose from the ideas in the box. Use adverbs or expressions of frequency in your answers.*

eat pizza	wear a suit	use a computer
eat raw fish	wear jeans	do laundry
clean your room	listen to opera	call your mother

EXAMPLE:
How often do you eat pizza?

Student #1
once or twice a week

Student #2
almost never

Student #3
about five times a week

8 DEALING WITH EMOTIONS

Work with a partner. In the conversation on pages 224 and 225, Yoko is angry at Carol. Yoko doesn't say anything. She leaves. How do you and you partner act? Ask each other the question:

"What do you usually do when you are _____?"

a. angry   **b.** sad   **c.** happy   **d.** bored   **e.** nervous   **f.** confused

EXAMPLE:
A: What do you usually do when you are angry?
B: When I'm angry, I usually shout.

9 HOW OBSERVANT ARE YOU?

Work with a partner.

Student A, study your classmates for one minute. Then close your eyes.

*Student B, ask your partner questions about the people in your class. Use the present progressive and the simple present tense. Use adverbs of frequency and the verbs **wear**, **sit**, and **do**.*

EXAMPLES:
B: What's Juan wearing?
A: He's wearing blue jeans and a white and black sweater.
B: Does Juan often wear blue jeans and a white and black sweater?
A: He often wears blue jeans, but he rarely wears a white and black sweater.

10 DO PEOPLE REALLY CHANGE?

Reread Exercise 6 on page 233. Discuss with your class: Do people really change?

NON-ACTION VERBS

GRAMMAR **IN CONTEXT**

WARM UP   Would you prefer a week in Bora Bora or Venice?

Bora Bora

Venice

Listen and read the conversation between Carol's parents, Pete and Elenore Winston. They are talking about a trip to the island of Bora Bora.

PETE: Any mail?

ELENORE: A couple of bills and a postcard from Bob and Valerie.

PETE: Where are they?

ELENORE: In Bora Bora.

PETE: Bora Bora? Where's that?

ELENORE: The South Pacific—it's a part of French Polynesia. Look at this photo. Isn't it fantastic?

PETE: Yes, it really is. Wow! It looks like a dream vacation.

ELENORE: Valerie says Bora Bora **has** perfect weather, white sand beaches, and wonderful snorkeling.

PETE: It really **sounds** terrific. Do you **remember** our trip to Curaçao?

ELENORE: Yes. The marine life was out of this world.

PETE: I know. I really **like** snorkeling. There's something marvelous about swimming underwater with the fish.

ELENORE: I **agree**. I **feel** completely relaxed when I snorkel. Oh Pete, this year let's go somewhere that has good snorkeling.

PETE: How about Bora Bora?

ELENORE: Bora Bora? It's so far away. It probably **costs** a fortune.

PETE: I **have** lots of frequent-flier miles. Let's see what it **costs**.

ELENORE: Okay.

GRAMMAR **PRESENTATION**
NON-ACTION (STATIVE) VERBS

STATE OF BEING	EMOTIONS	SENSES	NEEDS / PREFERENCES	MENTAL STATES	POSSESSIONS
be	love hate like dislike	hear see feel taste smell sound	want need prefer	agree disagree understand know remember believe think	have own belong owe cost

NOTES

EXAMPLES

1. Some verbs do not describe actions. These verbs are called **non-action** or **stative verbs**.

- I **have** frequent-flier miles.

2. Some non-action verbs express **emotions**.

- We **like** snorkeling.

3. Some non-action verbs describe **senses**.

- The music **sounds** romantic.

4. Some non-action verbs describe **mental states** and **thoughts**.

- Carol **knows** you.
- She **understands** you.

5. Some non-action verbs show **possession**.

- I **have** a red car.
- The book **belongs** to him.

6. Some non-action verbs express **needs** and **preferences**.

- I **prefer** black coffee.

7. Note that *be* is also a non-action verb.

- I **am** tired now.

8. We usually do not use non-action verbs in the present progressive (-*ing*) form, even when something is happening right now.

- I **own** a car.
  NOT ~~I'm owning a car.~~

9. Some non-action verbs can also be used as action verbs. In these cases the meanings of the verbs change, and they take the role of action verbs.

non-action
verb   action verb
- I **have** a new car. **I'm having** trouble with the engine.

action verb   non-action verb
- **I'm tasting** the turkey. It **tastes** good.

action verb
- **I'm thinking** about English grammar.

non-action
verb
- I **think** it's interesting.

FOCUSED PRACTICE

1 DISCOVER THE GRAMMAR

Underline the non-action verbs in the questions. Then match the questions with the answers.

___d___ **1.** Do you <u>like</u> golf?

_____ **2.** Do you love me?

_____ **3.** Do you smell any smoke?

_____ **4.** Does the pineapple taste good?

_____ **5.** Do you hear the birds?

_____ **6.** What do you see?

_____ **7.** Does she have time this morning?

_____ **8.** Do you know those men?

a. Nothing. It's too foggy.

b. Yes. They sound wonderful.

c. Yes. They're waiters at Star Cafe.

d. I prefer tennis.

e. Of course I do. My heart belongs to you.

f. No. I have a cold.

g. No. I think she's busy.

h. Yes. It's delicious.

2 AT THE TRAVEL AGENCY   Grammar Notes 1–3, 5–7

Elenore is at a travel agency. She is asking about tours to Bora Bora. Complete the conversation. Use the verbs in the box.

cost	prefer	know	need	remember	have	be

TRAVEL AGENT: May I help you?

   ELENORE: Yes. My husband and I are thinking about taking a trip to Bora Bora.

   ___Do___ you ___have___ any package tours there?

¹

   AGENT: Yes, we have a couple of tours that go to Bora Bora. Do you prefer an

   eight-day or ten-day tour?

   ELENORE: I _____ a ten-day one.

²

AGENT: Here's a brochure all about French Polynesia. Why don't you take it home and read it?

ELENORE: Thanks. Tell me, _____ it _____ a lot to go there?
3.

AGENT: Not really. There _____ tours for all budgets.
4.

ELENORE: Is there anything special I need to do now?

AGENT: You _____ to book early. That's about it.
5.

ELENORE: Okay. By the way, what do people speak in Bora Bora?

AGENT: French and Tahitian.

ELENORE: Tahitian? Is Bora Bora a part of Tahiti?

AGENT: Not exactly. Tahiti and Bora Bora are different islands. They're a part of Polynesia. But some people call all the islands of French Polynesia Tahiti.

ELENORE: I see. Well, I _____ some French from high school, but I don't
6.

_____ a word of Tahitian.
7.

AGENT: Here's a list of words in Tahitian.

ELENORE: Oh. Thank you very much. "Parahi."

AGENT: "Parahi."

English	Tahitian
Hello	La orana
How are you?	Eaha to oe huru?
I'm fine	Maita
Good-bye	Parahi
Thank you	Maururu
Yes	E
No	Aita
No problem	Aita pe'ape'a

③ BEFORE A TRIP   Grammar Notes 1–2, 5

Write sentences. Use the simple present or the present progressive.

1. to / camera / This / belong / me

 This camera belongs to me.

2. learn / Right now / Elenore / in Tahitian / a few words and phrases

_____

3. French / Pete / understand, not

_____

(continued on next page)

4. Elenore / plan, not / a trip / to Hawaii

_____

5. It / snow / now in New York

_____

6. in Bora Bora / Pete and Elenore / dream about snorkeling

_____

4 EDITING

Pete, Elenore, and their son, Doug, are waiting for dinner to be ready. Correct the mistakes in the conversation. There are mistakes in all the underlined words.

Doug: What's Mom doing?

Pete: I <u>~~no~~</u> know. *don't* I think she <u>practices</u> Tahitian.

Doug: You're joking!

Elenore: Pete, <u>are you remember</u> the word for "good-bye" in Tahitian?

Pete: "Parahi," right?

Elenore: Right. <u>You're having</u> a wonderful memory. Doug, what <u>do you do</u>?

Doug: I'm hungry. I <u>try</u> the soup. It<u>'s tasting</u> delicious, Mom.

Elenore: Good, but leave some room for dinner.

Doug: Okay, Mom.

Elenore: Pete, <u>do you knowing</u> our travel agent's last name?

Pete: I think it's Reza. Why?

Elenore: I <u>having</u> a few questions <u>I'm wanting</u> to ask her about our trip. She's sending us an itinerary this week.

Pete: When <u>is she needing</u> the deposit?

Elenore: She needs it before the fifteenth of this month.

Pete: Okay.

Elenore: Did you know there are no taxes in Bora Bora? And there's no tipping. And . . .

Doug: Hey, Mom. You'd better watch out. You don't want to become a Bora Bora bore.

COMMUNICATION PRACTICE

5 QUOTABLE QUOTES

Work with a partner. Read these sayings aloud. Give your opinion.

EXAMPLE:

A: Do you think absence makes the heart grow fonder?

B: Yes, I think so.

| I agree. | I don't agree. | I think so, too. | I don't think so. | I don't know. |

1. Absence makes the heart grow fonder.

2. Talk does not cook rice.

3. Smile and the world smiles with you.

4. A mother is a person who, seeing there are only four pieces of pie for five people, says she never liked pie.

6 HOW DO YOU FEEL ABOUT . . . ?

Work with a partner. Take turns telling each other your feelings about the items in the box. Use **I love**, **I like**, **I don't like**, **I hate**.

your family	romantic movies	TV talk shows	MTV
this city	warm weather	horror movies	baseball
English grammar	chocolate	flying	basketball

EXAMPLE:

A: How do you feel about this city?

B: It's very exciting. I love everything about it.

What do you know about your partner now? In what ways are you and your partner alike? In what ways are you different? Tell the class.

EXAMPLE:

A: We both love our families. I like this city, but my partner doesn't.

7 A SURVEY

Complete the questions. Use the ideas in parentheses or your own ideas. Then survey five classmates. Report the results to your class.

Do you know _____? (karate, tai chi)

Do you like _____? (snorkeling, sailing)

Do you remember the movie _____? (*Star Wars, The Sound of Music*)

Do you understand _____? (sign language, physics)

27 VERBS PLUS NOUNS, GERUNDS, AND INFINITIVES

GRAMMAR IN CONTEXT

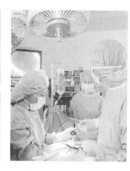

WARM UP What is your dream career? Why do you think people become clowns? carpenters? surgeons? politicians?

It's career day at Doug's high school. Former students are talking about their careers. Mona Reza is answering questions about the travel business. Listen and read the students' questions and Mona's answers.

1ST STUDENT: Ms. Reza, what do you **enjoy** about your job?

MONA REZA: Many things. But I especially **enjoy planning** trips to new places. First of all, I **like to read** and **learn** about my customers' destinations. Then I **try to give** my customers exactly what they want.

1ST STUDENT: What do you mean?

MONA: Well, some people **want to do** unusual things—things they don't do at home. Others **enjoy finding** bargains. They **want a "good deal."** Others **enjoy a beautiful hotel room** with a beautiful view. Still others **prefer to spend** their money on tours, gifts, and souvenirs.

2ND STUDENT: I'll bet you travel a lot.

MONA: I sure do. I'm away about two months a year.

2ND STUDENT: Do you ever **get tired of traveling**?

MONA: Never.

3RD STUDENT: What don't you **like** about your job?

MONA: Well, these days the airlines and the Internet are taking away a lot of business from the travel agencies. It's very competitive.

3RD STUDENT: What do I **need to do** to prepare for a job in the travel field?

MONA: Well, ask yourself these questions. **Am I interested in travel**? Do I **enjoy working** with people? **Am I good at working** with numbers and details? And remember, you **need to keep cool** even when an angry customer calls at 2:00 A.M. and says, "I'm in Australia and my bags went to Austria."

3RD STUDENT: Do you get angry?

Mona: No. I want to say, "Look, I didn't send your bags to Austria. I just booked your tour." But I never say that because I don't want to lose a customer. My customer is always right.

GRAMMAR **PRESENTATION**
VERBS PLUS NOUNS, GERUNDS, AND INFINITIVES

SUBJECT	VERB	OBJECT NOUN
I	like	music.

SUBJECT	VERB PHRASE	OBJECT NOUN
I	am interested in	music.

SUBJECT	VERB	GERUND (VERB + -*ING*)
I	like	singing.

SUBJECT	VERB PHRASE	GERUND (VERB + -*ING*)
I	am interested in	singing.

SUBJECT	VERB	INFINITIVE
I	like	to sing.

VERBS + GERUND	PHRASES + GERUND	VERBS + INFINITIVE	VERBS + INFINITIVE OR GERUND
enjoy finish keep	be interested in be tired of be good at be afraid of	agree need decide plan hope refuse want	like love prefer hate

NOTES	**EXAMPLES**
1. Some verbs, such as *enjoy, finish*, and *keep*, can be followed by a noun or a **gerund (base form of verb + *-ing*)**.	 noun • I **enjoy music**. gerund • I **enjoy singing**.
2. Some verbs, such as *want, need, try, plan*, and *refuse*, can be followed by a noun or an **infinitive (*to* + base form of the verb)**.	 noun • I **want a job**. infinitive • I want **to work**.
3. A noun or gerund also can follow these phrases: ***to be interested in*** ***to be tired of*** ***to be good at*** ***to be afraid of***	 noun • I'm **interested in law**. gerund • I'm **interested in studying law**. noun • She**'s good at art**.
4. Some verbs, such as *like, hate, dislike*, and *prefer*, can be followed by a noun, a gerund (*-ing* form), or an infinitive.	• I like **summer**. • I like **to swim**. • I like **swimming**.

FOCUSED PRACTICE

1 DISCOVER THE GRAMMAR

*Look at the underlined words. Label them **g** for gerund, **i** for infinitive, and **n** for noun or noun phrase.*

1. Are you interested in <u>art</u>? <u>science</u>? <u>computers</u>? <u>business</u>?
(above: n, n, n, n)

2. Do you enjoy <u>working</u> with people?

3. Do you prefer <u>to work</u> alone?

4. Do you like <u>to work</u> with your hands?

5. Are you interested in <u>helping</u> people?

6. Are you good at <u>detail work</u>?

7. Do you want <u>to make</u> a lot of money?

2 ACTING   Grammar Notes 1–2

Students at Kennedy High School are questioning Bob Roberts. He graduated five years ago and is hoping to be a successful actor. Complete the sentences with the gerund or the infinitive of the words in parentheses.

STUDENT: Do you enjoy _____acting_____?
                                  1. (act)

BOB: Yes. I love _____.
                          2. (act)

STUDENT: Is it hard to find work as an actor?

BOB: Very hard. Many people want _____ actors. You need
                                              3. (become)
_____ talent, patience, and luck.
      4. (have)

STUDENT: What do you do when you aren't working?

BOB: I'm a waiter. Many actors are waiters.

STUDENT: Do you ever think about changing careers?

BOB: No. I refuse _____ my dream. I keep _____ out for new
                            5. (give up)   6. (try)
parts. I think I'm good at _____ and I plan _____ it to
                                    7. (act)   8. (show)
the world.

3 **EDITING**

A student is applying for a job at Reza Travel Agency. Find and correct the errors in this first draft of a letter to Mona Reza.

Dear Ms. Reza,

I'd like to apply for a part-time job as an assistant at Reza Travel Agency.

I enjoyed ~~to hear~~ *hearing* you speak at Kennedy High School last week. Thank you for your honest and interesting answers to our questions about the travel business.

I am in my last year at Kennedy High School. Next year I hope to attend Baruch College. I want studying hotel and business administration.

I am interested in to work with people and learn more about the travel business. I have good computer skills and I'm fluent in Spanish and English. I am free on weekends and afternoons after 3:00 P.M.

I hope hear from you soon.

Sincerely yours,

Alex Pabon

COMMUNICATION PRACTICE

4 CATEGORIES

Work with a partner. Name something you like for each category. Your partner agrees or names something he or she prefers.

1. sports   **3.** movies   **5.** books
2. music   **4.** dessert   **6.** flowers

EXAMPLES:

Sports   *Music*

A: I like to play golf.   **A:** I like jazz.

B: I do, too.   **B:** I do, too.

     OR   OR

I prefer to play tennis.   I prefer classical music.

5 GOOD AT A JOB

Work with a partner. Talk about people who are good at their jobs—for example, a good parent, a good kindergarten teacher, a good doctor, or a good student. Write down your ideas. Compare your ideas with your classmates'.

EXAMPLES:

A good kindergarten teacher enjoys working with young children.

A good kindergarten teacher doesn't get tired of repeating things.

6 WHAT KIND OF JOB IS GOOD FOR YOU?

Work with a partner. Ask your partner the questions in Exercise 1 on page 246. Add your own questions. Talk about careers.

EXAMPLES:

A: Are you interested in art?

B: No. I'm interested in business.

A: What kind of business?

B: The music business.

A: That's interesting. Do you enjoy working with people?

B: Yes, I do.

A: What are you interested in doing?

B: I want to discover new music groups and help them become famous.

POSSESSIVE ADJECTIVES AND POSSESSIVE PRONOUNS

GRAMMAR **IN CONTEXT**

WARM UP   Is it easy for you to apologize? When? When is it difficult for you to apologize?

Listen and read the following conversation. Yoko, Carol, and Nancy are at the university library.

NANCY: Excuse me, Carol, but I think that's **mine**.

CAROL: What's **yours**?

NANCY: That yellow umbrella. The one you just put in **your** bag. It's **mine**.

CAROL: It's not **yours**. It's Yoko's.

NANCY: Whose?

CAROL: Yoko's. It's **hers**. My roommate's. There she is. Yoko, isn't this **your** umbrella?

YOKO: Yes. Uh, wait. No, it's not. **Mine** is right here under this chair.

CAROL: Oh, Nancy. I'm terribly sorry. I was sure it was **hers**. Oh, I see. It's exactly like **hers**.

NANCY: That's okay. Well, Yoko, you have great taste in umbrellas.

YOKO: Thanks. So do you.

GRAMMAR **PRESENTATION**
POSSESSIVE ADJECTIVES AND POSSESSIVE PRONOUNS

PRONOUNS					
POSSESSIVE ADJECTIVES	**POSSESSIVE PRONOUNS**	**POSSESSIVE ADJECTIVE**		**POSSESSIVE PRONOUN**	
my	mine	This is	**my** umbrella.	**Mine**	is blue.
your	your	That isn't	**your** hat.	**Yours**	is in the closet.
his	his	I'm not wearing	**his** coat.	**His**	is on the chair.
her	hers	We don't have	**her** book.	**Hers**	is at home.
our	ours	This isn't	**our** classroom.	**Ours**	is on the third floor.
their	theirs	That's not	**their** car.	**Theirs**	is in a garage.
its			**Its** name is Goldy.		

NOTES

EXAMPLES

1. A **possessive pronoun** replaces a **possessive adjective** and a **noun**.

- This isn't **my umbrella**. **Mine** is blue.

2. A noun never follows a possessive pronoun.

- This is my hat. This is **mine**.
  NOT ~~This is **mine** hat~~.

3. The verb that follows a possessive pronoun agrees with the noun it replaces.

- Her notebook is blue. = Hers **is** blue.
- Her notebooks are red. = Hers **are** red.

REFERENCE NOTE
See Unit 10 for a further discussion of possessive adjectives.

FOCUSED PRACTICE

① DISCOVER THE GRAMMAR

Change the underlined words to a possessive pronoun.

1. A: Is that your scarf?

    B: No, it's not <u>my scarf</u>. It's <u>his scarf</u>. <u>My scarf</u> is in my coat pocket.
                           mine
                            a.   **b.**   **c.**

    A: Oh.

2. A: Is this their house?

    B: No. <u>Their house</u> is next door.
               a.

    A: Whose house is this?

    B: It's <u>our house</u>.
              b.

    A: <u>Your house</u>?
             c.

    B: Yes, <u>our house</u>.
                 d.

3. A: Are these your sunglasses?

    B: No, they're <u>her sunglasses</u>.
                      a.

    A: <u>My sunglasses</u> are in my bag.
           b.

② POSSESSIONS Grammar Notes 1–2

Complete each sentence. Use the possessive adjective or the possessive pronoun.

A. 1. This is (my, mine) _____my_____ umbrella.

    2. (You, Yours) _____ is over there.

    3. It's next to (her, hers) _____ backpack.

    4. (Her, Hers) _____ backpack has many pockets.

    5. (My, Mine) _____ has only one pocket.

B. 1. Where is (their, theirs)_____ car?

    2. (Their, Theirs) _____ is in the garage.

    3. Is (your, yours)_____ car in the garage, too?

    4. No, (our, ours) _____ is on the street.

3 A TEENAGER'S DREAM

Complete the conversation. Use **you**, **your**, **mine**, *and* **yours**. *Then listen and check your work.*

Doug is smiling. It is six-thirty in the morning, and he's sleeping. He's dreaming. This is Doug's dream:

DOUG: What are these?

DAD: The key to _____ new red sports
1.

car.

DOUG: _____?
2.

MOM: Yes, _____. It's a present for
3.

_____ on _____
4.   5.

eighteenth birthday.

DOUG: Oh, wow! Are you sure?

DAD: Of course. Every young man needs a

sports car.

DOUG: You're so right!

4 EDITING

Find and correct the three mistakes in this conversation between Yoko and her classmate Carmen.

CARMEN: Is their class in room 304 today?

YOKO: No. Our is in room 304. Theirs are in this room.

CARMEN: Is that necklace new? I really like it, Yoko.

YOKO: Thanks, but it isn't mine necklace. It's my roommate's. She lent it to me.

COMMUNICATION PRACTICE

5 COMPARING LIVES

Work with a partner. Take turns. One of you reads the sentence. The other talks about his or her life.

> **EXAMPLES:**
> **A:** Yoko's hair is short and straight.
> **B:** Mine is short and curly.
>
> > OR
>
> My hair is short and curly now, but it was long and straight last year.
>
> **A:** Doug's school has more than 500 students.
> **B:** Ours has about 200 students.
>
> > OR
>
> Our school has about 200 students.

1. Yoko's hair is short and straight.

2. Doug's school has more than 500 students.

3. Yoko's eyes are brown.

4. Yoko's classes are fifty minutes long.

5. Yoko's family lives far away from her.

6. Yoko's classes meet five times a week.

7. Yoko's family has a sports car.

8. Yoko's grammar class has fifteen students.

9. Yoko's family speaks Japanese.

6 A GUESSING GAME

Student A, go to the front of the class and close your eyes. Student B, choose five objects that belong to different students and put them in front of Student A.

Student A, guess whose they are. Point and use a possessive pronoun. You get one point for a correct answer and one point for the correct use of a possessive pronoun.

> **EXAMPLE:**
> **A:** I think this pen is **his**. *(A points to B)*
> **B:** That's right. You get two points.
> **A:** I think this backpack is **yours**. *(A points to C)*
> **B:** That's wrong. It isn't mine. It's **hers**.

REVIEW OR SELFTEST

I. *Read each conversation. Circle the letter of the underlined word or group of words that is not correct.*

1. **A:** Excuse me, but you're using <u>my pen</u>. <u>Mine pen</u> is blue.   **A B C D**
       A   B

   <u>Yours</u> <u>is</u> gray.
      C   D

   B: Oh, excuse me. Here.

2. **A:** I <u>don't know</u> him very well. <u>Does he come</u> on time?   **A B C D**
      A   B

   B: I <u>don't think</u> so. He <u>comes usually</u> late.
         C   D

3. **A:** Does he <u>like black coffee</u>?   **A B C D**
              A

   B: No, <u>he doesn't</u>. He <u>prefers</u> <u>drink</u> coffee with milk
           B   C   D

   and sugar.

4. **A:** <u>How often</u> <u>are you sweeping</u> the floor?   **A B C D**
        A   B

   B: <u>Every evening</u>. I <u>usually</u> sweep it after dinner.
        C   D

II. *Match the questions with the answers.*

_____ **1.** What are Carol and Yoko doing?   **a.** At his friend's apartment.

_____ **2.** What do they usually do on   **b.** They're cleaning their
         Sunday afternoon?   apartment.

_____ **3.** Are they working hard?   **c.** Once or twice a week.

_____ **4.** Do they usually work hard?   **d.** Juan.

_____ **5.** Where is Bekir studying?   **e.** Yes, they are.

_____ **6.** Why is he studying there?   **f.** Because the apartment is quiet.

_____ **7.** Who is he studying with?   **g.** Yoko does, but Carol doesn't.

_____ **8.** How often do they study   **h.** They clean their apartment.
         together?

III. *Rewrite each sentence. Use the adverb or expression of frequency in parentheses.*

1. (every week) They go to the bank.

   _____

2. (rarely) She wears jeans.

   _____

3. (always) They watch TV at night.

   _____

4. (several times a year) We go to concerts.

   _____

5. (often) You are funny.

   _____

IV. *Write questions with* **How often***. Use the simple present tense.*

1. Carol / call her parents

   A: _____?

   B: Once a week.

2. We / get a free lunch

   A: _____?

   B: There are no free lunches.

V. *Choose the correct words to complete the conversations.*

1. **A:** How's the food?

   B: The chicken is terrible, but this pasta _____ delicious.
   (is tasting, tastes)

2. **A:** Why _____ you _____ a suit and tie?
   (are, do)   (wearing, wear)

   B: I have a job interview this morning. I _____ to look good.
   (am wanting, want)

3. **A:** _____ you _____ your first date?
   (Are, Do)   (remembering, remember)

   B: Yes. What about you?

4. **A:** _____ he _____ dinner now?
   (Is, Does)   (eating, eat)

   B: No. He _____ to eat dinner at 8:30.
   (is liking, likes)

5. **A:** Your plants are beautiful. How often _____
   (are, do)

   you _____ them?
   (watering, water)

   B: Once a week.

VI. *Complete the letter. Use the simple present tense, the present tense of* **be**, *or the present progressive.*

Dear Grandma Lulu,

How _____ you, and how _____ things in Miami? Today's newspaper
　　　　1. (be)　　　　　　　　　　　2. (be)

says it's 80 degrees and sunny in Miami. Here in Oregon it _____ 50 degrees,
　　　　　　　　　　　　　　　　　　　　　　　　　　　3. (be)

and it _____.
　　　4. (rain)

I like Oregon State University a lot. This semester my favorite course is art. I

_____ a wonderful professor. This month we _____ how to draw from live
5. (have)　　　　　　　　　　　　　　　　　6. (learn)

models. I _____ very well in this course, and I _____ to take another art
　　　7. (do)　　　　　　　　　　　　　　　　　8. (want)

course next term. My other courses are difficult, but I'm working hard and _____ okay.
　　　　　　　　　　　　　　　　　　　　　　　　　　　　　　　　9. (do)

Every evening I _____ to the library for three or four hours. I _____
　　　　　　　　10. (go)　　　　　　　　　　　　　　　　　　　11. (study, not)

all the time. Sometimes I _____ to my good friend Dan. Dan and I _____
　　　　　　　　　　　12. (talk)　　　　　　　　　　　　　　　　13. (like)

to talk about lots of things. He _____ a lot of interesting ideas.
　　　　　　　　　　　　　14. (have)

Thanks for the beautiful sweater. I _____ the color purple. I _____ the
　　　　　　　　　　　　　　15. (love)　　　　　　　　　16. (wear)

sweater now and it _____ very comfortable. Thanks so much. I can't wait to see
　　　　　　　17. (be)

you. Please write!

　　　　　　　　　　　　　　Love,
　　　　　　　　　　　　　　Carol

VII. *Complete the conversations. Use the words in the boxes.*

1. A: Why are you angry?

I	me	my	mine

B: That sweatshirt is _____. It's not yours. It belongs to _____. Mom
　　　　　　　　　　　　　a.　　　　　　　　　　　　　　　　　　　b.

gave it to _____. It's _____ favorite sweatshirt. _____ want to
　　　　　　c.　　　　　　　d.　　　　　　　　　　　　　　e.

wear it. You always wear my clothes.

2. A: Do _____ need an umbrella?
　　　　　　a.

you	your	yours

B: Yes. It's raining, and I don't have one.

A: Here's my umbrella.

B: Thanks, but I don't want to use _____.
　　　　　　　　　　　　　　　　　　b.

A: That's okay. I'm wearing _____ rain hat.
　　　　　　　　　　　　c.

3. A: Do you and your wife live

| we | us | our | ours |

alone in that big house?

   B: No, _____ don't. _____ married son and his wife live with
                      a.   b.

      _____. Their bedroom is on the second floor. _____ is on the first floor.
         c.   d.

4. A: Do you have a rabbit?

| it | its |

   B: Yes. _____ name is Lucky. _____ has brown and white fur.
                a.   b.

5. A: Do _____ live in that big house?
           a.

| they | their | them | theirs |

   B: Yes, but the house doesn't belong to _____. It's _____ parents'
                                       b.   c.

      house. They own a house, too, but _____ is very small.
                                      d.

VIII. *Write sentences. Use the simple present tense. Use infinitives or gerunds after the verbs.*

  1. Doug / want / meet his friends after school

    _____

  2. Pete / need / go to the dentist

    _____

  3. Carol and Yoko / enjoy / cook

    _____

  4. We / be tired of / play soccer

    _____

IX. *Correct these sentences.*

      She always
  1. ~~Always she~~ polishes her nails.

  2. I come usually late.

  3. How often are you sweeping the floor?

  4. He likes drink coffee.

▶ *To check your answers, go to the Answer Key on page 259.*

FROM GRAMMAR TO WRITING
ORGANIZATION: TIME MARKERS

1 *Look at these sentences. Which words talk about time?*

   1. He studies at home in the evening.

   2. At present I live on Bleeker Street.

Study this information about time sequence markers.

Time Sequence Markers You can organize your writing by using **time sequence markers**. Some common markers for the time of day are: **in the morning, in the afternoon, in the evening, at night**. Some common markers for the past, present, and future are: **in the past, at present, in the future**.	• Michele works **in the morning**. • **At present**, I'm a student.

2 *Read this story about a country doctor. Underline the time sequence markers. Then write about a day in the life of someone you know well.*

A Country Doctor

   Michelle Hirch-Phothong is a country doctor. Her day begins at six-thirty in the morning. At seven o'clock she is at the hospital. She visits her patients and discusses their problems with the nurses and other doctors. Michelle enjoys talking to her patients. She listens to them carefully and never rushes them.

   In the afternoon Michelle works at a clinic. The clinic is busy and patients are often worried and nervous. Michelle and the other doctors try to calm them down.

   At six o'clock in the evening Michelle leaves the clinic. She goes home and relaxes. Every evening at seven o'clock Michelle goes to "Bangkok in the Boondocks." That's my restaurant, and Michelle is my wife. Michelle and I enjoy a delicious Thai dinner alone. Sometimes, however, people come to the restaurant and tell Michelle their medical problems. I say, "Tell them to go to the clinic." But Michelle never sends them home without listening to their problems and offering them advice. Michelle is a wonderful doctor.

REVIEW OR SELFTEST
ANSWER KEY

I.
1. B
2. D
3. D
4. B

II.
1. b
2. h
3. e
4. g
5. a
6. f
7. d
8. c

III.
1. Every week they go to the bank. (They go to the bank every week.)
2. She rarely wears jeans.
3. They always watch TV at night.
4. Several times a year we go to concerts. (We go to concerts several times a year.)
5. You are often funny.

IV.
1. How often does Carol call her parents?
2. How often do we get a free lunch?

V.
1. tastes
2. are / wearing; want
3. Do / remember
4. Is / eating; likes
5. do / water

VI.
1. are
2. are
3. is ('s)
4. is raining ('s raining)
5. have
6. are learning
7. am doing ('m doing)
8. want
9. doing
10. go
11. don't study
12. talk
13. like
14. has
15. love
16. am wearing ('m wearing)
17. is ('s)

VII.
1. a. mine
   b. me
   c. me
   d. my
   e. I
2. a. you
   b. yours
   c. your
3. a. we
   b. Our
   c. us
   d. Ours
4. a. its
   b. It
5. a. they
   b. them
   c. their
   d. theirs

VIII.
1. Doug wants to meet his friends after school.
2. Pete needs to go to the dentist.
3. Carol and Yoko enjoy cooking.
4. We are tired of playing soccer.

IX.
2. I usually come late.
3. How often do you sweep the floor?
4. He likes to drink coffee. (He likes drinking coffee.)

REVIEW OF THE SIMPLE PAST TENSE; NEGATIVE QUESTIONS; THE FUTURE

PREVIEW

Pete Winston is talking to his 73-year-old mother, Lulu, on the telephone. Pete lives in New York City. His mother lives in Florida. It's Tuesday morning. Listen and read their conversation.

IS LOVE BLIND?

LULU: Hello.

PETE: Hi, Mom.

LULU: Hi, Pete, how are you?

PETE: Okay. How about you?

LULU: I'm just wonderful. Tell me. How are my grandchildren? Are Carol and Yoko getting along?

PETE: Oh yes.

LULU: And is Norma going to go to that convention next month?

PETE: Yes, yes.

LULU: When will Doug be in Miami?

PETE: He and Noah are flying there in the middle of March. Look, Mom, the kids are fine. But it's you I'm worried about. Where were *you* last night? I tried calling you until midnight. I was very worried.

LULU: Oh, I'm sorry. I was out. First I ate at a wonderful new Japanese restaurant. Then I went to the movies. The food was delicious and the movie was hilarious.

PETE: Oh, that's really nice. Were you with Bertha?

LULU: No.

PETE: Were you alone?

LULU: No, I wasn't.

PETE: Who were you with?

LULU: James Belmont.

PETE: James Belmont! Your photography teacher? Didn't you tell me he's a ladies' man? He's not for you. How could you go out with him?

LULU: Pete! Calm down. He's thoughtful and intelligent.

PETE: But Mom, isn't he a little young for you?

LULU: Good-bye, dear.

PETE: Wait, I'm sorry . . .

[Lulu hangs up]

PETE: I don't understand Mom. What in the world is she doing?

COMPREHENSION CHECK

Complete the sentences. Circle the right words.

1. Pete says, "Isn't he a little young for you?" Pete _____.
   a. thinks James is too young for his mother
   b. thinks James isn't too young for his mother
   c. wants to know if James is too young for his mother

2. At the end of the conversation Lulu _____.
   a. is angry at Pete
   b. is happy with Pete
   c. is worried about Pete

WITH A PARTNER

Practice the conversation on pages 260 and 261.

REVIEW OF THE SIMPLE PAST TENSE; NEGATIVE QUESTIONS

GRAMMAR **IN CONTEXT**

WARM UP   A May–December romance is one between people who are different ages. Do you know of any such romances?

Listen and read the following conversation.

GAIL: Sima, **isn't that an engagement ring**?

SIMA: Yes, it is.

GAIL: Wow! Congratulations. Let me see it. It's beautiful. I **didn't** even **know** you **had** a boyfriend.

SIMA: Well, it **happened** quickly. Phil and I **met** a year ago, but we **didn't date** until three months ago. Then last weekend Phil **gave** me this ring and we got engaged.

GAIL: It's really beautiful. **Did** you **meet** him at school?

SIMA: No. Remember when I **worked** at the bank last summer?

GAIL: Uh-huh.

SIMA: Well, Phil **was** the bank's director.

GAIL: The director? How old is he?

SIMA: Fifty-five.

GAIL: Fifty-five? **Isn't he a little old for you**? You're just twenty-eight.

SIMA: I know, but we're in love.

GAIL: Wow! **Weren't your parents surprised**?

SIMA: Well, actually they **were** upset. My Dad **yelled** and my Mom **cried**. But it's my life.

GAIL: Uh, well, I guess you're right. I just hope you know what you're doing.

GRAMMAR **PRESENTATION**
THE SIMPLE PAST TENSE; NEGATIVE QUESTIONS

AFFIRMATIVE OF *BE*		
SUBJECT	**VERB**	
I	**was**	at a restaurant last night.
We	**were**	

AFFIRMATIVE OF OTHER VERBS		
SUBJECT	**VERB**	
I	**went**	to a restaurant last night.
We		to a restaurant, too.

NEGATIVE OF *BE*		
SUBJECT	*WAS / WERE NOT*	
I	**wasn't**	at home last night.
They	**weren't**	

NEGATIVE OF OTHER VERBS			
SUBJECT	*DIDN'T*	**BASE FORM OF VERB**	
I	**didn't**	**stay**	home last night.
They			

YES / NO QUESTIONS WITH *BE*		
WAS / WERE	**SUBJECT**	
Was	he	at work two weeks ago?
Were	you	at a party last night?

YES / NO QUESTIONS WITH OTHER VERBS			
DID	**SUBJECT**	**BASE FORM OF VERB**	
Did	he	**return**	to work yesterday?
	you	**stay**	until midnight?

NEGATIVE QUESTIONS	
QUESTIONS	**ANSWERS**
Isn't he a student?	Yes, he is.
Aren't you from Korea?	Yes, I am. (Yes, we are.)
Wasn't he in class yesterday?	Yes, he was.
Didn't you work at a bank last year?	Yes, I did. (Yes, we did.)
Don't they live on Main Street?	Yes, they do.
Doesn't she have a younger sister?	Yes, she does.

NOTES	EXAMPLES
1. The **simple past tense** tells about events that happened in the past. For all verbs except *be*, the simple past tense form is the same for all persons.	• I **lived** in England last year. • She **lived** in England five years ago. • We **lived** in England in 1998.
2. The past tense of *be* has two forms: *was* and *were*.	• Mozart **was** a musician. • Renoir and Monet **were** painters.
3. There are regular and irregular verbs. The past tense of regular verbs end in *-d* or *-ed*.	regular verb • We **worked** at a restaurant. irregular verb • They **ate** there.
4. Use **contractions** in speaking and informal writing. Use *didn't* + **the base form** for negative statements with all verbs except *be*. Use *wasn't* or *weren't* for negative statements with the verb *be*.	• I **didn't understand**. • He **wasn't** in school. • They **weren't** alone.
5. For *yes / no* questions with *be*, reverse the subject and verb. For *yes / no* questions with all other verbs, use *did* + **the subject** + **the base form** of the verb.	• **Were you** late? • **Did you come** late?
6. Use **negative *yes / no* questions** to ask about something you already think is true. If the information is true, the person answers yes.	**A:** **Aren't** you from Korea? **B:** Yes, I am. **A:** **Didn't** you work at the library? **B:** No, I didn't.

REFERENCE NOTE
See Appendix 12, page A-13, for a list of common irregular verbs.

FOCUSED PRACTICE

1 DISCOVER THE GRAMMAR

Pete is talking to his mother again. Listen and read their conversation. Then underline all sentences in the past tense with **be**. *Circle all other past tense sentences. Put a check (✔) above negative questions.*

LULU: Hello.

PETE: Hi Mom.

LULU: Pete! It's one o'clock in the morning. What's wrong?

PETE: Nothing here. <u>But you weren't home all evening.</u>

⟨I left four messages on your machine⟩.

LULU: Oh, dear. I'm sorry. Didn't I tell you about the party?

PETE: No. What party?

LULU: The surprise party for James's friend. James gave a wonderful party for his

friend. He invited over forty people. And it was a real surprise.

PETE: That's nice, Mom. But I really don't think James is right for you.

LULU: Yes, dear.

PETE: I'm serious. Weren't you out with James the last two nights?

LULU: Uh-huh. Maybe you want to speak with James? He's here now.

PETE: What? Please, Mom. Take care of yourself.

LULU: Don't worry. Good-bye, dear.

PETE: Bye, Mom.

[Pete to Elenore]

PETE: Now I'm really upset. I want to speak to my friend Milt, the detective.

ELENORE: Aren't you making too much of this?

② PETE'S WORRIED   Grammar Note 2

Elenore and Pete are talking about Lulu. Complete the sentences with **'s, 'm, 're,
was,** *or* **were***.*

ELENORE: What's_____ wrong, Pete?
          1.

PETE: Now I _____ really worried about my mother. She _____ with James
          2.   3.

          last Monday. They _____ at a Japanese restaurant and the movies.
                            4.

          She_____ at a party with him on Tuesday. They _____ together on
             5.   6.

          Wednesday and Thursday. Now there _____ a message on our answering
                                            7.

          machine. They _____ on their way to Walt Disney World and Epcot Center.
                        8.

ELENORE: But Pete, your mom sounds so happy. Isn't that wonderful?

③ EPCOT CENTER   Grammar Notes 1–4

Complete the story. Use the simple present or simple past tense of each verb.

Epcot Center _____is_____ in
            1. (be)

Orlando, Florida. It _____
                     2. (be)

open every day of the year. Epcot

Center _____ two separate
       3. (have)

areas. One area _____
                4. (show)

things from all over the world.

The other area _____
               5. (have)

scientific exhibits.

     Lulu and James _____ to Epcot Center yesterday. They _____ there all
                    6. (go)   7. (stay)

day. They _____ many of the pavilions. They _____ Mexican and Chinese
          8. (visit)   9. (eat)

food. They _____ souvenirs from Morocco and _____ photos of
           10. (buy)   11. (take)

everything.

     The weather _____ good, but they _____ glad because the lines
                 12. (be, not)   13. (be)

_____ long. James and Lulu _____ everything about Epcot.
14. (be, not)   15. (enjoy)

4 CONFIRMING INFORMATION   Grammar Notes 5–6

Complete these negative questions.

1. A: _____Aren't_____ you tired of studying?

   B: No, I'm not.

2. A: _____ you speak a little Spanish?

   B: Yes, I do.

3. A: _____ he buy a motorcycle?

   B: No, he didn't.

4. A: _____ it hot yesterday?

   B: Yes, it was.

5 QUESTIONS   Grammar Notes 5–6

A. *Write* **yes / no** *questions.*

1. be / you / in class yesterday

   _Were you in class yesterday?_____

2. be / you / in Disney World / last year

   _____

3. take a vacation / last summer

   _____

4. study English / last year

   _____

5. see the film *Star Wars* / as a child

   _____

B. *Now use the words above and write negative* **yes / no** *questions.*

1. _____

2. _____

3. _____

4. _____

5. _____

COMMUNICATION PRACTICE

6 WEREN'T YOU IN CLASS YESTERDAY?

Work with a partner. Ask your partner the questions in Exercises 4 and 5. Use negative questions when you think you know the answer.

7 WHAT WERE YOU LIKE AS A CHILD?

Work with a partner. Ask your partner what he or she was like as a child. Look at Boxes A and B for ideas.

EXAMPLE:

A: When you were a child, were you talkative?

B: Yes. Once my teacher wrote a note to my mother, "Bernie never stops talking. He's very bright, but he needs to give other children a turn." What were you like as a child? Did you study hard?

A: No, I didn't. I began to study hard in high school.

A. Were you _____?	B. Did you _____?
athletic—uninterested in sports naughty—well behaved stubborn—easygoing talkative—quiet—shy	study hard play with dolls / guns / video games watch a lot of TV like music / art / dance fight with your brother / sister

8 GUESSING WHY

Work with a partner. Read each sentence together. Then give three possible reasons to explain why.

EXAMPLE:

A: John didn't go to work today.

B: He felt sick.

OR

He was lazy.

OR

His wife had a baby.

1. John didn't go to work today.
2. Our teacher was absent today.
3. A man bought his wife a ring.
4. Your boss yelled at you.
5. A man wore a mask.
6. Some children wore uniforms.

WH- QUESTIONS IN THE SIMPLE PAST TENSE

GRAMMAR **IN CONTEXT**

WARM UP   Do you like quiz shows? What kinds of questions do you like best? Questions about art? sports? literature? history? entertainment?

Carol and her boyfriend Dan are watching a new quiz show. Listen and read.

DAN: Is it 7:00 o'clock yet?

CAROL: Just about. Why?

DAN: That new quiz show "Win a Fortune" is on. It's good. Let's watch it.

CAROL: Okay.

HOST: Good evening and welcome to "Win a Fortune." With us tonight are John daSilva from Naples, Florida, and Amy O'Donnell from Racine, Wisconsin. John, Amy, press the button as soon as you know the answer. Then give three more correct answers on that topic and you win $5,000. Okay. Now. Our first question is in the field of art. **Who painted *The Night Watch*?**
[Amy buzzes]

HOST: Okay, Amy?

AMY: Rembrandt.

HOST: Good. Next, **in what century did Rembrandt live?**

AMY: The seventeenth century.

269

HOST: Great. Two down and two to go. **Where was Rembrandt born? In what country?**

AMY: In Holland.

HOST: Good. Now you have just one more question to answer. This one of course is a little more difficult. **What was Rembrandt's full name?**

AMY: Hmm. I . . . uh . . . I don't know.

DAN: It's Rembrandt van Rijn.

HOST: I'm so sorry, Amy. It's Rembrandt van Rijn.

CAROL: Hey, you're good, Dan.

HOST: Our next question is in the field of music. **Who married Yoko Ono?**
[John buzzes]

HOST: John?

JOHN: John Lennon.

HOST: Okay. Now, **what was the name of John Lennon's group?**

JOHN: The Beatles.

HOST: Good. Now John, remember, two more correct answers and you win $5,000. **Where did the Beatles come from?**

JOHN: Liverpool, England.

HOST: Right again. Now our final question. **When did the Beatles make their last appearance together?**

JOHN: Uh . . . Was it 1965?

DAN: It was 1966.

HOST: Gee, I'm sorry, John. You were almost correct. It was 1966. Okay, it's time for a new question.

CAROL: You're pretty smart, Dan. Why don't *you* go on the show?

DAN: Maybe I will.

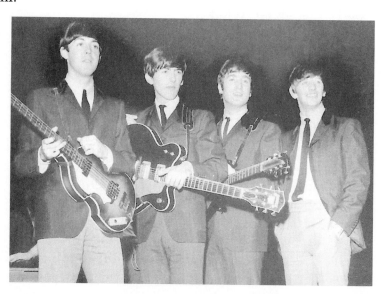

GRAMMAR **PRESENTATION**
WH- QUESTIONS IN THE SIMPLE PAST TENSE

WH- WORD	DID	SUBJECT	BASE FORM	ANSWERS
WH- QUESTIONS IN THE PAST				
When		she	**arrive**?	At 7:00 P.M. (She arrived at 7:00 P.M.)
What time		it	**land**?	At noon. (It landed at noon.)
Why		we	**leave**?	We had another job. (We left because we had another job.)
What	**did**	they	**do**?	They went to the mall.
Where		he	**stay**?	At his friend's house. (He stayed at his friend's house.)
How		I	**do**?	Wonderful. (You were wonderful. OR You did a wonderful job.)
Who(m)		you	**help**?	My brother. (I helped by brother.)

WH- WORD	WAS / WERE	SUBJECT		ANSWERS
WH- QUESTIONS IN THE PAST WITH BE				
When	**was**	she	in Rome?	Last summer. (She was in Rome last summer.)
What time	**was**	it?		Ten-thirty. (It was ten-thirty.)
Why	**were**	they	late?	They missed their bus. (They were late because they missed their bus.)
What	**was**	he?		A lawyer. (He was a lawyer.)
Where	**were**	we?		In Rome. (We were in Rome.)
How	**was**	I?		Great. (You were great.)
Who(m)	**were**	you	with?	My aunt. (I was with my aunt.)

WH- WORD	PAST FORM		ANSWERS
WH- QUESTIONS ABOUT THE SUBJECT			
Who	**found**	the money?	My boyfriend. (My boyfriend found the money.)
What	**happened**?		Nothing. (Nothing happened.)

NOTES	EXAMPLES
1. Most *wh-* **questions in the simple past tense** begin with the question word followed by *did* **+ the subject + the base form**.	• **Where did you go**? • **Why did he come** late? • **How did they get** here?

2. The simple past tense with *be* and all questions about the subject do not use *did*. They begin with the question word followed by the past tense form.	**PAST TENSE WITH *BE*** • **Where were** you? • **Who was** there? **QUESTIONS ABOUT THE SUBJECT** • **Who ate** the cake? • **What happened** next?

3. Questions and statements about birth use the phrase *to be born*.	**A:** When **was** Pablo Picasso **born**? **B:** Picasso **was born** in 1881. **A:** Where **were** Pablo Picasso and Salvador Dali **born**? **B:** Picasso and Dali **were born** in Spain.

REFERENCE NOTE
See Unit 20 for a more complete discussion of *wh-* questions in the past.

FOCUSED PRACTICE

1 DISCOVER THE GRAMMAR

Listen and read the conversation in Al Brown's English class.

BEKIR: Who's that man in the picture on the wall?
I mean the man with the funny white hair.

AL BROWN: That's George Washington. He's wearing a wig.
Wigs were the style in the 1700s.

BEKIR: Who was he?

AL BROWN: Washington was the first president of the
United States.

YOLANDA: Where was he born?

YOKO: Wasn't he born in Virginia?

AL BROWN: That's right.

BEKIR: When was he born?

AL BROWN: In 1732. He became the commander-in-chief
of the Continental Army during the American Revolution.

BEKIR: What was the war about?

AL BROWN: It was a war for independence from Great Britain.

YOKO: How was he as a leader?

AL BROWN: Excellent.

BEKIR: Why?

AL BROWN: Well, he surprised the British many times. And he was a good example for his
soldiers. He stayed with them during the bad times—like the long, cold winter
at Valley Forge.

BEKIR: How long did the war last?

AL BROWN: Eight years. Washington did a lot for our country. After the war, he was elected
the first president of the United States. He is called the father of our country.

BEKIR: He sounds like Ataturk. Ataturk was also a brilliant soldier and leader. He was
the father of modern Turkey.

YOKO: When did he rule?

BEKIR: From 1923 to 1938. He really changed Turkish life. Wasn't Simón Bolívar the
father of half a dozen countries in South America?

PEDRO: Yes, he was.

Now read the conversation and underline all the **wh-** *questions in the past.*

2 NEWS ABOUT LULU

Carol and Yoko are back at their apartment after their classes. Fill in the blanks with the questions in the box. Then listen and check your work.

How were your classes?	How's Grandma?
What's so funny?	Why was he so upset?
What was it about?	Where did they meet?
Where did they go?	

CAROL: Hi, Yoko. <u>How were your classes?</u>
1.

YOKO: Okay. Al Brown's class was interesting.

CAROL: _____
2.

YOKO: It was about leaders from different countries.

CAROL: Sounds good. Any mail?

YOKO: There's a letter from your mom.

[*Carol reads the letter and laughs.*]

YOKO: _____
3.

CAROL: My grandma Lulu has a boyfriend and my dad's worried. I have to call home.

ELENORE: Hello.

CAROL: Hi? Mom?

ELENORE: Hi, Carol.

CAROL: I got your letter. How's everything? _____?
4.

ELENORE: She's fine, at least I hope so.

CAROL: Tell me about her boyfriend.

ELENORE: Well, his name's James Belmont.

CAROL: _____
5.

ELENORE: He's Grandma's photography teacher. Grandma Lulu and James went away for a couple of days last week.

CAROL: No kidding! _____
6.

ELENORE: Epcot Center. Dad was upset.

CAROL: _____
7.

ELENORE: I'm not sure.

CAROL: Well, I think it's wonderful for Grandma to get out.

ELENORE: I hope you're right.

3 A CON MAN

*Use these words to write questions in the past. Then read the newspaper article
and answer the questions.*

1. Who / be / Todd Westin

   Who was Todd Westin?   He was a con man.

2. When / the police / arrest / him

3. Who / meet / Todd Westin / five years ago

4. Where / she / meet him

5. What / Westin / give her

6. Why / be / Sadie / grateful to Westin

7. What / happen / to her $30,000

8. Where / Westin / born

The Daily Times

CON MAN ARRESTED IN FLORIDA

Yesterday afternoon police arrested con man Todd Westin in the Palm Beach airport. The 51-year-old Westin stole over a million dollars from wealthy older women all over the United States.

Sadie Wills, 80, is one of twenty women who lost money because of Westin. She says, "Five years ago I met Westin at the library. He was always polite and friendly to me. He dressed well, read good books, and drove an expensive car. After a year he gave me some good advice about money. I made over $600. I was very grateful. Then he told me about a new investment. He offered to do the paperwork. I thought he was my friend. I trusted him, so I gave him $30,000. Last week I discovered that all my money was gone."

Westin was born in Chicago. He lived in four different states before coming to Florida. In every state Westin took money from women who trusted him.

4 JAMES AND LULU

Write **wh-** *questions in the past. Use the words below. Then read Pete and Elenore's conversation and answer the questions.*

1. Who / speak with Lulu

   Who spoke to Lulu   ?   Elenore spoke to Lulu   .

2. What / Lulu say about James

   _____?   _____.

3. What / happen to a few seniors in Lulu's community

   _____?   _____.

4. How / Lulu feel before

   _____?   _____.

ELENORE: Hi, Pete? It's Elenore. Listen, Pete, I have good news about Mom.

PETE: I'm ready for some good news. Did you tell her about that Florida con man?

ELENORE: Yes.

PETE: Well, what did she say?

ELENORE: She told me that James is not a con man. Anyway, James isn't her boyfriend. He's her business partner. They're starting a business.

PETE: A business? Why did she start a business? She doesn't need money.

ELENORE: Well, there were a few muggings in her community. Most of the victims were seniors.

PETE: I remember. Mom was upset about it. But what does that have to do with her business?

ELENORE: After the muggings, seniors stopped going out. Now James and Lulu are organizing safe trips for seniors. Anyway, Lulu sounds happy. She felt lonely before, but now she's not. She says that James is better than all the pills in the world.

PETE: Well, I'm still not sure about him.

ELENORE: Pete . . . come on. Trust your mother.

PETE: Okay, Elenore. Maybe I'm wrong. Maybe James is good for her.

COMMUNICATION PRACTICE

5 A QUIZ SHOW

Work in small groups. Prepare a quiz show. Write questions in the past tense.
Choose a host or hostess from your group. Choose contestants from classmates in
other groups.

EXAMPLE:

Who painted the *Mona Lisa*?

What was the *Titanic*?

When did India become independent?

Who wrote *War and Peace*?

(Answers on page 305)

6 INFORMATION GAP: GAME—WHO AM I?

Work with a partner.

Student A, your partner is a famous person from the past. Ask your partner
questions. Guess your partner's identity.

Student B, you are a famous person from the past. Turn to the Information Gap
on page 305 to find out who you are.

When / born
Where / born
What / be / your occupation
Where / begin your career
Who / discover / you
Where / be / you from 1958 to 1960
What / do / after that
When / die

7 PEOPLE OF THE PAST

Work in small groups. Each group member gathers facts about a famous person
from the past. Other group members ask questions about the person.

Tell the class some interesting facts you learned about the different people.

BE GOING TO FOR THE **FUTURE;** **FUTURE** AND **PAST TIME MARKERS**

GRAMMAR **IN CONTEXT**

WARM UP   Can you think of a reason why a person who needs a hearing aid doesn't get one? Do you know anyone who has a hearing aid?

Bertha and Lulu are going to spend the day together. Listen and read their conversation.

> I'm going to get a hearing aid.
>
> You're going to get a lemonade?

BERTHA: Hello.

LULU: Hi, Bertha. It's me, Lulu.

BERTHA: Hi, Lulu.

LULU: Listen, Bertha. James has an exhibit of photos at the Convention Center. I'd like to go. Are you free this morning?

BERTHA: Sorry. **I'm going to see** an ear, nose, and throat doctor.

LULU: What was that?

BERTHA: *[louder]* **I'm going** to the ear, nose, and throat doctor.

LULU: Oh. Why? You're not sick, are you?

BERTHA: No. **I'm going to get** a hearing aid.

LULU: What did you say? **You're going to get** a lemonade?

BERTHA: *[louder]* Not a lemonade—a hearing aid!

LULU: Oh, a hearing aid. Why?

BERTHA: Well, I have a little trouble hearing.

LULU: No you don't. These days everyone is whispering. Tell people to speak louder. I do. You don't need a hearing aid.

BERTHA: Why not? The new ones are small and comfortable.

LULU: Really?

BERTHA: Yes. I have an idea. Come with me to the doctor this morning. She's very nice and her office is near the Convention Center. In the afternoon we can see James's exhibit together.

LULU: All right. Listen. Don't forget your umbrella. They say **it's going to rain** today. **Are we going to meet** at the bus stop?

BERTHA: Okay. Let's meet at the bus stop at ten.

LULU: When?

BERTHA: Ten.

LULU: Bye.

GRAMMAR **PRESENTATION**
BE GOING TO FOR THE FUTURE; FUTURE AND PAST TIME MARKERS

AFFIRMATIVE / NEGATIVE STATEMENTS

SUBJECT + *BE*	*(NOT)*	*GOING TO*	BASE FORM OF VERB	
I'm				
You're				
He's She's	(not)	going to	study	tomorrow.
We're You're They're				
It's	(not)	going to	rain	tomorrow.

YES / NO QUESTIONS

BE	SUBJECT	*GOING TO*	BASE FORM OF VERB	
Am	I			
Are	you			
Is	he she	going to	study	next week?
Are	we you they			
Is	it	going to	rain	tomorrow?

SHORT ANSWERS

AFFIRMATIVE	NEGATIVE
Yes, you are.	No, you're not.
Yes, I am.	No, I'm not.
Yes, he is. Yes, she is.	No, he's not. No, she's not.
Yes, you are. Yes, we are. Yes, they are.	No, you're not. No, we're not. No, they're not.
Yes, it is.	No, it's not.

WH- QUESTIONS ABOUT THE SUBJECT

WH- WORD	BE	GOING TO	BASE FORM OF VERB
Who	is	going to	**come**?
What			**happen**?

SHORT ANSWERS

Lulu and Bertha.
They're going to see James' exhibit.

OTHER WH- QUESTIONS

WH- WORD	BE	SUBJECT	GOING TO	BASE FORM OF VERB
What	is	she		**do**?
Where	is	the plane		**land**?
When	are	you		**arrive**?
Why	are	you	going to	**leave**?
Who(m)	are	they		**see**?
How	am	I		**travel**?
How long	am	I		**work**?

SHORT ANSWERS

Meet her friend.
At the Los Angeles airport.
In the afternoon.
I want to.
Dr. Finkelstein.
By boat.
About two months.

TIME MARKERS
FUTURE TIME MARKERS

tomorrow	
tomorrow	morning afternoon evening night
next	week month year Monday weekend
in	2010 the twenty-second century twenty years two weeks a few days
today	
this	morning afternoon evening
tonight	

TIME MARKERS
PAST TIME MARKERS

yesterday		
yesterday	morning afternoon evening	
last	night week month year Monday weekend	
in	1992 the nineteenth century	
twenty years a year		ago
today		
this	morning afternoon evening	
tonight		

NOTES	**EXAMPLES**
1. There are different ways to express **future time**.	• We**'re going to buy** a car. • We**'re buying** a car tomorrow. • We**'ll buy** a car.
2. Use **be + going to** + base form of the verb for general facts in the future.	• The scientists **are going to meet** in Rome.
3. Use **be + going to** + base form of the verb to make predictions.	**FORTUNE TELLER:** You **are going to be** rich and famous.
4. Use **be + going to** + base form of the verb to talk about definite plans that were made before now.	**A:** Are you free this evening? **B:** No, we're not. We**'re going to visit** Aunt Valerie.
5. Always use the **base form** of the verb after *be going to*. Remember that the base form does not change.	• He's going to **buy** a car. • They're going to **buy** a car.
6. Use *probably* with *be going to* for the future to say that your plans are not definite.	• We**'re probably going to buy** a new car next month.
7. Use contractions of *be* in speaking and informal writing. ▶ **BE CAREFUL!** There are two ways to make negative contractions with pronouns + *be* for all forms except *I'm not*.	• **He's** going to buy a new car. • **He isn't** going to buy a motorcycle. <center>OR</center>• **He's not** going to buy a motorcycle.

(continued on next page)

8. Sometimes the **present progressive + a future time marker** are used for the future. This is especially true with the verb *go* and with other words of movement or transportation.

present progressive   time marker
- We**'re going** there **next week**.

     OR

- We**'re going to go** there next week.

- I**'m leaving** for Rome in two days.

     OR

- I**'m going to leave** for Rome in two days.

9. Some **time markers** are used only for the **past** or only for the **future**. Other time markers can be used for the past or the future.

past
- **Yesterday** I went to work.

future
- **Tomorrow** I'm not going to go to work.

past or future
- **In** 2020 he will be twenty-one years old.
- **In** 1996 they visited Taiwan.

REFERENCE NOTE
See Units 8 and 25 for a discussion of the present progressive.

PRONUNCIATION NOTE
When speaking, people often say "gonna" (/gənə/) for **going to**.

       I'm (/gənə/) visit her. They're (/gənə/) go to the theater.

("Gonna" is never used in writing.)

FOCUSED PRACTICE

1 DISCOVER THE GRAMMAR

Match the sentences.

_____ **1.** Yoko is homesick.

_____ **2.** Bertha has a hearing problem.

_____ **3.** Pete's raincoat is dirty.

_____ **4.** Lulu likes photography.

_____ **5.** The Winstons' car doesn't work.

_____ **6.** Bertha's friend Adele is very happy.

_____ **7.** It's late and I'm tired.

a. She's going to the ear, nose, and throat doctor next week.

b. I'm going to sleep in a few minutes.

c. She's going to a photography show tomorrow.

d. She's going to be a grandmother.

e. He's not going to wear it. He's going to take it to the cleaners.

f. She's going to call home this evening.

g. They're going to take it to the auto repair shop.

In which sentences is the present progressive used for the future? _____.

2 LULU AND BERTHA   Grammar Notes 3, 5–7

Listen to each situation. Circle the answer that describes what Lulu and Bertha are probably going to do.

1. They're probably going to _____.
 a. go to the photography show
 b. go to the doctor
 c. have lunch

2. They're probably going to _____.
 a. sit at the counter
 b. sit at a table
 c. sit on the floor

3. Lulu _____.
 a. and Bertha are both going to order dessert
 b. is probably going to order dessert, but Bertha isn't
 c. is probably not going to order dessert, but Bertha is

4. Lulu and Bertha are probably _____.
 a. going to leave a big tip
 b. going to leave a small tip
 c. not going to leave a tip

5. They're probably going to _____.
 a. take a bus
 b. take a taxi
 c. walk

❸ A TRIP TO SEATTLE

Next month Pete and Elenore's daughter Norma is going to go to a teachers convention in Seattle with a friend. Write questions about her plans. Use **be going to** *for the future.*

1. Norma / combine her convention with a short vacation?

_____

2. she / share a hotel room with her friend?

_____

3. How many days / they / spend sightseeing in Seattle?

_____

4. they / go to the top of the Space Needle and take a ferry boat to Puget Island?

_____

🔊 *Now listen and answer the questions.*

4 AT A COFFEE SHOP

Pete and Elenore are having lunch in a coffee shop. Complete the sentences with the verbs in parentheses. Use the simple past tense and **be going to** *for the future.*

PETE: The turkey looks good. _____Are_____ you ___going to order___ a turkey
                                                          1. (order)

sandwich?

ELENORE: No, just a salad.

PETE: What _____ you _____? Coffee?
                                          2. (drink)

ELENORE: No, I _____ three cups this morning. I _____ a glass
                              3. (have)   4. (have)

of lemonade with my salad.

PETE: How about dessert?

ELENORE: No, I _____ a big breakfast. I _____ dessert.
                              5. (eat)   6. (have, not)

PETE: Guess what I _____?
                              7. (order)

ELENORE: That's simple. A turkey sandwich on a roll with lettuce and tomato.

PETE: How _____ you _____?
                                          8. (know)

ELENORE: Just a good guess.

5 LULU'S PLANS

Look at Lulu's schedule for next week. Write questions. Use the present progressive for the future. Then answer the questions.

1. Lulu / go / to the dentist next Wednesday at 10:00

A: _Is Lulu going to the dentist next Wednesday at 10:00?_

B: _No, she isn't. She's going to the dentist next Monday at 10:30._

2. When / Lulu / meet / Bertha

A: _When is Lulu meeting Bertha?_

B: _Next Friday at 10:00._

3. What / Lulu / do / next Friday afternoon

A: _____

B: _____

4. Where / she / go / Thursday morning

A: _____

B: _____

5. When / she / do / volunteer work at the hospital

A: _____

B: _____

6. she / go / to a photography class on Tuesday

A: _____

B: _____

7. What / she / do / Monday morning

A: _____

B: _____

Monday
dentist— 10:30 A.M.

Tuesday
eye doctor— 2:00 P.M.

Wednesday
trip to Palm Beach— 9:30 A.M.

Thursday
hairdresser— 11:00 A.M. volunteer work at hospital— 2:30 P.M.

Friday
meet Bertha— 10:00 A.M. photography class— 1:00 P.M.

6 EDITING

Correct the mistakes in the conversations.

1. (3 mistakes)

    BERTHA: What are you doing?

    LULU: I'm preparing packages for Carol and Norma.

    BERTHA: Towels?

    LULU: Yes. I buy them last week, but I don't really need them. I'm go to the post office this afternoon. I'm going send them to Carol and Norma.

    BERTHA: You're a nice grandmother. Those towels are beautiful.

2. (2 mistakes)

    ELENORE: Doug, your hair is getting long. When you going to get a haircut?

    DOUG: I'm not. I like it this way. Soon I'm going have a ponytail.

3. (2 mistakes)

    CAROL: I'm really upset. I lost my wallet this morning.

    YOKO: Oh, no. What you going to do?

    CAROL: Nothing right now, but later this afternoon I'm go get a new ID card and a new library card.

4. (3 mistakes)

    LULU: Mmm. Those cupcakes smell good. When did you put them in the oven?

    BERTHA: Before twenty minutes. I take them out in ten minutes.

    LULU: Are you going frost them?

    BERTHA: I don't know.

    LULU: I know a recipe for delicious chocolate frosting.

    BERTHA: What about your diet?

    LULU: Hush up.

COMMUNICATION PRACTICE

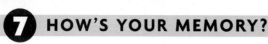

7 HOW'S YOUR MEMORY?

*Play a memory game with the class. Sit in a circle. The first student tells one
thing he or she is going to do after school. The next student tells about the first
student and about his or her plans.*

> **EXAMPLE:**
> **A:** After school I'm going to buy a watch.
> **B:** After school A is going to buy a watch. I'm not going to buy a watch. I'm
> going to study at the library.
> **C:** After school A is going to buy a watch and B is going to study at the library.
> I'm not going to buy a watch, and I'm not going to study at the library. I'm
> going to listen to my new tape.

Continue as long as each student remembers what the others have said.

8 TELL A STORY

Work with a partner. Continue this story. Tell your story to the class.

Mary was a poor and hardworking _____. For fifteen years Mary

_____ Sam Clark. Sam Clark died last month. To Mary's surprise,

Sam left Mary _____. Mary is going to make many changes.

She . . .

9 A BIG CHANGE IN YOUR LIFE

Work with a partner.

*Student A, talk about a change (a marriage, a graduation, a move, a new job)
that is going to take place in your life or in the life of someone you know well.*

Student B, ask your partner questions about the situation. Then change roles.

> **EXAMPLE:**
> **A:** My sister is going to get married next month.
>
> **Possible Questions**
> Who's she going to marry?
> Is she going to have a big wedding? Where is it going to be?
> Where's she going to live?

⑩ A GOOD TIME TO MEET

Work in small groups.

Write down the time and things you are going to do in the next three days.

TODAY	TOMORROW	THE DAY AFTER TOMORROW

Your group wants to meet some time today, tomorrow, or the next day. You need to find a time when everyone is free. Use **be going to** *or the present progressive for the future.*

EXAMPLE:

A: I'm free tomorrow at 2 o'clock. Are you doing anything at that time?

B: Yes, I'm going to visit my uncle. How about this evening at eight o'clock?

A: No, that's not a good time for me. How about tonight at nine o'clock?

B: That's good. How about you, C? Are you doing anything tonight at nine?

WILL FOR THE FUTURE

GRAMMAR **IN CONTEXT**

WARM UP Do you believe that winning a lot of money makes a person happy?

Listen and read this conversation between a TV news reporter and two lottery winners.

REPORTER: Good evening. Here with me now are our two lucky lottery winners, Susan Kerins and Jim Morris. So, Susan, now that you're very, very rich, what are you going to do?

SUSAN: Well . . . **I'll probably leave** my job. I'm a waitress. My customers are nice, but after fifteen years . . . I'm ready to see new places.

REPORTER: **Will** you **travel**?

SUSAN: I think so. **I'll probably go** to Ireland. That's where my grandparents were born. And **I'll buy** a big, beautiful house with room for all my friends and relatives.

REPORTER: Sounds wonderful. I bet **you'll find** you have a lot of friends and relatives. How about you, Jim, **what will you do** with all your money?

JIM: I think **I'll give** it **away**.

REPORTER: What was that? You**'ll give** it **away**? To whom?

JIM: To people who really need the money. **I'll ask** people to write to me and explain why they need money. And **I'll choose** the people who need it the most.

REPORTER: Wow! That's very unusual. And generous. Uh . . . what about your wife and family? Do you have any idea what they **will say** about this?

JIM: I'm sure **my wife will want** me to keep the money and **my family will be** very angry. But **I won't listen** to them.

REPORTER: Ladies and gentlemen, get out your pens and start writing those letters now. A letter to generous Jim may get *you* a lot of money. And now a word from our sponsor. Don't go away. **We'll be** back in two minutes with more details from "Generous Jim."

GRAMMAR **PRESENTATION**
Will FOR THE **Future**

SUBJECT	*WILL*	BASE FORM OF VERB	
I You He She It We You They	will	leave	tomorrow.

AFFIRMATIVE STATEMENTS

CONTRACTIONS

I will	→ **I'll**
you will	→ **you'll**
he will	→ **he'll**
she will	→ **she'll**
it will	→ **it'll**
we will	→ **we'll**
you will	→ **you'll**
they will	→ **they'll**

NEGATIVE STATEMENTS

SUBJECT	*WILL NOT (WON'T)*	BASE FORM OF VERB
I You He She It We You They	will not won't	travel.

YES / NO QUESTIONS

WILL	SUBJECT	BASE FORM OF VERB	
Will	I you he she we you they	paint	tomorrow?
Will	it	snow	tonight?

SHORT ANSWERS

AFFIRMATIVE	NEGATIVE
Yes, you **will**.	No, you **won't**.
Yes, I **will**.	No, I **won't**.
Yes, he **will**.	No, he **won't**.
Yes, she **will**.	No, she **won't**.
Yes, you **will**.	No, you **won't**.
Yes, we **will**.	No, we **won't**.
Yes, they **will**.	No, they **won't**.
Yes, it **will**.	No, it **won't**.

(continued on next page)

WH- QUESTIONS ABOUT THE SUBJECT		
WH- WORD	**WILL**	**BASE FORM OF VERB**
Who	will	**help**?
What		**happen**?

OTHER WH- QUESTIONS			
WH- WORD	**WILL**	**SUBJECT**	**BASE FORM OF VERB**
What		I	**do**?
Where		you	**go**?
When		he	**return**?
Who(m)	will	she	**visit**?
Why		it	**happen**?
How		we	**travel**?
How long		they	**study**?

NOTES

EXAMPLES

1. Use *will* for general facts about the future.

- The scientists **will meet** in Australia.

2. Use *will* to make predictions.

FORTUNE TELLER: You **will have** six children.

3. Use *will* for the future when you are deciding to do something at the time of speaking.

A: How much do those umbrellas cost?

B: Six dollars each.

A: That's a good price. **I'll take** two.

4. Use *will* to make a promise or give assurance.	• **I'll be** back in five minutes. • Don't worry. **We'll** help you.

5. Use *will* to ask for or to offer something.	**A: Will** you **help** me? **B:** I'**ll help**.

6. ***Won't*** is the contraction of **will + not**. It has two meanings. You can use *won't* to mean the negative future. You can also use *won't* to mean refuse(s) to.	• He **won't be** in school today. He's sick. • The child **won't eat** his vegetables.

7. Use the **base form** of the verb after *will* or *won't*. Remember that the base form does not change.	• The plane will **arrive** at 6:00 P.M. • The plane won't **be** late.

8. Use **contractions** of *will* with pronouns in speaking and in informal writing. Do not use contractions in affirmative short answers.	• **We'll** be there before three o'clock. • Will they be there? • Yes, they **will**. NOT ~~Yes, they'll.~~

9. To say that something is not definite, use ***probably*** with *will* for the future.	• She will **probably** visit Ireland in June.

FOCUSED PRACTICE

1 DISCOVER THE GRAMMAR

Read and underline the examples of **will** *for the future.*

DOUG: I'm starving. When <u>will</u> dinner <u>be</u> ready?

ELENORE: It won't be ready for half an hour.

DOUG: I guess I'll have a candy bar.

ELENORE: Don't. It'll spoil your appetite.

DOUG: No, it won't. Nothing spoils my appetite. Remember, I'm a growing boy.

What does **won't** *mean in this conversation?*

a. negative future

b. refuse to

2 A TRIP TO PALM BEACH Grammar Notes 1–2, 4, 6–9

Tamar Lyman is going on a trip to Palm Beach organized by Lulu and James. Listen to Tamar's conversation with Lulu. Write the group's activities for the trip. Use the phrases in the box.

> arrive home
> get on the bus
> have lunch
> leave for Palm Beach
> meet at the Star Diner
> arrive in Palm Beach

1. At nine o'clock, they'll ___meet at the Star Diner_____.

2. At ten o'clock, they'll _____.

3. At eleven o'clock, they'll _____.

4. At one o'clock, they'll _____.

5. At two o'clock, they'll probably _____.

6. At three o'clock, they'll probably _____.

3 THE WEATHER

Complete the conversation. Use the affirmative, negative, or question form of **will**
for the future and the verb in parentheses. Use contractions when possible.

BERTHA: Listen to that rain. It sure is raining hard. When ___will___ it ___stop___?
1. (stop)

LULU: Don't worry. It _____ long.
2. (last)

BERTHA: How do you know?

LULU: It never does.

BERTHA: What's the forecast for this afternoon?

LULU: It _____ warm and sunny.
3. (be)

BERTHA: Then I _____ the kitchen. I _____ to the beach instead.
4. (clean, not)   5. (go)

LULU: Good idea. I _____ you at the beach and I _____ you photos of
6. (meet)   7. (show)

my last trip.

BERTHA: Okay. _____ you _____ that novel you told me about?
8. (bring)

LULU: Of course. I _____ you at the usual spot at two o'clock.
9. (see)

BERTHA: See you then.

4 PROMISES AND REQUESTS

Rearrange the words to make statements or ask questions.

1. shortly / Someone / be with you / will

_____Someone will be with you shortly._____

2. you / Will / me / marry

_____

3. I / be / long / won't

_____

4. I'll / you / forget / never

_____

5. quiet / you / be / please / Will

_____

6. hurt / It / won't

_____

5 GRAND OPENING

*Read this advertisement for a new branch of the Superking Clothing store. Then write **wh-** questions with **will** about the underlined words.*

1. ___What will open on Main Street next Saturday?___

2. _____

3. _____

4. _____

5. _____

COMMUNICATION PRACTICE

6 A CLASS SURVEY ABOUT THE FUTURE

What do you think the future will be like? Check (✔) Yes, No, or Maybe for each question.

By the year 2100, do you think . . .

	Yes	No	Maybe
1. the climate in the United States will be different?	☐	☐	☐
2. the country you are now in will be a superpower?	☐	☐	☐
3. cars will use solar energy for power?	☐	☐	☐
4. the average person will live to be 100 years old?	☐	☐	☐
5. men and women will still marry?	☐	☐	☐
6. older people will live with their children?	☐	☐	☐
7. people will take vacations on the moon?	☐	☐	☐
8. men and women will have equal rights?	☐	☐	☐

Now take a class survey. One student reads the questions and asks, "How many checked Yes? No? Maybe?" for each question. Discuss each question and your class's predictions.

Did you find any interesting results?

7 WHAT DO YOU THINK?

Complete the questions. Then take turns asking your classmates their opinions.

1. Will _____ still be popular in _____? (Name something or someone that is popular now and a time in the future.)

2. Will _____ be a superpower in _____? (Write the name of a country and a year.)

3. Will _____ be the president of _____ in _____? (Write the name of a person, a country, and a year.)

Report your results to the class.

> **EXAMPLE:**
> I asked six people this question: "Will VCRs still be popular in ten years?"
> Four out of six students said, "Yes."

8 RESOLUTIONS

Many people in the United States make New Year's resolutions. New Year's resolutions are decisions or promises you make to yourself for the new year. Some examples are "I won't smoke anymore," "I won't come to work late anymore," "I'm going to answer letters right away," or "I'm not going to eat so much candy."

Write down three resolutions. Read your resolutions to the class. Then put all the resolutions in an envelope. Check the resolutions at the end of the term. How many students are keeping their resolutions?

9 FORTUNE TELLERS

*You are a fortune teller. Write a wonderful fortune. Use **will** or **be going to** for the future. Hang your fortune on the wall for the class to read.*

EXAMPLE:
You will be rich and famous. You're going to live in a beautiful home on a tropical island.

Number all the fortunes. Take turns reading the fortunes aloud. Then each student chooses his or her favorite fortune. Did many students choose the same fortune?

10 A PROVERB

Can you explain this proverb? Can you give an example from your life?

A small leak will sink a big ship.

REVIEW OR SELFTEST

I. *Circle the letter that best completes each sentence.*

1. Where _____ tomorrow night?   A B C D
   (A) you going
   (B) are you going
   (C) will you going
   (D) did you go

2. Where _____ last night?   A B C D
   (A) you went
   (B) are you going
   (C) did you go
   (D) did you went

3. Who _____ you at the airport yesterday?   A B C D
   (A) did meet you
   (B) is meeting you
   (C) met you
   (D) will meet

4. Will she _____ the car?   A B C D
   (A) to take
   (B) takes
   (C) take
   (D) going to take

5. Is he _____ his house?   A B C D
   (A) going to sell
   (B) going to sells
   (C) will sell
   (D) sold

6. How long _____ in Vermont?   A B C D
   (A) they going to stay
   (B) will they to stay
   (C) are they going to stay
   (D) they staying

II. *Complete these negative questions.*

EXAMPLE:
A: _____Aren't_____ you late?
B: No, I'm not. I'm on time.

1. A: _____ you go to the University of Michigan?

B: Yes, I did.

2. A: _____ you in Japan last year?

B: Yes, I was.

3. A: _____ she beautiful?

B: She certainly is.

4. A: _____ you Tom Cruise?

B: No, I'm not.

III. *Read the information in the box. Then complete the questions.*

Thomas Jefferson—1743–1826
Born—Virginia
Wrote—Declaration of Independence in 1776
Third president of the United States—1801–1809
Wife—Martha

1. A: _____ the third president _____?

B: Thomas Jefferson.

2. A: _____?

B: In 1743.

3. A: _____?

B: In 1826.

4. A: _____?

B: In Virginia.

5. A: _____?

B: In 1776.

6. **A:** _____?

   B: For eight years.

7. **A:** _____ his wife's name?

   B: Martha.

IV. *Complete the conversations. Choose from the words in parentheses.*

1. **CAROL:** I'm really tired of the rain. It _____ yesterday. It
   (rains, rained)
   _____ right now, and the weather report says
   ('s raining, rains)
   tomorrow it _____, too.
   (rains, 's going to rain)

   YOKO: Oh, no.

2. **NANCY:** Would you like to see the new art exhibit this afternoon?

   NORMA: I'm sorry, I can't. I _____ for a new sofa.
   ('m going to look, look)

   NANCY: How about on Wednesday?

   NORMA: Wednesday I _____ a haircut. I'm free on Thursday.
   (got, 'm getting)

   NANCY: Good. Let's go to the exhibit on Thursday.

   NORMA: I'd really like to.

3. **BERTHA:** _____ you _____ the news about
   (Do, Did)   (hear, heard)
   James? He _____ first prize for one of his photographs
   (won, 's winning)
   last week.

   TAMAR: I know. I _____ it's wonderful. What
   ('m thinking, think)
   _____ he _____ with the prize money?
   (is, does)   (going to do, do)

   BERTHA: He _____ Kenya.
   ('s going to visit, visits)

   TAMAR: Why Kenya?

   BERTHA: He _____ pictures of wild animals there.
   (takes, 's going to take)

4. **ELENORE:** Doug, _____ you _____ the video?
   (do, did)   (returning, return)

   DOUG: Not yet. I _____ it after dinner.
   ('ll return, return)

   ELENORE: Well, don't forget. The store _____ early on weekdays.
   (closes, closing)

   DOUG: Okay, Mom.

V. *Read the questions and complete the answers. Use the correct verb tenses. There may be more than one possibility.*

1. A: What did you say? Where are you going to go this afternoon?

   B: I _____ to the supermarket.

2. A: Did he go to the bank this morning?

   B: No, he _____ to the library.

3. A: When did she bake that cake?

   B: She _____ it early this morning.

4. A: When will you be back?

   B: I _____ back before midnight.

VI. *Correct the nine other mistakes in Elenore's conversation with her friend Denise.*

ELENORE: Hello.

DENISE: Hi, Elenore. This is Denise. I ~~did~~ called you this morning. You wasn't home.

ELENORE: I was at the bank. I be there for two hours this morning. The bank teller made a mistake. Then when I showed her the mistake, she got angry. And after that the bank's computer went down.

DENISE: That's awful. What you do?

ELENORE: I complained to the manager.

DENISE: Will she help?

ELENORE: No, she didn't. In fact, she did laugh and did say, "Put your money under your mattress!"

DENISE: Wow! What did you doing then?

ELENORE: I was very angry. I took all my money out of my account.

DENISE: Good for you.

ELENORE: Tomorrow I wrote a letter to the bank director. And I'm going put my money in the bank across the street.

FROM GRAMMAR TO WRITING
TIME CLAUSES WITH *WHEN*

❶ *How can you combine these sentences using* **when***?*

1. I was six years old. I loved to play with dolls.

_____

2. I will graduate next year. I will work for a newspaper.

_____

Study this information about present, past, and future time clauses.

TIME CLAUSES WITH *WHEN*

1. Time Clauses

We can combine two sentences that tell about time by using a **time clause** and a **main clause**. *When I was six years old* is a **time clause**. It is not a sentence and can never stand alone. It needs a main clause.

- I was six years old. I started school.

  time clause
- **When** I was six years old,

  main clause

  I started school.

2. Present Time Clauses

When we use **present time clauses**, both parts of the sentence are written in the **present**.

present   past
- When I **get** home, I **have** dinner.

3. Past Time Clauses

When we use **past time clauses**, both parts of the sentence are written in the **past**.

past   past
- When I **got** home, I **had** dinner.

4. Future Time Clauses

When we use a **future time clause**, the future time clause uses the **simple present**. The main clause uses the **future**.

        present   future

- When I **get** home, I **will have** dinner.
  (First I'll get home. Then I'll have dinner.)

5.

You can begin a sentence with the time clause or the main clause. When the time clause begins the sentence, you need a **comma** before the main clause. There is no comma when the main clause begins the sentence.

- When I got home, I had dinner.
- I had dinner when I got home.

- When I get home, I will have dinner.
- I will have dinner when I get home.

---

2   *Rewrite this paragraph using three time clauses.*

My Dream

    I was a child. I loved to play "make-believe" games. Sometimes I was a cowboy, and sometimes I was a prince. I became a teenager. I got a job at a video store. I saw many movies. I also made a couple of videos and I acted in all the school plays. Now I'm studying film and acting at school. I will finish college next year. I will move to Hollywood. I hope to become a movie star.

---

3   *Write a paragraph about yourself at different times of your life. Include a part about your future.*

REVIEW OR SELFTEST
ANSWER KEY

I.
1. B
2. C
3. C
4. C
5. A
6. C

II.
1. Didn't
2. Weren't
3. Isn't
4. Aren't

III.
1. Who was / of the United States?
2. When was he born?
3. When did he die?
4. Where was he born?
5. When did he write the Declaration of Independence?
6. How long was he president? (How long was he president of the United States?)
7. What was his wife's name?

IV.
1. rained / 's raining / 's going to rain
2. 'm going to look / 'm getting
3. Did / hear / won / think / is / going to do / 's going to visit / 's going to take
4. did / return / 'll return / closes

V.
1. 'm going / 'm going to go
2. went
3. baked
4. 'll be ('m going to be)

VI.
2. wasn't → weren't
3. be there → was
4. What you do? → What did you do?
5. Will she help? → Did she help?
6. did laugh → laughed
7. did say → said
8. What did you doing then? → What did you do then?
9. Tomorrow I write a letter → Tomorrow I'm going to write (Tomorrow I'll write) (Tomorrow I'm writing)
10. And I'm going put → And I'm going to put

INFORMATION GAP FOR STUDENT B   Unit 30, Exercise 6

Student B, you are Elvis Presley. Answer your partner's questions.

You were a popular singer. You were born in Tupelo, Mississippi, in 1935. You began singing in a local church, and you taught yourself to play the guitar. Sam Phillips, the president of Sun Records, discovered you in 1953. By 1956 you were the most popular performer in the United States. Soon after that you became popular all over the world. Your music combined country and western music with rhythm and blues. You spent two years, from 1958 to 1960, in the army. You appeared in several movies, but none were very successful. You died in 1977. You are known as the king of Rock and Roll.

Answers to Exercise 5 on page 277
1. Leonardo da Vinci.
2. A ship that sank on its first voyage.
3. 1946
4. Leo Tolstoy

NOUNS, ARTICLES, AND QUANTIFIERS; MODALS I

PREVIEW

Carol and Yoko are preparing for a party. Listen and read their conversation.

CAROL AND YOKO HAVE A PARTY

CAROL: Hi, Bekir. You're very early. It's only six. The party isn't until eight o'clock.

BEKIR: I know. I'm here to help. I have my car. I can go to the store for you.

CAROL: Oh, Bekir. That would be wonderful.

BEKIR: So what do you need?

CAROL: We need a lot of soda and chips. And I'd like a jar of hot salsa and a few cans of tuna fish.

BEKIR: Do you have enough ice?

CAROL: We have two trays, but we might need more.

BEKIR: I'll get a bag of ice.

CAROL: Great.

BEKIR: So, how much soda will you need?

CAROL: Get five big bottles.

BEKIR: How many bags of chips?

CAROL: One extra large one.

BEKIR: Tuna?

CAROL: Three cans.

[Bekir returns an hour later.]

BEKIR: Here you are. I couldn't get an extra large bag of chips, so I bought two smaller ones.

CAROL: That's fine, but there's a little problem here.

BEKIR: A problem? What's the matter?

CAROL: It's the tuna. This is tuna for cats.

BEKIR: Oh, no.

CAROL: It's okay. I'll return it.

BEKIR: I feel sick.

CAROL: Why? You didn't eat it.

BEKIR: Not today, but this is the tuna I usually eat.

[Yoko enters the room]

BEKIR: Meow. Meow.

YOKO: What's going on?

CAROL: Bekir's learning a new language.

COMPREHENSION CHECK

Check (✓) **That's right, That's wrong,** *or* **I don't know.**

	That's right.	That's wrong.	I don't know.
1. Bekir thinks the party is at six o'clock.	☐	☐	☐
2. Carol is glad that Bekir is going shopping for the party.	☐	☐	☐
3. Carol wants a lot of soda and chips.	☐	☐	☐
4. Bekir sometimes eats tuna fish.	☐	☐	☐
5. Bekir has a cat.	☐	☐	☐

WITH PARTNERS

Work with partners. Practice the conversation on pages 306 and 307.

COUNT AND NON-COUNT NOUNS AND QUANTIFIERS

GRAMMAR **IN CONTEXT**

WARM UP   There's a saying, "An apple a day keeps the doctor away." List five healthy and five unhealthy foods. Compare your list with a partner.

 *Listen and read the conversation.*

BEKIR: I'm getting hungry. Is there anything to eat?

YOKO: Carol made **some** soup yesterday. I think there's **a little** left.

CAROL: There's **a lot** left. I put **the** soup in **the** refrigerator. I'll heat it up and we can all have **some**.

BEKIR: Mmm. Carol, this soup is out of this world.

CAROL: Thanks. And it's healthy too. My sister gave me **the** recipe.

BEKIR: What's in it?

CAROL: **One** zucchini, **a few** carrots, **some** yams, and **an** onion.

BEKIR: When you say **"a few"** carrots, exactly how many do you mean?

CAROL: **Two** or **three**. I use what I have.

BEKIR: How many yams did you use?

CAROL: Not **many**. **Two** large ones.

BEKIR: What else?

CAROL: That's it. Just add **a little** salt.

BEKIR: **Any** pepper?

CAROL: I didn't use **any**, but you can. I never use **much** pepper. Anyway, put **the** vegetables in about **three** quarts of water, add **a** vegetarian bouillon cube, and cook the soup for **an** hour and **a** half.

BEKIR: Is that it?

CAROL: I guess so. Why?

BEKIR: Well, my aunt is **a** fabulous cook, but when we try to follow her recipes, **the** food never tastes the same.

CAROL: Why?

BEKIR: I don't know. My sister says my aunt always leaves **one** ingredient out of her recipes. My dad says it's because she puts her love in it.

GRAMMAR **PRESENTATION**
COUNT AND NON-COUNT NOUNS AND QUANTIFIERS

AFFIRMATIVE STATEMENTS

COUNT NOUNS

	ARTICLE NUMBER	SINGULAR NOUN
Carol wants	a	banana.
	an	apple.
	one	banana.
		apple.

NON-COUNT NOUNS

	QUANTIFIER	NON-COUNT NOUN
Carol needs	a little	help.
	some	
	a lot of	

	NUMBER QUANTIFIER	PLURAL NOUN
Carol has	seven	friends. books.
	a few	
	some	
	several	
	a lot of	
	many	

NEGATIVE STATEMENTS

COUNT NOUNS

	ARTICLE NUMBER	SINGULAR NOUN
I didn't buy	a	pear.
	an	apple.
	one	pear.
		apple.

	NUMBER QUANTIFIER	PLURAL NOUN
I didn't buy	two	pears.
	any	
	many	
	a lot of	

NON-COUNT NOUNS

	QUANTIFIER	NON-COUNT NOUN
I didn't buy	any	milk.
	much	
	a lot of	

THE DEFINITE ARTICLE

THE

I want **the** letter.
He has **the** mail.
She has **the** packages.

NOTES	EXAMPLES

1. Use *a, an*, or *one* before a singular **count noun**. Use *a* before a consonant sound. Use *an* before a vowel sound.

- I didn't use **a** potato. <small>count</small>
- I used **an** onion. <small>count</small>
- I used **one** zucchini. <small>count</small>

To form the plural of most count nouns, add *-s* or *-es*.

- We like carrot**s**.
- Bekir washed the dish**es**.

2. Some nouns cannot be counted. They are called **non-count nouns**. Do not put *a, an*, or a number (*one, two, three*) before a non-count noun. Do not add *-s* or *-es* to a non-count noun.

- There's **salt** on the table.
  NOT ~~There's a salt on the table.~~
  NOT ~~There's salts on the table.~~

3. You can use the definite article *the* before singular count nouns, plural count nouns, and non-count nouns.

- **The** onion is here. <small>count</small>
- **The** carrots are there. <small>count</small>
- **The** soup is delicious. <small>non-count</small>

4. Use *the* for specific things that the listener and speaker know about.

ALI: How was **the** party?
BEKIR: It was wonderful.

5. Use *the* when you talk about something for the second time.

- She cooked rice and soup. She ate **the** rice and put **the** soup in the refrigerator.

6. Use *some* with plural count nouns and non-count nouns in affirmative statements.

- I bought **some** carrots. <small>count</small>
- I drank **some** juice. <small>non-count</small>

Use *any* with plural count nouns and non-count nouns in negative statements.

- I didn't buy **any** potatoes. <small>count</small>
- I didn't use **any** pepper. <small>non-count</small>

7. Use *a few* for small amounts and *many* for large amounts with count nouns.

- I used **a few** carrots. <small>count</small>
- I used **many** yams. <small>count</small>

Use *a little* for small amounts and *much* for large amounts with non-count nouns.

- I only used **a little** salt. <small>non-count</small>
- I never use **much** pepper. <small>non-count</small>

▶ **BE CAREFUL!** *Much* is not usually used in affirmative statements. We usually use *a lot of* instead.

- I drank **a lot of** water. <small>non-count</small>
  NOT ~~I drank much water.~~

8. *A lot of* is used with both count and non-count nouns. *Lots of* is informal for *a lot of*.

- She made **a lot of** soup. <small>non-count</small>
- There was **lots of** soup in the refrigerator.

You can use a quantifier without a noun if the noun was named before.

- Is there **any** left?

▶ **BE CAREFUL!** Drop the *of* in *a lot of* when used without a noun.

- There's **a lot**.

9. USAGE NOTE: In informal speaking, some non-count nouns may be used as count nouns.

- I'd like **two coffees** and **two sodas**.
  (I'd like two containers of coffee and two cans of soda.)

REFERENCE NOTE
See Unit 5 for count nouns, *a*, and *an*.
See Appendix 7, pages A-7 and A-8, for rules about plural nouns.
See Appendix 9, page A-9, for a list of common non-count nouns.
See Appendix 10, page A-10, for a fuller discussion of the definite article *the*.

FOCUSED PRACTICE

1 DISCOVER THE GRAMMAR

Read the sentences. Circle the noun in each sentence. Then check (✔) whether the noun is a singular count noun, a plural count noun, or a non-count noun.

	Singular Count Noun	Plural Count Noun	Non-count Noun
1. She wants a little (milk).	☐	☐	☑
2. There are only a few eggs.	☐	☐	☐
3. There isn't much time left.	☐	☐	☐
4. There aren't many visitors here now.	☐	☐	☐
5. I used a lot of juice.	☐	☐	☐
6. He ate several carrots.	☐	☐	☐
7. They don't have a car.	☐	☐	☐
8. He has two radios.	☐	☐	☐
9. She ate an orange.	☐	☐	☐
10. We have only one telephone.	☐	☐	☐
11. There aren't any books over there.	☐	☐	☐
12. They ate some bread.	☐	☐	☐

2 PARTY PREPARATION
Grammar Notes 1–2, 6

Complete the sentences with **a**, **an**, *or* **some**.

1. Carol and Yoko are having _____*a*_____ party.

2. Carol's making _____ apple pie.

3. They borrowed two tables and _____ chairs for the party.

4. They put _____ chips and salsa on one table.

5. They put _____ soda and juice on the other table.

6. Yoko bought _____ flowers, and Carol bought _____ camera.

7. Bekir brought _____ CDs from his apartment.

3 DIFFERENT PLACES

Some classmates are describing their countries and cities. Complete the sentences with **isn't**, **aren't**, **much**, **many**, *and* **any**.

HUGO: There ___isn't___ ___any___ snow in San Juan, but there's a lot of rain in
1.   2.
September.

SOFIA: My city is not near an ocean, so there _____ _____ natural beaches.
3.   4.
However, there are a lot of swimming pools.

JOSE: There _____ _____ hospitals in my town, but many doctors live
5.   6.
there. All the doctors work at the hospital in the next town fifty miles away.

NICHOLAS: There _____ _____ crime and there _____ _____
7.   8.   9.   10.
poverty in my village. There are only a few robberies, and most people own
their own homes.

ALI: There _____ _____ cultural activities in my town. There's only one
11.   12.
theater and one museum, but housing is cheap and unemployment is low.

Do you know any places that fit the descriptions above?

4 APPLES AND HONEY

Complete each sentence in as many ways as possible using the words in the box.

a	an	one	Ø*	the	some	any	a few	many	a little	much	a lot of	two

1. I want _____ honey.

2. He wants _____ apple.

3. I want _____ apples.

4. He doesn't want _____ honey.

5. I don't want _____ apples.

6. They want _____ peach.

*leave blank

A, an, *and* **the** *were left out of these conversations. Listen and add them in the correct places.*

BEKIR: It's getting hot. Is there _an_ air conditioner in this room?

CAROL: Yes. air conditioner is in wall under that window.

BEKIR: What's that?

CAROL: My new camera.

BEKIR: Was camera expensive?

CAROL: No. It was very cheap. I just hope it works. I need battery. Yoko, are there any AA batteries in refrigerator?

YOKO: I'll check. . . . Uh . . . Yes. There's package of AA batteries here.

CAROL: Thanks.

   [Carol puts a battery in her camera.]

BEKIR: Well?

CAROL: Something's wrong. camera doesn't work.

YOKO: Maybe battery isn't good.

CAROL: Or maybe it's camera.

BEKIR: I have camera. I'll go home and get it.

CAROL: Thanks. I really want some pictures of party.

COMMUNICATION PRACTICE

6 INFORMATION GAP: COUNTRIES AND PRODUCTS

Student A, ask your partner questions to complete the sentences. Answer your partner's questions.

Student B, turn to the Information Gap on page 357 and follow the instructions there.

EXAMPLE:
What European country produces a lot of chocolate, cheese, and watches?

1. A European country that produces a lot of chocolate, cheese, and watches

   is _____.

2. Colombia is a South American country where you can find a lot of emeralds.

3. An African country that produces a lot of diamonds is _____.

4. A very large Asian country that produces a lot of rice is China.

5. _____ is a very large South American country that produces a lot of coffee.

6. Three Asian countries that manufacture a lot of computers and cars are Japan, Korea, and Taiwan.

7. Two countries that produce a lot of oil are _____ and _____.

7 OUR CITY: THE GOOD AND THE BAD

Work in small groups. Write ten good or bad things about the city or town you are in. Use the words in the box or add your own words. Use **a**, **one**, **a few**, **some**, **many**, **a lot of**, **any**, **a little**, *or* **much** *in each sentence.*

concert halls	museums	schools and universities
crime	noise	sports facilities
good hospitals	parks and gardens	taxis
job opportunities	pollution	traffic

EXAMPLES:
There's a wonderful concert hall here.
There isn't much pollution here.
There are many good schools and universities here.
There are only a few parks and gardens in this city.

Read your sentences to the class. Listen to your classmates' sentences. Were your ideas about the city or town the same as theirs?

QUESTIONS WITH *ANY* / *SOME* / *HOW MUCH* / *HOW MANY*; *QUANTIFIERS*; *CONTAINERS*

GRAMMAR **IN CONTEXT**

WARM UP Are you getting **enough** or **too little** sleep? Are you getting **enough** or **too little** exercise?

Listen and read the following from Health and Fitness *magazine.*

Health and Fitness

This week's *Health and Fitness* magazine has a questionnaire by nutritionist Dr. Diane Stone. Complete the questions and calculate your score. Send us your answers and receive a free copy of our newsletter, "News on Health and Fitness." Send to: Health and Fitness, Box 458, St. Paul, MN 55101.

RATE YOUR HEALTH

Measure your health and fitness. Put an X in the box next to your answer.

1. How much time do you spend exercising?

   a. at least an hour a day ☐
   b. about an hour three times a week ☐
   c. about an hour a week ☐
   d. less than an hour a week ☐

2. How much coffee do you drink?

   a. four or more **cups** (of coffee) a day ☐
   b. three cups a day ☐
   c. two cups a day ☐
   d. I don't drink any coffee. ☐

3. How many vegetables do you eat each day?

   a. six or more servings ☐
   b. about three servings ☐
   c. only two servings ☐
   d. I don't eat vegetables. ☐

4. How much candy do you eat each day?

   a. a lot ☐
   b. some ☐
   c. a little ☐
   d. none ☐

5. How much water do you drink each day?

   a. eight or more **glasses** ☐
   b. four glasses ☐
   c. two glasses ☐
   d. one or fewer ☐

6. How many vacations do you take a year?

   a. **a lot**, at least four a year ☐
   b. **a few**, about two or three ☐
   c. one ☐
   d. I don't take vacations. ☐

Scoring Key
BEST SCORE = 24
1. a = 4, b = 4, c = 2, d = 0
2. a = 0, b = 2, c = 4, d = 4
3. a = 4, b = 2, c = 1, d = 0
4. a = 0, b = 1, c = 4, d = 4
5. a = 4, b = 2, c = 1, d = 0
6. a = 4, b = 4, c = 1, d = 0

GRAMMAR **PRESENTATION**
QUESTIONS WITH *ANY* / *SOME* / *HOW MUCH* / *HOW MANY*; QUANTIFIERS, CONTAINERS, AND MEASURE WORDS

YES / NO QUESTIONS

	SINGULAR COUNT NOUN
Does Carol have	**a** raincoat?
	an umbrella?
	one sister?

	QUANTIFIER	PLURAL COUNT NOUN OR NON-COUNT NOUN
Do you want	**any**	apples?
	some	coffee?

QUESTIONS ABOUT QUANTITY

HOW MUCH	NON-COUNT NOUN	
How much	milk	do you need?
		did she buy?

ANSWERS
Two quarts. (Two quarts of milk.)
A carton. (A carton of milk.)

HOW MUCH	PLURAL COUNT NOUN	
How many	apples	do we need?
		did he buy?

ANSWERS
A lot.
One bag.
Two pounds.
One or two.

	VERB	TOO MANY / TOO MUCH	NOUN
We	bought	**too many**	**apples.**
There	is	**too much**	**noise.**

	VERB	ENOUGH	NOUN
We	have	**enough**	**books.**
	don't have		**time.**

	VERB	TOO FEW / TOO LITTLE	NOUN
We	bought	**too few**	**bananas.**
There	is	**too little**	**work.**

NOTES	EXAMPLES
1. We use *any* in *yes / no* questions with non-count nouns and plural count nouns. We can also use *some* in *yes / no* questions. We usually use *some* in *yes / no* questions when we want or expect the answer to be yes.	• Did you buy **any** milk? ^(non-count) • Did you buy **any** pencils? ^(count) • Would you like **some** milk? • Do you need **some** more eggs?

2. Use *how much* or *how many* to ask about quantity. You can use quantifiers, containers, or measure words (for specific quantities) in your answers. You can also use numbers in answering questions with *how many*.	• **How much** juice do you have?
	  A little.
	  A carton.
	  A gallon.
	
	• **How many** onions do you need?
	  A few.
	  A bag.
	  A pound.
	  Ten.

3. It is not necessary to repeat the noun after *how much* or *how many* if the noun was named before.	**A:** I need some money. **B:** **How much** do you need? (How much money do you need?) **A:** I bought some magazines. **B:** **How many** did you buy? (How many magazines did you buy?)
4. You can use measure words or containers to count non-count nouns. You can use measure words or containers with count nouns, too.	• Please get me **one quart of milk**. ^(non-count) • He drank **two glasses of milk**. ^(non-count) • I bought **a box of cookies**. ^(count)

5. *Enough* means the amount you need. Use *enough* before plural count nouns and non-count nouns.

Not enough means less than the amount you need. Use *not enough* before plural count nouns and non-count nouns.

- count
  We have **enough eggs**.
  (We need six eggs, and we have six eggs.)

- non-count
  We don't have **enough milk**.
  (We need three cups of milk, but we have only two cups of milk.)

6. *Too much* and *too many* mean more than the right amount. They usually have negative meanings. Use *too much* before non-count nouns. Use *too many* before plural count nouns.

Too little is the opposite of *too much*. *Too few* is the opposite of *too many*. Both *too little* and *too few* mean not enough.

- non-count
  He bought **too much milk**. We needed one quart, but he bought three quarts.

- count
  We ate **too many donuts**.

- There was **too little** time.
- There were **too few** books.

REFERENCE NOTE
See Appendix 9, page A-9, for a list of common containers and measure words.
See Unit 40 for a discussion of *too* and *enough* with adjectives.

FOCUSED PRACTICE

1 DISCOVER THE GRAMMAR

Match the sentences in column A with those in column B.

A

___e___ **1.** This soup tastes terrible.

_____ **2.** That company is not doing well.

_____ **3.** How many faxes do you receive in a day?

_____ **4.** I don't believe him.

_____ **5.** How much time do you spend away from the office?

_____ **6.** Do you have any news about their son?

_____ **7.** Don't buy that computer.

B

a. Yes. He's doing very well.

b. It costs too much.

c. There are too many bosses and too few assistants.

d. One or two.

e. We used too much water and not enough salt.

f. Four weeks each year.

g. He tells too many lies.

2 CONTAINERS AND MEASURE WORDS   Grammar Note 4

Complete the answers. Use the words in the box. (See Appendix 9, page A-9, for a list of containers and measure words).

cans	roll	box	loaf	bottle	piece	bag

A: Do you have a _____ of paper?
                              1.

B: Here.

A: Thanks. I want to make a shopping list before we go to the store.

B: Good idea. What do you think we need?

A: A few _____ of soup, a big _____ of soda, and a _____
                    2.   3.   4.
of pretzels.

B: Okay.

A: Is there anything special you want?

B: Yes. Let's get a _____ of cereal and a _____ of bread.
                        5.   6.

A: Good. And how about a _____ of film?
                              7.

B: Sure.

3 CAROL'S RECIPE FOR APPLE PIE   Grammar Notes 2, 4

 Carol baked an apple pie for her party. Yolanda asks for the recipe. First complete the questions with **much** *or* **many***. Then listen to the conversation. Listen again and circle the correct amounts.*

1. How __much__ flour did Carol use for the pie crust?
   a. two and a half tablespoons
   (b.) two and a half cups
   c. two and a half pints

2. How _____ oil did she use?
   a. a cup
   b. a pinch
   c. a tablespoon

3. How _____ water did she use?
   a. a pinch
   b. a quarter of an ounce
   c. a quarter of a cup

4. How _____ salt did she use?
   a. a gallon
   b. a pinch
   c. a cup

5. How _____ eggs did she use?
   a. one
   b. two
   c. three

6. How _____ apples did Carol use for the filling?
   a. eight
   b. two
   c. five

7. How _____ sugar did Carol use for the filling?
   a. one tablespoon
   b. one teaspoon
   c. one cup

8. How _____ flour did Carol use for the filling?
   a. two teaspoons
   b. two tablespoons
   c. two cups

4 QUESTIONS ABOUT QUANTITY Grammar Note 2

Complete the questions. Begin with **how much** *or* **how many** *and use the phrases in the box.*

> did you do last night
> do you buy in a month
> do you need for the tickets
> do you drink each day
> did you invite to your last party
> do you spend on your homework every night

1. _____ money _____?

2. _____ people _____?

3. _____ time _____?

4. _____ homework _____?

5. _____ glasses of water _____?

6. _____ CDs _____?

5 PRACTICING FORM Grammar Notes 1–6

Complete the sentences in as many ways as possible using the words in the box.

How much	How many	(not) enough	too little
too much	too few	any	too many
two bottles	a lot	a little	a few

EXAMPLE:
A: How much water did he drink?
B: Enough. OR Too little. OR . . .

1. **A:** _____ water did he drink?

   B: _____ .

2. **A:** _____ oranges did you buy?

   B: _____

3. **A:** Do you need _____ help?

   B: Yes. I need _____ of help.

6 YOKO'S WORRIES

Carol and Yoko are waiting for their friends to come to their party. Listen to their conversation and complete the sentences.

YOKO: How much milk is there?

CAROL: Don't worry. _____ _____. We have three quarts. Three quarts are
          1.
probably too much. No one drinks much milk at parties.

YOKO: _____ _____ _____ _____?
     2.

CAROL: There are only ten, but people don't usually sit. _____ _____
                         3.

_____ _____ _____? People drink a lot at parties.

YOKO: I think so. Bekir bought five bottles, and we had a few in the refrigerator. What

about music? _____ _____ _____ _____?
         4.

CAROL: Definitely. Dan brought us some last night. And Bekir brought some today. And we

have quite a few.

YOKO: Juice. _____ _____ _____ _____?
       5.

CAROL: Yes. Relax Yoko. We have _____ _____, _____
               6.

_____, and _____ _____.
               7.

YOKO: I guess you're right. I have a new thought. Will we have _____
                                         8.

_____?

7 TOO MUCH, TOO LITTLE

*Look at the pictures and complete
these conversations. Use* **too much,**
too many, *or* **too few.**

  1. A: Did you study at home?

    B: No.

    A: Why not?

    B: _____

(continued on next page)

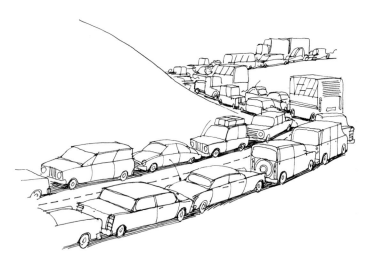

2. A: Why did you drive through the city?

B: _____ on the highway.

3. A: I don't like this area. Let's move.

B: What's wrong?

A: There _____ bugs here.

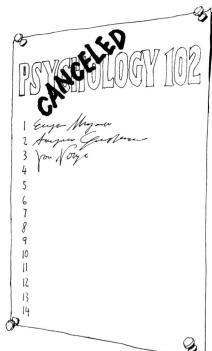

4. A: Why did they cancel the class?

B: _____. Only three students registered for the class.

COMMUNICATION PRACTICE

8 A WEEK'S GROCERIES

Work in small groups. Your group is going to buy food for one week. Make a list of all the items you will need. Next to each item, write how much you will buy.

Meat and Fish	Vegetables and Fruit	Bread and Cereals	Dairy Products and Eggs
beef—4 pounds	broccoli	dinner rolls	yogurt

Compare your list with the other groups'.

> **EXAMPLE:**
> **A:** Did you buy any meat?
> **B:** Yes, we bought four pounds. How much meat did you buy?
> **A:** None.

Which group bought the most food? Which group bought the healthiest food? Did any group buy a lot of junk food? Did your group forget to buy anything?

9 A CLASS SURVEY

Write two questions that begin with **How much** *or* **How many**. *Survey your classmates. Compare the answers of the men and the women.*

> **EXAMPLES:**
> How many hours do you sleep each night?
>
> OR
>
> How much time do you spend listening to music?

Study your results. Report interesting results to the class.

10 PROBLEMS AROUND THE WORLD

Work in small groups. Talk about problems in different parts of the world. Use **too much**, **too many**, **too little**, **too few**, *or* **not enough**. *The words in the box may be helpful.*

crime	oil	water	cultural activities	food
pollution	rain	traffic	schools	jobs

EXAMPLES:

There are too few doctors in Alaska.

There isn't enough rain in the Mojave Desert.

11 LETTER TO THE EDITOR

Work in small groups.

First read this letter to the editor. Then complete the sentences.

> To the editor:
>
> I enjoy reading your paper almost every day, but please don't add any more sections. These days information is cheap and easy to get. We have radios, TVs, computers, faxes, cell phones, e-mail, and the Internet. In addition, there is always snail mail. And let's not forget regular phones and, of course, newspapers. Information is wonderful, but too much information causes problems. People don't have enough time to think things through. Most of us get too much mail, too many faxes, too many phone calls, and too many news reports. We need time to stop and think. We need less information, not more.
>
> Sincerely yours,
> Gabrielle Lowe

1. Ms. Lowe thinks there isn't enough _____.

2. Ms. Lowe thinks there's too much _____.

3. Ms. Lowe thinks there are too many _____.

Do you agree or disagree with the author?

CAN AND COULD FOR ABILITY AND POSSIBILITY; MAY I, CAN I, AND COULD I FOR POLITE REQUESTS

GRAMMAR **IN CONTEXT**

WARM UP Can you build muscles in three weeks?

Doug and Noah are returning home from school. Listen and read the conversation.

SALESMAN:	Step right this way, everybody. Right this way. Come and get Paul's Muscle Builders. For only $10.95 you too **can build** big muscles. And in only three weeks you too **can look** like him.
STUDENT:	**Can I** have a bottle?
SALESMAN:	Certainly, sir. Here you go.
SECOND STUDENT:	I'll take two.
THIRD STUDENT:	**May I** see one of your bottles?
SALESMAN:	Sure.
DOUG:	Hey, Noah. What do you think? Sounds pretty good, doesn't it?
NOAH:	Come on. Are you serious? You **can't** possibly **build** muscles in three weeks. At least not safely. A couple of years ago my cousin took pills for a year. I **couldn't see** any more muscles. But he began to have kidney problems.
DOUG:	Well, this guy is making a fortune. Look at all the kids buying his formula. Maybe it works.
NOAH:	Trust me, it doesn't.
	[The next week]
DOUG:	Hey, Noah. Look at this. Isn't this the guy who sold the Muscle Builder pills?
NOAH:	Uh-huh. That's him.
DOUG:	The police arrested him for selling drugs to minors.

GRAMMAR **PRESENTATION**
CAN AND *COULD* FOR ABILITY AND POSSIBILITY; *MAY I*, *CAN I*, AND *COULD I* FOR POLITE REQUESTS

AFFIRMATIVE AND NEGATIVE STATEMENTS

SUBJECT	CAN (NOT) / COULD (NOT)	BASE FORM OF VERB
I You He She It We You They	can can't could couldn't	swim.

CONTRACTIONS

cannot → **can't**
could not → **couldn't**

YES / NO QUESTIONS

CAN / COULD	SUBJECT	BASE FORM OF VERB
Can Could	you she	dance? finish the test?

SHORT ANSWERS

AFFIRMATIVE	NEGATIVE
Yes, I can. Yes, she could.	No, I can't. No, she couldn't.

QUESTIONS

MAY / CAN / COULD	I	BASE FORM OF VERB
May Can	I	help you?
May Can Could		(please) borrow your dictionary?

SHORT ANSWERS

AFFIRMATIVE	NEGATIVE
Yes, please.	No, thanks.
Yes, of course.	No, I'm sorry, I'm using it.

NOTES

1. Modals are words that come before verbs. They change the meanings of the verbs in some way. For example, modals can express ability or possibility. Or modals can ask for or give permission.

EXAMPLES

- I lift weights every day. (*Routine*)
- I **can** lift 50 pounds. (*Ability*)
- I **might** join a gym. (*Possibility*)
- **May** I see that ad? (*Permission*)

2. The modals *can*, *could*, and *may* are followed by the **base form of the verb**.

modal base form
- He **can paint**.
- She **could speak** French.
- **May** I **see** your newspaper?
  Not ~~He can to paint. She could to speak French. May I to see your newspaper?~~
  Not ~~He can paints. She could speaks French. May I sees your newspaper?~~

3. *Can, could,* and *may* have different meanings. *Can* expresses **ability in the present**. *Can't* is the negative of *can*.

- I **can** understand English.
- I **can't** understand Arabic.

4. *Could* expresses **ability in the past**.

Couldn't is the negative of *could*.

- In high school Pete **could run** 100 meters in one minute. Now he can't.
- Last year I **couldn't speak** English. Now I can.

5. *Can* and *could* also express **possibility in the future**.

- We **can go** there by bus.
- We **could visit** him tonight.

6. Use *Can I, Could I,* or *May I* to make **polite requests**.

- **Can I** (please) borrow your pen?
- **Could I** (please) borrow your pen?
- **May I** (please) borrow your pen?

Usage note: *May* is more formal than *can* or *could*.

- **May I** help you?
- **Can I** help you?

Pronunciation Note
When *can* is followed by a base-form verb, we usually pronounce it /kən/ and stress the base-form verb. We can **dánce**. In sentences with *can't* followed by a base-form verb, we stress both *can't* and the base-form verb. We **cán't dánce**.

Reference Note
See Unit 37 for a discussion of using *could* and *would* to make polite requests.

FOCUSED PRACTICE

1 DISCOVER THE GRAMMAR

Match the sentence in column A with a possible reason in column B.

<table>
<tr><td align="center">**A**</td><td align="center">**B**</td></tr>
<tr><td>__c__ **1.** She can lift 100 pounds.</td><td>**a.** There's a lot of noise here.</td></tr>
<tr><td>_____ **2.** She can't smell the roses.</td><td>**b.** I knew that wasn't true.</td></tr>
<tr><td>_____ **3.** I couldn't see the chalkboard.</td><td>**c.** She's very strong.</td></tr>
<tr><td>_____ **4.** We couldn't work on Sunday.</td><td>**d.** She has a cold.</td></tr>
<tr><td>_____ **5.** I can't hear you.</td><td>**e.** I forgot my glasses.</td></tr>
<tr><td>_____ **6.** You couldn't fool me.</td><td>**f.** The building was closed.</td></tr>
</table>

2 LISTENING: STRESS *CAN* AND *CAN'T*

Listen and repeat the sentences. Listen again and complete the sentences. Then listen and mark the stress.

1. Bekir ____can séw____, but he ____cán't cóok____.

2. Doug _____ 50-pound weights, but Noah _____.

3. Dan _____ tennis. He _____ basketball, too.

4. Jung Hee _____ English newspapers and write good English compositions.

5. Jung Hee _____ English, too.

6. Jung Hee just _____ English well.

7. Who _____ to the party?

8. Who _____ to the party?

9. How _____ I _____ to your house from here?

10. You _____ the bus, but you _____.

3 AN AMAZING DOG

Yoko is talking to Dina. Yoko's dog, Rocky, is nearby. He's scratching his stomach. Listen to the conversation. Then read each sentence and check **That's right**, **That's wrong**, *or* **I don't know.**

	That's right.	That's wrong.	I don't know.
Dina says:			
1. Poopsie can sit.	☑	☐	☐
2. Poopsie can spit.	☐	☐	☐
3. Poopsie can't roll over.	☐	☐	☐
4. Poopsie can't dance.	☐	☐	☐
5. Poopsie can talk.	☐	☐	☐
Yoko thinks:			
6. Dina is not telling the truth.	☐	☐	☐

4 BEFORE AND AFTER

Complete the sentences. Use **can**, **can't**, **could**, *or* **couldn't**.

1. Lulu feels great. She goes to aerobics class twice a week. When she began six months ago, she __*couldn't*__ exercise
   a.
   for more than fifteen minutes. Now she _____ exercise for an hour.
   b.
   She also lost some weight. Now she _____ wear a skirt she _____
   c.   d.
   wear before.

2. A few months ago I didn't know much English. I _____ understand English very well. I _____ speak at all. I
   a.   b.
   _____ write only a few words. Now I _____ understand a lot more and I
   c.   d.
   _____ say many things. I _____ also write simple compositions.
   e.   f.

3. I _____ go to the library yesterday because I was busy, but I _____ go later
   a.   b.
   today. _____ you meet me at the library at 2:30?
   c.

5 INVENTIONS

Read the chart and complete the sentences. Use **could**, **couldn't**, **can**, *or* **can't** *and the verbs in the box. Then listen and check your work.*

see	watch	listen to	use
speak	learn	record	

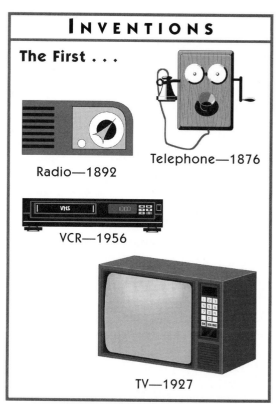

INVENTIONS

The First . . .

Radio—1892

Telephone—1876

VCR—1956

TV—1927

1. By 1890 people ___could speak___ to their

   friends on the telephone, but they

   ___couldn't see___ them on a picture phone.

2. By 1925 people _____ the radio,

   but they _____ TV.

3. By 1950 people _____ TV, but they

   _____ programs on a VCR.

4. Today people _____ many

   wonderful machines, but they still

   _____ a language while they sleep.

6 EDITING

Correct the errors. Add **can** *in two places to correct the sentences.*

A: May I ⨉ help you?

B: Yes, please. I see one of those electronic dictionaries?

A: Here you are. This dictionary can translates words into five languages.

B: Does it give the pronunciation, too?

A: Oh, yes. You can see the spelling and hear the word, too.

B: Sounds perfect. Do can I pay by check?

A: Sorry, you use a credit card or cash, but we can't take checks.

COMMUNICATION PRACTICE

7 WHAT CAN YOU DO?

Work with a partner. Ask each other these questions.

1. Can you say "I love you" in more than five languages?

2. Can you understand the formula e = mc²?

3. Can you program a VCR?

4. Can you name all the colors of the flags of eight countries?

5. Can you stand on your head?

6. Can you pronounce the word "xylophone"?

7. Can you spell a word that begins with "m" and describes a person who does tricks?

Report interesting results to the class.

8 APOLOGIES AND EXCUSES

*Work with a partner. Complete the sentences with **can't** or **couldn't**. Then make up two excuses for each situation. Role-play your excuses to the class. The class decides on the best excuse.*

1. I'm so sorry I ___couldn't___ get back to you.

   I lost your telephone number.

   I was busy all day.

2. I'm really sorry I _____ lend you any money at this time.

   _____

   _____

3. I'm sorry I _____ come to your party last night.

   _____

   _____

❾ POLITE REQUESTS

*Work with a partner. Act out these
situations. Begin with* **May I** *or*
Can I. *Continue each conversation
with your partner.*

1. Student A is a police officer. Student B was driving very fast.
   The police officer stops the driver.
2. Student A is a salesperson. Student B is a customer.
3. Student A is entering a country. Student B is a customs official.
4. Student A needs some money. Student B is a classmate.

EXAMPLE:

POLICE OFFICER: May I see your driver's license?

DRIVER: Certainly. Here it is, officer.

POLICE OFFICER: Thank you. Do you know the speed limit here is 55 miles
per hour?

DRIVER: Uh . . . no, sir. I didn't see the sign.

POLICE OFFICER: Well, . . .

❿ PROVERBS

What do these proverbs mean? Do you agree or disagree with them?

1. "An ambitious man can never know peace."
   J. Krishnamurti

2. "When a man gets angry, he cannot be in the right."
   Chinese proverb

3. "Those who cannot remember the past are condemned to repeat it."
   George Santayana

4. "One father can support twelve children, but twelve children cannot support one father."
   French proverb

Do you know any proverbs? Do you know where they are from?

MAY OR *MIGHT* FOR **POSSIBILITY**

GRAMMAR **IN CONTEXT**

WARM UP   Do you watch the weather report on TV, listen to it on the radio, or read it in the newspaper? How often is the report wrong?

Listen and read the conversation. Elenore, Doug, and Pete are talking about the weather.

ELENORE: Shh. The weather report is on next.

METEOROLOGIST: Good evening, everyone. This is Mike Hersh with today's weather report. Anyone with plans to be outdoors tomorrow or Tuesday **might not welcome** this news. The weather will continue to be unseasonably cold and windy. And heavy rain will begin tonight or tomorrow. There **may be** flooding on the highways. So, if you can, take public transportation. And don't put away those umbrellas too soon. Our meteorologists predict more rain for Wednesday. By Thursday the weather **may become** milder with only a 20 percent chance of showers. We **might** even **see** some sun. But until then my best advice is: Stay indoors with a good book or video.

DOUG: I guess that means no soccer tomorrow.

PETE: Don't be too sure. You **may** still **have** a game. The weather forecaster is often wrong. Remember yesterday. He predicted a beautiful day, and it was awful. And last week he said we **might have** a major snowstorm. It turned out to be sunny and dry.

DOUG: You **may be** right. But I have a feeling that this time he's on target.

ELENORE: I just hope you don't play in the rain.

DOUG: We **may**. The last time it rained we played an entire game. You know, we're not a group of wimps.

GRAMMAR **PRESENTATION**
MAY OR *MIGHT* FOR POSSIBILITY

		AFFIRMATIVE / NEGATIVE STATEMENTS			
SUBJECT	**MAY / MIGHT**	**(NOT)**	**BASE FORM OF VERB**		
I You He She We You They	**may** **might**	**(not)**	**take**	a vacation in June.
It	**may** **might**	**(not)**	**rain**	tonight.

NOTES

EXAMPLES

1. Use *may* or *might* to express **possibility about the future or the present**. *May* and *might* have almost the same meaning, but *may* means something is a little more possible than *might*.

- I **might** be late. (It's possible.)
- I **may** be late. (It's more possible.)
- I'll **probably** be late. (It's likely.)
- I **will** be late. (It's definite.)

2. Use *may* (but not *might*) to **give**, **refuse**, **or ask for permission**.

- You **may** use a pencil to take this test.
- You **may not** use your dictionary during this test.
- **May** I use your pen?

3. BE CAREFUL! Do not use *may* or *might* to ask *yes* / *no* questions about possibility.

- Will you go to the party?
  NOT ~~Might you go to the party?~~

4. *May* and *might* are followed by the base-form verb. There are no contractions for *may* or *might*.

- We **might go** to the movies.
  NOT ~~We might to go to the movies.~~
  NOT ~~He might goes to the movies.~~
  NOT ~~He mightn't go to the movies.~~

FOCUSED PRACTICE

1 DISCOVER THE GRAMMAR

Match the sentences in column A with the sentences in column B.

A

___d___ **1.** It's definitely going to rain.

_____ **2.** There's an 80 percent chance of rain.

_____ **3.** There's a 50 percent chance of rain.

_____ **4.** There's a 10 percent chance of rain.

_____ **5.** It's definitely not going to rain.

B

a. It probably won't rain.

b. It'll probably rain.

c. It won't rain.

d. It will rain.

e. It may rain.

2 DEFINITE OR POSSIBLE   Grammar Notes 1, 4

Choose the correct words to complete the conversations.

1. **NORMA:** Remember, the movie begins at seven o'clock. Please don't be late.

    NANCY: Don't worry. We <u>'ll be</u> _____ there.

(may be, 'll be)

2. **BOB:** I wonder why Pete isn't here.

    ROGER: Well, yesterday he looked pale. He _____ sick.

(may be, is)

3. **ELENORE:** Do you think there's something wrong with that man?

    PETE: I don't know. He _____ help.

(might need, needs)

4. **DAN:** Uh-oh. The car _____. What's wrong?

a. (won't start, may not start)

    JON: Try again. It _____. Just keep trying. That happens

b. (will be cold, may be cold)

    sometimes. Don't forget, this car is almost ten years old.

❸ TOO GOOD TO BE TRUE

Complete the conversation. Use the statements in the box.

> I may get one.
> May I help you?
> They might not be made well.
> Or they might come without some necessary parts.

NOAH: Look at this ad. These new computers sound great. They're cheap and they have a lot of memory. _____ .
1.

DOUG: I'd think twice before getting one.

_____ .
2.

_____ . They're
3.

too cheap.

NOAH: Well, I'm going to find out.

SALESPERSON: _____ ?
4.

NOAH: Yes, I'm interested in those computers you advertise.

SALESPERSON: You mean the ones for $395?

NOAH: Uh-huh.

SALESPERSON: Sorry. That was a misprint. Those machines are actually $1,395.

❹ POSSIBILITIES

Complete the conversations with the affirmative or negative of **may** *or* **might** *and a verb from the box.*

> rain   need   be   have

1. A: Take your umbrella. It _____ may rain _____ this afternoon.

   B: But the forecast was for sun.

   A: Just take a look at those clouds.

2. A: Start dinner without me. I _____ home before nine.

   B: Oh that's okay. I'll wait.

   A: Are you sure it's okay?

   B: I'm positive.

3. A: Adele looks very upset.

   B: She is. She _____ an operation.

   A: Oh, that's too bad. I hope it's not serious.

   B: It's not, but it's still an operation.

4. A: I don't understand him. Why is he studying part time?

   B: He _____ enough money to study full time.

   A: I never thought of that. You're probably right.

5 PACKING FOR A TRIP Grammar Notes 1, 4

Pete and Elenore are packing for a trip to Oregon and California. Elenore is a light packer—she travels with very few clothes. Pete is the opposite. Listen to their conversation. Then tell why Pete is taking each item.

1. boots: _They may want to go mountain climbing._ _____

2. three sweaters: _____

3. two watches: _____

4. two cameras: _____

5. a hair dryer: _____

COMMUNICATION PRACTICE

6 THINK ABOUT THE POSSIBILITIES

Work with a partner. Read the situation. Think of several possibilities and discuss them.

EXAMPLE:

1. The person may be sick or depressed.
   OR
   The person might be very busy.

1. A person isn't eating as much as usual.
2. A person usually wears a suit to work. Today the person is wearing jeans.
3. A person usually takes the bus. Today the person is walking.
4. A baby is crying.
5. A person found a watch.

7 NAMES

Work in small groups. Read the list of the names of students in an ESL class. Guess their nationalities. The nationalities listed in the box may be helpful.

Austrian	French	Japanese	Senegalese
Canadian	German	Korean	Swiss
Chinese	Greek	Puerto Rican	Thai
Colombian	Haitian	Russian	Turkish
Dominican	Israeli	Saudi Arabian	Venezuelan
Egyptian	Italian		

EXAMPLE:

Pierre Laporte
He may be French.
He might be Canadian.

1. Yuriko Shinohara _____
2. Ratatamanoon Dulyanunt _____
3. Roberto Alvarado _____
4. Paul Steiner _____
5. Ilana Ben Ohr _____
6. Sung Eun Park _____
7. Wei Liang Chang _____
8. Mohammed Ghoneia _____
9. Maria Angelica Riviera _____
10. Rita Inslicht _____
11. Merlina Pappas _____
12. Irina Statyevskaya _____

Compare your guesses with the other groups' guesses. Then check your answers on page 357.

8 YOUR PLANS FOR TONIGHT

Work with a partner. Take turns asking about each other's plans for tonight. Ask questions with **be going to** *for the future. Give answers with* **Yes, I am**; **Yes, I'll probably . . .** ; **I may . . .** ; **I might . . .** ; *or* **No, I'm not**. *Explain your answers. Use the ideas in the box or your own ideas.*

EXAMPLE:
watch TV

A: Are you going to watch TV tonight?

B: Yes, I am. I always watch TV at night.
OR
Yes, I'll probably watch TV tonight. I usually watch TV at night.
OR
I may watch TV tonight. There's a good show on channel 13 at nine o'clock.
OR
I might watch TV tonight. I'm busy, but there's a good show on at nine o'clock.
OR
No, I'm not. I'm going to a concert tonight.

> watch TV
> cook dinner
> go shopping
> eat at a Chinese restaurant
> listen to the news
> play tennis
> go dancing

9 THINK ABOUT IT

Voltaire, an eighteenth-century French philosopher, said, "I may disapprove of what you say, but I will defend to the death your right to say it."

What did Voltaire mean? Do you agree with him?

DESIRES, INVITATIONS, REQUESTS: WOULD LIKE, WOULD YOU LIKE...?, WOULD YOU PLEASE...?

GRAMMAR **IN CONTEXT**

WARM UP   The average age of marriage is rising in the U.S. Is it rising or falling in other countries?

AVERAGE AGE OF MARRIAGE IN THE UNITED STATES		
	men	**women**
1900	25.9	21.9
1950	22.8	20.3
1997	26.8	25.0

Molly Murdock is a modern-day matchmaker. Listen and read the answers that one client gave Murdock.

WISHES

Could you please think carefully before you answer?
Mark only the things you feel strongly about.

	I'd love to	I'd hate to
have a sports utility vehicle	☑	☐
have a sports car	☐	☐
have a lot of children	☑	☐
have a country home	☑	☐
have an apartment in a large city	☐	☑
go camping	☑	☐
go to the opera	☐	☑
stay home and take care of my children	☑	☐
hire a baby-sitter to take care of my children	☐	☑
have my spouse take care of our children	☐	☐
be famous	☐	☐
be rich	☐	☐
spend my free time writing, painting, or composing music	☐	☐
have a large circle of friends	☐	☐
have a small circle of close friends	☑	☐

Would you please check (✓) the four most important items for you?
I'd like my spouse (husband or wife) **to be** _____.

_____ generous	✓ kind and helpful to others	_____ rich
_____ ambitious	✓ a good cook and homemaker	_____ creative
_____ traditional	✓ honest and sincere	_____ intelligent
_____ modern	_____ famous	✓ practical

GRAMMAR **PRESENTATION**
DESIRES, INVITATIONS, REQUESTS: *WOULD LIKE, WOULD YOU LIKE . . . ?, WOULD YOU PLEASE . . . ? / COULD YOU PLEASE . . . ?*

DESIRES: AFFIRMATIVE STATEMENTS

SUBJECT	WOULD LIKE	
I You He She We You They	**would like**	some coffee. to visit him.

CONTRACTIONS WITH *WOULD*

I would → **I'd** he would → **he'd** she would → **she'd**	we would → **we'd** you would → **you'd*** they would → **they'd**

You is both singular and plural.

WH- QUESTIONS

WH- WORD		WOULD	SUBJECT	LIKE	
What					to drink?
Where					to stay?
When					to leave?
Who		**would**	you	**like**	to sit next to?
How					your meat?
How much	sugar				in your tea?
How many	cookies				to have?

ANSWERS

Some tea, please.
At a hotel.
At nine-thirty.
Bill.
Well done.
One teaspoon.
One or two, please.

INVITATIONS AND OFFERS

WOULD	SUBJECT	LIKE	
Would **Would**	you you	**like** **like**	some fruit? to join us?

SHORT ANSWERS

AFFIRMATIVE	NEGATIVE
Yes, thank you. Yes, I would.	No, thanks.

POLITE REQUESTS

WOULD YOU PLEASE / COULD YOU PLEASE	BASE FORM OF VERB	
Would you please **Could you please**	lend	me your pen?

NOTES	**EXAMPLES**
1. ***Would like*** is a polite way of saying *want*. USAGE NOTE: Use contractions in speaking and informal writing.	• I **would like** a sports car. • **I'd** like a sport utility vehicle.
2. *Would like* can be followed by **a noun**. *Would like* can be followed by **an infinitive**. *Would like* can also be followed by a noun or an object pronoun plus an infinitive. In this case, the subject wants someone else to do something.	• I'd like **a sailboat**. <small>noun</small> • She'd like **to marry** a generous man. <small>infinitive</small> • She'd like **her husband to be** honest and sincere. <small>noun + infinitive</small>
3. Use ***Would you like*** for polite invitations or offers to do something.	• **Would you like** to dance? • **Would you like** some soda? • **Would you like** me to help you?
4. We don't usually use *would like* in short answers to invitations or offers with *Would you like*.	**A:** Would you like some coffee? **B:** **No, I don't want any, thank you.** OR **B:** **No, thanks.** NOT ~~No, I wouldn't like any, thank you.~~
5. In Unit 21, you learned how to make polite requests using *Please* + a base-form verb. ***Would you please*** and ***Could you please*** + **a base-form verb** are two other ways of making polite requests.	• Please close the window. • **Would you please close** the window? • **Could you please close** the window?

PRONUNCIATION NOTE
You never pronounce the "l" in the word *would*. *Would* is pronounced like the word *wood* / wʊd /. (*Would you* often sounds like / wʊdyə /.)

FOCUSED PRACTICE

1 DISCOVER THE GRAMMAR

Read the conversation between Molly and a new client.

MOLLY: So, John, you enjoy writing and painting. Would you like to meet a writer or painter?

JOHN: Oh no, Molly. I don't want to meet a writer or painter. I'd like to meet a successful accountant or businessperson.

MOLLY: Why an accountant or businessperson?

JOHN: Well, I'd like my wife to work and earn a lot of money. I'd like to stay home and write and paint.

MOLLY: I see. So would you like to take care of the house?

JOHN: No. I'd like to write and paint.

MOLLY: What about a family? Would you like to have children?

JOHN: Children? Not really, but if my wife wants them, it's OK. Of course she'll take care of them.

MOLLY: And you'll write and paint?

JOHN: That's the picture.

MOLLY: Well, John, I'm afraid I just can't help you.

Check (✔) each true statement.

_____ **1.** John would like to be an accountant or businessperson.

_____ **2.** John would like his wife to be an accountant or businessperson.

_____ **3.** John would like to have children.

_____ **4.** John would like to stay home and take care of the house.

2 A BIRTHDAY GIFT   Grammar Notes 1–4

Listen to the conversation. Then write what the wife doesn't want and what she would like.

The wife doesn't want _____

The wife would like _____

In your opinion, is this a good advertisement?

3 TWO RESTAURANTS

Complete the conversations with **I'd like**, **Would you like**, *or* **Could you please**.

Conversation 1

SERVER: Ready to order?

CUSTOMER: Yes. _____<u>I'd like</u>_____ two eggs, scrambled, and a large orange juice.
1.

SERVER: _____ some potatoes with the eggs?
2.

CUSTOMER: Yes, please. Home fries.

SERVER: Okay. Coffee?

CUSTOMER: No. I'll take tea.

Conversation 2

SERVER: Are you ready, sir?

CUSTOMER 1: Yes, I think so.

SERVER: _____ something to drink?
3.

CUSTOMER 1: _____ some ginger ale. No ice, please.
4.

CUSTOMER 2: And _____ bring us some bread?
5.

SERVER: Of course. And what _____ to drink, sir?
6.

CUSTOMER 2: _____ a glass of Perrier™.
7.

SERVER: Very good. We have a few specials that are not on the menu. We have a

delicious squash soup for six dollars, a striped bass with grilled zucchini

for twenty-five dollars, and a chicken breast in mushroom sauce for

twenty-one dollars.

CUSTOMER 1: That soup sounds good. I'll try it.

CUSTOMER 2: And _____ to begin with a salad.
8.

SERVER: Very good.

Now circle the right answers.

9. The server in the first conversation is getting an order for _____.
   a. breakfast in a coffee shop   b. dinner in an expensive restaurant

10. The second conversation takes place at _____ restaurant.
    a. a fast food   b. an expensive   c. a cheap

4 AT CAROL AND YOKO'S PARTY Grammar Notes 1–5

Listen to this conversation between Yoko and some friends at her party. Then circle the answer that best completes each sentence.

1. Juan would like _____.
   a. some more sushi
   b. the recipe for sushi *(circled)*

2. Yoko _____.
   a. doesn't want to give Juan the recipe for sushi
   b. would like to give Juan the recipe for sushi

3. Yolanda would like _____.
   a. some more sushi
   b. the recipe for sushi

4. Yolanda would like _____.
   a. to have something to drink
   b. to have a glass of soda

5. Dina _____.
   a. would like to stay, but she can't
   b. would like to dance, but she can't

6. Dina would like _____.
   a. her cat
   b. her coat

5 DESIRES, INVITATIONS, AND REQUESTS Grammar Notes 1–5

Read each response. Then write the correct question or request. Use the questions in the box.

> What would you like to drink?
> Would you like to dance?
> Would you please pass the salt?
> How much coffee would you like?
> Would you like to have some pizza?
> How many glasses of soda would you like?
> I'm fixing the cabinet. Could you please answer the telephone?
> What would you like us to do with the dirty glasses?
> Would you like some help?

1. A: Would you like to have some pizza?

   B: No, thanks. I'm not hungry. I had a big dinner.

(continued on next page)

2. A: _____

    B: Oh, I'd really be grateful. I'm terrible at math.

3. A: _____

    B: Okay, but I hope your neighbors aren't calling to complain about the noise.

4. A: _____

    B: Please put them in the sink.

5. A: _____

    B: Not too much. Just half a cup. I drank four cups this morning.

6. A: _____

    B: Here it is. Would you like the pepper, too?

7. A: _____

    B: I'm sorry, I can't. I have a bad ankle.

8. A: _____

    B: Two, please. We're both thirsty.

9. A: _____

    B: Just a glass of water, please.

---

6 PULLED IN ALL DIRECTIONS   Grammar Notes 1–3

Pete arrived home from work. Listen to the conversation between Pete and Elenore. Then listen again and circle the answer that best completes the sentence.

1. Doug would like Pete to _____.

    a. help him with housework   **(b.)** help him with homework   **c.** help him with magic

2. Valerie and Bob would like Pete to _____.

    a. go camping with them   **b.** go bowling with them   **c.** go shopping with them

3. Lulu would like Pete to _____.

    a. meet her later tonight   **b.** call her tomorrow night   **c.** call her later tonight

4. Elenore would like Pete to _____.

    a. make some fish   **b.** buy some fish   **c.** try some fish

COMMUNICATION PRACTICE

7 INVITATIONS

Work with a partner. Take turns. Invite your partner to do something. Your partner can accept or refuse. Use the suggestions in the box or make up your own.

Would you like to _____ ?

> **EXAMPLE:**
> **A:** Would you like to come to my house for dinner?
> **B:** Sure. What time?
>
>   OR
>
> I'd really like to, but I can't. I have lots of homework and a big test tomorrow. I need to study.

> come to my house for dinner
> go shopping together
> go to the movies
> have lunch together
> play tennis
> study English together

8 POLITE REQUESTS

Work with a partner. Read the situations. Take turns making polite requests. Answer each other's requests.

> **EXAMPLE:**
> Your neighbor's radio is on. He is listening to loud music. You are trying to study.
> **A:** I have a lot of homework to do, and I can't do it with music playing. Could you please turn down the volume on your radio?
> **B:** Oh, I'm so sorry. I didn't mean to disturb you.

1. You're at the dinner table. The salt is in front of John.

2. You don't understand some math problems. Your friend is very good in math.

3. You're a teacher. Class is almost over. You want your students to hand in their tests.

4. You forgot your eraser. Your classmate has an eraser.

5. Your neighbor's parrot wakes you up at five o'clock every morning.

PART IX

REVIEW OR SELFTEST

I. *Read each conversation. Circle the letter of the underlined word or group of words that is not correct.*

1. **A:** Why did you leave your job?   A B C D

   B: I had too <u>much</u> problems.
                    A

   A: What will you do?

   B: I <u>may</u> <u>take</u> a short vacation, and then I <u>may</u> go back
          B   **C**   **D**

   to school.

2. **A:** <u>May</u> you get me <u>a few</u> things at the supermarket?   A B C D
          A   **B**

   B: Sure. What do you need?

   A: <u>Some milk</u>, bread, and <u>bananas</u>.
          C   **D**

3. **A:** <u>How much</u> <u>sugar</u> did you put in the coffee?   A B C D
          A   **B**

   B: <u>Too</u> <u>many</u>. Let me get you another cup.
          C **D**

   A: No, it's okay. I like it sweet.

4. **A:** What's the best way to get to the theater?   A B C D

   B: Well, there are several possibilities. You <u>would</u> <u>take</u>
                                                    A   **B**

   a bus, a train, or a taxi.

   A: I guess <u>I'll</u> <u>take</u> the train. It's cheap and fast.
                  C   **D**

5. **A:** <u>Would you</u> <u>like</u> <u>some</u> more cake?   A B C D
          A   **B**   **C**

   B: Oh, yes. This cake's delicious.

   A: How about you?

   B: No. I <u>wouldn't like</u> any.
                D

II. *Complete the sentences. Choose from the words in parentheses.*

1. He met _____ _____ at the concert.
              (a few, a little)   (friend, friends)

2. There isn't _____ _____ in the freezer.
                  (some, any)   (ice cream, ice creams)

3. I bought _____ _____ at the post office.
　　　　　　　　　(some, any)　　　　　　(stamp, stamps)

4. There is only _____ _____ left.
　　　　　　　　　(a few, a little)　　　　　(time, times)

5. He doesn't have _____ _____.
　　　　　　　　　　(many, much)　　　　　(money, moneys)

6. We eat _____ _____.
　　　　　　　(lots, lots of)　　　(vegetable, vegetables)

7. We need _____ _____ about your bank accounts.
　　　　　　　　(an, some)　　　(information, informations)

8. _____ _____ did you deliver?
　　(How much, How many)　(furniture, furnitures)

9. _____ _____ of milk did the baby drink today?
　　(How much, How many)　　(bottle, bottles)

10. I couldn't finish my homework. I didn't have _____
　　　　　　　　　　　　　　　　　　　　　　　　(too much, enough)

_____.
　(time, times)

11. I'm leaving. There are _____ _____ in the kitchen.
　　　　　　　　　　(too much, too many)　　(cook, cooks)

12. The soup isn't very good. I used _____ _____.
　　　　　　　　　　　　　　　(too few, too little)　　(salt, salts)

III. *Complete the conversations. Use* **how much** *or* **how many**.

A: Mmm. This French toast is delicious. How did you make it?

B: It's simple.

A: Listen, I'm a terrible cook. Tell me exactly what you did.

B: Okay. What do you want to know?

A: _____ eggs did you use?
　　　　　　1.

B: Two or maybe three.

A: _____ slices of bread?
　　　　　　2.

B: Two.

A: _____ butter?
　　　　　　3.

B: About half a teaspoon, I guess. I'm not really sure.

A: _____ salt?
　　　　　　4.

B: Just a pinch.

A: You're a good cook, but your directions are really bad.

IV. *Complete the sentences. Use the nouns in the box.*

> bowl   cup   gallon   jar   piece   pound

1. He bought a _____ of milk. He has five children, and they all drink a lot of milk.

2. I usually have a _____ of cereal for breakfast.

3. He always drinks a _____ of tea after his dinner.

4. I'm washing the floor because I dropped a _____ of grape jelly and I don't want the floor to be sticky.

5. I bought a _____ of meat for the barbecue, but I need to get some more.

6. He wrote the number on a _____ of paper, but he can't find it.

V. *Complete the letter. Use the words in parentheses. Change count nouns to the plural when necessary.*

Dear Mom and Dad,

   I'm thoroughly exhausted. Yoko and I had a wonderful party last night. We had lots
of _____ and terrific _____. At first Yoko was upset
        1. (food)   2. (music)
because there were only _____ people, but by nine o'clock there were
                             3. (a few, a little)
more than fifty people. _____ of the _____ from
                     4. (Many, Much)   5. (student)
Yoko's ESL class brought food from their countries. Everything was delicious.

   Today I don't have _____ for anything but schoolwork. I have
                     6. (time)
several _____ and a lot of _____ this week.
       7. (test)   8. (homework)
   Send my love to Doug, and thanks for the _____. Everything is
                         9. (money)
so expensive.

                          Love,

                          Carol

VI. *Complete the conversations. Use* **can**, **can't**, **may**, **could**, **couldn't**, **would**, *or* **'d**.
In some cases, more than one answer is correct.

    1. A: _____ you like some coffee?

       B: No, thanks. I had two cups at home and I _____ drink any more.

    2. A: Is your English improving?

       B: Oh, yes. Last year I _____ read, write, or speak a word of English. Now

          I _____ understand a lot and I _____ say what I want to.

    3. A: Did you send that package?

       B: Not yet. We _____ go to the post office yesterday because it was

          closed, but we _____ go this afternoon. It's open today.

    4. A: Excuse me. I _____ like to return this sweater.

       B: Do you have the receipt?

       A: No, I'm sorry. I don't.

       B: Well, in this store you _____ return anything without a receipt.

    5. A: _____ I help you?

       B: Yes, I'm looking for a gray wool sweater.

    6. A: _____ you like to dance?

       B: Yes, thank you.

    7. A: _____ I please borrow your pen for a minute?

       B: Of course. Here it is.

    8. A: _____ you please translate this sentence?

       B: Sure. No problem.

VII. *Complete the conversations. Choose from the words in parentheses.*

    1. A: Is Pete busy all day?

       B: I'm not sure. He _____ be free in the afternoon.
                   (may, 'll)

    2. A: These boxes are very heavy.

       B: I _____ help you carry them.
           (may, 'll)

(continued on next page)

3. A: Would you please explain that math problem to me?

    B: I _____ try to help you.
                   ('ll, might)

    A: Thanks.

4. A: What kind of vegetables are you going to grow in your garden this year?

    B: I'm not sure. We _____ grow tomatoes and cucumbers. They usually do
                      (may, won't)

    well. One thing is certain. We _____ grow carrots. They never do well.
                               (may not, won't)

5. A: Where's Noah?

    B: Don't worry. He _____ be back in a few minutes. He just went to
                   ('ll, won't)

    the store.

6. A: What level is Mr. Brown going to teach next semester?

    B: He _____ probably teach the advanced course.
             (may, 'll)

7. A: I need some quarters for the laundry. Do you have any?

    B: I'll see. I don't have any in my wallet, but I _____ have some in my pocket.
                            (may, 'll)

VIII. *Correct these sentences.*

                 many
1. We bought too ~~much~~ eggs.

2. She did some homeworks last night.

3. She doesn't need some apples.

4. They put a few salt and pepper on the pasta and it tasted fine.

5. There are too few doctor in Alaska.

6. A week ago he can't ride a bicycle, but now he can ride very well.

7. Would you please to help me?

8. Is test on Monday?

▶ *To check your answers, go to the Answer Key on page 357.*

FROM GRAMMAR TO WRITING
A BUSINESS LETTER

1 *Work with a partner. Look at the business letter on page 356 and answer the questions. Read the rules and check your work.*

1. Where does your address belong?

_____

2. Where does the date belong?

_____

3. Where does the name and the address of the person you're writing to belong?

_____

4. How do you address the person you are writing to?

_____

5. What do you do in the first sentence?

_____

6. What does the last full line of the letter often say?

_____

7. How do you end the letter?

_____

Business Letter Form

When we write a business letter, we follow a certain form. Use this form for all letters that are not to friends or relatives.

1. Write your address at the top left of the page.
2. Write the date below your address.
3. Skip at least two lines. Write the name and address of the person you are writing to on the left margin below your address.
4. When you write a letter, it's best to write to a person by name. If you don't know the person's name, you may write "Dear Sir/Madam:" or "To Whom It May Concern:"; be sure to use a colon (:) after the name.
5. Tell what you want in your first sentence.
6. In the last line of your letter you usually thank the person you are writing to.
7. You may end a letter with "Sincerely yours" or "Yours truly."

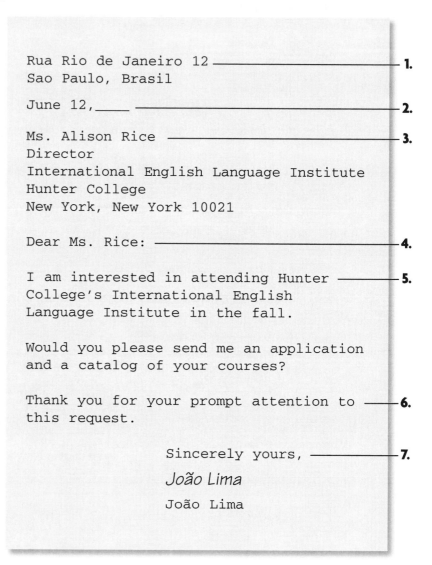

```
Rua Rio de Janeiro 12 ——————————— 1.
Sao Paulo, Brasil

June 12,____ ———————————————————— 2.

Ms. Alison Rice  ———————————————— 3.
Director
International English Language Institute
Hunter College
New York, New York 10021


Dear Ms. Rice: ————————————————— 4.


I am interested in attending Hunter ——— 5.
College's International English
Language Institute in the fall.

Would you please send me an application
and a catalog of your courses?

Thank you for your prompt attention to ——— 6.
this request.

                    Sincerely yours, ———— 7.

                    João Lima

                    João Lima
```

2 *Write one of the following business letters. Follow the form of the letter in Exercise 1.*

1. Ask for a bulletin of courses and an application for a language program.
2. Ask for a list of moderately priced apartments near the language program.

REVIEW OR SELFTEST
ANSWER KEY

I.
1. A   3. D   5. D
2. A   4. A

II.
1. a few friends
2. any ice cream
3. some stamps
4. a little time
5. much money
6. lots of vegetables
7. some information
8. How much furniture
9. How many bottles
10. enough time
11. too many cooks
12. too little salt

III.
1. How many   3. How much
2. How many   4. How much

IV.
1. gallon   3. cup   5. pound
2. bowl   4. jar   6. piece

V.
1. food   4. Many   7. tests
2. music   5. students   8. homework
3. a few   6. time   9. money

VI.
1. Would; can't
2. couldn't; can; can
3. couldn't; can
4. 'd like; can't
5. May; (Can)
6. Would
7. Could; (May); (Can)
8. Could; Would

VII.
1. may   5. 'll
2. 'll   6. 'll
3. 'll   7. may
4. may; won't

VIII.
2. She did some **homework** last night.
3. She doesn't need **any** apples.
4. They put a **little** salt and pepper on the pasta and it tasted fine.
5. There are too few **doctors** in Alaska.
6. A week ago he **couldn't** ride a bicycle, but now he can ride very well.
7. **Would** you please help me? (eliminate "to")
8. Is **the** test on Monday?

INFORMATION GAP FOR STUDENT B   Unit 33, Exercise 7

Answer your partner's questions. Ask your partner questions to complete the sentences.

1. A European country that produces a lot of chocolate, cheese, and watches is Switzerland.

2. _____ is a South American country where you can find a lot of emeralds.

3. An African country that produces a lot of diamonds is South Africa.

4. A very large Asian country that produces a lot of rice is _____ .

5. Brazil is a very large South American country that produces a lot of coffee.

6. Three Asian countries that manufacture a lot of computers and cars are _____ , _____ , and _____ .

7. Two countries that produce a lot of oil are Saudi Arabia and Iran.

Answer to Exercise 7 on page 340
1. Japanese   4. Austrian   7. Chinese   10. Swiss
2. Thai   5. Israeli   8. Senegalese   11. Greek
3. Puerto Rican   6. Korean   9. Colombian   12. Russian

COMPARISONS;
THE PAST PROGRESSIVE

PREVIEW

Elenore and Pete are having dinner. Listen and read their conversation.

YOU CAN WIN MORE BEARS WITH HONEY

ELENORE: Pete, didn't you get my message?

PETE: What message?

ELENORE: I called your office this afternoon and left a message for you to call home.

PETE: Sorry. I never got it.

ELENORE: I was calling to find out how your speech went.

PETE: I think it went very well. Everyone laughed at my jokes and clapped for a long time.

ELENORE: Great. You know, I'm not crazy about that new assistant of yours. Bob was much better. The phone rang six times before she picked up.

PETE: Six times?

ELENORE: Uh-huh. Bob always answered on the second ring. I must say your new assistant has a pleasant voice, but she wasn't as friendly as Bob, and half the time she spoke too softly.

PETE: That's really too bad. Sally's a super typist. She types quickly and accurately. And that combination is hard to find.

ELENORE: Did many people apply for the job?

PETE: No, only one other person. Sally had much more experience and better references than the other woman.

[the next evening]

ELENORE: You know, Pete, I spoke to Sally again. Today she answered the phone immediately. She was much friendlier and much more confident than yesterday. Did you complain?

PETE: No, I didn't. She remembered your call and felt awful about forgetting to tell me.

ELENORE: So, what did you say?

PETE: I said, "Sally, my wife thinks you have a lovely voice. She enjoyed talking with you."

ELENORE: What's that expression? "You can win more bears with honey." Pete, you really handled the situation well.

PETE: Thanks, Elenore. That's nice to hear.

COMPREHENSION CHECK

Write **True (T)** *or* **False (F)** *next to each sentence.*

_____ **1.** Pete complained to his assistant because she let the phone ring six times.

_____ **2.** Many people applied for the job as Pete's assistant.

_____ **3.** Elenore thinks Pete's former assistant was better on the telephone than Sally is.

_____ **4.** Elenore thinks Pete was smart not to complain to Sally.

_____ **5.** "You can win more bears with honey" means you can accomplish more by being nice than by being critical.

WITH A PARTNER

Practice the conversation on pages 358 and 359.

COMPARATIVE FORM OF ADJECTIVES

GRAMMAR **IN CONTEXT**

WARM UP   Imagine you are choosing an assistant and a boss. List five qualities you would like to find in an assistant and five qualities you would like to find in a boss. Use the suggestions in the box, or write your own ideas.

dependable	organized
enthusiastic	honest
intelligent	calm
hard-working	thoughtful
fair	generous
punctual	
creative	(your own ideas)

An assistant:

1. _____

2. _____

3. _____

4. _____

5. _____

A boss:

1. _____

2. _____

3. _____

4. _____

5. _____

Listen and read the conversation between Pete and Elenore.

PETE: Where were you? I was beginning to worry.

ELENORE: Oh, I met Michelle Sobel. She was really upset.

PETE: Oh?

ELENORE: Ron didn't get that promotion.

PETE: Again? Oh, no. Who got it?

ELENORE: Steve.

PETE: Steve Smith? Isn't he a lot **younger than** Ron?

ELENORE: A lot. And he's **less experienced**, too.

PETE: Well, why didn't Ron get the promotion? He's bright and well spoken.

ELENORE: Actually, I think he's **more intelligent than** Steve. I really don't know what happened. Maybe Ron's not a good team player. Steve gets along well with everyone, and he's very enthusiastic. Ron can be difficult. And he can also be quite stubborn.

PETE: Probably because he's right. I don't think that's why Steve got the job.

ELENORE: Why do you think he did?

PETE: Steve's probably willing to work for **less money than** Ron. Companies can pay younger people with **less experience** lower salaries.

ELENORE: That's awful.

PETE: It is.

[A few months later]

ELENORE: Pete, you'll never guess who I ran into. Ron Sobel.

PETE: Oh, how's he doing?

ELENORE: Great. Remember when he didn't get that promotion?

PETE: Sure.

ELENORE: Well, he left his job and started his own company. He's doing fabulously. He's **much happier** and **much more enthusiastic** than he was before.

PETE: That's terrific. I'm really happy for him.

GRAMMAR **PRESENTATION**
COMPARATIVE FORM OF ADJECTIVES

	COMPARATIVE FORM OF ADJECTIVE	THAN	
Ron is	old**er** bus**ier**	than	**Steve**.
	more careful		

	IRREGULAR COMPARATIVE FORM OF ADJECTIVE	THAN	
The new computer is	**better** **worse**	than	the old one.
His new office is	**farther**		

NOTES

EXAMPLES

---

1. Use the **comparative form of an adjective +** ***than*** to compare two people, places, or things.

- I'm **taller than** she is.

---

2. USAGE NOTE: In formal English, use the subject pronoun after *than*.

- Steve's younger than **he** is.   *subject pronoun*

OR

- Steve's younger than **he**.

In informal English, you can use the object pronoun after *than*.

- Steve's younger than **him**.   *object pronoun*

3. To form the comparative of **short (one-syllable*) adjectives**, add **-er** to the adjective. Add only **-r** if the adjective ends in **e**.

When a one-syllable adjective ends in **a consonant**, **vowel**, and **consonant (CVC)**, double the last consonant and add **-er**.

- (old) I'm old**er** than my sister.
- (large) His office is large**r** than his assistant's.

  CVC
- (thin) Elenore is thi**nner** than Lulu.

  CVC
- (hot) Yesterday was ho**tter** than today.

---

4. To form the comparative of most **adjectives** of **two** or **more syllables**, add **more** before the adjective and **than** before the person or thing you are comparing.

- (generous) He is **more generous than** his brother.
- (famous) Today Michael Douglas is **more famous than** his father, Kirk Douglas.

---

5. To form the comparative of two-syllable adjectives that end in **-y**, change the **y** to **i** and add **-er**.

busy → bus**ier**
- (busy) We are **busier** than they are.

funny → funn**ier**
- (funny) The movie was **funnier** than the book.

---

6. These are exceptions to the preceding notes. *Tired* and *bored* are one-syllable adjectives that follow the pattern of long adjectives.

Quiet and *simple* are two-syllable adjectives that follow the pattern of one-syllable adjectives.

- Today I'm **more tired than** I was yesterday.
- The children were **more bored than** the adults.

- He's **quieter than** his sister.
- This lesson is **simpler than** the next one.

---

*A syllable is a word or part of a word that contains one vowel sound. *Old* has one syllable.
Older has two syllables: *old + er*.

(continued on next page)

7. *Less* is the opposite of *more*. You can also use *not as* + **adjective** + *as* for such comparisons.

- A car is **more expensive than** a bicycle.
- A bicycle is **less expensive than** a car.
- A bicycle is **not as expensive as** a car.

8. The adjectives *good, bad,* and *far* have irregular comparative forms.
good—better
bad—worse
far—farther

- I think his new movie is good, but his old one was **better**.
- I think that book is bad, but the film is **worse**.
- Both museums are far from here, but the art museum is **farther** than the natural history museum.

9. Use *much* to make comparisons stronger.

- I am **much** taller than you are.
- This book is **much** more interesting than that other book.

10. BE CAREFUL! Always compare the same things.

- **Lulu's name** is shorter than **Elenore's name**.

  OR

- **Lulu's name** is shorter than **Elenore's**.

  NOT ~~Lulu's name is shorter than Elenore.~~ (You are comparing names, not people.)

REFERENCE NOTE
See Unit 40 for a discussion of *not as* + adjective + *as*.

FOCUSED PRACTICE

① DISCOVER THE GRAMMAR

A. *Write the comparative form of each of these words.*

1. fast _____faster_____

2. big_____

3. pretty _____

4. strong _____

5. expensive _____

6. funny _____

7. generous _____

8. tired _____

9. bored_____

10. quiet _____

11. simple _____

12. far _____

B. 📼 *Pete's new assistant, Sally, has an eight-year-old son named Rick. Rick is playing with his friend Jimmy at the playground. Complete their conversation with the comparative form of the correct words from above. Then listen and check your work.*

JIMMY: Let's race.

RICK: Okay.

> *[The boys race. Jimmy wins the race.]*

JIMMY: I won. I'm ___faster than___
1.

you are.

RICK: So? I can lift this rock and you can't. I'm _____ you.
2.

JIMMY: See this watch? It costs $100. It's _____ your watch.
3.

RICK: So what? My uncle is six feet tall, and he weighs 200 pounds. He's _____
4.

your uncle.

JIMMY: Well, my mom won a beauty contest in high school. She's _____
5.

your mom.

RICK: No, she isn't.

JIMMY: Yes, she is. And my mom knows 200 jokes. She's _____ your mom, too.
6.

RICK: Well, my grandparents give me presents every month. They're _____
7.

your grandparents.

JIMMY: How do you know? Look, there's Bob. Hey Bob, want to race?

2 JIMMY AND RICK

	HEIGHT	WEIGHT	AGE
Rick	4 feet 2 inches or 127 centimeters	57 pounds or 25.9 kilograms	8
Jimmy	4 feet 4 inches or 132 centimeters	69 pounds or 31.3 kilograms	8½

Read the chart. Then write sentences comparing Rick and Jimmy. Use the adjectives in the box.

tall	short	old	young	heavy	thin

1. Rick is shorter than Jimmy.

2. _____

3. _____

4. _____

5. _____

6. _____

3 JOB INTERVIEWS

Last week Pete interviewed Sally Cooper and Gail Finger. Listen to their interviews. Then compare Sally and Gail. Use the words in parentheses.

1. (experienced—more) Sally is more experienced than Gail.

2. (experienced—less) _____

3. (talkative—more) At the interview _____ was _____

4. (talkative—less) At the interview _____ was_____

5. (young) _____

6. (polite) _____

7. (bad—much) In my opinion, _____

8. (good—much) In my opinion, _____

4 **TWO APARTMENTS**   **Grammar Notes 1–4, 6, 8, 10**

A. *Sally is looking for an apartment for herself and her son, Rick. She is considering two apartments. One apartment is in the center of Manhattan near her job, and the other is in Queens.*

Look at the two ads. Write the abbreviation next to the word.

ing, center of town, near to station **$1,400**	schools **$1,100**
Manhattan Apartment 3 rms/1 lg bdrm, older building, center of town, convenient to all **$1,400 mo.**	**Queens Apartment** 4 rms/2 bdrms, 2 bths/ modern building/quiet location/nr schools and parks **$1,300 mo.**
Manhattan Apartment 7 rms/2 lg bdrms, relatively newer building, center of	Queens Condo 5 rms/3 bdrms, 3 baths/modern kitchen/mod

1. rooms = _____

2. large = _____

3. bedrooms = _____

4. baths = _____

5. near = _____

6. month = _____

B. *Now write the sentences comparing the two apartments. Use the words in parentheses.*

1. (large) The apartment in Queens is larger than the one in Manhattan. _____

2. (expensive) _____

3. (quiet) _____

4. (modern) _____

5. (convenient to Sally's job) _____

6. Give your opinion:
(good) In my opinion _____
for Sally and her son.

COMMUNICATION PRACTICE

5 INFORMATION GAP: POPULAR SAYINGS

Student A, read these three sayings aloud. Your partner will find an illustration that matches each saying. Then listen to your partner's sayings and find an illustration that matches your partner's sayings.

Student B, look at the Information Gap on page 399 and follow the instructions there.

Sayings:

Half a loaf is better than none.

His eyes are bigger than his stomach.

His bark is worse than his bite.

Illustrations:

Try and finish that report before you leave today.

His book changed the world.

Why don't we work together? I'm sure we'll get more done.

6 COMPARING CITIES

A. *Each student names a city he or she knows well. The teacher writes the names on the blackboard. (Do not name the city you are in.)*

B. *Now the class names adjectives that describe cities, people, and climates. The teacher writes the adjectives on the blackboard.*

> **EXAMPLE:**
> **CITIES:** clean, dangerous, crowded
> **PEOPLE:** friendly, polite, helpful
> **CLIMATES:** warm, dry, humid

C. *Each student writes questions comparing the cities on the blackboard to the city you are in. Students can use the adjectives on the blackboard or choose their own. Then students ask each other questions comparing the cities.*

> **EXAMPLES:**
> You are now in San Francisco.
> **A:** Is Paris cleaner than San Francisco?
> **B:** I don't think so. In my opinion, San Francisco is cleaner than Paris.
> **C:** Is the climate in Tokyo warmer than the climate in San Francisco?
> **D:** Well, in the winter San Francisco is warmer than Tokyo, but in the summer Tokyo is much hotter than San Francisco.

ADVERBS OF MANNER AND COMPARATIVE FORMS OF ADVERBS

GRAMMAR **IN CONTEXT**

WARM UP   How do you feel about public speaking?

Listen and read this article about public speaking.

Public Speaking
by Nadine Chan

A well-known speech writer said, "The mind is a wonderful thing. It starts working the minute you're born and never stops . . . until you get up to speak in public."

Many well-educated people never speak in public. But anyone who can speak **well** in private conversation can learn to give a good public speech. Just remember three things: instruct, entertain, and inspire. Author Bob Rosner likes to say, "It's ha-ha and ah-hah."

When you instruct, speak **briefly**, **slowly**, and **clearly**. Don't speak too **long**. And don't speak too **fast**. Try to speak **clearly** and present ideas simply with good examples.

Use humor whenever possible. When people laugh, they relax. And remember that really great speeches inspire and move an audience. Know about your audience and touch their emotions.

I gave my first public speech fifteen years ago. I wanted to impress my audience so I told them a lot of facts. I used big words and long sentences. I spoke **quickly** and **seriously**, and I didn't use any humor because I wanted to be taken seriously.

My speech was a disaster. The next time I spoke, a friend helped me prepare my speech. This time I spoke much **more slowly** and **clearly**. I focused on three ideas and gave lots of examples. I added humor and I spoke **more sincerely** and **more emotionally**. I included personal experiences and I used simple words. The applause was long and loud. When I sat down, I knew I had connected with my audience. And I felt good. They gave me their time. And I gave them a speech to remember.

GRAMMAR **PRESENTATION**
ADVERBS OF MANNER; COMPARATIVE FORM OF ADVERBS

COMMON ADVERBS OF MANNER

ADJECTIVE + -LY	SAME FORM AS ADJECTIVE	IRREGULAR ADVERB
accurately badly briefly carefully clearly fluently freely well loudly neatly quickly quietly seriously slowly softly	early fast hard late long	well

COMPARATIVE FORM OF ADVERBS

		MORE + ADVERB	THAN	
Nadine	typed	**more carefully**	**than**	John.
	spoke	**more intelligently**		

		ADVERB + -ER	THAN	
Sally	types	fast**er**	**than**	Gail.
	works	hard**er**		

	IRREGULAR COMPARATIVE FORM OF ADVERB	THAN	
The fish tastes	**better**	**than**	the meat.
Pete sings	**worse**		Doug.

NOTES	**EXAMPLES**
1. Adverbs of manner describe action verbs. They say **how** or **in what manner** something happens. The adverb often comes at the end of the sentence.	• She walks **fast**. • He spoke **slowly**.

2. Most adverbs of manner are formed by adding *-ly* to the adjective.	• She's a adjective
	  She's a **careful** driver.
	• adverb
	  She drives **carefully**.

3. Some adverbs of manner have the same form as adjectives. ▶ **BE CAREFUL!** Some words that end in *-ly* are **adjectives**, not adverbs. A few of these are *lively, lovely, ugly, lonely,* and *friendly*. These adjectives have no adverb form.	adjective adverb • She's a **fast** typist. She types **fast**. • She's a **hard** worker. She works **hard**. adjective • She's a **friendly** person.

4. *Well* is the adverb for the adjective *good*. *Well* is also an adjective that means "in good health."	• She's a good speaker.
	      adverb
	• She speaks **well**.
	
	      adjective
	• I feel **well**.

(continued on next page)

5. Some verbs, called **linking verbs**, are followed by **adjectives**, not by adverbs of manner. Use adjectives after the linking verbs *appear, be, become, feel, look, seem, smell, sound,* and *taste.*

- These eggs **taste good**.
  (linking verb) (adjective)
- The music **sounds beautiful**.
  (linking verb) (adjective)
- You **look tired**.
  (linking verb) (adjective)

---

6. To form the **comparative of adverbs** that end in *-ly*, add *more* before the adverb. For other adverbs, add *-er* to the adverb.

Early is an exception; the comparative form is *earlier*.

- He drives **more slowly** than his wife.
- I worked **longer** than you did.
- She arrived **earlier** than he did. NOT ~~She arrived more early than he did.~~

---

7. The adverbs *well* and *badly* have irregular comparative forms.
well—better
badly—worse

- Bob typed well, but Sally types **better**.
- He sang badly, and he danced **worse**.

---

8. BE CAREFUL! *Hard*, not *hardly*, is the adverb of manner for the adjective *hard*.

Hardly means very little.

- She's a **hard** worker. *(adjective)*
- She works **hard**. *(adverb)*
- She **hardly** ate anything.

FOCUSED PRACTICE

1 DISCOVER THE GRAMMAR

Underline the adverb in each sentence. Then write the adjective form.

1. That waitress worked <u>quickly</u>. _____quick_____

2. Sally types well. _____

3. Norma speaks Spanish fluently. _____

4. Yoko dresses neatly. _____

5. Dan drives fast. _____

6. Does Noah drive dangerously? _____

7. Who sings badly? _____

8. The mail arrived early. _____

9. It rained hard last night. _____

2 ADJECTIVES OR ADVERBS   Grammar Notes 1–2, 4–5

Complete each sentence. Use the adjective or adverb in parentheses.

1. He writes _____well_____.
   (good / well)

2. She sings _____.
   (beautiful / beautifully)

3. It tastes _____.
   (good / well)

4. That's a _____ picture.
   (beautiful / beautifully)

5. He usually does _____ on written tests but _____ on oral ones.
   (bad / badly)   (good / well)

6. Please open the door _____.
   (slow / slowly)

7. The first act was very _____, but the second act was lively and interesting.
   (slow / slowly)

❸ UNDERSTANDING INTONATION   Grammar Notes 1–2

Study the words in the box. Use your dictionary for any new words. Then listen to the speakers. Describe how they're speaking.

sarcastically	nervously	jokingly	quietly	sadly

Speaker 1. _____   **Speaker 4.** _____

Speaker 2. _____   **Speaker 5.** _____

Speaker 3. _____

❹ PETE'S ASSISTANT   Grammar Notes 1–4

Listen to the conversation between Elenore and Pete. Then choose the best adverb to complete each sentence.

1. Sally works _____.
   (hard, slowly, sloppily)

2. She types _____.
   (slowly, carelessly, fast)

3. She takes shorthand _____.
   (slowly, quickly, sloppily)

4. She doesn't take phone messages _____.
   (well, badly, carelessly)

Important Message

Date: 5/30   Time: 10:15 A.M.

For: Pete Winston   From: Mr. Hen

Telephone: 555-3232

Message: Wants to meet you

6/2 at 1 P.M.

Taken By: SMJ

❺ A BETTER WAY   Grammar Notes 6–7

Complete the sentences. Use the comparative form of the adverbs in the box.

badly	carefully	early	late	quickly	slowly	well

1. Don't add those numbers in your head. A calculator can add much ___more quickly___ than you can.

2. You speak very fast. I can't understand you. Please speak _____.

3. We missed the train today. Tomorrow we will wake up _____.

4. Denise is a careless driver. Ask Elenore to drive. She drives _____.

5. He's a good dancer, but she dances much _____.

6. Don't let Ron or Carol sing. Ron sings badly, and Carol sings _____.

7. Monday Pete arrived thirty minutes late. Tuesday he arrived even _____.

COMMUNICATION PRACTICE

6 INTONATION

Work with a partner. Take turns reading the following sentence in the ways listed.

I love English grammar.

Say it . . .

1. fast
2. slowly
3. nervously
4. angrily
5. happily

6. questioningly
7. convincingly
8. loudly
9. sarcastically
10. sadly

Can your partner guess how you are speaking? Try one or two other sentences in front of the class.

7 EXPRESSING OPINIONS

Work in groups. Write comparative questions. Then discuss the answers. Does everybody in your group have the same opinion?

1. doctors / work hard / teachers _Do doctors work harder than teachers?_

2. be / doctors / honest / lawyers _____

3. be / love / important / money _____

4. rich people / work hard / poor people _____

5. rich people / live long / poor people _____

6. be / doctors / important / teachers _____

7. women / work hard / men _____

8. women / live long / men _____

9. be / women / emotional / men _____

10. women / cry easily / men _____

11. be / soccer / exciting / baseball _____

40 ADJECTIVE + *ENOUGH* / *TOO* / *VERY*; *AS* + ADJECTIVE / ADVERB + *AS*

GRAMMAR **IN CONTEXT**

WARM UP   A *perfectionist* tries to do a perfect job. It's always good to try and do one's best, but being a perfectionist may not always be good. Why?

Listen and read this conversation between Sally and her sister Penny. Sally and Penny are at a grocery store. Sally is choosing a honeydew melon.

PENNY: Sally, are you ready? It's getting late.

SALLY: No. I can't find a good honeydew melon.

PENNY: Why not? There's a huge selection. They all look **very good** to me. Here's a nice one.

SALLY: No, it's **way too small**.

PENNY: What about this one here?

SALLY: It's almost **the same size as** the other one.

PENNY: Oh. Well, here's one. Is it **big enough**?

SALLY: It's **too big**.

PENNY: Take the one in the corner. It's the perfect size.

SALLY: You're right, but it's a little **too soft**. It may be overripe.

PENNY: Okay. Here. This one is harder.

SALLY: It's **too hard**.

PENNY: Sally, you're choosing a honeydew, not a husband. You're **much too fussy**.

SALLY: I'm **very fussy**, but I'm not **too fussy**. I like to get good food for Rick and me. Anyway, I think I'll get a pineapple. This one looks and smells good. Wait. No. It's a little **too ripe**. Here. This one isn't **as ripe**, and it smells delicious. It's perfect.

PENNY: It's about time.

GRAMMAR **PRESENTATION**
ADJECTIVE + *ENOUGH* / *TOO* / *VERY*; AS + ADJECTIVE / ADVERB + AS; THE SAME + NOUN + AS; THE SAME AS; DIFFERENT FROM

ADJECTIVE + *ENOUGH*			
	ADJECTIVE	**ENOUGH**	(*TO* + BASE FORM OF VERB)
The pineapple is	**ripe**	**enough**	(to eat).
The grade was**n't**	**high**		(to pass).

TOO + ADJECTIVE			
	TOO	**ADJECTIVE**	(*TO* + BASE FORM OF VERB)
The job was	**too**	**difficult**	(to do).

VERY + ADJECTIVE		
	VERY	**ADJECTIVE**
I'm	**very**	**tired**.

AS + ADJECTIVE / ADVERB + AS				
	AS	**ADJECTIVE / ADVERB**	**AS**	
Sally is	**as**	**tall**	**as**	Elenore.
Is Sally		**friendly**		Carol?
Gail doesn't type		**quickly**		Sally.

THE SAME + NOUN + AS				
	THE SAME	**NOUN**	**AS**	
Elenore is	**the same**	**size**	**as**	Norma.
My compositions were		**length**		yours.
My eyes are		**color**		his.
My suitcase was		**weight**		theirs.
Doug is		**height**		Noah.
Yoko has		**umbrella**		Nancy.
Mr. Brown teaches		**courses**		Ms. Alvarez.

THE SAME AS

	THE SAME AS	OBJECT
My last name is	the same as	your last name.
My initials are		yours.

DIFFERENT FROM

	DIFFERENT FROM	OBJECT
An orange is	different from	a tangerine.
Pine trees are		oak trees.
My hat is		your hat.

NOTES

EXAMPLES

---

1. *Enough* means sufficient. It has a positive meaning. Use *enough* after an adjective.

Not enough means not sufficient. It has a negative meaning.

A: Was the speech **short enough** for you?

B: No, it was**n't short enough**.

---

2. *Too* means more than necessary. It has a negative meaning. Use *too* before an adjective.

To intensify the meaning of the adjective, use *much too*. In informal conversation we also use *way too* to intensify the meaning.

A: What's wrong?

B: The speech was **too long**.

OR

The speech was **much too long**.

The movie was **way too long**.

---

3. An **infinitive** can follow an **adjective + enough**. An **infinitive** can follow **too + an adjective**.

- He's **old enough to drive**. *(infinitive)*
- She's **too tired to drive**.

---

4. *Very* intensifies the meaning of an adjective. *Very* comes before an adjective.

- I'm **very** tall.

▶ **BE CAREFUL!** Both *very* and *too* intensify the meaning of an adjective, but *too* has a negative meaning and *very* doesn't.

- He's **very** young. = He's really young. (It may be positive or negative.)

- He's **too** young. = He's too young to do something. (to drive, to work, etc.)

---

5. Use *as* **+ adjective / adverb +** *as* to express equality.

- Sally is **as tall as** Elenore. They are the same height.
- I work **as hard as** you do.

Use *not as* **+ adjective / adverb +** *as* to express inequality.

- Sally is **not as tall as** her sister.
- They **don't type as well as** we do.

Use *yes / no* questions with *as* **+ adjective / adverb +** *as* to ask if a person or thing is the same as or more than another in some way.

A: Is Carol **as tall as** Elenore?
B: Yes, she is. She's even taller.

---

6. Use *the same* **+ noun +** *as* and *the same as* to say that two things are exactly alike.

- My eyes are **the same color as** my brother's.
- Carol Winston's initials are **the same as** Charles Wu's.

The opposite of *the same as* is **different from**.

- My new car is **different from** my old one.

REFERENCE NOTE
See Unit 34 for a discussion of the use of *too* and *enough* with nouns.

FOCUSED PRACTICE

① DISCOVER THE GRAMMAR

Match the sentences.

__e__ **1.** I couldn't wear that sweater.
I wear a large. It was a medium.

_____ **2.** She burned her tongue when
she drank the coffee.

_____ **3.** They didn't like the soup.

_____ **4.** They both have blue eyes.

_____ **5.** They say that opposites attract.

_____ **6.** Turtles move more slowly
than rabbits.

a. He's very different from his wife.

b. They aren't as fast as rabbits.

c. His eyes are the same color as hers.

d. It wasn't hot enough.

e. It was too small.

f. It was too hot.

② WORD ORDER PRACTICE   Grammar Notes 1–4

Unscramble these sentences.

1. to vote / She's / enough old

   She's old enough to vote.

2. hot / swimming / to go / It isn't / enough

   _____

3. too / This steak / is / to eat / tough / much

   _____

4. to see / you / The doctor / busy / is / too

   _____

5. weren't / the refrigerator / They / enough / strong / to move

   _____

6. way / restaurant / too / That / expensive / is

   _____

❸ WHICH SYMBOLS ARE THE SAME?

*Look at the symbols and complete the sentences. Use **the same as** or **different from**.*

	A	B	
1.	ΩΩ≈ç√	ΩΩ≈ç√	A is ___the same as___ B.
2.	^®˜´	^®˜´	A is _____ B.
3.	∂å□^å	∂å□^ø^å	A is _____ B.
4.	µøµµ¥	µøµµ¥	A is _____ B.

❹ LOU DIDN'T GET A PROMOTION

Lou is a graphic artist at an advertising agency. He works in the same building as Sally. Complete the conversation between Sally and Lou. Use the phrases in the box.

> as hard as she does
> as fast and dependable
> the same university as Mary
> as talented as she is
> the same amount of experience as she does

SALLY: Lou, what's wrong? You seem to be upset.

LOU: I am. I didn't get the promotion. Mary did. I work _____.
  1.

SALLY: I know. And you really are talented.

LOU: I'm certainly _____.
  2.

SALLY: That's true.

LOU: And I hand in every project on time. I'm just _____.
  3.

SALLY: What about her background and experience?

LOU: We've got the same degrees. I even went to _____.
  4.

  And I have _____.
  5.

SALLY: Well, why do you think she got the job?

LOU: I think it's because she's a woman.

SALLY: What? That's a switch. It's usually just the opposite.

5 **WHY LOU DIDN'T GET THE PROMOTION** Grammar Notes 1–2, 4

Listen to the directors of Lou's company discuss Mary and Lou. Then explain why Lou didn't get the promotion.

1. Lou is too _____.

2. Nobody's work is _____ for him.

3. He's not _____ Mary.

6 **EXPRESSIONS IN ENGLISH** Grammar Note 5

Look at the pictures and complete the sentences.

1. He is never nervous. He never shouts or gets angry. He's as cool as a ___cucumber___.

2. She never says a word. She just sits and smiles. She's as quiet as a _____.

3. The fruit at Sam's Market is delicious. Each piece of fruit is as sweet as _____.

4. You can believe her. She's very honest. Her word is as good as _____.

5. What a strong woman! She can lift 100 pounds. She's as strong as a _____.

6. She doesn't weigh much at all. She's as light as a _____.

7. Look at him. He thinks he's grand. He's as proud as a _____.

7 TOO OR VERY

Complete the sentences with **too** *or* **very**.

1. Don't wear that skirt. It's _____*too*_____ short to wear to a job interview.

2. That's a nice blouse. The color is _____ beautiful.

3. Bekir can't reach the box. It's on the top shelf. He's _____ short. Ask Ali.

   He's _____ tall.

4. Your composition is _____ interesting and well written. Please read it to

   the class.

5. I can't lift the sofa. It's _____ heavy for me to lift. Ask Bekir. He's

   _____ strong.

6. We can't vote. We're _____ young.

8 EDITING

Correct four mistakes in the use of the comparative in this conversation.

PETE: So, how's the apartment search going?

SALLY: It's not easy. I'm still staying with my sister. I'm considering two apartments, one

in Queens and one in Manhattan.

PETE: How do they compare?

SALLY: The apartment in Queens is enough big, but it's very farther from the office.

PETE: And the Manhattan apartment?

SALLY: It's very small and it isn't as quiet than the one in Queens, but it's in Manhattan.

And I love Manhattan.

PETE: Which apartment is more expensive?

SALLY: The Queens apartment isn't expensive as the one in Manhattan, but if you add the

cost of transportation, they're the same price.

PETE: Well, good luck.

SALLY: Thanks.

COMMUNICATION PRACTICE

9 MORE THAN NECESSARY

Work with a partner. Complete these sentences.

I'm too tired to _____.

I'm not too tired to _____.

I'm too old to _____.

I'm not old enough to _____.

I'm not too young to _____.

I'm young enough to _____.

It's too late to _____.

It's not too late to _____.

I'm too shy to _____.

I'm not tall enough to _____.

I'm lucky enough to _____.

10 SIMILARITIES

Take five minutes. Walk around your classroom. Find classmates who are like you in some way. Write their names in the blanks.

1. I was born in the same month as _____.

2. I have the same color eyes / hair as _____.

3. I like the same kind of music / books / movies as _____.

4. I have the same number of sisters / brothers as _____.

THE PAST PROGRESSIVE

GRAMMAR IN CONTEXT

WARM UP Do you like surprise visitors, or do you prefer to have people call before visiting?

It's Sunday morning. Doug and his mother, Elenore, are talking about the night before. Listen and read their conversation.

DOUG: Morning, Mom. Did you and Dad enjoy the party?

ELENORE: Don't ask.

DOUG: Why?

ELENORE: We thought that Dad's new boss, Sheila, and her husband, Bob, **were having** a party last night. We arrived at 8. When Bob opened the door, he **was expecting** a delivery from the Chinese restaurant. He **was wearing** pajama bottoms and an old T-shirt. Sheila **was standing** in front of a mirror. She **was wearing** a bathrobe and a green facial mask.

DOUG: Oh, no.

ELENORE: Everyone was really embarrassed.

DOUG: What about Dad? What did he say?

ELENORE: He turned to me and said, "Elenore, you didn't tell me it was a costume party."

DOUG: Was it a costume party?

ELENORE: No. Sheila laughed and said, "Pete, we're not having a costume party, and our party is next Saturday night." We showed up on the wrong day!

DOUG: What did Dad say?

ELENORE: He said, "Oh, oh, oh, oh."

DOUG: Well, does Dad still have a job?

ELENORE: Yes, but only because Sheila has a good sense of humor.

GRAMMAR **PRESENTATION**
PAST PROGRESSIVE: AFFIRMATIVE AND NEGATIVE STATEMENTS, YES / NO QUESTIONS AND ANSWERS, WH- QUESTIONS

AFFIRMATIVE AND NEGATIVE STATEMENTS

SUBJECT	PAST TENSE OF *BE*	BASE FORM OF VERB + -*ING*	
I	**was (not)**		
You	**were (not)**		
He She It	**was (not)**	**sleeping**	at ten last night. when you **called**. while you **were working**.
We You They	**were (not)**		

YES / NO QUESTIONS

PAST TENSE OF *BE*	SUBJECT	BASE FORM OF VERB + -*ING*
Was	I	
Were	you	**laughing?**
Was	he she	
	it	**raining?**
Were	we you they	**laughing?**

SHORT ANSWERS

	AFFIRMATIVE			NEGATIVE	
	you	**were.**		you	**weren't.**
Yes,	I he she it	**was.**	No,	I he she it	**wasn't.**
	you we they	**were.**		you we they	**weren't.**

WH- QUESTIONS

WH- WORD	WAS / WERE	SUBJECT	BASE FORM OF VERB + -*ING*
Where	**was**	he	going?
What	**were**	they	doing?

NOTES	**EXAMPLES**
1. Use the **past progressive** to show that an action was in progress at a specific time in the past.	• They **were working** at seven o'clock last night.
2. To form the past progressive, use **the past form of *be* + the verb + *ing***. Add *not* after *was* or *were* to form the negative. USAGE NOTE: Use the contractions *wasn't* and *weren't* in informal speaking and writing. ▶ **BE CAREFUL!** The past progressive is not usually used with non-action verbs.	• We **were sleeping** all morning. • I **was not singing** in the shower. • He **wasn't working** on Saturday. • We **weren't watching** the time. • We understood the lesson. NOT ~~We were understanding the lesson.~~

3. Use the **past progressive** and the **simple past** in one sentence to show that one event (the simple past event) interrupted another (the past progressive event). *phone rang* **Now** Past ——X—— Future *was sleeping*	past progressive • I **was sleeping** when the phone simple past **rang**. (The ring interrupted my sleep.)

4. You can change the order of the two parts of a sentence describing a continuous action and an interruption. When you begin with the continuous action, do not use a comma between the two parts. When you begin with the interruption, add a comma between the two parts.	continuous action • I **was driving** across the bridge interruption when I **got** a flat tire. • When I **got** a flat tire, I **was driving** across the bridge.
5. *While* means "during the time that." Use *while* before a past progressive event.	• **While** I was driving across the bridge, a car hit my car.
6. Use the past progressive for two actions that continued in the past. ***While*** expresses the idea that the two actions were happening at the same time.	• **While** they **were laughing**, she **was crying**.

FOCUSED PRACTICE

1 DISCOVER THE GRAMMAR

Choose the best way to complete the sentences.

___c___ **1.** They were sleeping

_____ **2.** I was skiing

_____ **3.** I was cooking

_____ **4.** She was petting the dog

_____ **5.** I was eating a carrot

_____ **6.** We were driving to work

_____ **7.** He was standing in the canoe

_____ **8.** I was dreaming about my boyfriend

a. when it turned over and we fell in the water.

b. when I burned my finger.

c. when the doorbell rang.

d. when a truck banged into our car.

e. when he called me on the telephone.

f. when it growled and bit her hand.

g. when I fell and broke my ankle.

h. when my tooth fell out.

2 AND THE REST IS HISTORY   Grammar Notes 1–2

Complete the sentences. Use the simple past tense or the past progressive of each verb in parentheses. Then listen and check your work.

1. **Sir Isaac Newton:** I ___was sitting___ under a tree when an apple ___fell___ on
                     a. (sit)   b. (fall)

   my head. That's when I first understood the concept of gravity.

2. **Benjamin Franklin:** I _____ a kite when lightning _____. I was
                                     a. (fly)   b. (strike)

   the first to show the connection between electricity and lightning.

3. **Johann Strauss:** I wrote a beautiful waltz, but I couldn't think of a name for it. I

   _____ to think of a name for it when I _____ out the window and
              a. (try)   b. (look)

   _____the beautiful Danube River. I called my waltz "The Blue Danube Waltz."
       c. (see)

4. **René Descartes:** I _____ about what makes me me when suddenly I
                                 a. (think)

   _____, "I *think*, therefore I am."
       b. (realize)

❸ PLEASANT AND UNPLEASANT SURPRISES Grammar Notes 1–4

Use the words below to write sentences. Decide which action was in progress and which action interrupted. Use the past progressive and the simple past tense.

Pleasant Surprises

1. I / dig in my garden / I find an old gold watch

   I was digging in my garden when I found an old gold watch.

2. They / run into some old friends / they / travel in Europe

3. He / meet his future wife / he / study English

Unpleasant Surprises

4. She / break her toe / she / play basketball

5. He / cut his chin / he / shave

6. He / eat dinner / he / hear about a murder in his neighborhood

❹ AT THE SAME TIME Grammar Notes 5–6

*Use **while** and the past progressive to connect these actions.*

1. I / take difficult final exams / my friend / take a wonderful vacation

   While I was taking difficult exams, my best friend was taking a wonderful vacation.

2. It / rain in Paris / it / snow in Quebec

3. They / have fun / we / work

❺ ALIBIS Grammar Notes 1–4

Victor Rodriguez was murdered last night. The police believe the murder occurred at 7:00 P.M. They are questioning three neighbors: Mr. Smith, Ms. Brown, and Mr. Clapp. Listen to the conversations. Then listen again and write down what each person was doing when the murder occurred.

1. Mr. Smith _____ 2. Ms. Brown _____ 3. Mr. Clapp _____

6 SOMEONE STOLE NORMA'S CAR

Complete the conversation. Use the correct form of the verbs in parentheses. Use the simple present tense, the present progressive, the future, the simple past tense, and the past progressive. Then listen and check your work.

PETE: Hello.

NORMA: Hi, Dad. _____ you busy?
1. (be)

PETE: No, not really. I _____ just _____ at the paper when you
2. (look)
called. What's going on?

NORMA: I'm okay, but you _____ my story. Someone _____ my car.
3. (believe, not)   4. (steal)

PETE: Oh, no! How _____ it _____?
5. (happen)

NORMA: Yesterday I _____ home from work when someone in an old car
6. (drive)
_____ my new car. I _____ hurt, but I _____ out
7. (hit)   8. (be, not)   9. (get)
to check my car. The man in the other car _____ out of his car, too. I
10. (get)
_____ to exchange addresses with him. I _____ over to his
11. (expect)   12. (walk)
car when he _____ over to my car. Then he _____ in my car
13. (run)   14. (get)
and _____ away.
15. (drive)

PETE: No! I _____ it. What _____ you _____ then?
16. (believe, not)   17. (do)

NORMA: I _____ his car to the police station. I _____ my car to them.
18. (take)   19. (describe)
Now they _____ to find the guy.
20. (try)

PETE: But you _____ a car to get to work. What _____ you
21. (need)
_____ on Monday?
22. (do)

NORMA: While I _____ home from the police station, I _____ a
23. (return)   24. (meet)
friend from work. I _____ him my story and he _____ to
25. (tell)   26. (offer)
lend me his second car. But I feel terrible. I _____ usually so careful.
27. (be)

PETE: I _____. You always _____ your car. What a terrible story!
28. (know)   29. (lock)

NORMA: Well, I _____ the police later today. I _____ and let you
30. (call)   31. (call)
know what happens.

PETE: Okay. Bye, Norma. Take care of yourself.

COMMUNICATION PRACTICE

 GAME: WHAT WE WERE DOING WHEN THE TELEPHONE RANG

Play a game with the class. Sit in a circle. Think about the last telephone call you received. The first student tells what he or she was doing when the telephone rang. The second student tells if he or she was doing the same thing as the first student. Continue around the circle until everyone has a turn.

> **EXAMPLE:**
> **A:** I was doing my homework when the telephone rang.
> **B:** I wasn't doing my homework. I was sleeping when the telephone rang.
> **C:** When the telephone rang, I was sleeping, too.

Now try to tell what everyone was doing.

> **EXAMPLE:**
> **A:** B and C were sleeping, and I was doing my homework when the telephone rang.

 MEMORY GAME

Divide the class into two groups. The students in Group A go to the front of the room. Each student acts out one of the activities in the box (or his or her own activity). The students in Group B watch carefully and take notes about what each student is doing.

argue with a classmate	sew
bow	sleep
comb your hair	sneeze
dance	sweep the floor
drink a cup of hot coffee	swim
erase the chalkboard	tell someone a secret
play cards with a classmate	walk a dog
play ping-pong with a classmate	whistle
put on lipstick	write on the chalkboard

The students in Group A sit down. Then they ask the students in Group B **yes / no** *and* **wh-** *questions about their activities. They use the past progressive in their questions.*

> **EXAMPLE:**
> **Group A student:** Was Maria sweeping the floor?
> **Group B student:** Yes, she was.
> **Group A student:** What was Bekir doing?

(continued on next page)

Group B student: He was erasing the blackboard.

Group A student: What was I doing?

Group B student: You were telling Juan a secret.

Now the students in Group B act out activities and ask the students in Group A past-progressive questions about their activities.

❾ MEMORIES

Work in small groups. Read these students' memories of special events. Tell your group your own memory of a special event. Use the past progressive to tell what you were doing when the event occurred. Then use the simple past to tell what you did after the event occurred.

EXAMPLES:

1. At midnight on December 31, 1999, I was watching spectacular fireworks on TV. We were eating, laughing, and talking about the coming century. After midnight we continued to eat, laugh, and talk until 4:00 A.M. on January 1.

2. There was an earthquake in my hometown three years ago. I was sleeping when it occurred. I woke up and ran to the basement of my building. Fortunately, nobody was hurt.

3. There was a blackout in my city a few months ago. I was taking a test when all the lights went out. The blackout lasted for two hours. My classmates and I took a different test the next day.

4. Two years ago I was eating dinner at a restaurant when my girlfriend asked me to marry her. My girlfriend is now my wife.

REVIEW OR SELFTEST

I. *Read the questions. Circle the letter of the correct words to complete the sentence.*

1. A: Who's taller, you or your sister?　　　　　　　　　　A　B　C
　　B: I'm _____.
　　　　(A) taller she is
　　　　(B) more tall than she is
　　　　(C) taller than she is

2. A: Did you buy the red coat or the blue one?　　　　　A　B　C
　　B: The blue one. The red coat was _____.
　　　　(A) too expensive
　　　　(B) as expensive
　　　　(C) much expensive

3. A: Why do you prefer to work at night?　　　　　　　　A　B　C
　　B: It's _____.
　　　　(A) much quieter than during the day
　　　　(B) more quieter than during the day
　　　　(C) as quiet as the day

4. A: How does she drive?　　　　　　　　　　　　　　　A　B　C
　　B: _____.
　　　　(A) Very careful
　　　　(B) Much more careful
　　　　(C) Very carefully

5. A: Did you compare the prices of the two motorcycles?　A　B　C
　　B: Yes. The black one is _____.
　　　　(A) more expensive than the blue one
　　　　(B) as expensive than the blue one
　　　　(C) expensive enough

6. A: Why can't he get a driver's license?　　　　　　　　A　B　C
　　B: He isn't _____.
　　　　(A) too old
　　　　(B) old enough
　　　　(C) enough old

II. *Circle the letter that completes the sentence.*

1. A: What was he doing last year at this time?　　　　　A　B　C
　　B: He _____.
　　　　(A) worked
　　　　(B) was working
　　　　(C) 's working

(continued on next page)

2. A: What was she doing when you rang her doorbell?   **A B C**
   B: She _____.
     (A) took a shower
     (B) is going to take a shower
     (C) was taking a shower

3. A: Who was painting the kitchen?   **A B C**
   B: Tom and I _____.
     (A) were
     (B) was
     (C) paint

4. A: What happened while you were sleeping?   **A B C**
   B: A bird _____.
     (A) is flying into my bedroom
     (B) was flying into my bedroom
     (C) flew into my bedroom

III. *Complete the sentences. Use the comparative form of the words in the box.*

comfortable	easy	fast	hot	old
dangerous	expensive	friendly	late	

1. Sally is thirty-eight years old. Bob is forty-five years old. Bob is _____ than Sally.

2. Yesterday it was 70 degrees. Today it is 85 degrees. Today it is _____ than it was yesterday.

3. This morning Sally and I spoke for a long time. We had a nice conversation. She was _____ today than she was yesterday.

4. Pete bought new chairs for his office. Everyone likes them. They are big, and the material is soft. The old chairs were small, and the material was rough. The new chairs are _____ than the old ones.

5. The new chairs cost $600. The old ones cost $300. The new chairs are _____ than the old ones were.

6. Pete leaves work at 6:00. Sally leaves work at 5:30. Pete leaves _____.

7. Sally types sixty words a minute. Gail types thirty words a minute. Sally types _____ than Gail.

8. That problem looks very complicated, but it's _____ than it looks.

9. There are many football injuries. There aren't many ping-pong injuries. Football is _____ than ping-pong.

IV. *Complete the conversations. Choose from the words in parentheses.*

1. **A:** How does he drive?

   B: _____ and _____.
      (Slow, Slowly)   (careful, carefully)

2. **A:** Why did everyone listen to her?

   B: She sang more _____ than the others.
                    (beautiful, beautifully)

3. **A:** Who painted that _____ picture?
                        (beautiful, beautifully)

   B: I did.

4. **A:** Something smells _____. Is it the soup?
                        (good, well)

   B: I don't know. I have a cold.

5. **A:** He types very _____.
                     (good, well)

   B: I know, but she types _____.
                             (well, better)

6. **A:** That's a _____ interesting ring. Where did you get it?
               (too, very)

   B: I didn't buy it. It was a present.

7. **A:** Why do you always take the bus?

   B: It's impossible to walk there. It's _____ far.
                                         (too, very)

V. *Complete the questions. Use* **than**, **as**, *or* **from**.

1. Is love more important _____ money?

2. Is love as important _____ money?

3. Do dogs live longer _____ cats?

4. Are dogs very different _____ cats?

5. Is your first name the same _____ your father's?

6. Is your new apartment farther from your office _____ your old apartment?

7. Does he have the same initials _____ his wife?

8. Are children less honest _____ adults?

VI. *Complete the sentences. Use the simple past tense or the past progressive of the verbs in parentheses.*

1. The telephone (ring) _____ while I (take) _____ a shower. When I (get) _____ to the phone, it was too late.

2. We (walk) _____ along Fifth Avenue in New York City when we (meet) _____ an old neighbor.

3. When the visitors (arrive) _____ , she (sleep) _____ .

4. Our dog hates loud noises. When the workers (start) _____ drilling the hole, the dog (hide) _____ under the bed.

5. It (rain) _____ when I (fall) _____ and (break) _____ my finger.

6. Who (drive) _____ when the accident (happen) _____ ?

7. (watch) _____ you _____ the news on TV when your father (call) _____ ?

8. While I (walk) _____ to the library, I (find) _____ a gold ring.

VII. *Correct these sentences.*

1. A teenager is different ~~as~~ ^from^ a young child.

2. I am going to exchange the shoes. They aren't enough big.

3. The coffee is cool enough for she to drink now.

4. Your necklace is too beautiful.

5. This semester there are less students than there were last semester.

6. Lulu Winston's last name is longer than Bertha Bean.

7. I'm more beautiful my sister.

8. She's a too good student.

▶ *To check your answers, go to the Answer Key on page 399.*

From Grammar to Writing
The Order of Adjectives before Nouns

---

1 *Complete the sentence with the words in parentheses.*

1. I was walking down the street when I saw a _____.
(funny / monkey / brown / little)

2. Everyone was looking at Maria's _____.
(red / dress / beautiful / silk)

Study this information about the order of adjectives before nouns.

THE ORDER OF ADJECTIVES BEFORE NOUNS

1. Opinion (beautiful)	**3. Shape** (square)	**5. Color** (red)	**7. Material** (silk)
2. Size (big)	**4. Age** (new)	**6. Origin** (French)	**8. Noun** (scarf)

1. We use adjectives to describe nouns. Descriptions make writing more lively. They also help the reader form mental pictures. When **several adjectives** come before a noun, they follow a **special order**.	• I saw a **beautiful young** woman. NOT: ~~I saw a young beautiful woman~~.

2. Use *and* to connect adjectives from the same category.	• The shirt was *cotton* **and** *polyester*. • The blouse was *red* **and** *white*.

3. Use commas between adjectives that give similar information.	• It was a difficult, complicated exam.

2 *Write the words in parentheses in the correct order.*

1. (red, big, delicious) He was eating a _____ apple.

2. (Italian, new, leather, brown) His cashmere coat was not as expensive as her

_____ jacket.

3. (silver, Mexican, two-hundred-year-old) They were looking for

_____ bowls.

3 *Read the story.*

Detective Work

Several years ago I was walking down the street when I saw my father's brand new shiny blue car. I expected to see my father, but to my surprise a young woman with short, curly bright red hair was behind the wheel of the car. I saw an empty taxi nearby and I got in quickly. I said dramatically to the driver, "Follow that new blue car." And I told the driver why.

The taxi driver had a car phone, and I told him to call the police. Soon we heard the siren of the patrol car and a loudspeaker. The police told the woman to pull over. We pulled over too. I immediately said to the woman, "That's not your car. It's my father's."

The woman smiled calmly and said, "Oh. You're Mr. Abbot's younger son. I recognize you from your picture."

Before I could say another word, the woman explained that she was my father's new assistant. My father had asked her to take his computer to the main office to get it fixed. He lent her his car. We called my father and he confirmed her story. The police laughed and the taxi driver laughed. I was too embarrassed to laugh. That was the beginning and the end of my career as a detective.

Now write your own story.

Begin,

I was walking down the street when I saw _____

REVIEW OR SELFTEST
ANSWER KEY

I.
1. C
2. A
3. A
4. C
5. A
6. B

II.
1. B
2. C
3. A
4. C

III.
1. older
2. hotter
3. friendlier
4. more comfortable
5. more expensive
6. later
7. faster
8. easier
9. more dangerous

IV.
1. Slowly / carefully
2. beautifully
3. beautiful
4. good
5. well / better
6. very
7. too

V.
1. than
2. as
3. than
4. from
5. as
6. than
7. as
8. than

VI.
1. rang / was taking
2. were walking / met
3. arrived / was sleeping
4. started / hid
5. was raining / fell / broke
6. was driving / happened
7. Were / watching / called
8. was walking / found

VII.
2. I am going to exchange the shoes. They aren't **big enough**.
3. The coffee is cool enough for **her** to drink now.
4. Your necklace is **very** beautiful.
5. This semester there are **fewer** students than there were last semester.
6. Lulu Winston's last name is longer than Bertha **Bean's**.
7. I'm more beautiful **than** my sister.
8. She's a **very** good student.

INFORMATION GAP FOR STUDENT B   Unit 38, Exercise 5

Listen to your partner's sayings and find an illustration that matches each saying.
Then read your sayings and your partner will find an illustration that matches.

Illustrations:

His boss often yells, but he's really fair. He's much nicer than people think.

Billy usually puts a lot of food on his plate, but he doesn't eat much.

Don't wait for a better job, Sally. Take this job. It's better than not having a job at all.

Sayings:

The pen is mightier than the sword.

Two heads are better than one.

The sooner, the better.

MODALS II; THE SUPERLATIVE

PREVIEW

Carol, who is in Oregon, is speaking to her parents in New York. Listen and read their telephone conversation.

CAROL'S NEWS

ELENORE: Hello.

CAROL: Hi. Mom?

ELENORE: Hi, Carol. How are you?

CAROL: Fine. Listen, Mom, I have some very important news. Is Dad on the extension?

ELENORE: No. Should I get him?

CAROL: Yes. I have something very special to tell you.
[*pause*]

PETE: Hi, Carol. What's up?

CAROL: Mom, Dad, you'd better sit down.

PETE: Okay. Now, what's this all about?

CAROL: Mom, Dad, I'm engaged.

PETE: You're what?

CAROL: I'm engaged to Dan.

ELENORE: That's . . . uh, wonderful, but isn't it sudden?

CAROL: Oh, no. We met in October, and we see each other all the time.

PETE: Well, tell us about Dan.

CAROL: He's the most handsome guy in the world. His eyes are big and bright. His hair is thick and wavy. His shoulders are very broad, and he has the cutest dimples in the world.

PETE: Okay. He's gorgeous. But what does he do?

CAROL: Oh, he's a poet and . . .

PETE: *[interrupting]* A poet? Carol, can he earn a living?

CAROL: Don't worry, Dad. You have to meet him. We're really in love. And I have some more news. You and Mom are going to be . . .

PETE AND ELENORE: Hello?

ELENORE: Carol? Carol? Are you still there? Pete, we just got cut off! What should we do?

PETE: We'd better call her back. Hang up and I'll try.
[pause]

PETE: *[to Elenore]* I can't get through.

ELENORE: We'd better wait near the phone until she calls back.

CAROL: *[to Yoko]* Oh, Yoko. I must call my parents immediately. We just got disconnected. I was beginning to tell them about Dan when the phone went dead. What a time for the phone not to work. I can't get a dial tone.

COMPREHENSION CHECK

Check (✔) **That's right, That's wrong,** *or* **I don't know.**

	That's right.	That's wrong.	I don't know.
1. Carol met Dan last summer.	❑	❑	❑
2. Pete's not happy to hear Dan's a poet.	❑	❑	❑
3. Carol got angry and hung up on her parents.	❑	❑	❑
4. Elenore and Pete are going to fly out to Oregon.	❑	❑	❑
5. Yoko thinks Carol should marry Dan.	❑	❑	❑

WITH PARTNERS

Practice the conversation on pages 400 and 401.

SHOULD, SHOULDN'T, OUGHT TO, HAD BETTER, AND HAD BETTER NOT

GRAMMAR **IN CONTEXT**

WARM UP Your friend wrote a novel and asked you to read it. You read it, but didn't like it. Your friend asks your opinion of his book. What should you say?

Listen and read this conversation.

PETE: What's that?

ELENORE: My cousin Jeremy's writing a novel. I'm reading pages from his book.

PETE: Oh, the one he was telling us about. The one about his mother?

ELENORE: Uh-huh.

PETE: How is it?

ELENORE: Uh . . .
Well, uh . . .

PETE: That bad?

ELENORE: I'm afraid so.

PETE: What are you going to tell him?

ELENORE: I don't know. **What should I say**?

PETE: You **shouldn't lie**. You **ought to tell** him what you really think.

ELENORE: He'll feel terrible.

PETE: Well, tell him the truth in a kind way. Then tell him about John Grisham.

ELENORE: The novelist?

PETE: That's right—the one who writes about law firms. Did you know that Grisham sent his first novel to about fifteen publishers, and none of them wanted it?

ELENORE: Really?

PETE: Uh-huh.

ELENORE: Well, I think **I'd better call** Jeremy today.

PETE: Don't call him. Meet him and tell him in person.

ELENORE: That's a good idea.

GRAMMAR PRESENTATION

MODALS: *SHOULD, SHOULDN'T, OUGHT TO, HAD BETTER,* AND *HAD BETTER NOT*

SHOULD, SHOULDN'T, OUGHT TO AFFIRMATIVE AND NEGATIVE STATEMENTS

SUBJECT	SHOULD	BASE FORM OF VERB
I You He She It We You They	**should shouldn't should not ought to**	**help**.

YES / NO QUESTIONS

SHOULD	SUBJECT	BASE FORM OF VERB	
Should	I you he she we you they	**call**?	
Should	it	**stay**	here?

SHORT ANSWERS

	AFFIRMATIVE			NEGATIVE	
Yes,	you I he she you we they it	**should**.	No,	you I he she you we they it	**shouldn't**.

(continued on next page)

WH- QUESTIONS ABOUT THE SUBJECT

WH- WORD	SHOULD	BASE FORM OF VERB
Who	should	call?
What	should	happen?

OTHER WH- QUESTIONS

WH- WORD	SHOULD	SUBJECT	BASE FORM OF VERB
What		I	do?
Where		he	go?
When		she	begin?
Why	should	it	help?
Who(m)		we	write to?
How long		you	stay?
How		they	travel?

HAD BETTER
AFFIRMATIVE STATEMENTS

SUBJECT	HAD BETTER	BASE FORM OF VERB	
You	had better	take	an umbrella.
We	'd better	wait	by the phone.

NEGATIVE STATEMENTS

SUBJECT	HAD BETTER	NOT	BASE FORM OF VERB	
You	had better		come	late again.
We	'd better	not	forget	to mail the letter.

CONTRACTIONS

I had better → **I'd better**	we had better → **we'd better**
you had better → **you'd better**	you had better → **you'd better**
he had better → **he'd better**	they had better → **they'd better**
she had better → **she'd better**	

NOTES	EXAMPLES
1. Use *should* to give advice or talk about what is right to do.	• I **should** study for the test. • He **should** give his seat to that man.
Use *should not* for the negative.	• She **should not** lie.
Use the contraction *shouldn't* in speaking and informal writing.	• She **shouldn't** lie.
2. *Should* is followed by **the base form of the verb**.	• She **should finish** school first. NOT ~~She should to finish school.~~ NOT ~~She should finishes school.~~
3. *Should* + base form refers to the present or future.	• I should go to the library **now**. • We should call them **tomorrow**.
4. *Ought to* means the same as should. ▶ **BE CAREFUL!** *Ought to* is rarely used in questions or negative statements.	• You **ought to** *(should)* see that new movie. It's great. • **Should** I see that new movie? NOT ~~Ought I to see that new movie?~~
5. USAGE NOTE: Use *I think* or *Maybe* before *you should* to sound more polite.	• **I think** you should call your mother. • **Maybe** you should see a doctor.

(continued on next page)

6. Use **had better** to give advice. *Had better* is stronger than *should*. It implies that something bad might happen if you don't follow the advice.

- You **had better** pay the bill. (You may have trouble if you don't.)
- He **had better not** forget his plane ticket. (He may not be able to get on the plane without his ticket.)

Use contractions of *had better* in speaking and in informal writing.

- **We'd better** call the doctor.

7. *Had better* is followed by the **base form of the verb**.

- **He'd better help** her.
  NOT ~~He'd better to help her.~~
  NOT ~~He'd better helps her.~~

8. To make a sentence with *had better* negative, add **not** before the base form of the verb.

- **He'd better *not* come** late again.

9. *Had better* is used to talk about the present or the future. The *had* in *had better* does not refer to the past.

- **I'd better** finish the dishes **now**.
- **She'd better** go to work **tomorrow**.

FOCUSED PRACTICE

1 DISCOVER THE GRAMMAR

Match the sentences.

___c___ **1.** The water is dripping under the sink.

_____ **2.** He trusts you.

_____ **3.** The roads are slippery.

_____ **4.** He repeats what he hears.

_____ **5.** The car is making funny noises.

a. You shouldn't lie to him.

b. We'd better drive carefully.

c. I should call a plumber.

d. Should I take it to the repair shop?

e. You'd better not tell him any secrets.

2 WHAT SHOULD WE DO?   Grammar Notes 1–5

Pete and Elenore are waiting for a phone call from their daughter Carol. She was telling them about the man she wants to marry when the phone went dead. Listen and complete the sentences.

> I'd like the number of "Dan the poet."

ELENORE: Pete, I'm worried. ___What should we do___?
                                          1.

_____ Dan?
          2.

PETE: We don't know his phone number.

ELENORE: Call information.

PETE: We don't know his last name. _____ for, "Dan the poet"?
                                                    3.

ELENORE: Maybe _____ out to Oregon. Carol's so young. She's just a baby.
                          4.

PETE: Elenore! Carol's not so young. She's almost twenty-one.

ELENORE: Maybe _____ Milt. He lives nearby. He could visit her.
                          5.

PETE: Elenore, this is not like you. You always say *I* should be more trusting. Well,

now _____ Carol, and you _____ to
              6.   **7.**

conclusions. Let's wait for her to call us back.

ELENORE: Well, okay. I guess you're right.

3 YOU SHOULDN'T POINT AT PEOPLE

Complete the sentences. Use **should** *or* **shouldn't**.

1. You _____shouldn't_____ point at people. It isn't polite.

2. Pete thinks they _____ trust Carol.

3. You _____ wear a seat belt in a car. Seat belts save lives.

4. They _____ drive so fast. It's dangerous.

5. We _____ take umbrellas. There are a lot of dark clouds.

4 ADVICE WITH *OUGHT TO*

Complete the sentences. Use **ought to**. *Choose from the verbs in the box.*

| buy | clean | send | wear | congratulate |

1. You _____ought to wear_____ boots. There's a lot of snow.

2. I _____ my uncle a birthday card. His birthday is next Monday.

3. She _____ her apartment. It's very dirty.

4. We _____ Noah. He graduated from high school last week.

5. He _____ a new coat. The coat he's wearing is old and torn.

5 ADVICE WITH *HAD BETTER*

Complete the sentences with **'d better** *or* **'d better not**.

1. We _____ hide. The police are nearby.

2. You _____ tell Dad about the car until he finishes dinner.

3. I don't trust him. We _____ check his references.

4. Grandma Lulu wasn't feeling well yesterday. I _____ call her today and find out how she is.

6 EDITING

A. *Correct these conversations by adding* **should** *or* **shouldn't**.

1. A: Is that Jon's watch?

    B: Yes. I _⋀ *should* return it to him. He may need it.

2. A: You're very low on gas. You get some gas before you go on your trip.

    B: You're right.

3. A: Be careful. You have a bad back. You lift that heavy chair.

    B: You're right. I won't lift it.

4. A: They stand up in the canoe. It's dangerous.

    B: You're right. Someone tell them.

B. *Correct these conversations by adding* **'d better** *or* **'d better not**.

1. A: She failed the last test. She study harder for the test next week or she may not pass the course.

    B: She knows.

2. A: What did the police say?

    B: They said, "You leave town. We may want to speak to you again."

3. A: What time does she go to sleep?

    B: Early. You call her after eleven o'clock.

COMMUNICATION PRACTICE

7 DECISIONS

Work in small groups. Read each problem. Choose a solution or write your own.
Talk about your answers.

1.

2.

1. I like my job and I like my boss, but my boss always calls me "honey." I don't like that. What should I do?

   a. When your boss calls you "honey," you should call him "babe."

   b. You should tell your boss, "Please don't call me 'honey.' Call me (your name)."

   c. You'd better not say anything. It's not important, and these days many people are looking for jobs.

   d. _____

2. My husband loves parties. At parties, he talks to everyone but me. I'm shy with large groups of people. I never know what to say. I hate to go to these parties. What should I do?

   a. You should ask people about themselves. People usually love to talk about themselves.

   b. You shouldn't go to large parties. Tell your husband to go alone.

   c. You should have small parties and invite people you are comfortable with.

   d. _____

8 ADVICE FROM FRIENDS

Listen and read about Dr. Smith's problem and the advice from her friends. Do you agree with the advice of the first, second, or third friend? Do you have another idea? Discuss the situation with a partner.

Dr. Sarah Smith is a heart specialist and her husband, Derek, is an engineer. They live in Georgia. The director of a hospital in Maryland offered Dr. Smith a job. The new job is more exciting than her present job, and the salary is higher. Dr. Smith would love to take the job. The problem is that Mr. Smith likes his job and doesn't want to move. He could get a job in Maryland, but they have a lot of friends and relatives in Georgia and their five-year-old daughter is happy at her school. The Smiths asked some friends for advice. They all had different ideas.

FIRST FRIEND: Sarah, I really don't think you should move to Baltimore. Derek would be very unhappy. You'd better wait for an opportunity in Atlanta.

SECOND FRIEND: I think you should move to Baltimore. Derek, you should give Sarah the chance to advance in her career. You shouldn't hold her back.

THIRD FRIEND: Sarah ought to take the job for one year and fly home on weekends.

9 **SAYINGS**

Work in small groups. Read these sayings. Then use **should**, **shouldn't**, **ought to**, **had better**, *or* **had better not** *to explain them.*

EXAMPLE:

"Look before you leap" means that you shouldn't jump into things. You ought to plan ahead.

1. Look before you leap.
2. Count your blessings.
3. Don't put off for tomorrow what you can do today.
4. A stitch in time saves nine.
5. The early bird catches the worm.
6. Honesty is the best policy.

🔟 CULTURAL DOS AND DON'TS

Every culture has different ideas of what people should *and* shouldn't *do. Even people from the same country may have different ideas if they are of different ages or from different parts of the country. Work in small groups. Compare ideas about the following subjects.*

Is it okay to blow your nose at the dinner table?

Is it okay to call a waiter by snapping your fingers or clapping your hands?

Is it ever okay to spit in public?

Is it good to smile a lot?

Is it okay to have silences during a conversation?

Is it okay to talk a lot? to talk very loud?

Is it okay to touch other people (slap them on the back, touch their arm, etc.)?

Is it okay to ask about age, weight, income, political ideas?

Make a list of what you **should**, **shouldn't**, **had better**, *or* **had better not** *do in different places.*

EXAMPLES:
In the United States, when you are invited for dinner you shouldn't arrive more than ten minutes late.

In the United States, you shouldn't ask people how much money they make.

43 HAVE TO, DON'T HAVE TO, MUST, MUSTN'T

GRAMMAR **IN CONTEXT**

WARM UP   People learn languages in different ways. How do you like to learn a foreign language? What do you believe helps you?

Listen and read the conversation these people are having about how they learn languages.

EMIKO: When I start to learn a new language, I like to listen to the language for a long time before I say a word.

PEDRO: Not me. I like to listen, but I also like to practice speaking from the first day.

OTTO: I **must learn** one thing at a time. I don't like to start a new lesson until I understand an old one perfectly.

PEDRO: I'm just the opposite. I **don't have to learn** everything perfectly. I think it's okay to make mistakes at first. Many mistakes disappear in time.

EMIKO: I don't like to speak English with classmates. You just learn their mistakes. I think you should only speak English with your teacher.

PEDRO: I disagree. I think you **have to speak** with classmates. That way, you practice a lot more than if you only speak to the teacher.

MOHAMMED: You **don't have to learn** grammar. As long as people understand you, correct grammar doesn't matter.

OTTO: I disagree completely. You **have to learn** grammar to speak correctly. Learning grammar gives you confidence and helps you understand how the language works.

EMIKO: I think you **must learn** perfect pronunciation.

PEDRO: I disagree. You **mustn't worry** about speaking perfectly. You should try to speak so that people can understand you without difficulty.

OTTO: You ought to look up every word in a dictionary. That way, you will learn a lot of new words.

PEDRO: Well, it's okay to use a dictionary, but first you **have to try** and guess the meaning of words. You shouldn't look up every word in a dictionary.

GRAMMAR **PRESENTATION**
MODALS: *HAVE TO, DON'T HAVE TO, MUST, MUSTN'T*

HAVE TO / DON'T HAVE TO

AFFIRMATIVE STATEMENTS			
SUBJECT	HAVE TO / HAS TO	BASE FORM OF VERB	
I You	have to		
He She	has to	understand	grammar.
We You They	have to		
It	has to	stand	near a window.

NEGATIVE STATEMENTS				
SUBJECT	DO NOT / DOES NOT	HAVE TO	BASE FORM OF VERB	
I You	don't			
He She	doesn't	have to	work	today.
We You They	don't			
It	doesn't	have to	stand	on a table.

YES / NO QUESTIONS				
Do / Does	**Subject**	**Have to**	**Base Form** of verb	
Do	I you	have to	read	the whole book?
Does	he she			
Do	you we they			
Does	it		be	a five-page report?

SHORT ANSWERS	
Affirmative	**Negative**
Yes, I do.	No, I don't.
Yes, you do.	No, you don't.
Yes, he does.	No, he doesn't.
Yes, she does.	No, she doesn't.
Yes, you do.	No, you don't.
Yes, we do.	No, we don't.
Yes, they do.	No, they don't.
Yes, it does.	No, it doesn't.

MUST / MUSTN'T

AFFIRMATIVE AND NEGATIVE STATEMENTS			
Subject	**Must**	**Base Form** of verb	
I You He She We You They	**must mustn't (must not)**	**arrive**	early.
It	**must**	**stand**	near the light.

NOTES	EXAMPLES
1. Use *have to* and *must* to talk about necessity. *Have to* is more common in spoken English.	• You **have to** pay your rent before the fifth of the month. • You **must** pay your rent before the fifth of the month.
NOTE: We usually use *have to*, not *must*, in questions.	• **Do** we **have to** pay a tax on tea? • **Does** he **have to** return the video today?
▶ **BE CAREFUL!** The verb *have* is different from the modal *have to*.	• He **has** a new computer. • He **has to** buy a printer.
2. Use *don't have to* or *doesn't have to* when there is no necessity. (You have a choice.)	• You **don't have to** make a reservation at that restaurant. *(You can go to the restaurant without a reservation.)* • He **doesn't have to** pay now. *(He can pay later.)*
3. *Must not*, or the contraction *mustn't*, means that you are not allowed to do something. (You don't have a choice.)	• You **must not** cross the street when the light is red. • You **mustn't** enter.
4. The past of *have to* and *must* is **had to**.	• I **had to** return the video yesterday. *(The video was due back yesterday.)*

FOCUSED PRACTICE

1 DISCOVER THE GRAMMAR

Match the sentences.

__c__ **1.** To drive,

_____ **2.** To enter the United States,

_____ **3.** In order to vote in the United States,

_____ **4.** To be an interpreter at the United Nations,

_____ **5.** To practice medicine,

a. you must be eighteen years old, but you don't have to have a high school diploma.

b. you must have a medical degree, but you don't have to know Latin.

c. you must have a driver's license, but you don't have to know how to change a tire.

d. you must have a passport, but you don't have to be a U.S. citizen.

e. you must speak three languages, but you don't have to have a degree in international affairs.

2 THE VALUE OF TESTS   Grammar Note 1

Complete the conversation with **have**, **has**, *or* **have to**.

A: Would you like to go to the movies this afternoon?

B: I can't. I _____have_____ a test tomorrow. I _____ study all afternoon.
         _____1.   2.

A: What do you _____ study?
                      3.

B: Grammar. I _____ review the modals. We always _____ review
                    4.   5.

tests on Fridays.

A: Do you _____ memorize grammar rules?
                 6.

B: Oh, no. We _____ use the grammar to answer questions. We really
                    7.

_____ understand it.
    8.

A: Does your teacher give a lot of tests?

B: Yes. He _____ a short test after we study every grammar point. I like tests.
                 9.

That way, I always review what I learn.

A: Well, to each his own. I don't really care for tests.

3 IS THERE A CHOICE?

Complete the sentences with **have to**, **has to**, **don't have to**, *or* **doesn't have to**.

1. At this store you can't use a credit card. You _____*have to*_____ use cash.

2. You can't wear jeans to the interview. You _____ wear a suit.

3. This ticket is good anytime. You _____ use it today.

4. We _____ do any homework tonight. Tomorrow's a holiday.

5. He'd like to stay out later, but he _____ be home before midnight.

6. She _____ buy the book. She can borrow it from the library.

7. They _____ pay their rent before the first of the month. Otherwise,
they pay a penalty.

8. He doesn't need much sleep. He _____ sleep more than five hours
a night.

4 UNDERSTANDING SIGNS

*Read these signs. Then explain the signs. Use the words in the box on page 420
and begin with* **You have to**, **You must**, **You mustn't**, *or* **You don't have to**.

1. ID Required

2. No Smoking

3. Black Tie Optional

4. Do Not Enter

5. No Bare Feet Allowed

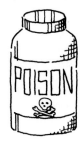

6. Poison

(continued on next page)

smoke
wear shoes
wear a tuxedo
show identification
drink the contents of this bottle
enter this room

1. You have to show identification to enter the dance club.

2. _____

3. _____

4. _____

5. _____

6. _____

5 EDITING

Correct the mistakes in each sentence.

1. They couldn't understand me at first. I have to repeat everything three times.

2. Now that they are managers, they had to work late several times a week.

3. You mustn't wear a fancy outfit. Jeans are okay.

4. To get to the museum, you have turn left at the third traffic light on this road.

5. She has a beautiful dress for the wedding, but she have to buy a pair of shoes.

6. You mustn't to go through a red light.

COMMUNICATION PRACTICE

6 RULES AT SCHOOL

Work in small groups. Make a list of rules at a school you know well. Use **have to** *and* **don't have to**. *Then discuss these rules with the people in your group.*

EXAMPLE:

> **Kennedy Elementary School (Grades 1–6)**
>
> Children have to wear uniforms.
>
> Children have to walk in the hallways. They mustn't run.
>
> They don't have to study a foreign language. They begin studying a foreign language in the seventh grade.

A: I think uniforms are a good idea. Rich and poor students wear the same clothes.

B: I agree. But I think students should study a language before the seventh grade. It's important to know more than one language.

Now talk about a school you attended in the past. Use **had to** *and* **didn't have to**.

A: When I went to primary school, I didn't have to wear a uniform.

B: I did, and I hated it.

7 CHORES AND ALLOWANCES

Work in small groups. Discuss the ideas below.

Some parents give their children an *allowance*, that is, money to spend on small things they may want or need. In exchange, the children have to do chores.

Did you get an allowance? Did you have to do any chores in order to get your allowance? What chores did you have to do as a child? For example, did you have to make your bed, clean your room, fix things around the house, or watch a younger sibling? Is an allowance a good idea or a bad one?

> **EXAMPLE:**
>
> **A:** I got a small allowance, but I had to clean my room before I got it.
>
> **B:** I did, too. I also had to watch my younger sister a lot of the time. Did you have to take care of a younger sister or brother?
>
> **A:** No, I was the baby in the family. What do you think about allowances?

SUPERLATIVE FORM OF ADJECTIVES AND ADVERBS

GRAMMAR **IN CONTEXT**

WARM UP   *In Happiness,* a recent best seller, author Sean Mallory says that for most people the forties and fifties are the best years of their lives. Do you agree? Why or why not?

Reporter Carol Evans is interviewing people. She wants to know what they see as the best and worst times of a person's life. Listen and read the comments by the following people.

José Arias
30 years old / business consultant

"Charles Dickens' *A Tale of Two Cities* begins, 'It was **the best** of times. It was **the worst** of times.' That's what the teenage years are like. You usually feel **the happiest** and **saddest** during those years. It's usually **the most idealistic** time of your life. You believe anything is possible."

Sophie Inslight
85 years old / housewife

"For me, my early twenties were **the happiest** years. My children were very young and I loved taking care of them. We were poorer than at any other time, but it didn't matter much. It was **the best** time of my life. **The hardest** time was the time after my husband passed away twenty-five years ago. He was **the kindest**, **the most generous**, and **the most honest** man you could find."

Emma Orsini
50 years old / teacher

"**The best** years of a person's life are the years when a person is **the freest**. A person can decide what he or she wants to do. **The worst** time is when a person is dependent on others."

Ken Woodward
65 years old / retired lawyer

"I definitely agree with Sean Mallory. The forties and fifties are **the best** years of a person's life. People in their forties and fifties are usually at the height of their careers. They're still active and involved in a lot of things. **The worst** years are the teenage years. I wouldn't repeat those years for anything."

Jessica Wright
17 years old / high school student

"I think twelve is **the nicest** time for most people. At twelve you usually don't have any real responsibilities and you have lots of free time to do what you want. I remember the summer when I was twelve. My friends and I played and laughed all day long. We had **the best** time of our lives."

GRAMMAR **PRESENTATION**
SUPERLATIVE FORMS OF ADJECTIVES AND ADVERBS

SUBJECT	VERB	SUPERLATIVE ADJECTIVE / ADVERB	
Doug	is	**the youngest**	in his family.
Doug	ran	**the fastest**	of all.
Book One	is	**the easiest**	in the series.
The A Bus	arrived	**the earliest**.	
The Porsche	is	**the most expensive**	car in the garage.
He	drives	**the most carefully**	of the group.
Noah	lives	**the farthest**	from school.
Doug	is	**the best**	soccer player on the team.
That	was	**the worst**	year of her life.

NOTES

EXAMPLES

1. Use the **superlative** form of adjectives and adverbs to compare three or more people, places, or things.

- (adjective: tall) He is **the tallest** in the class.
- (adverb: beautiful) She sings **the most beautifully** of all.

2. To form the superlative of **short (one-syllable) adjectives** or **adverbs**, add **-est** to the adjective or adverb and **the** before the adjective or adverb.

If the adjective or adverb ends in **e**, add **-st**.

If a one-syllable adjective ends in a consonant, a vowel, and a consonant (CVC), double the final consonant before adding **-est**.

- (adjective: fast) She is **the fastest** typist of all.
- (adverb: fast) He runs **the fastest** of all.

- (adjective: large) Alaska is **the largest** state in the United States.
- (adverb: late) All the Winstons slept late, but Doug slept **the latest** of all.

(CVC)
- (adjective: big) She has the **biggest** backpack in the class.

3. To form the superlative of **two-syllable adjectives** that end in *y*, drop the *y* and add *-iest* to the adjective. Add *the* before the adjective. The adverb *early* follows the same form.

- (adjective: happy) What was **the happiest** time of your life?
- (adverb: early) Who arrived **the earliest**?

4. To form the superlative of **long adjectives** or **adverbs** that end in *ly*, use *the most* before the adjective or adverb.

- (adjective: interesting) It was **the most interesting** time of my life.
- (adverb: openly) He speaks **the most openly** of all.

5. Some adjectives and adverbs have **irregular** superlative forms:

ADJECTIVE	ADVERB	COMPARATIVE FORM	SUPERLATIVE FORM
good	well	better (than)	**the best**
bad	badly	worse (than)	**the worst**
far	far	farther (than)	**the farthest**

- The thirties are **the best** years of your life.
- He worked **the best** when he was on his own.
- What was **the worst** year of your life?
- Who lives **the farthest** from school?

6. After the superlative, you can use **a prepositional phrase** to identify the group you are talking about.

- He's the tallest **in the class**.
- She's the most generous one **of all**.

7. *One of the* often comes before a superlative adjective. The adjective is followed by a plural noun.

- He is **one of the richest men** in the world.
- She is **one of the most intelligent** women in the country.

REFERENCE NOTE
See Units 38 and 39 for a complete discussion of adjectives and adverbs.

FOCUSED PRACTICE

Listen and read the conversation. Underline the superlative form of all adjectives and adverbs.

ELENORE: Doug, please don't use the phone.

DOUG: Why not? . . . You two look a little strange. Is everything okay?

ELENORE: Carol just told us she's engaged to Dan.

DOUG: Oh, that? I know all about Dan.

PETE: You do? Please tell us.

DOUG: He's <u>the most handsome</u> guy on campus.

PETE: Uh-huh. Do you have any other information?

DOUG: He drives the coolest car. He has the biggest and best collection of CDs, and he knows the most exciting places to go.

ELENORE: Great. How do you know so much about Dan?

DOUG: Carol told Dino's sister, and Dino told me.

PETE: Did she happen to say anything more about Dan?

DOUG: Oh yeah, I forgot. He has the cutest dimples in the world.

PETE: Great.

2 FACTS

Complete the sentences with the superlative form of the adjectives in the box.

small	near	cold	high	long	large	short

1. Winter is _____the coldest_____ season of the year.

2. The Nile River in Egypt is _____ river in the world.

3. Mount Everest is _____ mountain in the world.

4. February is _____ month of the year.

5. The blue whale is _____ mammal in the world.

6. Mercury is _____ planet.

7. Mercury is also _____ planet to the sun.

3 DESCRIBING THINGS

Use **one of the** *+ the superlative and the plural form of the noun in parentheses.*
Choose from the words in the box.

important	good	cold	interesting	big	cheap

1. A: Did you enjoy *Life is Beautiful*?

   B: It was excellent. It was _____*one of the best videos*_____ in the store.

(video)

2. A: How's the food at Burger Hut?

   B: Okay if you like fast food. The prices are good. It's

   _____ in the neighborhood.
   (restaurant)

3. A: Gee. The pollution here is awful.

   B: Not just here. It seems to be all over. Pollution is

   _____ in the world.
   (problem)

4. A: Brrr. It's cold. I think it's way below freezing.

   B: You're right. Today is _____ of the year.
   (day)

5. A: How's the book you bought?

   B: Great. I can't put it down. It's _____ of the year.

(book)

6. A: Is New Year's Day the most important holiday of the year?

   B: I'm not sure, but it's certainly _____ of the year.

(holiday)

4 COMPARISONS

Form questions. Use the comparative or superlative form of the adjective or adverb.

1. Is / your best friend / tall / you

   Is your best friend taller than you?

2. Is / New Year's Day / important holiday / in your country

   _____

3. Is / a diamond / hard / a pearl

   _____

4. Is the giraffe / tall animal in the world

   _____

5. Does / your best friend / work hard / you

   _____

6. Is July / hot month of the year in the country where you were born

   _____

7. Is April / rainy season of the year in the country you are in now

   _____

8. Does your best friend / sing beautiful / you

   _____

9. Is your father / generous person in your family

   _____

5 CAROL SPEAKS WITH HER PARENTS   Grammar Notes 1–2, 7

Carol finally reaches Pete and Elenore. Listen and complete the conversation.

ELENORE: Hello.

CAROL: Hi, Mom.

ELENORE: Carol! We tried to call many times. The line was always busy. I'm so glad you reached us. Carol, when we got interrupted, you said Dad and I were going to be something. What was that all about?

CAROL: You and Dad are going to be grandparents. Yoko's dog, Rocky, is going to be a father and I'm getting one of the puppies. But listen, before you ask other questions, let me tell you about Dan and me.

ELENORE: Please.

CAROL: Dan's father has _____ in Portland, and Dan is going to work
                                         1.
for him. Dan is _____ I know, and he writes beautifully. He
                              2.
writes _____ love poems, but they're just for me.
              3.

ELENORE: Well, that's good to hear. But what about you? You're only twenty years old. This
is _____ of your life. Today most women want a career.
          4.
Shouldn't you finish your education first? Don't you want to live on your own?
You're much too young to get married. And you're certainly too young to be a
parent. Don't you agree?

CAROL: Mom, remember, you got married at twenty. And you don't understand. I'm in
love. Nothing else matters. Besides, I'm planning to go to school and work after
I'm married.

PETE: Well, we just want _____ for you.
                                         5.

CAROL: I know, Dad. Dad, Dan is _____.
                                                      6.

PETE: Is there anything we can do for you?

CAROL: Yes. Get some groceries. I invited Dan to spend a few days with all of us in New
York. I hope that's okay with you?

ELENORE: Of course it is. It's wonderful.

COMMUNICATION PRACTICE

6 YOUR THOUGHTS

Work with a partner. First write the questions together. Then take turns asking and answering the questions. Use the superlative or **one of the +** *the superlative and a plural noun in answering the questions.*

1. What / good restaurant / in town

   A: What's the best restaurant in town?

   B: I don't know if it's the best restaurant in town, but *China Grill* is one of the best restaurants in town.

2. What / easy way to earn a lot of money

3. What / interesting TV show / on the air now

4. When / good time to get a college degree

5. Who / famous leader in the world today

6. What / good way to save money

7 COMPLIMENTS

Work with a partner. Use superlatives to say something nice about each person in your class.

> **EXAMPLES:**
> Yolanda is the most helpful person in our class.
> Bekir is the funniest. He has the best sense of humor.
> Maria is the most understanding.
> Mr. Brown is the most patient person in our class.

8 CITIES

Each student writes on the blackboard the name of a city he or she knows well. Other students ask questions about that city. Use the superlative form of the words in the box.

> popular sport
> important holiday
> rainy / hot / cold month
> interesting section
> good university / restaurant / hospital
> important industry
> beautiful section

EXAMPLE:

HERMAN: What's the most popular sport in Paris?

PIERRE: I'm not sure, but soccer is one of the most popular sports in Paris. How about in Lima?

HERMAN: Soccer is definitely the most popular sport in Lima. Everyone there loves soccer.

9 WORLD PROBLEMS

Work in small groups. Learn the meaning of the words in the box. Make a list of the five biggest problems in the world today. You may look at the suggestions in the box or use your own ideas. Read your list to the class. Compare your list with the lists of other groups. Discuss.

> poverty   hunger   inflation   pollution   crime   corruption   illiteracy

EXAMPLE:

Poverty is one of the biggest problems in the world today.

⑩ TRIVIA

Work in small groups. Answer the questions. Compare your answers with those of the other groups.

1. The hottest city in the United States is _____.
   a. Los Angeles, California
   b. Key West, Florida
   c. Houston, Texas
2. Where do people pay the highest income tax? In _____.
   a. Switzerland
   b. the United States
   c. Sweden
3. What is the largest animal in the world?
   a. the blue whale
   b. the elephant
   c. the hippopotamus
4. Which animal runs the fastest over a short distance?
   a. the lion
   b. the llama
   c. the cheetah
5. What is the largest planet in our solar system?
   a. Pluto
   b. Mercury
   c. Jupiter
6. Which word do we say the most?
   a. I
   b. and
   c. yes
7. What is the most densely populated place?
   a. Toronto
   b. Calcutta
   c. Miami
8. What is the tallest building in the United States?
   a. the Sears Tower in Chicago, Illinois
   b. the World Trade Center in New York City
   c. Texas Commerce Plaza in Houston, Texas
9. What independent state has the smallest population?
   a. Hawaii
   b. Vatican City
   c. Greenland
10. What is the most populated country in the world?
    a. China
    b. Russia
    c. India

Check your answers on page 440.

Now write your own trivia question for the class.

REVIEW OR SELFTEST

I. *Circle the letter of the correct answer to complete each sentence.*

1. Who's _____ person in your family?   A B C
   (A) the most kind
   (B) kinder than
   (C) the kindest

2. Who speaks _____?   A B C
   (A) the most polite
   (B) the most politely
   (C) the politest

3. The ending is _____.   A B C
   (A) the most important part of the book
   (B) the most important part than the book
   (C) the most important of the book part

4. She arrived _____.   A B C
   (A) the most early
   (B) the earlier
   (C) the earliest

5. My old painting was good. My new painting is better, but   A B C
   your new painting is _____ of all.
   (A) the best
   (B) the most better
   (C) the most good

6. Who lives _____ from school?   A B C
   (A) the farther
   (B) the most far
   (C) the farthest

II. *Match the sentences.*

_____ **1.** I lost my passport.

_____ **2.** I'd like to get a
driver's license.

_____ **3.** My cough is getting worse.

_____ **4.** I don't have a computer.

_____ **5.** Can you remember what
jobs we did as children?

_____ **6.** That medicine is
very important.

a. You had to wash the dishes
and I had to dry them.

b. You mustn't forget to take it every day.

c. You'd better report it right away.

d. You should see a doctor.

e. You have to pass a written test
and a road test.

f. You don't have to use one for
your composition.

III. *Complete the sentences. Use the affirmative or negative form of the words in
parentheses.*

1. We _____ take the test now. We can take it next month
(have to)
if we prefer.

2. His sister is in trouble. He _____ help her.
(should)

3. You _____ put metal in a microwave oven.
(must)

4. I _____ get some milk today. The stores will be
(had better)
closed tomorrow.

5. She _____ work this Sunday, but she will be off next Monday.
(have to)

6. We _____ call and wish them a happy anniversary.
(ought to)

7. His old boots have holes. He _____ get some new ones.
(should)

8. We _____ forget to take the chicken out of the freezer. We're going to
(had better)
cook it tonight.

9. You _____ stop at the red light.
(must)

10. I _____ wear a suit. I can come in jeans.
(have to)

11. They have a big problem with their neighbor. They _____ see a lawyer.
(should)

IV. *Add* **to** *to the sentences where necessary.*

1. Would you like _____ try some pasta?

2. He ought _____ see a doctor.

3. She shouldn't _____ take so many pills.

4. He has _____ go to the dentist next Thursday.

5. You'd better not _____ wait for me. I won't be ready for a long time.

6. We couldn't _____ understand his letter.

7. She has _____ two children.

8. We might not _____ have school next Tuesday afternoon.

9. He doesn't have _____ cook. There's a cafeteria nearby.

10. We mustn't _____ use that camera.

V. *Complete the conversation. Choose from the words in parentheses.*

ELENORE: What's the problem, Doug?

DOUG: It's my English homework. I _____ write a three-page essay.
1. (may, have to)

ELENORE: When is it due?

DOUG: We _____ hand it in until the day after tomorrow, but I'd like
2. (have to, don't have to)

to finish it today. I _____ a big soccer game tomorrow night.
3. (have, have to)

I _____ get home before eleven o'clock.
4. (might not, mustn't)

ELENORE: What are you going to write about?

DOUG: That's the problem. We _____ write about anything, and I
5. (can, had better)

_____ decide on a topic.
6. (shouldn't, can't)

ELENORE: Write about soccer.

DOUG: Soccer?

ELENORE: Why not?

DOUG: Well, I _____ write about the terrible time I caught the ball
7. (should, could)

by mistake and my team lost the game.

ELENORE: That's a good idea. *(continued on next page)*

DOUG: Or I _____ write about the time our team won all the games.
               8. (might, ought to)
       Thanks, Mom.

ELENORE: No problem.

VI. *Complete the sentences. Use the superlative or comparative form of each adjective or adverb in parentheses.*

1. (bad) It was _____ storm of the century.

2. (bad) Today he felt _____ he felt yesterday.

3. (fast) Do you walk much _____ he does?

4. (fast) Who is _____ runner in your family?

5. (interesting) What was _____ part of the film?

6. (funny) That is _____ show on TV this season.

7. (funny) He is _____ his brother.

8. (handsome) Carol thinks Dan is _____ man in the world.

9. (good) The new answering machines are _____ the old ones.

10. (good) What is _____ answering machine in your store?

11. (fresh) The bread at the bakery is _____ the bread at the supermarket.

12. (intelligent) She is one of _____ people in her company.

VII. *Correct these sentences.*

1. He is one of the best student͜s in the school.

2. Should she gets a new job?

3. We don't have eat in the cafeteria because there's a good coffee shop nearby.

4. She'd better register for the new course last week.

5. She ought to finds a better job.

6. She shouldn't does her homework at the last minute.

7. He doesn't has to bring the money today.

8. What should we doing about the extra books?

9. Who's the most tallest one in the class?

10. It's one of the most expensive restaurant in town.

▶ *To check your answers, go to the Answer Key on page 440.*

FROM GRAMMAR TO WRITING EXPRESSING AND SUPPORTING AN OPINION

1 *Read the following sentences. Write* **O** *next to sentences that express an opinion and* **F** *next to sentences that express a fact.*

_____ **1.** The average age at which people get married is increasing.

_____ **2.** I believe young children forget things quickly.

_____ **3.** The Himalayas are the highest mountains in the world.

_____ **4.** John was looking for a gift for his father all day Sunday.

_____ **5.** Children shouldn't watch violent videos.

Study the information about expressing and *supporting an opinion.*

Expressing and Supporting an Opinion	
1. You can express your opinion by using expressions such as:	
In my opinion	• **In my opinion**, it's wrong to spank a child.
I believe	• **I believe** tests are harmful.
I think	• **I think** tests are helpful.
Better than / Its better to . . . than to	• Some tests are **better than** others.
	• **It's better to** give **than to** receive.
Should / Shouldn't	• Parents **shouldn't** spank their children.

2. After you express your opinion, give reasons to support your opinion. For example:

Opinion
In my opinion, it's wrong to spank children.

Support
When adults use physical force, children think physical force is okay.

2 *Read the e-mail message and the response.*

Subject: Customs
From: "Sara Kim" <sarakim@aol.com>
To: "Pat Pro" <pgs8@prodigy.com>

Hi Pat,
I need some help.

I'm new to San Francisco, and I need some help.

My neighbor is very friendly and helpful. Yesterday she invited me to a barbeque at her home next Sunday. I accepted the invitation, but I have three questions. First of all, what should I wear? Second, do I have to bring a gift or is that not necessary? And, if I bring a gift, what should I buy? Also, the barbecue is for two o'clock. What time should I arrive, at two exactly, a little after two, or at three? And finally, what do you think I should wear? You lived in California for a year. Please help me out.

Hope all is well with you in London. Regards to Gerald.

Warmest wishes,
Sara

Subject: Customs
From: "Pat Pro" <pgs8@prodigy.com>
To: sarakim@aol.com

Dear Sara,
Barbecues are usually more casual than other dinners, so you don't have to wear special clothes. You can wear jeans or a casual skirt. As far as a gift goes, stick with chocolates, flowers, or cake. As a student, you probably don't have to bring anything, but it's certainly a nice idea to bring something. As far as the time, I'd stay close to the time she invited you. It's possible some people will arrive later, but you shouldn't come too late.

I hope you have a great time at the barbeque.

I was sad to leave San Francisco, and I'm sure you'll grow to love the city. I still miss it a lot.

Best wishes,
Pat

3 *Now read this e-mail message and respond to it. Give your opinion along with reasons to support it.*

Subject: A birthday gift for a fifteen-year-old
From: "Joe Perry" <joeperry@aol.com>

Hi Ron,
I have a problem. It's my cousin's 15th birthday. He wants a video game, and I want to get it for him, but his mother is very much against it. She thinks violent video games have a bad effect on young people. The game involves killing the enemy. There is a lot of violence in it. But my cousin is one of the most non-violent young people I know. He never gets into fights. He's a good student. He has a lot of friends. I think there's no reason not to get him what he wants. On the other hand, I don't want to get his mom angry. What do you think I should do?

Thanks for your advice.
Joe

PART

XI

REVIEW OR SELFTEST
ANSWER KEY

I.
1. C
2. B
3. A
4. C
5. A
6. C

II.
1. c
2. e
3. d
4. f
5. a
6. b

III.
1. don't have to
2. should
3. mustn't
4. 'd better (had better)
5. has to
6. ought to
7. should
8. 'd better not (had better not)
9. must
10. don't have to
11. should

IV.
1. to
2. Ø
3. to
4. Ø
5. Ø
6. Ø
7. to
8. Ø

V.
1. have to
2. don't have to
3. 'd like
4. might not
5. can
6. can't
7. could
8. might

VI.
1. the worst
2. worse than
3. faster than
4. the fastest
5. the most interesting
6. the funniest
7. funnier than
8. the most handsome
9. better than
10. the best
11. fresher than
12. the most

VII.
2. Should she **get** a new job?
3. We don't have **to** eat in the cafeteria because there's a good coffee shop nearby.
4. She **had to** register for the new course last week.
5. She ought to **find** a better job.
6. She shouldn't **do** her homework at the last minute.
7. He doesn't **have** to bring the money today.
8. What should we **do** about the extra books?
9. Who's **the tallest** one in the class? (eliminate **most**)
10. It's one of the most expensive **restaurants** in town.

Answer to Exercise 10 on page 432
1. b
2. c
3. a
4. c
5. c
6. a
7. b
8. a
9. b
10. a

REVIEW OF VERB TENSES AND MODALS

FOCUSED PRACTICE

① TEENAGERS AND THEIR PARENTS

Pete is talking to his wife, Elenore, on the telephone. He is upset with their teenage son, Doug. Complete the conversation. Choose the correct verb forms and modals. Then listen to the conversation and check your work.

ELENORE: Hello.

PETE: Well, finally.

ELENORE: Pete?

PETE: Yes, it's me. I finally _____reached_____ you.
1. (was reaching, reached)

ELENORE: What _____ you _____ about?
2. (do, are)   3. (talk, talking)

PETE: I _____ to call you at 10:00, at 12:00, and at 2:00.
4. ('m trying, tried)

I _____ _____ you because the line
5. (can't, couldn't)   6. (reach, reached)

_____ always busy. _____ Doug
7. (be, was)   8. (Was, Is)

on the phone again?

ELENORE: I guess so.

PETE: I _____ _____ him. Every day he
9. (don't, 'm not)   10. (understand, understands)

_____ to his friends for hours. Yesterday when I
11. (talks, talking)

_____ him a few questions, he _____
12. (ask, asked)   13. ('s answering, answered)

every question with one word.

ELENORE: Many teenagers _____ like that.
14. (are, were)

PETE: Well, I _____. When I was a teenager,
15. ('m not, wasn't)

I _____ hours on the phone. I _____
16. (didn't spend, don't spend)   17. (go, went)

to school. Then after school I _____ _____.
18. (had better, had to)   19. (work, works)

I _____ play all day.
20. (couldn't, shouldn't)

ELENORE: But Pete. You always say, "I _____ my children to work as
21. (don't want, won't want)

hard as I did."

(continued on next page)

PETE: I _____, but Doug _____ grateful.
22. (know, 'm knowing)   23. (isn't, wasn't)

He's so lucky he _____ _____ and
24. (doesn't have to, isn't having to)   25. (works, work)

_____. He doesn't understand that.
26. (study, studies)

ELENORE: Not now, but one day in the future he _____.
27. ('ll understand, understands)

PETE: I guess you're right. Do I sound very old?

ELENORE: No, just a little old-fashioned.

② TEENAGERS AND THEIR PARENTS

*Doug and his friend Noah are talking about their parents. Complete the
conversation. Choose the correct verb forms and modals. Then listen to the
conversation and check your work.*

NOAH: What's up, Doug? _____Don't_____ you _____like_____ the music?
1. (like, not)

DOUG: I like it. I _____was_____ just _____ about something else. You know,
2. (think)

Noah, after high school I _____ _____ a job and move away.
3. (may, may not)   4. (get)

NOAH: Really? You mean, you _____ to college?
5. (go, not)

DOUG: Uh-huh. But listen, _____ a word about this to my parents. My Dad and
6. (say, not)

I _____ things very differently. He _____ I _____
7. (see)   8. (think)   9. (should, shouldn't)

_____ all the time. But I _____ to enjoy life.
10. (study)   11. (want)

NOAH: My mom is a lot like that, too. What's worse, she still _____ I'm a child.
12. (think)

Last Saturday night I _____ home a little late. My mom
13. (come)

_____ about it for two hours. Then on Sunday my grandma
14. (complain)

_____ us. I _____ my jeans. My grandma _____
15. (visit)   16. (wear)   17. (like, not)

them and we were going to a restaurant so my mom _____ me to
18. (tell)

change my clothes. I don't think my mom or my grandma _____
19. (could, should)

_____ me what to wear.
20. (tell)

DOUG: I _____ with you. You're absolutely right.
21. (agree)

❸ A TELEPHONE CALL

Noah's mother, Rita Steiner, is speaking to Pete Winston. Complete the telephone conversation in your own words. Then listen to their conversation.

PETE: Hello.

RITA: Hello, Pete. _____ Rita, Noah's mom.
　　　　　　　　　　　1.

PETE: Hi, _____. How _____?
　　　　　　2.　　　　　　　　　3.

RITA: Okay, thanks. How _____?
　　　　　　　　　　　　　4.

PETE: Fine.

RITA: _____ Elenore _____?
　　　　5.　　　　　　　　　　　6.

PETE: She's out now, but _____ back in an hour.
　　　　　　　　　　　　　7.

RITA: Please _____.
　　　　　　　　8.

PETE: Okay. Bye.

RITA: _____.
　　　　9.

❹ NOAH'S CHANGING

Elenore returns Rita Steiner's call. Complete their conversation. Use the correct form of modals and the correct form of the verbs in the box.

apologize	have	put
be	help	see
come	listen	visit
do	love	wear (two times)
go	need	

RITA: Hello.

ELENORE: Hi, Rita? Elenore.

RITA: Hi, Elenore.

ELENORE: Is everything okay?

RITA: I guess so, but I _____*need*_____ some advice. Lately, Noah and I
　　　　　　　　　　　　　　1.
_____*can't*_____ agree about anything.
　2. (can, can't)

ELENORE: That _____ strange. He's a teenager. Just yesterday Doug and Pete
　　　　　　　　3. (not)

(continued on next page)

_____ a terrible argument. But, you know, in our home, Noah is
      4.

always polite. We _____ to have him here.
              5.

RITA: Noah? That's great to hear. At home, he's not so polite. In the past Noah always

_____ with chores and _____ to me. He _____
  6.   **7.**   **8.**

his homework on time and he _____ nice clothes. Now I
                      9.

_____ recognize him. Last weekend, when my mother
10. (can, can't)

_____ us, he _____ torn, dirty jeans. And the day before
  11.   **12.**

he came home two hours late. He _____ and when I complained,
                        13. (not)

he got angry. Elenore, you have three children. Tell me, what _____
                                14. (might, should)

I do?

ELENORE: Listen, Doug and Noah _____ to a soccer game tomorrow. Why don't
                15.

you _____ here for dinner? I _____ have any answers,
      16.   **17. (might not, should not)**

but we can _____ our heads together and maybe come up with some
              18.

good ideas. Then we _____ look at Noah's and Doug's pictures from a
              19. (can, had to)

few years ago and remember the "good old days."

RITA: Elenore, thanks. That would be great. I _____ you tomorrow night.
                                20.

COMMUNICATION PRACTICE

5 THE GENERATION GAP

Work with a partner. Discuss the years when you were a teenager. What did you have to do? What couldn't you do? What did you and your parents disagree about? (If you are a teenager, what do you have to do? What can't you do? Do you and your parents disagree about some things?)

EXAMPLE:
When I was a teenager, I had to study almost all the time. I couldn't stay out late on school nights. I had to do my homework before I watched TV. I often wanted to go out on school nights, but my parents never let me.

6 A GROUP TRIP

Work in small groups. Imagine each person has $500. Plan a trip together. Complete the sentences. Tell the class about your trip.

1. We'd like to go _____

2. With $500, we can / could _____

3. We can't _____

4. We'd better bring _____

5. We'd better not _____

6. We ought to _____

7. We have to _____

8. We don't have to _____

9. We might _____

EXAMPLE:
We'd like to go camping in Yosemite National Park.
With $500, we can (could) probably stay for three weeks.
(We're in Michigan.) We can't afford to fly to California. We'll have to take a bus.
We'd better bring along a tent, sleeping bags, backpacks, and sunscreen.
We'd better not bring too many things.
We ought to bring a camera and buy a guidebook about Yosemite National Park.
We have to make a reservation. Yosemite is always crowded.
We don't have to bring fancy clothes. We won't need any. We don't have to bring food. We can buy food there.
We might spend a night in San Francisco on our way home.

7 PROBLEM SOLVING

Work in small groups. Read each problem. Choose a solution or write your own.
Talk about your answers.

1. My teenage daughter never gets off the phone. Our telephone is always busy. What should I do?

   a. You should get a second telephone line.

   b. You should give her a time limit of thirty minutes a day.

   c. You should be glad she has friends. Let her talk on the phone.

   d. You _____.

2. I lent my seventeen-year-old son my car. He had an accident. He was driving fast and hit a street lamp. He's okay, but it will cost $1,000 to fix the car. He doesn't have enough money to pay for the repairs, but he could get a part-time job. What should I do?

   a. You should tell him to get a part-time job to pay for the repairs.

   b. You should tell him to be more careful in the future. You should pay for the repairs.

   c. You shouldn't lend him your car in the future.

   d. You _____.

8 HOW MUCH FREEDOM SHOULD TEENAGERS GET?

Work in small groups. Discuss the following ideas.

1. Teenagers learn from their mistakes. Parents should give their teenagers freedom to make mistakes.

2. Teenagers need to learn by example. Parents should have strict rules. Rules help teenagers become responsible adults.

Does your group agree with the first idea or the second one? Why? Tell your class your ideas. Listen to the other groups' ideas.

> **EXAMPLES:**
> 1. Our group believes teenagers need the freedom to make mistakes. Teenagers have to discover who they really are. They should be allowed to take risks. Parents shouldn't make too many rules, or else teenagers will do things secretly.
> 2. Our group believes that teenagers need and want rules. Sometimes they ask to do what others are doing, but they secretly hope their parents will say no to them.

Then write about a time when you learned from a mistake or a time when you took a big risk.

OR

Write about a time when your parents said you couldn't do something you really wanted to do.

REVIEW OF VERB TENSES AND COMPARISONS

FOCUSED PRACTICE

1 NEW YORK AND CORVALLIS

Carol invited her boyfriend, Dan, to spend a few days with her in New York. Carol and Dan arrived in New York from their school in Corvallis, Oregon, three days ago. It's 7:00 P.M. They are having dinner with Carol's parents, Elenore and Pete, and Carol's brother, Doug.

Complete the conversation. Use the correct form of each verb in parentheses. Then listen to the conversation and check your work.

PETE: Well, Dan, what _____do_____ you _____think_____ of New York?
1. (think)

DAN: It _____ great. I love the people, the buildings, the stores, and the
2. (be)

food. I _____ everything about it!
3. (love)

DOUG: You do? Why?

DAN: It's so alive! Corvallis _____ a nice small town, but it's too quiet for
4. (be)

me. My parents _____ I should go to school there because it's clean,
5. (decide)

safe, and near our family's home and business, but I _____ big cities
6. (prefer)

like New York.

CAROL: I _____ you. I love Corvallis. You know, clean, safe towns
7. (understand, not)

_____ hard to find, and the scenery in Corvallis is beautiful. Also,
8. (be)

the people are friendly. Here in New York people _____ always in a
9. (be)

hurry. New Yorkers _____ fast. They _____ fast. They
10. (talk)   11. (walk)

even _____ fast.
12. (eat)

DAN: But New York is special!

ELENORE: Carol never liked New York, Dan, but I do. In my opinion, it's the greatest city

in the world. By the way, what _____ you two _____
13. (do)

earlier today?

DAN: First we _____ along Fifth Avenue. After that we _____ to
14. (walk)   15. (go)

Rockefeller Center and the Museum of Modern Art. Then we _____
16. (ride)

the subway. It wasn't too bad.

(continued on next page)

Doug: Wow! You're brave!

Carol: Doug, _____ so mean and _____ so much. You're eating
$\quad\quad\quad$ 17. (be, not) $\quad\quad\quad\quad\quad$ 18. (eat, not)

all the meat. _____ some for us.
$\quad\quad\quad\quad$ 19. (Leave)

Doug: I'm a growing boy. Look, it _____ outside.
$\quad\quad\quad\quad\quad\quad\quad\quad$ 20. (snow)

[Everyone looks outside.]

Carol: No, it's not. Hey, Doug, you just _____ the last potato.
$\quad\quad\quad\quad\quad\quad\quad\quad\quad\quad\quad$ 21. (take)

Elenore: Don't worry. There _____ more food in the kitchen.
$\quad\quad\quad\quad\quad\quad\quad\quad$ 22. (be)

Dan: Mrs. Winston, the roast beef is delicious.

Elenore: Thanks, Dan.

Doug: _____ it now, Dan. When our sister Norma is here, we usually
$\quad\quad\quad$ 23. (enjoy)

_____ meat. She's a vegetarian.
$\quad\quad$ 24. (have, not)

Dan: I know. Carol _____ me.
$\quad\quad\quad\quad\quad\quad\quad$ 25. (tell)

Doug: Right now Norma _____ for animal rights. She stops every woman
$\quad\quad\quad\quad\quad\quad\quad\quad$ 26. (protest)

in a fur coat and hands her pictures of dead animals and articles about

animal rights.

Elenore: Norma _____ strong beliefs.
$\quad\quad\quad\quad\quad$ 27. (have)

**Carol &
Doug:** We _____.
$\quad\quad\quad$ 28. (know)

[The telephone rings. Elenore answers the phone.]

Elenore: Hello? Hi, Norma. How's everything? What? No! Really? Oh, my!

Pete: What's going on?

Elenore: Norma _____ on the news later tonight.
$\quad\quad\quad\quad\quad$ 29. (be)

Dan: How exciting!

Doug: Well, things are never quiet around here! Maybe the police _____
$\quad\quad\quad\quad\quad\quad\quad\quad\quad\quad\quad\quad\quad\quad\quad\quad$ 30. (arrest)

her and put her in jail.

Elenore: Doug!

2 COMPARING PLACES

Read the conversation on pages 447 and 448 again. Write comparative sentences. Use the words in parentheses.

What do you think Carol would say about Corvallis and New York? Carol would probably say:

1. (clean) ___Corvallis is cleaner than New York._____

2. (beautiful) _____

3. (noisy) _____

4. (friendly) People in Corvallis _____

5. (walk, fast) People in New York _____

6. (talk, fast) People in New York _____

7. (eat, fast) People in New York _____

3 MORE COMPARISONS

Complete the sentences. Use **as . . . as**, **the same . . . as**, **too**, **enough**, **from**, **to**, **than**, *or* **of**.

1. Dan thinks Corvallis is a nice town, but it's _____too_____ quiet for him.

2. Dan thinks Corvallis isn't _____ exciting _____ New York.

3. In Corvallis there are fewer people _____ there are in New York.

4. Doug is about _____ weight _____ Dan.

5. Carol can't wear those shoes. Her feet are _____ big.

6. Doug is fifteen years old. He's _____ young _____ drive a car.

7. Doug isn't old _____ to get a driver's license.

8. New York City is different _____ Corvallis.

9. Corvallis has fewer people _____ New York.

10. Elenore thinks New York City is one _____ the greatest places in the world.

11. New York has more schools and hospitals _____ Corvallis.

12. There is less crime in Corvallis _____ there is in New York.

COMMUNICATION PRACTICE

4 CRITICISM

Write about a place or a thing that you don't like. Give five reasons why you think it's so bad. Read your sentences to your partner. Then listen to your partner's sentences.

EXAMPLE:

Our school cafeteria is one of the worst places to eat in this city.

1. The food is very greasy.

2. The food is expensive, too.

3. The portions are too small.

4. There aren't enough cashiers, so the lines are very long.

5. In addition, it's one of the noisiest and dirtiest places in our school.

5 CITY LIFE, SUBURBAN LIFE, SMALL TOWN LIFE

Work in small groups. Discuss the advantages and disadvantages of

• life in a big city

• life in a small town

• life in a suburb

Then choose one of these statements. Write a paragraph to support your opinion. Read your paragraph to the class.

1. It's best for people to live in a big city.

2. It's best for people to live in a small town.

3. It's best for people to live in a suburb.

REVIEW OF VERB TENSES, NOUNS, AND QUANTIFIERS

FOCUSED PRACTICE

1 A PICKPOCKET

It's Sunday afternoon. Pete is speaking to his mother, Lulu, who lives in Florida. Complete the conversation. Choose the correct verb forms, nouns, and quantifiers. Then listen to the conversation and check your work.

PETE: Hi, Mom. How are you?

LULU: So-so. Actually, I __'m__ _____ a little upset.
  1. ('m, was)

PETE: Why? What _____?
  2. (did happen, happened)

LULU: Someone _____ my wallet.
  3. (stole, was stealing)

PETE: Oh, no. How _____ it _____?
  4. (did, does)   5. (happen, happens)

LULU: I _____ on the bus when someone _____ my wallet.
  6. (rode, was riding)   7. (took, was taking)

It was in my handbag.

PETE: Where were you going?

LULU: I _____ home from Bertha's house. I had my wallet at Bertha's house.
  8. (was returning, return)

I _____ Bertha pictures of all of us. I also _____ my
  9. (showed, show)   10. (had, was having)

wallet when I got on the bus. I _____ my senior citizen's card to the
  11. (showed, show)

bus driver. But when I got home, I _____ my handbag and my wallet
  12. (open, opened)

_____ there.
  13. (wasn't, won't be)

PETE: _____ you _____ a lot of _____ in it?
  14. (Do, Did)   15. (have, had)   16. (money, moneys)

LULU: No, not _____. I _____ only _____
  17. (many, much)   18. (have, had)   19. (a few, a little)

_____.
  20. (dollar, dollars)

PETE: _____ there any identification in your wallet?
  21. (Was, Were)

LULU: Yes, there was—my senior citizen's card, my Medicare card, and my credit card.

PETE: _____ you _____ your credit card?
  22. (Did, Do)   23. (cancel, canceled)

LULU: No, not yet. At first I _____ _____ upset to do anything.
24. (was, am)   25. (too, very)

Later when I _____ to call, I _____ a busy signal.
26. (try, tried)   27. (get, got)

PETE: Well, it _____ _____ important to keep trying. But
28. ('s, 'll be)   29. (too, very)

_____ about the wallet or the money. The important thing is
30. (not to worry, don't worry)

that you are okay.

LULU: I know. You _____ right. I'm really most upset because I
31. ('s, 're)

_____ those pictures of all of us. I _____ and
32. (lose, lost)   33. ('ll call, call)

_____ my credit card in a few minutes.
34. (cancel, canceled)

PETE: I _____ terrible about this. I _____ about you a lot. I
35. (feel, 'll feel)   36. (worry, worried)

_____ bad we live so far apart.
37. (feel, felt)

LULU: I do, too. But that's life. Please _____ about me. I'm fine.
38. (don't worry, don't you worry)

PETE: I _____ again later this afternoon and see how you are.
39. (call, 'll call)

LULU: Okay, Pete. Bye.

PETE: Bye, Mom.

2 A HAPPY ENDING

Pete calls his mother again. Complete their conversation. Choose the correct verb forms, nouns, and quantifiers. Then listen to the conversation and check your work.

LULU: Hello.

PETE: Hi, Mom. How are you now? _____ you _____ about
1. (Are, Did)   2. (calling, call)

your credit card?

LULU: Yes, I took care of everything.

PETE: Good. _____ you _____ anything? Do you have
3. (Are, Do)   4. (need, needing)

_____ _____ in the house?
5. (enough, too much)   6. (food, foods)

LULU: I _____ a thing. James _____ here a while ago. He
   7. (don't need, 'm not needing)   8. ('ll be, was)

brought _____ _____. He got _____
      9. (a few, a little)   10. (grocery, groceries)   11. (a few, a little)

_____, _____ _____, _____
  12. (meats, meat)   13. (a few, a little)   14. (potatoes, potato)   15. (a few, a little)

_____, _____ _____, and some
  16. (onions, onion)   17. (a few, a little)   18. (carrot, carrots)

_____. Right now I _____ and tonight we
  19. (fruit, fruits)   20. (cook, 'm cooking)

_____ a nice dinner together and forget about my wallet.
 21. ('re going to have, have)

PETE: Well, now I'm glad that James is your friend.

LULU: I _____ so happy to hear you say that. James *is* special. When he was
   22. ('m, was)

here earlier, we _____ a long talk. We _____ really very
        23. ('re having, had)   24. ('re, 'll be)

happy together, and we would like to get married. I _____ there is a
                                              25. ('m knowing, know)

big age difference, and I know there may be problems, but in many ways we're

really a wonderful match.

PETE: You know, Mom, a few months ago I _____ worried that you were
                                    26. ('m, was)

dating James. But I see you're much happier. I think it's great. I _____
                                                            27. (hoped, hope)

you two will be very happy.

LULU: Thanks.

PETE: I _____ you again tomorrow.
   28. ('ll call, called)

LULU: I _____ to speak with you, but I _____ you're
   29. (love, 'm loving)   30. (know, knew)

_____ busy. You don't
  31. (very, too)

have to call. _____ my
           32. (Give, Giving)

love to Elenore and Doug. I

_____ to Carol last week.
  33. ('ll speak, spoke)

She sounds very happy. I can't wait to

meet Dan.

PETE: He seems very nice. It's really

wonderful: My daughter and my mother

are getting married.

COMMUNICATION PRACTICE

3 PROBLEMS OF SENIOR CITIZENS

Work with a partner. Discuss the problems of senior citizens. Do senior citizens have special problems with crime, money, health, and transportation? Talk about senior citizens you know.

EXAMPLE:

I live in the countryside. In my community there are many senior citizens. There isn't much crime, but many senior citizens have problems with transportation. When they can't drive, they can't get to stores or hospitals. Taxis are expensive, so they depend on other people to take them places.

4 LIVING TOGETHER

Work in small groups. Discuss the following question: What do you think are the advantages and disadvantages of grandparents, parents, and children living together? Consider the viewpoints of the grandparents, the parents, and the children.

EXAMPLE:

When grandparents, parents, and children live together, the children have the security of a larger family. Sometimes parents are busy with their careers, and grandparents have more time to listen to and help children.

Then choose one of these statements. Write a paragraph to support your opinion. Read your paragraph to the class.

1. Families should live together. It's better for all people.

2. When grandparents, parents, and children live together, there are many problems.

5 WEDDINGS

Work in small groups. Talk about traditional weddings in different countries.
Answer these questions.

1. Are weddings small or big?

   How long are the weddings?

2. What do people wear to weddings?

3. What do people do at weddings?

4. What do people bring as gifts?

5. Who usually pays for the wedding?

6. Where do the bride and groom go

   after the wedding?

Now work alone. Write about a wedding in your country.

EXAMPLE:

In my country, some people have very small, simple weddings. Others have big, elaborate parties. At a traditional wedding, the bride usually wears a long white gown. The groom wears a tuxedo. After the ceremony, people eat and drink and dance. Sometimes relatives and friends give short speeches about the bride, the groom, and their families. Guests give the bride and groom money or presents for their home. Usually the bride's family pays for the wedding, but it is not a rule. Sometimes the groom's family pays for the wedding, and sometimes the bride and groom pay for their own wedding. After the wedding the bride and groom usually go away for a week on a honeymoon.

APPENDICES

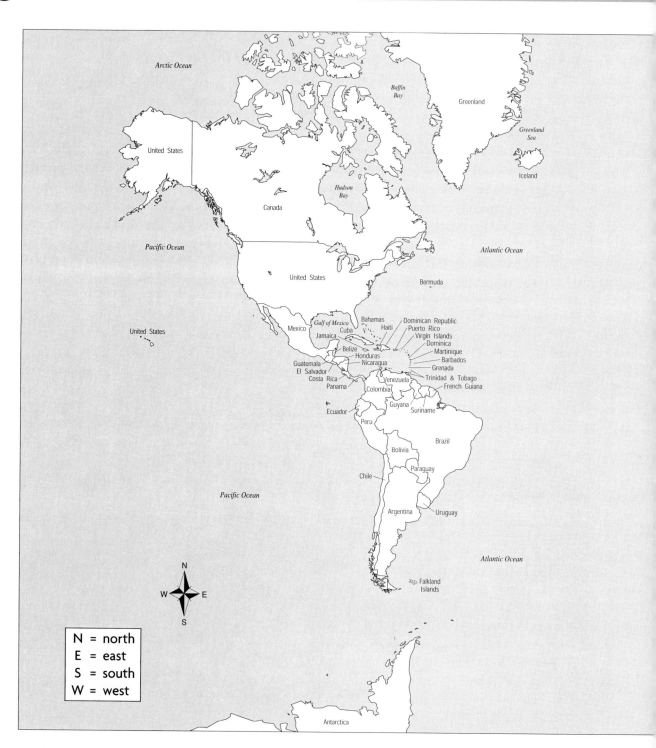

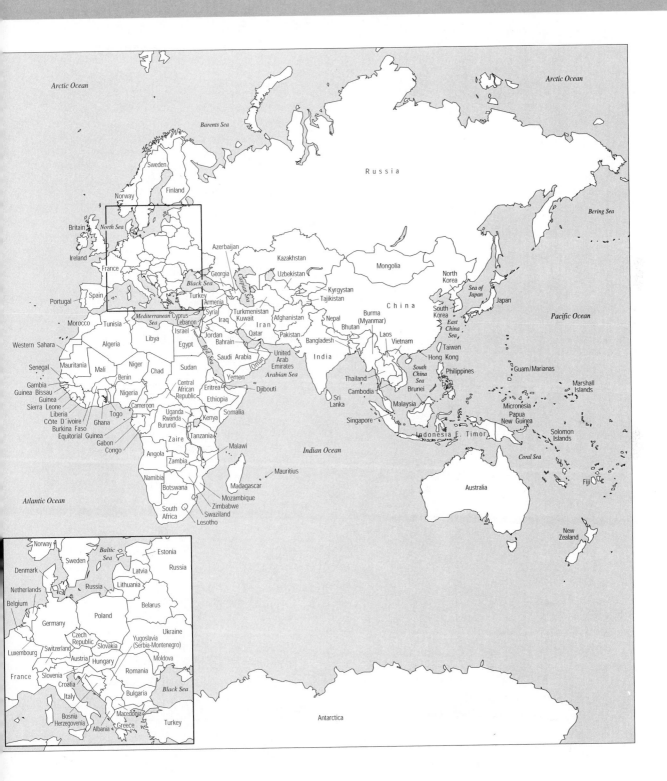

Arctic Ocean

Barents Sea

Arctic Ocean

Bering Sea

Russia

Sweden

Finland

Norway

Britain

North Sea

Ireland

France

Azerbaijan

Kazakhstan

Mongolia

North Korea

Sea of Japan

Japan

Portugal

Spain

Georgia

Black Sea

Caspian Sea

Uzbekistan

Kyrgystan

Tajikistan

China

South Korea

Pacific Ocean

Turkey

Armenia

Morocco

Tunisia

Mediterranean Sea

Cyprus

Syria

Lebanon

Israel

Iraq

Kuwait

Qatar

Afghanistan

Nepal

Bhutan

Burma (Myanmar)

East China Sea

Taiwan

Hong Kong

Western Sahara

Algeria

Libya

Egypt

Jordan

Bahrain

Iran

Pakistan

Bangladesh

Laos

Vietnam

Senegal

Mauritania

Mali

Niger

Chad

Sudan

Red Sea

Saudi Arabia

Oman

United Arab Emirates

Yemen

Arabian Sea

India

South China Sea

Philippines

Guam/Marianas

Marshall Islands

Gambia

Guinea Bissau

Guinea

Sierra Leone

Liberia

Côte D´ivoire

Burkina Faso

Equitorial Guinea

Benin

Nigeria

Central African Republic

Eritrea

Ethiopia

Djibouti

Thailand

Cambodia

Brunei

Sri Lanka

Malaysia

Micronesia

Papua New Guinea

Togo

Ghana

Cameroon

Uganda

Rwanda

Burundi

Kenya

Somalia

Singapore

Indonesia

E. Timor

Solomon Islands

Gabon

Congo

Zaire

Tanzania

Malawi

Indian Ocean

Coral Sea

Angola

Zambia

Fiji

Namibia

Madagascar

Mauritius

Australia

Atlantic Ocean

Botswana

Mozambique

Zimbabwe

South Africa

Swaziland

Lesotho

New Zealand

Norway

Sweden

Baltic Sea

Estonia

Denmark

Russia

Latvia

Russia

Netherlands

Russia

Lithuania

Belgium

Belarus

Germany

Poland

Czech Republic

Slovakia

Ukraine

Luxembourg

Switzerland

Austria

Hungary

Yugoslavia (Serbia-Montenegro)

Moldova

France

Slovenia

Romania

Croatia

Italy

Bulgaria

Black Sea

Bosnia Herzegovenia

Macedonia

Albania

Greece

Turkey

Antarctica

3 Numbers, Temperature, Months, Days, Seasons, Titles

CARDINAL NUMBERS

1 = one	11 = eleven	21 = twenty-one
2 = two	12 = twelve	30 = thirty
3 = three	13 = thirteen	40 = forty
4 = four	14 = fourteen	50 = fifty
5 = five	15 = fifteen	60 = sixty
6 = six	16 = sixteen	70 = seventy
7 = seven	17 = seventeen	80 = eighty
8 = eight	18 = eighteen	90 = ninety
9 = nine	19 = nineteen	100 = one hundred
10 = ten	20 = twenty	200 = two hundred
		1,000 = one thousand
		1,000,000 = one million
		10,000,000 = ten million

EXAMPLES:

Cardinal Numbers

That book has seventy-seven pages.
There are thirty days in April.
There are six rows in the room.
She is twelve years old.
He has four children.

ORDINAL NUMBERS

1st = first	11th = eleventh	21st = twenty-first
2nd = second	12th = twelfth	30th = thirtieth
3rd = third	13th = thirteenth	40th = fortieth
4th = fourth	14th = fourteenth	50th = fiftieth
5th = fifth	15th = fifteenth	60th = sixtieth
6th = sixth	16th = sixteenth	70th = seventieth
7th = seventh	17th = seventeenth	80th = eightieth
8th = eighth	18th = eighteenth	90th = ninetieth
9th = ninth	19th = nineteenth	100th = one hundredth
10th = tenth	20th = twentieth	200th = two hundredth
		1,000th = one thousandth
		1,000,000th = one millionth
		10,000,000th = ten millionth

EXAMPLES:

Ordinal Numbers

It's his seventy-seventh birthday.
It's April thirtieth.
He's in the sixth row.
It's her twelfth birthday.
Bob is his first child. Mary is his second. John is his third, and Sue is his fourth.

TEMPERATURE

We measure the temperature in degrees (°).

Changing from degrees Fahrenheit to degrees Celsius:

$$(F° - 32) \times 5/9 = °C$$

Changing from degrees Celsius to degrees Fahrenheit:

$$(9/5 \times °C) + 32 = F°$$

DAYS OF THE WEEK

Weekdays	Weekend
Monday	Saturday
Tuesday	Sunday
Wednesday	
Thursday	
Friday	

MONTHS OF THE YEAR

Month	Abbreviation	Number of Days
January	Jan.	31
February	Feb.	28*
March	Mar.	31
April	Apr.	30
May	May	31
June	Jun.	30
July	Jul.	31
August	Aug.	31
September	Sept.	30
October	Oct.	31
November	Nov.	30
December	Dec.	31

*February has 29 days in a leap year, every four years.

THE SEASONS	TITLES

THE SEASONS

Spring—March 21st–June 20th

Summer—June 21st–September 20th

Autumn or Fall—September 21st–December 20th

Winter—December 21st–March 20th

TITLES

Mr. (Mister) / mɪstər /unmarried or married man

Ms. / mɪz /   unmarried or married woman

Miss. / mɪs /   unmarried woman

Mrs. / mɪsɪz/   married woman

Dr. (Doctor) / daktər / doctor (medical doctor or Ph.D.)

4 Time

It's one o'clock.
(It's 1:00.)

It's five after one.
(It's 1:05.)

It's one-ten.
It's ten after one.
(It's 1:10.)

It's one-fifteen.
It's a quarter after one.
(It's 1:15.)

It's one twenty-five.
It's twenty-five after one.
(It's 1:25.)

It's one-thirty.
It's half past one.
(It's 1:30.)

It's one forty-five.
It's a quarter to two.
(It's 1:45.)

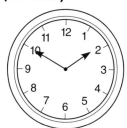

It's one-fifty.
It's ten to two.
(It's 1:50.)

TALKING ABOUT TIME

1. You can ask about time this way:

- **A: What time is it?**
- **B:** It's one o'clock.

2. **A.M.** means before noon
(the hours between midnight and noon).

- It's 10:00 **A.M.**

P.M. means after noon
(the hours between noon and midnight).

- It's 10:00 **P.M.**

BE CAREFUL! When people say 12:00 A.M.,
they mean midnight. When people say
12:00 P.M., they mean noon.

3. We often write time with numbers.

- It's one o'clock = It's **1:00**.
- It's two-twenty = It's **2:20**.

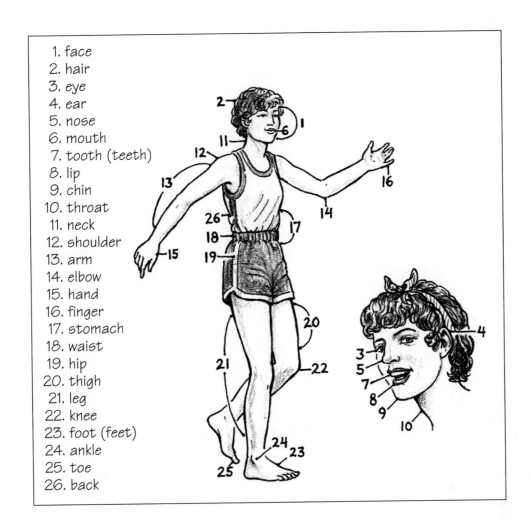

1. face
2. hair
3. eye
4. ear
5. nose
6. mouth
7. tooth (teeth)
8. lip
9. chin
10. throat
11. neck
12. shoulder
13. arm
14. elbow
15. hand
16. finger
17. stomach
18. waist
19. hip
20. thigh
21. leg
22. knee
23. foot (feet)
24. ankle
25. toe
26. back

Medical Problems

I have a backache.
I have an earache.
I have a headache.
I have a sore throat.
I have a stomachache. (I'm nauseous; I have diarrhea; I'm constipated.)
I have a fever.
My nose is running.
I have a cough.
I have a pain in my back.
My neck hurts.

U.S. Holidays (Federal and Legal Holidays and Other Special Days)

January
*New Year's Day — January 1st
*Martin Luther King, Jr.'s Birthday — January 15th (observed on the closest Monday)

February
Valentine's Day — February 14th
*George Washington's Birthday — February 22nd (observed on the closest Monday)

March

April
April Fools' Day — April 1st

May
Mother's Day — the second Sunday in May
*Memorial Day — May 30th (observed on the last Monday in May)

June
Flag Day — June 14th
Father's Day — the third Sunday in June

*federal legal holidays

July
*Independence Day — July 4th

August

September
*Labor Day — the first Monday in September

October
*Columbus Day — October 12th (observed on the closest Monday)
Halloween — October 31st

November
Election Day — the first Tuesday after the first Monday in November
*Veterans' Day — November 11th
*Thanksgiving — the fourth Thursday in November

December
*Christmas — December 25th
New Year's Eve — December 31st

Canadian Holidays (Legal and Public Holidays)

January
New Year's Day — January 1st
Sir John A. Macdonald's Birthday — January 11th

February
Valentine's Day — February 14th

March
*St. Patrick's Day — the Monday nearest March 17th

March or April
*Good Friday
*Easter Monday

April
April Fool's Day — April 1st

May
Mother's Day — the second Sunday in May
Victoria Day — the Monday preceding May 25th

June
Father's Day — the third Sunday in June

St. John the Baptist's Day — the Monday nearest June 24th (only in Quebec)

July
Canada Day — July 1st

August
Civic Holiday — the first Monday in August (celebrated in several provinces)
Discovery Day — the third Monday in August (only in the Yukon)

September
Labor Day — the first Monday in September

October
Thanksgiving Day — the second Monday in October
Halloween — October 31st

November
Remembrance Day — November 11th

December
Christmas Day — December 25th
Boxing Day — December 26th

*Many Americans in the United States observe these religious holidays too. However, these days are not official U.S. holidays.

SPELLING RULES

1. Add *-s* to form the plural of most nouns.

- student—student**s**
- picture—picture**s**
- chief—chief**s**

2. Add *-es* to form the plural of nouns that end in *ss*, *ch*, *sh*, and *x*. (This ending adds another syllable.)

- class—class**es**
- watch—watch**es**
- dish—dish**es**
- box—box**es**

3. Add *-es* to form the plural of nouns that end in *o* preceded by a consonant.

EXCEPTION: Add *s* to plural nouns ending in *o* that refer to music.

- potato—potato**es**

- piano—piano**s**
- soprano—soprano**s**

4. Add *-s* to form the plural of nouns that end in *o* preceded by a vowel.

- radio—radio**s**

5. To form the plural of words that end in *y* preceded by a consonant, change the *y* to *i* and add *-es*.

- dictionary—dictionar**ies**
- fly—fl**ies**

6. To form the plural of words that end in *y* preceded by a vowel, add *-s*.

- boy—boy**s**
- day—day**s**

7. To form the plural of certain nouns that end in *f* or *fe*, change the *f* to *v* and add *-es*.

- half—hal**ves**
- loaf—loa**ves**
- knife—kni**ves**
- wife—wi**ves**

8. Some plural nouns are irregular.

- woman—women
- child—children
- person—people
- mother-in-law—mothers-in-law
- man—men
- foot—feet
- tooth—teeth

9. Some nouns do not have a singular form.

- (eye) glasses
- clothes
- pants
- scissors

10. Some plural nouns are the same as the singular noun.

- Chinese—Chinese
- fish—fish
- sheep—sheep

PRONUNCIATION RULES

1. The final sounds for regular plural nouns are / s /, / z /, and / ɪz /.

2. The plural is pronounced /s/ after the voiceless sounds / p /, / t /, / k /, / f /, and / ө /.
   - cups
   - hats
   - works
   - cuffs
   - myths

3. The plural is pronounced /z/ after the voiced sounds / b /, / d /, / g /, / v /, / m /, / n /, / ŋ /, / l /, / r /, and / ð /.
   - crabs
   - cards
   - rugs

4. The plural *s* is pronounced / z / after all vowel sounds.
   - day—days
   - toe—toes

5. The plural *s* is pronounced / ɪz / after the sounds / s /, / z /, / ʃ /, / ʒ /, / ʧ /, and / ʤ /.(This adds another syllable to the word.)
   - races
   - causes
   - dishes

8 Possessive Nouns

1. Add *'s* to form the possessive of singular nouns.
   - Lulu**'s** last name is Winston.

2. To form the possessive of plural nouns ending in *s*, add only an apostrophe (').
   - The girl**s'** gym is on this floor.
   - The boy**s'** locker room is across the hall.

3. In hyphenated words (*mother-in-law, father-in-law,* etc.) and in phrases showing joint possession, only the last word is possessive in form.
   - My sister-in-law**'s** apartment is big.
   - Elenore and Pete**'s** apartment is comfortable.

4. To form the possessive of plural nouns that do not end in *s*, add *'s*.
   - The men**'s** room is next to the water fountain.

5. To form the possessive of one-syllable singular nouns that end in *s*, add *'s*.
   - **James's** apartment is beautiful.

   To form the possessive of words of more than one syllable that end in *s*, add an *'* or an *'s*.
   - **McCullers's** novels are interesting.
     OR
   - **McCullers'** novels are interesting.

6. **BE CAREFUL!** Don't confuse possessive nouns with the contraction of the verb *be*.
   - **Carol's** a student. = **Carol** *is* a student.
   - **Carol's** book is open. = **Her** book is open.

Common Non-count Nouns*

Liquids	Food	Too small to count	School subjects
milk	bread	sugar	math
coffee	cheese	salt	history
oil	lettuce	pepper	geography
juice	broccoli	cinnamon	biology
soda	ice cream	rice	chemistry
water	butter	sand	music
beer	mayon-	baking powder	
	naise	cereal	
	ketchup	spaghetti	
	jam	wheat	
	jelly	corn	
	fish		
	meat		
	sour cream		
	soup		

City problems	Weather	Gases	Abstract ideas	Others
traffic	snow	oxygen	love	money
pollution	rain	carbon dioxide	beauty	mail
crime	ice	nitrogen	happiness	furniture
	fog	air	luck	homework
			advice	information
			help	jewelry
			noise	garbage
			time	toothpaste
				paper

*Some nouns can be either count or non-count nouns.

I'd like some **chicken**. (non-count)
There were three **chickens** in the yard. (count)

Did you eat any **cake**? (non-count)
I bought a **cake** at the bakery. (count)

Common Containers, Measure Words, and Portions

a bottle of (milk, soda, catsup)
a bowl of (cereal, soup, rice)
a can of (soda, beans, tuna fish)
a cup of (hot chocolate, coffee, tea)
a foot of (snow, water)
a gallon of (juice, gas, paint)
a head of (lettuce)
an inch of (snow, rain)
a loaf of (bread)

a pair of (pants, skis, gloves)
a piece of (paper, cake, pie)
a pint of (ice cream, cream)
a quart of (milk)
a roll of (film, toilet paper, paper towels)
a slice of (toast, cheese, meat)
a tablespoon of (flour, sugar, baking soda)
a teaspoon of (sugar, salt, pepper)
a tube of (toothpaste, glue)

1. *The* is the definite article. You can use *the* before singular count nouns, plural count nouns, and non-count nouns.

- **The** hat is red.
- **The** hats are red.
- **The** coffee is hot.

2. Use *the* for specific things that the listener and speaker know about.

- **A:** How was **the** test?
- **B:** It was easy.

- **A:** Would you like to read **the** paper?
- **B:** Yes, thanks.

3. Use *the* when the speaker and listener know there is only one of the item.

- **A:** Is there a cafeteria in this school?
- **B:** Yes, **the** cafeteria is on the third floor.

4. Use *the* when you are talking about part of a group.

- Meat is usually expensive, but **the** meat at Ron's Butcher Shop is cheap and delicious.

5. Use *the* when you talk about something for the second time.

- **A:** What did you buy?
- **B:** Some apples and some pears. **The** apples were bad, but **the** pears were delicious.

6. Use *the* before the plural name of a whole family.

- **The** Winstons live in New York City.

7. Use *the* before the names of oceans, rivers, mountain ranges, seas, canals, deserts, and zoos.

- **The Pacific Ocean** is on the West Coast.
- **The Mississippi River** is the longest river in the United States.
- We visited **the Rocky Mountains.**
- Where is **the Dead Sea**?
- The boat went through **the Suez Canal**.
- **The Sahara Desert** is growing.
- We visited **the San Diego Zoo**.

8. Use *the* with phrases with *of* when there is only one of the item that follows *the*.

- Paris is **the capital of France**.
- I attended **the University of Michigan**.

    BUT

- He drank **a** cup of tea.

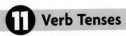

THE PRESENT TENSE OF *BE*

SINGULAR		
SUBJECT	***BE***	
I	**am**	
You	**are**	a student.
He She	**is**	
It	**is**	in the United States.

PLURAL		
SUBJECT	***BE***	
We You They	**are**	in the United States.

THE PAST TENSE OF *BE*

SINGULAR			
SUBJECT	***BE***		**TIME MARKER**
I	**was**		
You	**were**	at a restaurant	last night.
He She It	**was**		

PLURAL			
SUBJECT	***BE***		**TIME MARKER**
We You They	**were**	at a restaurant	last night.

THE PRESENT PROGRESSIVE

SUBJECT	***BE***	**BASE FORM OF VERB + *-ING***
I	**am**	
You	**are**	
He She It	**is**	working.
We You They	**are**	

THE SIMPLE PRESENT TENSE

SUBJECT	VERB
I You We They	**work.**
He She It	**works.**

THE SIMPLE PAST TENSE

SUBJECT	BASE FORM OF VERB + -ED / -D / -IED
I You He She It We You They	**worked.** **arrived.** **cried.**

THE PAST PROGRESSIVE

SUBJECT	PAST TENSE OF BE	BASE FORM OF VERB + -ING
I He She It	**was**	**working.**
We You They	**were**	

WILL FOR THE FUTURE

SUBJECT	WILL	BASE FORM OF VERB	
I You He She It We You They	**will**	**work**	tomorrow.

BE GOING TO FOR THE FUTURE

SUBJECT	BE	GOING TO	BASE FORM OF VERB	
I	**am**			
You	**are**			
He She	**is**	**going to**	**work**	tomorrow.
You We They	**are**			
It	**is**	**going to**	**rain**	tomorrow.

⑫ Base Forms and Past-Tense Forms of Common Irregular Verbs

Base form	Past-tense form	Base form	Past-tense form	Base form	Past-tense form
become	became	go	went	sell	sold
begin	began	grow	grew	send	sent
bite	bit	hang	hung	shake	shook
blow	blew	have	had	shoot	shot
break	broke	hear	heard	shut	shut
bring	brought	hide	hid	sing	sang
build	built	hit	hit	sit	sat
buy	bought	hold	held	sleep	slept
catch	caught	hurt	hurt	speak	spoke
choose	chose	keep	kept	spend	spent
come	came	know	knew	stand	stood
cost	cost	lead	led	steal	stole
do	did	leave	left	swim	swam
draw	drew	lend	lent	take	took
drink	drank	lose	lost	teach	taught
drive	drove	make	made	tear	tore
eat	ate	meet	met	tell	told
fall	fell	pay	paid	think	thought
feed	fed	put	put	throw	threw
feel	felt	quit	quit	understand	understood
fight	fought	read*	read*	wake	woke
find	found	ride	rode	wear	wore
fly	flew	ring	rang	win	won
forget	forgot	run	ran	write	wrote
get	got	say	said		
give	gave	see	saw		

*Pronounce the base form / rɪd /. Pronounce the past-tense form / rɛd /.

⑬ The Present Progressive: Spelling Rules

1. Add **-ing** to base form of the verb.

- drink—drink**ing**
- eat—eat**ing**
- see—see**ing**

2. If a verb ends in a silent **e**, drop the final **e** and add **-ing**.

- smil**e**—smil**ing**

3. If a one-syllable verb ends in a consonant, a vowel, and a consonant (CVC), double the last consonant before adding **-ing**.

However, do not double the last consonant if it is a **w**, **x**, or **y**.

CVC

sit—sit**ting**

CVC

run—run**ning**

- sew—se**w**ing
- play—pla**y**ing
- mix—mi**x**ing

4. In two-syllable words that end in a consonant, a vowel, and a consonant (CVC), double the last consonant only if the last syllable is stressed.

- a**d**mit—admi**tt**ing (last syllable is stressed)
- whisper—whispe**r**ing (last syllable is not stressed)

SPELLING RULES FOR THE THIRD-PERSON SINGULAR AFFIRMATIVE

1. Add **-s** to form the third-person singular of most verbs.

- Pete works. I work too.
- Doug wears sweatshirts. I wear shirts.

Add **-es** to words that end in **ch, s, sh, x,** or **z.**

- Norma teaches Spanish. I teach English.
- Lulu washes her cloths on Tuesday. Elenore and Pete wash their clothes on Sunday.

2. When a base-form verb ends in a consonant + *y*, change the *y* to *i* and add **-es.**

- I study at home. Carol studies at the library.

Do not change the *y* when the base form ends in a vowel + *y*. Add **-s.**

- Dan plays tennis. I play tennis, too.

3. Some verbs have irregular forms for the third-person singular.

- I have   He **has**.
- I do.   She **does**.
- I go.   It **goes**.

PRONUNCIATION RULES FOR THE THIRD-PERSON SINGULAR AFFIRMATIVE

1. The final sound for the third-person singular form of the simple present tense is pronounced / s /, / z /, or / ɪz /. The final sounds of the third-person singular are the same as the final sounds of plural nouns. See Appendix 7 on pages A-7 and A-8.

/ s /	/ z /	/ ɪz /
talks	loves	dances

2. *Do* and *say* have a change in vowel sound.

- I say. / seɪ /
- I do. / du/
- He says. / sɛz /
- He does. / dʌz /

SPELLING RULES

1. If the verb ends in an *e*, add *-d*.

2. If the verb ends in a consonant, add *-ed*.

3. If a one-syllable verb ends in a consonant, a vowel, and a consonant (CVC), double the last consonant and add *-ed*.

However, do not double the last consonant if it is a *w*, *x*, or *y*.

4. If a two-syllable verb ends in a consonant, a vowel, and a consonant (CVC), double the last consonant only if the last syllable is stressed.

5. If the verb ends in a consonant + *y*, change the *y* to *i* and add *-ed*.

6. If the verb ends in a vowel + *y*, do not change the *y* to i. Add *-ed*.

EXCEPTIONS: *pay—paid, lay—laid, say—said*

- arrive—arrive**d**
- rain—rain**ed**

- like—like**d**
- help—help**ed**

CVC

hug—hu**gged**

CVC

rub—ru**bbed**

- bow—bo**wed**
- mix—mi**xed**

- play—play**ed**

- refér—refe**rred** (the last syllable is stressed)
- énter—enter**ed** (the last syllable is not stressed)

- worry—worr**ied**
- carry—carr**ied**

- play—pla**yed**
- annoy—anno**yed**

PRONUNCIATION RULES

1. The final sounds for regular verbs in the past tense are / t /, / d /, and / ɪd /.

2. The plural is pronounced / t / after the voiceless sounds / f /, / k /, / p /, / s /, / ʧ /, and / ʃ /.

- laughed
- licked

- missed
- watched

- wished
- sipped

3. The final sound is pronounced / d / after the voiced sounds / b /, / g /, /ʤ /, / l /, / m /, / n /, / r /, / ŋ /, / ð /, / ʒ /, / v /, and / z /.

- rubbed
- hugged
- judged
- pulled

- hummed
- banned
- occurred
- banged

- bathed
- massaged
- lived
- surprised

4. The final sound is pronounced / d / after vowel sounds

- played
- skied

- tied
- snowed

- argued

5. The final sound is pronounced /ɪd / after the letters "t" and "d." /ɪd / adds a syllable to the verb.

- want—wanted
- rest—rested

- instruct—instructed
- attend—attended

COMPARATIVE FORM (USED TO COMPARE TWO PEOPLE, PLACES, OR THINGS)

Sally	is	older busier more industrious	than	her sister.
	types	faster more quickly		

SUPERLATIVE FORM (USED TO COMPARE THREE OR MORE PEOPLE, PLACES, OR THINGS)

Sally	is	the	oldest busiest most industrious	of the three.
	types		fastest most quickly	

EQUATIVE FORM (USED TO SHOW THAT TWO PEOPLE, PLACES, OR THINGS ARE THE SAME)

Sally	is	as	tall busy industrious	as	Bob.
	types		fast quickly		

FUNCTION	MODALS	EXAMPLES
to make polite requests	**would like** **May I . . .** **Can I . . .** **Would you (please)** **Could you (please)**	I**'d like** to buy a gold bracelet. **May I** help you? **Can I** please see your paper? **Would you** please lend me your pen? **Could you** please help me?
to express possibility (present or future)	**may** **might**	Take an umbrella. It **may** rain. We **might** visit my cousin this evening.
to express future possibility	**can** **could**	How **can** I get to the library? You **could** go by bus or by train.
to talk about the future	**will**	He **will** be three years old next week.
to express present ability	**can**	I **can** type fifty words a minute.
to express past ability	**could**	I **could** run very fast ten years ago.
to express necessity in the present or future	**must** **have to**	You **must** pay the rent by the first of the month. She **has to** work today.
to express past necessity	**had to**	We **had to** read two new chapters for today.
to express advisability	**should** **ought to** **had better**	He **should** see a doctor. He doesn't sound very good. We **ought to** study today. They**'d better** return my money.
to promise or assure	**will**	I**'ll be** there at 10.
to express strong prohibition	**mustn't**	You **mustn't** smoke near the chemical factory.
to indicate that something is not a requirement	**don't / doesn't have to**	You **don't have to** type your composition. She **doesn't have to** wear a suit at her office.

These are the pronunciation symbols used in this text. Listen to the pronunciation of the key words.

VOWELS		CONSONANTS			
Symbol	**Key Word**	**Symbol**	**Key Word**	**Symbol**	**Key Word**
i	beat, feed	p	pack, happy	ʃ	ship, machine, station, special, discussion
ɪ	bit, did	b	back, rubber		
eɪ	date, paid	t	tie	ʒ	measure, vision
ɛ	bet, bed	d	die	h	hot, who
æ	bat, bad	k	came, key, quick	m	men
ɑ	box, odd, father	g	game, guest	n	sun, know, pneumonia
ɔ	bought, dog	tʃ	church, nature, watch	ŋ	sung, ringing
oʊ	boat, road	dʒ	judge, general, major	w	wet, white
ʊ	book, good	f	fan, photograph	l	light, long
u	boot, food, student	v	van	r	right, wrong
ʌ	but, mud, mother	θ	thing, breath	y	yes, use, music
ə	banana, among	ð	then, breathe		
ɚ	shirt, murder	s	sip, city, psychology		
aɪ	bite, cry, buy, eye	z	zip, please, goes		
aʊ	about, how				
ɔɪ	voice, boy				
ɪr	deer				
ɛr	bare				
ɑr	bar				
ɔr	door				
ʊr	tour				

INDEX

This index is for the full and split editions. All entries are in the full book. Page numbers for Volume A of the split edition are in black. Page numbers for Volume B are in color.